LAW AND REGULATION OF CRYPTOCURRENCIES AND CRYPTOASSETS

LAW AND REGULATION OF CRYPTOCURRENCIES AND CRYPTOASSETS

SECOND EDITION

ANDREW HAYNES AND PETER YEOH

Routledge
Taylor & Francis Group
LONDON AND NEW YORK

Designed cover image: wacomka/Getty Images ®

Second edition published 2026
by Routledge
4 Park Square, Milton Park, Abingdon, Oxon, OX14 4RN

and by Routledge
605 Third Avenue, New York, NY 10158

Routledge is an imprint of the Taylor & Francis Group, an informa business

First edition published by Routledge 2020

British Library Cataloguing-in-Publication Data
A catalogue record for this book is available from the British Library

Library of Congress Cataloging-in-Publication Data
Names: Haynes, Andrew, 1953– author. | Yeoh, Poh Seng, 1949– author.
Title: Law and regulation of cryptocurrencies and cryptoassets / Andrew Haynes and Peter Yeoh.
Description: Second Edition. | Abingdon, Oxon [UK] ; New York, NY : Routledge, 2026. | Includes bibliographical references and index.
Identifiers: LCCN 2025028786 | ISBN 9781032667379 (hardback) | ISBN 9781032667362 (paperback) | ISBN 9781032667416 (ebook)
Subjects: LCSH: Cryptocurrencies—Law and legislation.
Classification: LCC K4433 . H39 2025 | DDC 343/.032—dc23/eng/20250618
LC record available at https://lccn.loc.gov/2025028786

ISBN: 978-1-032-66737-9 (hbk)
ISBN: 978-1-032-66736-2 (pbk)
ISBN: 978-1-032-66741-6 (ebk)

DOI: 10.4324/9781032667416

Typeset in Times New Roman
by Apex CoVantage, LLC

CONTENTS

TABLE OF CASES

TABLE OF STATUTES

United States

TABLE OF REGULATIONS

ABBREVIATIONS

5AMLD	5th Anti-Money Laundering Directive
PACTE	action plan for business growth and transformation
AMLCTF	Anti-Money Laundering and Counter-Terrorism Financing Amendment Bill 2017 (Australia)
AML	anti-money laundering procedures
AA	ASIC Act
AFS	Australian financial services
AFSL	Australian Financial Services License
ASIC	Australian Securities and Investments Commission
AUSTRAC	Australian Transaction Reports and Analysis Centre
ATO	The Australian Taxation Office
BIS	Bank for International Settlements
BoE	Bank of England
BEPS	base erosion and profit shifting
CSA	Canadian Securities Administrators
CGT	capital gains tax
CIMA	Cayman Islands Monetary Authority
CBDC	central bank digital currency
CBOE	Chicago Board Options Exchange
CME	Chicago Mercantile Exchange Inc.
CBIRC	China Banking and Insurance Regulatory Commission
CIS	collective investment scheme
CFPB	Consumer Finance Protection Bureau
CPMI	Committee on Payments and Market Infrastructures
CFTC	Commodities Futures Trading Commission
CEA	Commodity Exchange Act
CRS	Common Reporting Standard
CA	Corporations Act
CTF	counter-terrorism financing
CAT	Cryptoassets Taskforce (UK)
CTP	cryptoasset trading platforms
DCEP	Digital Currency Electronic Payment (China)
DDR	digital depository receipts
DIA	Digital Innovation Authority Act (Malta)

DLT	distributed ledger technology
DOJ	US Department of Justice
EFTA	Electronic Fund Transfer Act of 1978
EMRs	Electronic Money Regulations 2011
EDD	enhanced due diligence
EBA	European Banking Authority
ECB	European Central Bank
ECBCTF	ECB Crypto-Assets Task Force
EC	European Commission
EIOPA	European Insurance and Occupational Pensions
EP	European Parliament
ESMA	European Securities and Markets Authority
ESAs	European supervisory authorities
ETF	exchange traded funds
BaFin	Federal Financial Supervisory Authority (Germany)
FAA	Financial Advisers Act (Cap. 110) (Singapore)
FATF	Financial Action Task Force
FCA	Financial Conduct Authority
FinCEN	Financial Crimes Enforcement Network
FINRA	Financial Industry Regulatory Authority
FIEA	Financial Instruments and Exchange Act (Japan)
FIT	financial instrument test
FINMA	Financial Market Supervisory Authority (Switzerland)
FSAP	Financial Sector Assessment Programmes
FSC	Financial Services Commission (Korea)
FSB	Financial Stability Board
FATCA	Foreign Account Tax Complaint Act (US)
GST	goods and services tax
HMRC	HM Revenue and Customs
HMT	HM Treasury
ICO	initial coin offerings
IIROC	Investment Industry Regulatory Organization of Canada
ITO	initial token offerings
IVFAOs	initial virtual financial assets offerings (Malta)
IRS	Inland Revenue Service
IMF	International Monetary Fund
IOSCO	International Organization of Securities Commissions
IAMAI	Internet and Mobile Association of India
ICT	Investment Contract Test (Canada)
JBA	The Japanese Blockchain Association
JFSA	Japan Financial Services Agency
JVCEA	Japanese Virtual Currency Exchange Association
KYC	know your customer procedures
KYT	know your transaction
LOLR	lender of last resort

LA	Libra Association
LETS	local exchange trading system
MFSA	Malta Financial Services Authority
MGA	Malta Gaming Authority
MIS	managed investment scheme
MiFID	Markets in Financial Instruments Directive
MAS	Monetary Authority of Singapore
MROS	Money Laundering Reporting Office Switzerland
ML/TF	money laundering/terrorism funding
NCAs	national competent authorities
NYSDFS	New York State Department of Financial Services
NIFA	National Internet Finance Association (China)
NASAA	North American Securities Administrators Association
OECD GBPF	OECD 2019 Global Blockchain Policy Forum
OCEO	Office of Consumer Education and Outreach (part of CFTC)
OECD	Organisation for Economic Co-operation and Development
PSA	Payment Services Act (Japan)
PSB	Payments Services Bill
PBOC	People's Bank of China
PCL	Proceeds of Crime Law (Cayman Islands)
PRA	Prudential Regulation Authority
RFBs	relevant financial businesses
IIROC	Regulatory Organisation of Canada
RS	regulatory sandbox
RBI	Reserve Bank of India
SFA	Securities and Futures Act (Japan or Singapore)
SEC	Securities and Exchange Commission
SAR	South Korea, Taiwan, Singapore, and Hong Kong
SCAV	Standing Committee on the Assessment of Vulnerabilities
SIF	State Secretariat for International Finance
SARs	suspicious activity reports
SIFI	systemically important financial institutions
FCA	UK Financial Conduct Authority
UCC	Uniform Commercial Code
UNODC	UN Office on Drugs and Crime
SEC	US Securities and Exchange Commission
VAT	value-added tax
VC	venture capital
VASP	virtual asset service providers
V20	Virtual Asset Service Providers Summit
VFAs	virtual financial assets
VFAA	Virtual Financial Assets Act (Malta)
WTO	World Trade Organization

DEFINITION OF KEY TERMS APPLIED IN CRYPTOASSETS AND DECENTRALISED FINANCE (DeFi)

The EU version is adopted and extracted for use in this book, as this is deployed in jurisdictions where cryptoassets and DeFi are widely applied.[1]

Algorithmic stablecoin. A stablecoin that aims to maintain its peg without maintaining reserve assets, instead relying on an on chain algorithm and/or smart contract that manages the supply of tokens in circulation. A common feature is a set relationship to a second cryptoasset token, wherein trading between the stablecoin and second token is intended to offer arbitrageurs profitable opportunities to return the stablecoin to its peg. The algorithm fails, however, if both the stablecoin and the cryptoasset token simultaneously drop in price, resulting in what is colloquially called a "death spiral".

Asset-backed token. A cryptoasset that represents an interest in a physical asset.

Blockchain. A form of distributed ledger in which details of transactions are held in the ledger in the form of blocks of information. A block of new information is attached to the chain of pre-existing blocks via a computerised process (commonly called a consensus mechanism) by which transactions are validated (by participants in the network).

Cryptoasset. A type of private sector digital asset that depends primarily on cryptography and distributed ledger or similar technology. It can be transferred and stored electronically, without the need for trusted intermediaries.

Central bank digital currencies (CBDCs) are publicly accessible digital forms of fiat currencies issued by the state and with legal tender status.[2]

1 European Systemic Risk Board (ESRB) (2023), "Crypto-assets and decentralized finance", *ESRB*, May 2023, pp. 68–69, www.esrb.europa.eu/pub/pdf/reports/esrb.cryptoassetsanddecentralisedfinance202305~9792140acd.en.pdf, accessed 11/05/2023.

2 Tan, B. (2023), "Central bank digital currency and financial inclusion", IMF Working Paper WP/23/69, March 2023, pp. 1–57; Bank for International Settlements (BIS) (2018), "Central bank digital currencies", *BIS*, March 2018, www.bis.org/cpmi/publ/d174.pdf, accessed 11/05/2023.

These are not cryptoassets. However, they could enable users to store and exchange value outside banks in a regulated way. Early non real life examples beyond ideas is the proposed e-krona from the Swedish Central Bank. The two main kinds of CBDCs are retail and wholesale CBDCs.[3] *Retail CBDCs* are mainly used by individuals essentially as digital cash and assured by the insight that the currency is issued and backed by the country's central bank. This innovation could potentially replace the need to carry physical currency and reduce economic rents associated with transacting in the legacy financial systems. Wholesale CBDCs are mainly employed by financial institutions, like banks. The use of CBDCs would enable banks to make payments in a faster and more automated way. Cross-border transactions could become faster and more reliable. China, Cambodia, the Bahamas, Eastern Caribbean, and Nigeria are the five countries that have implemented CBDCs across the globe.[4]

Consumer tokens are inherently consumptive in nature, because their intrinsic features are designed to serve as, or provide access to, a particular set of goods, services, or content. The most well-known example of a consumer token is probably Ether, which was marketed, was sold, and serves as "fuel" for the Ethereum blockchain. Examples include Ether, Waves, and BItshares.

Cryptoasset trading platform. Any trading platform where cryptoassets can be bought and sold, regardless of the platform's legal status.

Cryptography. The conversion of data into private code using encryption algorithms, typically for transmission over a public network.

Decentralised autonomous organisation (DAO). A blockchain enforced organisational structure that emphasises community, as opposed to centralised, governance. It involves mechanisms such as decision making based on votes by "governance token" holders rather than control by management or a board of directors.

Decentralised applications (dApps). Software applications built from smart contracts, often integrated with user interfaces using traditional web technology. These run on peer-to-peer networks or blockchain networks instead of centralised servers.

Decentralised finance (DeFi). A set of alternative financial markets, products, and systems that operate using cryptoassets and "smart contracts" (software) built using distributed ledger or similar technology.

Decentralised exchange (DEX). A decentralised finance protocol that creates markets for exchanging one cryptoasset for another.

3 Corporate Finance Institute (CFI) (2023), "What is central bank digital currency (CBDC)", https://corporatefinanceinstitute.com/resources/cryptocurrency/central-bank-digital-currency-cbdc/, accessed 11/05/2023.

4 Deloitte (2023), "Central bank digital currencies: Building block of the future of value transfer", https://www2.deloitte.com/content/dam/Deloitte/in/Documents/financial-services/in-fs-cbdc-noexp.pdf, accessed 11/05/2023.

Digital asset. A digital instrument that is issued or represented through the use of distributed ledger or similar technology. This does not include digital representations of fiat currencies.

Distributed ledger technology (DLT). A means of saving information through a distributed ledger, that is, a repeated digital copy of data available at multiple locations. It enables the operation and use of distributed ledgers. The definition of a DLT is similar to, but not the same as, that for blockchain technology.[5] A blockchain is one kind of DLT, though not every distributed ledger is a blockchain. Some DLTs do not share all the data with all the participants in the way that blockchains do.

Financial asset tokens (digital tokens) are designed to work as a medium of exchange within a limited ecosystem and to offer additional features, such as representing the right to access products, services, or ownership of assets (e.g. shares, bonds). They are hosted on top of an existing public DLT and typically issued in ICOs (initial coin offerings), a means for fundraising that avoids traditional intermediaries, such as banks, venture capital, and stock exchanges. Examples include Eos, Tron (TRX), and Tether (USDT).

Fintech. Technology-enabled innovation in financial services that could result in new business models, applications, processes, or products with an associated material effect on the provision of financial services.

Global stablecoin. A stablecoin with a potential reach and use across multiple jurisdictions and which could become systemically important in and across one or many jurisdictions, including as a means of making payments.

Mining. A means to create new cryptoassets, often through a mathematical process by which transactions are verified and added to the distributed ledger.

Oracle. A third party service enabling smart contracts to access external data, on chain or off chain, that may be an input for that smart contract's functionality.

Proof of stake (PoS). A decentralised consensus mechanism that requires members of a network to stake (lock up) cryptoasset units in order to obtain the right to validate transactions. Validators are rewarded by newly created cryptoasset units. The probability of a participant being chosen to validate a block of transactions is based on the amount of staked cryptoassets. PoS was created as a less energy intensive alternative to proof of work, the original consensus mechanism used to validate transactions and add new blocks to the blockchain.

Payment tokens (cryptocurrencies) are tokens whose intrinsic features are designed to serve as a general-purpose store of value, medium of exchange or means of payment, and/or unit of account.

5 Winston & Strawn LLP (2023), "What is distributed ledger technology?", www.winston.com/print/v2/content/1022948/distributed-ledger-technology.pdf, accessed 11/05/2023.

Similar to a currency and designed to work, as frequently referred to, as a "coin" or "digital money". This does not require traditional intermediaries for exchange and production. Legal status as a currency is controversial. Examples of these include Bitcoin (BTC) and Ripple (XRP).

Proof of work (PoW). A decentralised consensus mechanism that requires members of a network to expend effort solving an arbitrary mathematical puzzle in order to gain the right to append a block of validated transactions to the chain. The probability of a participant being chosen to validate a block of transactions is related to the computing power expended by the participant in solving the puzzle. The goal of PoW is to increase the cost of manipulating the ledger. PoW is used widely for validating transactions on blockchains.

Protocol. Specific combinations of cryptoassets, smart contracts, and user applications that are necessary for specific decentralised finance applications, including any related functional components, such as user interfaces, oracles, governance and voting mechanisms, developing grants and foundations, and financial assets, such as tokens, treasuries, and funds. Some of these components may be automated, and some may be carried out by individuals and entities.

Smart contract. A collection of code and data that is deployed using cryptographically signed transactions on the blockchain network. The smart contract is executed by nodes within the blockchain network; all nodes much derive the same results for the execution, and the results of execution are recorded on the blockchain.

Stablecoin. A cryptoasset that aims to maintain a stable value relative to a specified asset or a pool or basket of assets.

Tokens. These are legal instantiations of a share of an asset, a set of permissions, or a set of claims that are held by the bearer or bearers of said token. A token might take a physical from – such as a lottery ticket – or it might be a digital representation of a physical asset (e.g. factional ownership of real estate or of luxury goods, such as cars or paintings), a set of permissions (e.g. the right for a one-off or perpetual discount for goods/services on an online platform), or a set of claims (e.g. the electronic representation of a debt contract). Digital tokens exist within a variety of network forms, including the traditional "hub and spoke" architecture, in which a central entity maintains token network activity; however, the primary interest of this definition is the particular subset of digital tokens that exists within distributed or decentralised networks popularly referred to as "cryptoassets".[6]

6 European Central Bank (ECB) (2018), "Cryptocurrencies and tokens", *ECB*, September 2018, www.ecb.europa.eu/paym/groups/pdf/fxcg/2018/20180906/Item_2a_-_Cryptocurrencies_and_tokens.pdf, accessed 11/05/2023.

Total value locked (TVL). A common metric of the size of decentralised finance protocols. It measures the value of cryptoassets or other tokens that have been transferred to the smart contracts underlying a decentralised finance protocol. Since these protocols differ in design, TVL is not a standardised measure, and reported values for specific protocols can vary substantially. The two main kinds of CBDCs are wholesale CBDC and retail CBDC. Retail CBDCs are mainly used by individuals essentially as digital cash and assured by the insight that the currency is issued and backed by the country's central bank.

Unbacked cryptoassets. Cryptoassets that are neither tokenised traditional assets nor stablecoins.

Wallet. An application or device for storing the private keys providing access to the cryptoasset. *Hosted wallets* are typically services where the keys are held by a third-party provider on behalf of the client, while *unhosted wallets* typically enable the users to hold and use the keys themselves.

Wallet provider. A firm that offers wallet services to holders of cryptoassets. These may involve holding private keys so that they are accessible online to the client in order to initiate transactions ("hot" storage) or keeping the keys offline ("cold" storage).

Sources: Financial Stability Board (2022a), Azar et al. (2022), and Regulation (EU) 2022/858 of the European Parliament and of the Council of 30 May 2022 on a pilot regime for market infrastructures based on distributed ledger technology, and amending Regulations (EU) No 600/2014 and (EU) No 909/2014 and Directive 2014/65/EU.

CHAPTER 1

Introduction and overview

The spectacular price changes that have taken place with regard to cryptocurrencies over recent years have attracted a great deal of public and professional attention. Periodic price crashes have also highlighted the risk involved for those investing money in them, which in turn has attracted the attention of banking and financial services regulators and central banks.[1] This interest has also expanded to the blockchain based system that they operate on and some of the other types of instruments that are now issued and traded on a similar basis.

Cryptoassets as a tracked movement began using a digital ledger known as blockchain. Its first known transaction was buying two large pizzas in Jacksonville, Florida, for 10,000 Bitcoins. Bitcoin's value increased steadily throughout the 2010s, taking parity with the US dollar in April 2011, before peaking in at US$1,242 on 29 November 2013. It had tripled again by 20 October 2021, taking the value of the original two pizzas to almost US$670 million.[2] This kind of growth transformed the crypto market from a specialist niche into a type of get rich quick scheme for enthusiastic investors. However, at the same time, algorithm experts and other technologists were indicating that blockchain had the potential for a much wider range of uses.[3] Cryptos enable the migration from centralised to decentralised finance, removing the need for banks and other financial institutions in the process. However, the abstract nature of crypto markets, together with the extreme volatility of assets, meme coins, and so on, renders them significantly more vulnerable to behavioural bias than other centralised assets. This in turn raised concerns over these activities' impact on existing financial systems.[4]

1 Morris, C. (2017), "Winklevoss twins used Facebook payout to become bitcoin billionaires", *Fortune*, 04/12/2017, https://fortune.com/2017/12/04/winklevoss-twins-bitcoin-billionaires/, accessed 21/01/2018.

2 Cronqvist, H. & Pely, D. J. (2024), "Introduction", in Cronqvist, H. & Pely, D. J. (eds.), *The Elgar companion to decentralized finance, digital assets, and blockchain technologies*, Cheltenham, Edward Elgar.

3 Shoetan, P. O. (2024), "Blockchain's impact of financial security and efficiency beyond cryptocurrency uses", *International Journal of Management & Entrepreneurship Research*, 6(4): 1211–1235.

4 Khan, A. & Sandner, P. (2024), "DeFi: An overview of use cases and a status quo analysis of the ecosystem", in Cronqvist, H. & Pely, D. J. (eds.), *The Elgar companion to decentralized finance, digital assets, and blockchain technologies*, Cheltenham, Edward Elgar.

DOI: 10.4324/9781032667416-1

Aside from this financial or "market" risk, there are those who unwittingly lost their highly valued Bitcoin and other cryptocurrencies due to lack of care. These include one man who accidentally lost his computer, together with the Bitcoin stored in it, in a UK council landfill because of complaints by his then girlfriend of the endless computer whirring in the mining process,[5] and others who could no longer retrieve their Bitcoins because of forgotten passwords. Altogether, the quantity of Bitcoin lost could be as high as 21 million, with a total estimated value of US$240 billion.[6] Some of those who lost their Bitcoins took to retrieving them from toxic landfill sites and hacking their own Bitcoin vaults.[7] These and other similar cases narrate the loss of a small fortune when measured at the price operating in early 2018. Tales are also told of those who bought cheaply in the early days and who were sitting comfortably on very large apparent profits, with monetary gains exceeding 1,000%, before the rapid decline in prices over the course of 2018 and 2021.[8] The initial price surge contributed to a surge in the 'fear of missing out syndrome', thereby propelling more to use their savings and even borrowings to participate so as not to miss out on the illusion of easy gain.[9] This may re-emerge if another price surge takes place, and indeed it did, albeit relatively modestly, in 2020–21 and 2024.

Bad news comes in other forms than price reductions, for example, the sporadic occasional hacks and thefts[10] in association with money laundering and other illicit activities.[11] One example is a South Korean college student who committed suicide after losing money as a result of trading in Bitcoin.[12] Also, more than £108,000 in Bitcoin were paid by victims of the WannaCry ransomware attack that crippled parts of the NHS, including businesses in 150 countries worldwide.[13]

---

5 Smith, A. (2017), "Man threw away laptop with bitcoin that is now worth £74 million", *Metro*, 09/12/2017, https://metro.co.uk/2017/12/09/man-threw-away-laptop-with-bitcoin-that-is-nowworth-74-million-7145361/, accessed 21/01/2018.

6 www.reddit.com/r/Bitcoin/comments/ih6dkqd/an_estimated_25_million_Bitcoin_240billion_are?rdt=42169, accessed 23/02/2025.

7 Umoh, R. (2017), "3 of the craziest things people are doing to recover their lost bitcoins", *CNBC*, 21/12/2017, www.cnbc.com/2017/12/21/3-crazy-things-people-are-doing-to-recoverlost-bitcoin.html, accessed 21/01/2018.

8 Blatchford, E. (2017), "Is it too late to invest in bitcoin? For those wondering if they've missed the money-making boat", *The Huffington Post Australia*, 25/08/2017, www.huffington-post. com.au/2017/08/22/is-it-too-late-to-invest-in-bitcoin_a_23156491/?guccounter=1, accessed 21/01/2018.

9 Bosotti, A. (2017), "Bitcoin craze: 'Fear of missing out' trade will lead to 'DRAMATIC' falls in bitcoin value", *Express*, 31/12/2017, www.express.co.uk/finance/city/898512/Bitcoin-news-price-update-value-fall-cryptocurrency-fomo-market-prices-finance-business, accessed 21/01/2018.

10 Roberts, J. J. (2017), "How bitcoin is stolen: 5 common threats", *Fortune*, 08/12/2017, https://fortune.com/2017/12/08/bitcoin-theft/, accessed 21/01/2018.

11 Bloomberg, J. (2017), "Using bitcoin or other cryptocurrency to commit crimes? Law enforcement is onto you", *Forbes*, 28/12/2017, www.forbes.com/sites/jasonbloomberg/2017/12/28/using-bitcoin-or-other-cryptocurrency-to-commit-crimes-law-enforcement-is-onto-you/, accessed 21/01/2018.

12 Kwak, Y.-S. (2018), "Man commits suicide after loss on cryptocurrency", *The Korea Times*, 01/02/2018, www.koreatimes.co.kr/www/nation/2018/02/121_243438.html, accessed 03/02/2018.

13 Gibbs, S. (2017), "WannaCry: Hackers withdraw £108, 000 of bitcoin ransom", *The Guardian*, 03/08/2017, www.theguardian.com/technology/2017/aug/03/wannacry-hackers-

Investors, whether sophisticated or not, are attracted by the possibility of rapid and high returns from cryptocurrencies. As for businesses, with the excitement and hype around Bitcoin and blockchain, there is the associated emotional element which has affected the share prices in crypto companies, in a manner reminiscent of the dot-com boom. One such example was the surging share price of LongFin, which specialises in trade finance and which went public on 13 December 2017 on Nasdaq. When LongFin announced that it was buying a blockchain related venture called Ziddu.com, its share price shot up by more than 1,000%, causing its own founder to call the price surge unwarranted.[14] According to Jordan Rochester, a Nomura analyst, the level of speculative mania had reached a point in 2017 where share prices had been boosted by businesses simply inserting "blockchain" onto the end of their names.[15] Blockchain is the technology underpinning Bitcoin and other cryptocurrencies.

This text is inspired by extensive writings on the themes of cryptocurrencies and cryptoassets that, for unknown reasons, do not include a comprehensive breakdown of these instruments, coupled with an explanation of the current and proposed legal and regulatory situation.

As explained in Chapter 2, cryptocurrencies and assets have come to capture the imagination of individuals, businesses, and more recently, regulators across the world. They have fired the dreams and ambitions of many others looking for quick wealth. Indeed, many cryptoassets – in particular Bitcoin – enthusiasts buy them for their potential to increase spectacularly in value, rather than as a medium of exchange. Their lack of guaranteed value and their digital nature imply that transactions in them would involve several inherent unique risks extending from regulatory to security, insurance, fraud, market, and tax issues, while the blockchain technology supporting them could unleash various innovative gains in the digital economy.[16]

The advent of Bitcoin and other cryptoassets thus led to both opportunities and risks for businesses and investors, something common to most innovations in their initial trajectory.[17] There were huge gains, running beyond 1,000%, from Bitcoin punting. This resulted in the spectacular run of Bitcoin from less than US$1,000 to an all-time high of US$19,500 by 1 January 2017, a hefty surge of 1,824% before the later 80% decline, and then, in turn, relative price stability followed by mid-2019, rising to US$96,577.76 by 22 February 2025.[18]

withdraw-108000-pounds-bitcoin-ransom, accessed 21/01/2018.

14 Bullock, N. & Wigglesworth, R. (2017), "Blockchain fervour evokes memories of dotcom bubble", *Financial Times*, 19/12/2017, www.ft.com/content/40ec964a-e429-11e7-8b99-0191e45377ec, accessed 21/01/2018.

15 Ibid note [14], Bullock & Wigglesworth (2017).

16 IMF-FSB (2023), "IMF-FAB synthesis paper: Policies for crypto-assets", IMF-FSB 07/09/223, file:///F:/Crypto-assets-CC-OpportiniteisRisksIMFFSB23.pdf, accessed 08/09/2023.

17 International Monetary Funds (IMF) (IMF), "G20 note on the macrofinancial implication of cryptoassets", *IMF*, February 2023, file:///F:/g20-report-macrofinancial-implications-crypto-assets-february23.pdf, accessed 15/05/2023.

18 Morris, D. Z. (2017), "Bitcoin hits a new record high, but stops short of US$20,000", *Fortune*, 17/12/2017, https://fortune.com/2017/12/17/bitcoin-record-high-short-of-20000/, accessed 12/02/2018.

Bitcoin prices received a further boost from Wall Street regulated futures trading, including the imminent implementation of the Lightning Network.[19] The Chicago Board Options Exchange (CBOE) and the Chicago Mercantile Exchange Inc. (CME) launched their respective futures product on 10 and 18 December 2017. New all time highs quickly appeared, and new price predictions became harder to form, with regular commentators advising new investors to learn more about cryptocurrencies before committing.[20]

Bitcoin's stellar price movement is accompanied by an even greater switchback ride by 13 other main cryptocurrencies. For example, for 2018 and 2019, Ripple gained 36,018%, then dropped by 59.3% of the previous total; Dash up 9,265%, then down 70.18% of that; Ethereum up 9,162%, then down 85.84% of that amount; Litecoin up 5,056%, before losing 70.53% of that; and OmiseGo up 3,315% before dropping 90.49%, compared to Bitcoin's gain of 1,318% at the end of 2017 before losing 59.3% of its highest amount.[21] These other cryptocurrencies joined the Bitcoin bandwagon with wider oscillations because of their much smaller capital base.

The common denominator tying the different crypto systems together is the public ledger or blockchain shared between network participants and the employment of native tokens to incentivise participants for manning the network in lieu of a central authority. They differ in the level of innovation.[22] The majority are mainly clones of Bitcoin, while other cryptocurrencies feature different block time, currency supply, and issuance themes, reflecting little to no innovation. These are commonly referred to as "altcoins", as exemplified by Dogecoin and Ethereum Classic. Others, while drawing on some Bitcoin concepts, offer novel and innovative features with substantive differences and comprise two main species, namely, those that exist on additional layers built on top of existing blockchain systems, and those offering new public blockchain systems.

As of 2015, Bitcoin accounted up to about 86% of the total cryptocurrency market capitalisation, but this fell to less than 58% in early 2025.[23] [24] The major growth in overall market cap in 2017 has been driven by altcoins like Ripple, Ether, Stellar, and little-known Tron. The extreme Bitcoin price volatility that occurred shows that those who committed financially close to its peak just before Christmas 2017 suffered significant losses in 2018. Hence, while there

---

19 Suberg, W. (2017), "Bitcoin hits $20,000 per coin, capping year of enormous growth", *Coin Telegraph*, 17/12/2017, https://cointelegraph.com/news/bitcoin-hits-20000-per-coin-cappingyear-of-enormous-growth, accessed 12/02/2018.

20 Suberg, W. (2017), "Another day, another thousand dollars: Bitcoin hits $15k", *Coin Telegraph*, 07/12/2017, www.cointelegraph.com/news/another-day-another-thousand-dollars-bitcoin-hits-15k, accessed 12/02/2018.

21 Wong, J. I. (2018), "Here are the top 10 cryptoassets of 2017 (and bitcoin's 1,000% rise doesn't even make the list)", *Quartz*, 01/01/2018, www.qz.com/1169000/ripple-was-the-best-performing-cryptocurrency-of-2017-beating-bitcoin/, accessed 02/02/2018.

22 Hileman, G. & Rauchs, M. (2017), *Global cryptocurrency benchmarking study*, Cambridge, Cambridge Centre for Alternative Finance.

23 Ibid note [22], Hileman & Rauchs (2017).

24 www.coingecko.com/en/global-charts#:~:text=The%20global%20cryptocurrency%20percentage%20cap,@%20Bitcoin%20dominance%20of%2057.6%25, accessed 22/02/2025.

are opportunities for speculative gains, equally there are risks attached to Bitcoin investing. Many people buy cryptocurrencies for their value rather than as a medium of exchange. Their lack of guaranteed value and digital nature implies that transacting in cryptocurrency involves several inherent unique risks, extending from regulatory to security, insurance, fraud, market, and tax.[25]

The 2018 to 2023 years continue to reflect price volatility for Bitcoin and other cryptoassets,[26] but also accompanied by fraud and related risks in some cases. The former led to the launching of Bitcoin futures trading.[27] The latter culminated in the FTX fiasco that led to its CEO and founder facing fraud charges.[28] Within the context of these frauds, Bitcoin reached an all time high of US$65,000 in November 2021 (connected to the launch of Bitcoin ETF in the United States), but declining to US$27,948 as of 9 October 2023 as FTX filed for bankruptcy.[29] The price outlook for cryptoassets, in particular, has few metrices that allow for forecasting, especially when market rumour has it that only a few cryptoasset holders own a large part of available supply. Referred to as "whales", these larger holders are said to account for 2% of anonymous ownership accounts while owning about 92% of Bitcoin. Further, most people using cryptoasset-related services worldwide are retail rather than institutional clients. This suggests that outlooks on whether Bitcoin prices would fall or grow are hard to measure, as movements from one large whale already have a significant impact on the market.[30]

Chapter 3 spotlights the wider use of blockchain technology in other innovative applications, as has been witnessed in healthcare, in supply chain management, and for the purposes of identification and authentication.[31] The aim is to ascertain just how wide ranging its use could be and the opportunities that it presents. Indeed, blockchain as a distributed ledger stores information that makes it extremely hard, if not impossible, for the system to be altered, hacked, or manipulated. The blockchain technology logs transactions in a digital ledger that is shared across the network, and owing to this, the ledger cannot be altered in any way. Accordingly, transactions involving anything of value,

25 Investopedia (2018), "Bitcoin", *Investopedia*, www.investopedia.com/terms/b/bitcoin.asp, accessed 02/02/2018.

26 Bouteska, A. & Harasheh, M. (2023), "Bitcoin volatility and the introduction of bitcoin futures: A portfolio construction approach", *Finance Research Letter*, 57: 104200–1044210.

27 Duggan, W. & Adams, M. (2023), "What are bitcoin futures? How do they work?", *Forbes Advisor*, 20/04/2023, www.forbes.com/advisor/investing/cryptocurrency/what-are-bitcoin-futures/, accessed 15/05/2023.

28 Levine, S. (2023), "FTX founder Sam Bankman-Fried charged with 12 counts in new indictment: Bankman-Fried was previously charged with eight counts including fraud and money laundering in FTX collapse case", *The Guardian*, 23/02/2023, www.theguardian.com/business/2023/feb/23/ftx-sam-bankman-fried-cryptocurrency-exchange-charges, accessed 15/05/2023.

29 De Best, R. (2023), "Bitcoin BTC/USD price history up until Oct 09, 2023", *Statista*, 10/10/2023, www.statista.com/statistics/326707/bitcoin-price-index/, accessed 10/10/2023.

30 Ibid note [29], De Best (2023).

31 Widjaja, G., Keshat, I. & Byeon, H. (eds.) (2023), *Applications beyond cryptocurrencies-non-financial use cases for blockchain technology*, EBook Xoffencer International Publication, 18/09/2023, file:///C:/Users/user/Downloads/EbookApplicationsBeyondCryptocurrencies-Non-financialusecasesfor.pdf, accessed 20/09/2023.

such as transactions in land, in cars, and general property transactions could be recorded on the blockchain.[32] Its five key characteristics – namely, distributed, secure, transparent, consensus based, and having a programmable platform – enable the technology to achieve this. Blockchain technology is used in these business cases in part because of the savings in terms of time and the increased security available. However, owing to its decentralised and other features, it might be challenging to scale it for employment in large scale applications. Other constraints pertain to its high energy consumption, its complexity, the general lack of knowledge relating to its functions, regulatory barriers, and the absence of agreed international standards. Thus far, in both the governmental and business landscapes, blockchain technology is identified with cryptoassets or cryptocurrencies and relatively less with other business uses. Bitcoin, the first speculative cryptocurrency, was initially launched as a global means of payment in 2009 and is widely perceived as the first digital asset, or cryptoasset. It is a digital representation of value made possible by cryptography and blockchain. Its original aim was to serve a mechanism for transferring value without the use of a bank or other trusted third-party entity. These cryptoassets or digital asses are categorised into cryptocurrencies, crypto commodities, and crypto tokens. Cryptocurrencies such as stablecoins are pegged to stable assets, like the US dollar, and are said to be becoming a critical component in decentralised finance (DeFi). In contrast, blockchain technology has been initially developed as a protocol for a peer-to-peer electronic cash system.[33] Chapter 3, therefore, looks at the wider potential impact of blockchain and puts the rest of the work in a wider context at the start of what may well be a journey that significantly affects business areas such as finance, banking, and financial services.

Chapter 4 discusses the controversies surrounding Bitcoin and its later imitators intended to function as global digital currencies and as an alternative to the existing fiat currency regime. There are those who would argue that cryptocurrencies' mission to be the future global digital currencies would eventually be realised,[34] whilst others, including world renowned economists, have claimed otherwise.[35] The ongoing debates between the two sides as to whether cryptocurrency amounts to money are therefore explored. Regardless of how different jurisdictions view cryptocurrencies, they have been employed for various purposes across many economies, from the emerging to the advanced.

32 Roman, D. & Schmid, G. (2017), "Beyond bitcoin: A critical look at blockchain-based systems", *MDPI*, 1: 1020015–1020046.

33 Library of Congress (2023), "Cryptocurrency & blockchain technology", https://guides.loc.gov/fintech/21st-century/cryptocurrency-blockchain, accessed 15/05/2023.

34 Arnold, M. (2017), "Six global banks join forces to create digital currency", *Financial Times*, 31/08/2017, www.ft.com/content/20c10d58-8d9c-11e7-a352-e4gf43c5825d, accessed 02/02/2018.

35 Roubini, N. (2018), "Blockchain's broke promises", *Project Syndicate*, 26/01/2018, www.project-syndicate.org/commentary/why-bitcoin-is-a-bubble-by-nouriel-roubini-2018-01?utm_sources=Project+Syndicate+, accessed 02/02/2018.

Chapter 5 deals with the ramifications of the current situation in various parts of the world and considers the problems that may arise in the context of cryptocurrencies and cryptoassets. The countries themselves are considered in terms of the stability of their fiat currencies and their democracies: those that are positioning themselves as crypto hubs, those that have a tradition of innovation, those that may well end up setting the regulatory standards, and those with competing agendas. This chapter therefore takes a look at the more notable "hot spots" around the world, and in particular the world's most crypto-friendly cities, to ascertain how widespread Bitcoin and other cryptocurrencies are applied across the world.[36] Insights drawn from these could, together with the conclusions that can be drawn from the economies that discouraged the use of cryptocurrencies, help provide some answers as to why regulators in both advanced and emerging economies are watching. This is not altogether surprising, with Nobel economics laureates[37] and others in global platforms[38] advising against widening their use.

Chapter 6 considers the various international bodies which have taken positions on this issue and considers their views. It covers the Group of 20 Nations (G20),[39] the Organisation for Economic Co-Operation and Development (OECD),[40] the International Monetary Fund (IMF),[41] the Financial Stability Board (FSB),[42] the Bank for International Settlements (BIS),[43] the International

36 Guibourg, C. (2016), "Which cities have the most businesses accepting bitcoin? London, New York, San Francisco among the world's 11 most bitcoin-friendly cities", *City AM*, 18/01/2016, www.cityam.com/232552/what-cities-have-most-businesses-accepting-bitcoin-london-new-york-san-franscisco-among-the-world's, accessed 02/02/2018.

37 Frank, J., Chian, K. & Ciolli, J. (2017), "PAUL KRUGMAN: Bitcoin is a more obvious bubble than housing was", *Business Insider*, 15/12/2017, www.businessinsider.com/paul-krugmansays-bitcoin-is-a-bubble-2017-12?r=US&IR=T, accessed 02/02/2018.

38 Kharpal, A. (2018), "Bitcoin is getting bashed at Davos but the crypto world is fighting back", *CNBC*, 26/01/2018, www.cnbc.com/2018/01/26/bitcoin-criticized-at-wef-in-davos-but-cryptocurrency-world-fights-back.html, accessed 02/02/2018.

39 G20 (2023), "Communique: Fourth G20 finance ministers and central bank governors meeting October 2023/Marakesh, Morocco", www.g20.org/content/dam/gtwenty/gtwenty_new/document/Final_G20_FMCBG_October_2023_Communique.pdf, accessed 25/10/2023.

40 OECD (2023), "Crypto-asset reporting framework and amendments to common reporting standard", www.oecd.org/tax/exchange-of-tax-information/crypto-asset-reporting-framework-and-amendments-to-the-common-reporting-standard.pdf, accessed 09/10/2023.

41 IMF (2023), "IMF policy paper: Elements of effective policies for crypto assets", www.elibrary.imf.org/downloadpdf/journals/007/2023/004/007.2023.issue-004-en.xml, accessed 12/02/2023; Hacibedel, B. & Pereaz-Saiz, H. (2023), "Assessing macrofinancial risks from crypto assets", IMF WP/23/214, September 2023, www.imf.org/en/Publications/WP/Issues/2023/09/30/Assessing-Macrofinancial-Risks-from-Crypto-Assets-539473, accessed 30/09/2023.

42 Financial Stability Board (FSB) (2023), "IMF-FSB synthesis paper: Policies for crypto-assets", file:///F:/cryptoassets-CC-FSB-IMFJointPaper23.pdf, accessed 08/09/2023.

43 Bank for International Settlements (BIS) (2023), "Financial stability risks from cryptoassets in emerging markets economies", BIS Papers No. 138, August 2023, file:///F:/cryptoassets-CC-BIS23.pdf, accessed 08/09/2023.

Organization of Securities Commissions (IOSCO),[44] the Financial Action Task Force (FATF),[45] and the World Economic Forum (WEF).[46]

Chapters 7 and 8 respectively cover the position taken by national regulators in the advanced Western economies of the United States,[47] the UK,[48] the EU,[49] and Australia, and those in major Asian economies, such as China,[50] Japan,[51] South Korea,[52] India,[53] and Singapore, amongst others. In turn, in Chapter 9 the capacity of crypto to operate under Islamic law and the regulatory policies adopted in Islamic states are analysed, including the attitudes displayed in a range of states.

Chapter 10, the concluding chapter, not only draws together the conclusions that can be reached from contents of the preceding chapters but also goes on to consider how matters are likely to develop in the future. The chapter therefore assesses the cryptocurrency evolutionary process, spells out its key opportunities and risks, gauges the extent of its applications across major emerging and advanced economies, deliberates on the feasibility of cryptocurrencies as global virtual currencies, examines the main regulatory approaches employed thus far, and finally reflects on what the real potentials of cryptocurrencies and cryptoassets are, and in particular the growing applications of blockchain technology beyond the cryptocurrency boundary.

---

44 International Organization of the Securities Commission (IOSCO) (2023), "IOSCO establishes global approach to address risks in decentralized finance", www.iosco.org/news/pdf/IOSCONEWS706.pdf, accessed 09/09/2023; IOSCO (2023), "Policy recommendations for crypto and digital asset markets: Consultation report", IOSCO May 2023, www.iosco.org/library/pubdocs/pdf/IOSCOPD734.pdf, accessed 11/05/2023; IOSCO (2023), "IOSCO sets the standard for global crypto regulation", www.iosco.org/news/pdf/IOSCONEWS693.pdf, accessed 26/05/2023.

45 Financial Action Task Force (FATF) (2023), "Targeted update on implementation of the FATF standards on virtual asset service providers", *FATF*, June 2023, www.fatf-gafi.org/content/dam/fatf-gafi/guidance/June2023-Targeted-Update-VA-VASP.pdf.coredownload.pdf, accessed 18/07/2023.

46 World Economic Forum (WEF) (2023), "Pathways to the regulation of crypto-assets: A global approach", *WEF*, May 2023, https://www3.weforum.org/docs/WEF_Pathways_to_the_Regulation_of_Crypto_Assets_2023.pdf, accessed 21/06/2023.

47 Price, M. & Schroeder, P. (2018), "U.S. regulators to back more oversight of virtual currencies", *Reuters*, 06/02/2018, www.reuters.com/article/us-global-bitcoin-congress/u-s-regulators-to-back-more-oversight-of-virtual-currencies-idUSKBN1FP2FJ, accessed 08/02/2018.

48 BBC (2017), "UK government mulls bitcoin regulation", *BBC*, 04/12/2017, www.bbc.co.uk/news/technology-42223577, accessed 02/02/2018.

49 Meyer, D. (2017), "Here's when Europe's new bitcoin rules will come into effect", *Fortune*, 04/12/2017, https://fortune.com/2017/12/04/eu-bitcoin-anti-money-laundering-uk/, accessed 02/02/2018.

50 Gibbs, S. (2018), "Bitcoin continues rapid slide as Russia and China stoke regulatory fears", *The Guardian*, 17/01/2018, www.theguardian.com/technology/2018/jan/17/bitcoin-continues-slide-drop-russia-china-regulatory-fears-cryptocurrency, accessed 02/02/2018.

51 Yagami, K. (2017), "Japan: A forward thinking bitcoin nation", *Forbes*, 02/11/2017.

52 De, N. (2018), "Report: South Korea eyes joint crypto regulations with China, Japan", *Coin Desk*, 09/01/2018, www.coindesk.com/report-south-korea-eyes-joint-crypto-regulations-withchina-japan, accessed 02/02/2018.

53 De, N. (2017), "India's supreme court prods government on bitcoin regulation", *Coin Desk*, 16/11/2017, www.coindesk.com/indias-supreme-court-calls-government-regulate-bitcoin, accessed 02/02/2018.

CHAPTER 2

Cryptocurrencies and assets, opportunities and risks

2.1 Introduction

A *cryptocurrency* is a digital or virtual currency employing cryptography to provide security and verify transactions on its network, and at the time of writing, the dominant species is Bitcoin.[1] They all operate on the basis of *cryptography*, which is the "practice and study of techniques for secure communication in the presence of third parties" employed in multiple places to provide security for the crypto network.[2] It primarily consists of mathematical and computer science algorithms applied to encrypt and decrypt information and is used in crypto addresses, hash functions, and the blockchain.

A cryptocurrency is not issued by a central authority but is a peer-to-peer blockchain based system, and it is therefore argued that it is immune from government interference or manipulation. That said, the same arguments were put forward concerning the internet in its early days,[3] and the view proved false. However, the reason in that instance was that the internet has key points of control and operators had to be located in a physical space, which brought them within the control of state governments.[4] This control, though, has been of limited success, with the result that child pornography and arms sales, amongst other criminal activities, still take place on the web. As De Filippi and Wright[5] have pointed out, blockchain has taken us back to the start of this problem, because blockchain is based on autonomous transactionally operating code based rules. The whole decentralised, peer-to-peer basis renders the state law making process potentially marginal, and it is this, rather than just the legal and regulatory issues of utilising cryptocurrencies and assets (discussed later), which is the greatest potential threat that blockchain based systems pose.

1 Bitcoin (2018), "Bitcoin glossary", *Bitcoin*, 16/01/2018, www.bitcoin.com/get-started/bitcoin-glossary, accessed 12/02/2018.

2 Ibid note [1], Bitcoin (2018).

3 Post, D. G. & Johnson, D. R. (1997) "Chaos prevailing on every continent: Towards a new theory of decentralized decision-making in complex systems", *Chicago-Kent Law Review*, 73: 1055–1099.

4 Goldsmith, J. & Wu, T. (2006), *Who controls the internet? Illusions of a borderless world*, Oxford University Press, pp. 142–161.

5 De Filippi, P. & Wright, A. (2018), *Blockchain and the law: The rule of code*, Harvard University Press, p. 51.

DOI: 10.4324/9781032667416-2

Bitcoin is an electronic peer-to-peer (P2P) cash system. Bitcoin Cash (BCH) and Bitcoin Core (BTC) represent the two main versions of Bitcoin. BCH is digital money offering very fast transaction times with low fees, while BTC has proved to be of limited use as money because of extremely high fees and slow transaction times.[6] A *blockchain* is a cryptographically secured public ledger shared among a distributed network of validating computers, each running common software that guides them to a consensus on the legitimacy of new entries and prevents anyone from unilaterally rewriting that agreed record.[7] This is how the technology solves the Double spend problem. *Double spending* occurs when someone tries to send a Bitcoin transaction to two different recipients simultaneously. However, when Bitcoin transactions are confirmed, it is nearly impossible to double spend. This further means that the more confirmations a transaction has, the harder it is to double spend the Bitcoin. Bitcoin and other cryptocurrencies are related to cryptography insofar as they employ mathematics to secure information. Within Bitcoin, cryptography generates and secures wallets, signs all transactions, and verifies each and every transaction in the blockchain. Even in the event of the blockchain becoming corrupted, or part of the network failing, it is possible to reconstruct it from the records kept elsewhere by others. It is thus unusually resilient.[8]

Digital currencies, or cryptocurrencies, represent something more than the digitisation of money. It is a way to reconstruct trust,[9] an innovative response by its designer to the erosion of trust in the banking system when the 2007/8 global financial crisis unfolded.[10] Some claim Bitcoin to be items of inherent value, like gold or cash. They differ from fiat money, such as the US dollar or the Japanese yen, in that they are decentralised, virtual stores of value and are transacted over the internet by different entities in anonymous fashion. Cryptocurrencies are therefore not controlled or supported by any bank or central authority. Their unique features[11] enable them to achieve financial transactions with no spatial constraints or middle party interventions, transactions finality,

---

6 Ibid note [1], Bitcoin (2018).

7 Casey, M. (2016), "How bitcoin and the blockchain are challenging the global economic order", Paper Presented at the 2016 MIT Consumer Dynamics Conference MIT Industrial Liaison Programme, 07/12/2016, http://ilp.mit.edu/images/conferences/2016/consumer/presentations/Casey.2016.CD.pdf, accessed 12/02/2018.

8 De Filippi, P. & Wright, A. (2018), *Blockchain and the law: The rule of code*, Harvard University Press, p. 2.

9 Shin, L. (2016), "Why a Wall Street Journal currency reporter didn't understand money until he learned about bitcoin", *Forbes*, 20/09/2016, www.forbes.com/sites/laurashin/2016/09/20/why-a-wall-street-journal-currency-reporter-didnt-understand-money-until-he-learned-about-Bitcoin/, accessed 12/02/2018; Vigna, P. & Casey, M. J. (2015), *Cryptocurrency: How bitcoin and digital money are challenging the global economic order*, New York, St. Martin's Press.

10 Crotty, J. (2009), "Structural causes of the global financial crisis: A critical assessment of the new 'financial architecture'", *Cambridge Journal of Economics*, 33(4): 563–580.

11 D'Alfonso, A., Langer, P. & Vandelis, Z. (2016), "The future of cryptocurrency: An investor's comparison of Bitcoin and Ethereum", Ryerson University Working Paper, 17/10/2016, www.econoist.com/sites/default/files/the_future_of_cryptocurrency.pdf, accessed 12/02/2018.

economical transaction costs, and the capacity to publicly verify transactions on the internet.

It is debatable as to whether they are "money". The classic definition for *money* is that from Mann, who said that it must function as:

(a) a medium of exchange;
(b) a measure of wealth, or as a standard for contractual obligations;
(c) a store or value of wealth; and
(d) a unit of account.[12]

However, as he went on to remark, "'money' can have very different meanings in different contexts".[13] So the classic definition of *money* seems to encapsulate cryptocurrencies as well as the traditional fiat currencies. The only remaining definitional issue is that the right to regulate money lies with sovereign states,[14] who have the capacity to restrict the right, delegate it, or transfer it.[15] The last point becomes critical in the context of the regulation of cryptocurrencies, an area examined later in the book.

This book maintains a focus on Bitcoin, the maiden, and still by far the most successful, cryptoasset for now. Bitcoin, designed by Satoshi Yakamoto, was launched into use mainly among software aficionados in 2008.[16] The attention then was largely confined to this small crypto partisan community, until it broke into public consciousness in 2013. This was the year that the digital currency evolved from a subcultural phenomenon into the mainstream of business, economics, and finance.[17] [18] A wider range of goods and services could then be purchased by Bitcoins as an increasing number of merchants signed up. This caused Bitcoin price to surge from US$13 per Bitcoin in January 2013 to US$1,242 at the end of November 2013 and reached US$8,510 by 1 June 2019[18] and $87,041 by 25 February 2025.[19] There are now 19.96 million Bitcoins in circulation,[20] but as the rate at which new Bitcoins will be created is being halved every four years, there will only be a maximum of 24 million coins issued.[20] Still, it remains

12 Proctor, C. (2005), *Mann on the legal aspect of money*, 7th edition, Oxford, Oxford University Press, p. 10.

13 Ibid note [12], Proctor (2005), p. 10.

14 Carreau, D. & Juillard, P. (2003), *Droit international économique*, Dalloz-Sirey.

15 Brownlie, I. (1973), *Principles of international law*, 6th edition, Oxford, Oxford University Press, Chapter 15.

16 Ibid note [9], Vigna & Casey (2015).

17 Christensen, N. (2013), "2013: Year of the bitcoin", *Forbes*, 10/12/2013, www.forbes.com/sites/kitconews/2013/12/10/2013-year-of-the-Bitcoin, accessed 12/02/2018.

18 Bitcoins (2018), "Bitcoin price chart with historic events", *99 Bitcoins*, 11/12/2019, www.99Bitcoins.com/price-chart-history, accessed 12/02/2018.

19 Market Summary, "Bitcoin", www.google.search?q=Bitcoin+current+price&sca_esv=ac-f673aa48e31f36&sxsrf=AHTn8zoyLhIICYG96z7ceot3Np_xI-1ZjQ%3A1740508495040&source=hp&ei=Tw2, accessed 25/02/2025.

20 www.nerdwallet.com, accessed 25/02/2025.

enigmatic, just like its shadowy designer, whose official identity remains a mystery to this day.

Increasingly, as Bitcoin prices continue to oscillate, the Bitcoin excitement that had earlier gained traction as a potential global digital currency began to shift focus to the blockchain technology underpinning it. Besides supporting cryptocurrencies, such as Bitcoin, blockchain technology is used for verifying and recording transactions. This public online ledger is now increasingly perceived as having the potential to reshape the global financial system and possibly have a significant impact on other industries too.[21] Bitcoin has gained imitators and adherents as well,[22] although it has its critics, including a Nobel economics laureate, who called it "a bubble, a scam or Ponzi scheme".[23] Being a relatively new technology, it will only survive with the support of optimists and faith in its business applications[24] and despite critics who argue that, despite a decade of existence, its only main contribution is as a payment mechanism that is more suited for business to business (B2B) use.[25]

2.2 Cryptocurrencies and blockchain

It could be helpful to step back to see the initial agenda of Bitcoin's designer so as to provide a balanced assessment of Bitcoin's potential. On 31 October 2008, Satoshi Nakamoto emailed a Bitcoin white paper to several hundred members of an obscure mailing list comprising cryptography experts and enthusiasts with the following abstract:

> A purely peer-to-peer version of electronic cash would allow online payments to be sent directly from one party to another without going through a financial institution. Digital signatures provide part of the solution, but the main benefits are lost if a trusted third party is still required to prevent double spending. We propose a solution to the double spending problem using a peer-to-peer network. The network timestamps transactions by hashing them into an ongoing chain of hash-based proof-of-work, forming a record that cannot be changed without redoing the proof-of-work. The longest chain not only serves as proof to the sequence of events witnessed, but proof that it came from the largest pool of CPU power. As long as a majority of CPU power is controlled by nodes that are not cooperating to attack the network, they'll generate the longest chain and outpace attackers. The network itself requires

21 Tapscott, D. & Tapscott, A. (2016), *Blockchain revolution: How the technology behind bitcoin is changing money, business, and the world*, New York, Penguin Random House.

22 Douma, S. (2016), "Bitcoin: The pros and cons of regulation", Universiteit Leiden Project Paper, 12/06/2016, https://openaccess.leidenuniv.nl/bitstream/handle/1887/42104/Bitcoin%2C%20The%20Pros%20and%20Cons%20of%20Regulation.pdf?sequence=1, accessed 12/02/2018.

23 Frank, J., Chin, K. & Ciolli, J. (2017), "Paul Krugman: Bitcoin is a more obvious bubble than housing was", *Business Insider*, 15/12/2017, www.businessinsider.com/paul-krugman-saysBitcoin-is-a-bubble-2017-12, accessed 12/02/2018; Deen, A. (2017), "Should you invest in bitcoin? Here are the pros and cons", *Equities*, 03/05/2017, www.equities.com/news/should-you-invest-in-Bitcoin-the-pros-and-cons, accessed 12/02/2018.

24 Ibid note [21], Tapscott & Tapscott (2016).

25 Roubini, N. (2018), "Blockchain's broken promises", Project Syndicate Paper, 26/01/2018, www.project-syndicate.org/commentary/why-Bitcoin-is-a-bubble-by-nouriel-roubini-2018-01?barrier=accesspaylog, accessed 28/01/2018.

> minimal structure. Messages are broadcast on a best effort basis, and nodes can leave and rejoin the network at will, accepting the longest proof-of-work chain as proof of what happened while they were gone.[26]

To this day, the identity of this emailer has not been formally established, such that most believe that it is the pseudonym used by an entity, an individual, or a group of individuals who seek anonymity for their own reasons. As has been pointed out,[27] this is essentially a combination of preceding ideas by others, though the end result is certainly innovative.[28]

Blockchain seems to work effectively for Bitcoin.[29] When payments are effected with a physical coin, the party handing it over will not be able to spend it again. Preventing double spending in a digital currency like Bitcoin is more complicated. In a typical Bitcoin transaction, one party uses Bitcoins to buy goods using their private key to transfer ownership of the currency. Word of the transaction is sent through the Bitcoin network to "miners" with powerful computers. The miners employ trial and error computations to solve a puzzle created by combining data about recent transactions. The first to locate the unique number that unlocks the puzzle earns the right to bundle the transactions into a confirmed batch, known as a block. The successful miner is rewarded with newly minted Bitcoin, but only after other miners confirm that the block's transactions do not contain any attempts to spend the same funds twice. This may be Bitcoin's Achilles heel, as once a certain number of Bitcoins have been issued, further issues of the currency will terminate. After that, an alternative way will be needed to validate transactions, and that will require payment by the users, something that will make the currency less attractive.

The blockchain acts as a public ledger, showing all transactions, though the identities of participants are obscured. Each block has a cryptographic link to the previous one. Every addition of a new linked block to the chain makes it harder for a rogue miner to steal Bitcoin by rewriting the sequence of transactions. Fink[30] defines it as "a database that is replicated across a network of computers updated through a consensus algorithm" and

> a shared and synchronized digital database that is maintained by an algorithm and stored on multiple nodes (the computers that store a local version of the distributed ledger). Blockchains can be imagined as a peer-to-peer network with the nodes serving as the different peers.[31]

---

26 Nakamoto, S. (2008), "Bitcoin: A peer-to-peer electronic cash system", Bitcoin White Paper, 31/10/2018, http://satoshinakamoto.me/whitepaper/, accessed 09/02/2020.

27 Narayanan, A. & Clark, J. (2017), "Bitcoin's academic pedigree: The concept of cryptocurrencies is built from forgotten ideas in research literature", *ACM Queue*, 15(4), 29/08/2017, https://queue.acm.org/detail.cfm?id=3136559; Atkinson, R. & Ezell, S. (2012), *Innovation economics: The race for global advantage*, Yale University Press.

28 Fink, M. (2019), *Blockchain, regulation and governance in Europe*, Cambridge, Cambridge University Press, p. 147.

29 Kharif, O. & Leising, M. (2018), "Bitcoin and blockchain", *Bloomberg*, 2/11/2018, www.bloomberg.com/quicktake/Bitcoins, accessed 29/01/2018.

30 Ibid note [28], Fink (2019), pp. 1.31, 6.

Thus, the construction looks like the following diagram. The central block at the bottom is the original arrangement, and each participant adds their own block as they engage in a transaction. Each transaction includes the cryptographic hash of the prior block, thus connecting them together. These blocks are each made up of several component parts:

- A header
- The version number
- A hash using standard cryptographic functions[31] (a kind of unique electronic fingerprint)
- A hash of the previous block
- A time stamp
- The body, made up of the previous transactions

Other information may also be added to it. The protocol of the relevant cryptocurrency or asset will link these together sequentially.

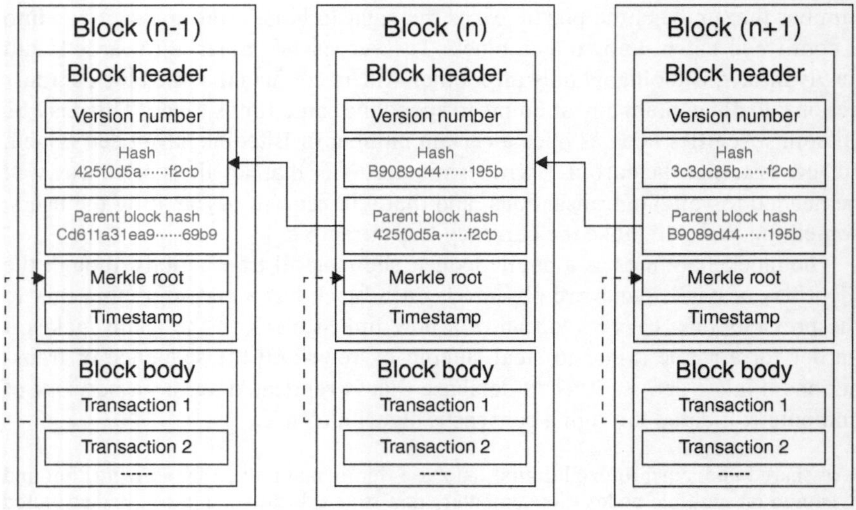

Figure 2.1 The process of cryptocurrency sales.[32]

31 De Phillipi, P. & Wright, A. (2018), *Blockchain and the law: The rule of code*, Harvard University Press, p. 22; Carter, J. L. & Wegman, M. N. (1979), "Universal classes of hash functions", *Journal of Computer and System Sciences*, 18(2): 143–154. ISSN 0022-0000; C/Users/andre/OneDrive/Documents/Articles/Islamic%20Blockchain/Blockchain%20structure%20_%20Download%20S, accessed 28/05/2024.

32 Raikwar, M., Gligoroski, D. & Kralevska, K., "SoK of Used Cryptography in Blockchain", https://doi.org/10.1109/ACCESS.2019.2946983, accessed 11/03/2025.

The blockchain acts as a public ledger showing all transactions, although it is not normally possible to determine the identities of participants. The construction thus takes on the following shape.

Forks can be added to the structure so that not all successive transactions remain the same. This is done by someone adding a different software component, resulting in what is called a "hard fork". Hard forks are not reversible and involve all the miners in updating their clients. Once this is done, those who do not implement the alteration to their part of the blockchain can no longer use it. Soft forks introduce voluntary changes to the software and can be reversed. They occur when the majority of the miners impose their approach on any dissenting minority. After that, transactions on the old software will be added to the previous structure, and the ones carried out on the new software will be added to the blockchain that has split off from the original construction. Either way, the blockchain becomes progressively longer and safer from interference after the event with each transaction.

Thus, the structure then looks like this:

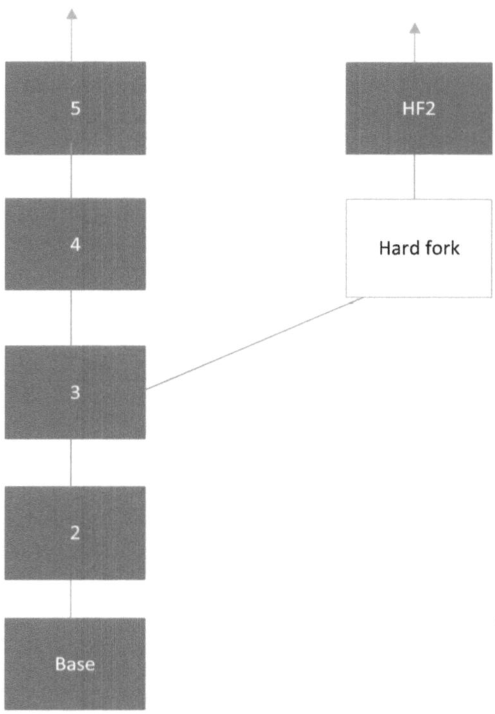

Figure 2.2 Blockchain and fork structure.

Bitcoin economic opportunities flow from Bitcoin and related cryptocurrency business applications. An empirical global study suggests the following:[33]

1. Unique active numbers of cryptocurrency wallets,[34] including Bitcoin, currently stand at around 560 million in 2024.[35] Many, however, are believed to be inactive. It is impossible to calculate how many people work in cryptocurrency businesses as, there are so many such operations around the world. Crypto.com alone had more than 4,000 employees by mid-2023.[36]
2. Crypto exchanges[37] have the highest number of operating entities and employ more people than others in this industry. There are 254 major ones, with a 24 hour trading value of over $1.2 trillion.[38]
3. The lines between wallets and exchanges are increasingly blurring. Some 52% of wallets surveyed provide an integrated exchange feature, of which 80% offer a national-to-cryptocurrency exchange service. The majority of wallets, in contrast, do not control access to user keys.[39]
4. Even as 79% of payment companies enjoy existing relationships with banking institutions and payment networks, the difficulty of obtaining and maintaining these relationships is cited as the sector's biggest challenge. National to cryptocurrency payments, on average, constitute two thirds of total company transaction volume, while national-to-national currency transfers and cryptocurrency to cryptocurrency payments account for 27% and 6%, respectively.
5. Some 79% of large miners rate their influence on protocol development as high to very high, compared to 51% of small miners. Publicly known mining facilities are geographically dispersed, but a significant concentration can be observed in particular Chinese provinces.

As of 27 August 2024, cryptoassets valuation stood at approximately US$2.3 trillion,[40] of which Bitcoin still dominates with a market cap of US$1.73 trillion, or 58.1% of the total cryptocurrency market.[41] As of 17 February 2020,

33 Hileman, G. & Rauchs, M. (2017), *Global cryptocurrency benchmarking study*, Cambridge, Cambridge Centre for Alternative Finance.

34 The Bitcoin wallet replaces Bitcoin addresses with a secret number (the private key) which acts as access to a store from which the owner can retrieve the Bitcoin by using that access code. This can be held on a laptop, desktop, or smartphone, or for a fee, they can be held by a specialist company on their software system.

35 www.triple-a.io>cryptocurrency-ownership-data, accessed 14/04/2025.

36 www.wikipedia.org/wiki/Crypto.com, accessed 25/02/2025.

37 The exchanges are online markets for buying and selling the relevant cryptocurrency, in the same way that an online stock exchange enables people to buy and sell shares.

38 https://coinmarketcap.com>rankings>exchanges, accessed 25/2/2025.

39 www.jbs.cam.ac.uk>uploads>2020/08, accessed 25/2/2025.

40 www.henleyglobal.com/newsroom/press-releases/crypto-wealth-report-2024, accessed 14/4/2025.

41 www.coingecko.com>global-charts, accessed 25/2/2025.

the top ten cryptocurrencies by market capitalisation were, in declining order of size: Bitcoin, Ethereum, XRP, Bitcoin Cash, Bitcoin SV, Tether, Litecoin, EOS, Binance Coin, and Tezos.[42] Given the general volatility of cryptoassets, in particular Bitcoin,[43] their respective order of ranking could change daily. The number of users is projected to reach 328.8 million by 2028.[44]

While various forces drive daily price fluctuations in equities, ultimately it is changes in the expectation of corporate earnings that have the most influence. For Bitcoin and other cryptoassets, there is no such earnings yardstick, only the waxing and waning of enthusiasm for a potentially revolutionary assets class for which at times the sky might seem to be the limit.[45] The return and volatility characteristics of Bitcoin compare starkly with those of the Standard and Poor's 500. The 30 day volatility of Bitcoin in between 2010 and 2021 never rose above 8.26% or fell below 2.49%. In most years, it was between 4% and 5%.[46] Bull market years in equities, such as 2013, when the S&P 500 rose 29.6%, and 2017, when it gained 19.4%, invariably come about when volatility is low. The S&P had a volatility rate of 11.2% in 2013, much lower than the 41% in 2008, when the benchmark dived by 38.5%. The 2008 and 2013 differences can be attributed to a marked shift in both reported and anticipated corporate profits, suggesting that dividend earnings drive equity prices.[47]

In the case of cryptocurrencies, and in particular Bitcoin, there are no interest payments or earnings, and there is no consensus valuation framework.[48] There is rather a rampant enthusiasm and the powerful fear of missing out interspersed with periods of panic. Captivating tales of substantial wealth generated over a very short period inspire fresh capital into the market.[49] The rush to purchase boosts prices even higher. This leads to a frenetic and positive volatility spiral where Bitcoin emerges as the poster child for self-reinforcing price momentum and speculation. Ignoring fundamental valuation guidance, price action drives demand that further drives the price before an inevitable price correction then occurs.[50]

---

42 https://coinmarketcap.com, accessed 17/02/2020.

43 Burger, D. (2017), "Bitcoin has become so volatile it looks like an ETF on steroids", *Bloomberg*, 29/06/2017, www.bloomberg.com/news/articles/2017-06-29/Bitcoin-s-becomeso-volatile-that-it-looks-like-a-steroidal-etf, accessed 02/02/2018.

44 Pradhan, D. (2024), "Top cryptocurrency statistics and trend in 2024", *Forbes Advisor*, 21/05/2024, www.forbes.com/advisor/in/investing/cryptocurrency/cryptocurrency-statistics/, accessed 22/05/2024.

45 Curnutt, D. (2018), "Cryptocurrencies steal volatility away from stocks", *Bloomberg*, 12/01/2018, www.bloomberg.com/opinion/articles/2018-01-11/cryptocurrencies-steal-volatility-away-from-stocks, accessed 02/02/2018.

46 https://bitbo.bio/volatility/, accessed 25/02/2025.

47 Ibid note [45], Curnutt (2018).

48 Ibid note [45], Curnutt (2018).

49 Ambler, A., Au-Yeang, A., Chung, G., Kauflin, J., Konrad, A., Shin, L. & Vardi, N. (2018), "The richest people in cryptocurrency", *Forbes*, 07/02/2018, www.forbes.com/richest-in-cryptocurrency, accessed 18/02/2018.

50 Ibid note [45], Curnutt (2018).

The "sky is the limit" syndrome has been observed over the past two decades, including the dot-com era of 1998 and 1999, crude oil in 2008, and gold in 2011.[45] In each of these, the spot price implied volatility moved dramatically higher with the fear of missing out, leading to a strong price surge. In the dot-com boom, for example, the Nasdaq 100 Index jumped by 85% in 1998, and 102% in 1999. The volatility of the technology index was 33% in that span, a sharp increase from the prior two year period. The impact of the 2008 crude oil and the US debt ceiling crisis suggests much of the same.

These three historical narratives appear to resemble the current risk dynamic in Bitcoin and other cryptocurrencies; a seductive, path breaking narrative and the resulting price action become sufficiently persuasive to demand action.[51] This positive relationship between price and volatility makes it almost impossible for investors to initiate a bearish bet, as the risks of being wrong are simply too great. This was the case for tech stocks in the late 1990s, where earnings became irrelevant to the valuation narrative. Indeed, volatility to both the upside and the downside is almost likely when fundamentals are superseded by the alluring story and the power of price momentum.[52]

Though with the high capitalisation mentioned earlier, Bitcoin is still small in scale when compared to other conventional asset instruments. The total value of all the world's coins and banknotes is estimated at US$7.6 trillion, the world's gold estimated at US$7.7 trillion basing on US$1,275 per ounce, and the total value of the world's money or broad money is estimated at US$90.4 trillion.[53] The world stock market capitalisation stood at about US$65.6 trillion,[54] and the daily foreign exchange market at about US$5.5 trillion[55] also dwarfed Bitcoin capitalisation at that time. At the end of 2024, cryptocurrencies accounted for less than 0.5% of global assets.[56] The challenge for Bitcoin is to achieve higher market capitalisation, though this is not easy, based on current trends. Much depends on the pace of adoption across the world, the acceleration of business application cases, and the kind of regulatory initiatives forthcoming from national and international regulators.

Meanwhile, the general public became interested following media stories telling how, at one point, various notable personalities had become so-called cryptoasset billionaires, largely because of their holdings of various cryptocurrencies, but mainly Bitcoin.[57] Based on cryptoasset prices on 27 August 2024,

---

51 Ibid note [45], Curnutt (2018).

52 Ibid note [45], Curnutt (2018).

53 Kaminska, I. (2017), "What happens when bitcoin's market cap overtakes world GDP?", *Financial Times*, 07/12/2017, https://ftalphaville.ft.com/2017/12/07/2196526/what-happens-when-Bitcoins-market-cap-overtakes-world-gdp/, accessed 18/02/2018.

54 Iskyan, K. (2016), "China's stock markets have soared by 1,479% since 2003", *Business Insider*, 06/11/2016, www.businessinsdier.com/world-stock-market-capitalizations-2016-11, accessed 18/02/2018.

55 McGeever, J. (2016), "Daily FX trading volume falls 5.5 pct to $5.1 trillion-BIS", *Reuters*, 01/09/2016, https://uk.reuters.com/article/bis-currency-idUKL8N1BC4PL, accessed 18/02/2018.

56 www.forbes.com/digital-assets/crypto-prices?sh=53fac33252478, accessed 25/02/2025.

57 Ibid note [49], Ambler, Au-Yeang, Chung, Kauflin, Konrad, Shin & Vardi (2018).

there were 325 crypto billionaires,[58] as opposed to 2,781 billionaires generally. Empirical examination of implied volatility spillovers and connectedness between Bitcoin and a wide menu of conventional financial assets, such as US equity market, gold, crude oil, emerging markets, and so on, from 8 January 2019 to 20 January 2022 suggests higher connectedness during COVID-19, but very low connectedness after the vaccine is available, signalling recovery in financial markets, besides indicating that Bitcoin is a strong transmitter of volatility during COVID-19.[59] Bitcoin Cash all time high price in 2017 has since never came close to that position.[60]

It seems that the blockchain based currency is here to stay and that these virtual assets have real, albeit volatile and speculative, value. Black market transactions, tax avoidance by entities, and sanctions dodging by countries like North Korea fan part of the demand, but this includes widespread excitement over the technology and the ideological aspiration for money free from interventions of whimsical nation states.

Following on from the analysis of fluctuations in cryptocurrency prices, three other issues arise: variations in cryptocurrency prices relative to other geographic areas, price variations relative to fluctuations in fiat currencies, and finally, whether or not the same approach in fluctuations in cryptocurrencies show price variations correlating with the Black–Scholes formula,[61] which explains price changes in certain derivative contracts[62] that correlate with underlying price volatility in the commodities the derivative relates to.

2.3 Price variations relative to other geographic areas

One recent analysis[63] illustrates that there are significant price variations in cryptocurrencies between states. Indeed, the variation between them was much higher than within them. This arises because of the fact that there is no central exchange on which to compare prices at any moment in time. The analysis only consisted of viewing Bitcoin prices,[64] but it is rational to suppose that the principle will carry over to cryptocurrencies generally. The price of crypto was 3% higher in South Korea than in the United States in February 2025,[65] with similar gaps between the United States on one hand and Japan and Europe on the other.

58 US billions, that is, $100 million.

59 Di, M. & Xu, K. (2022), "COVID-19 vaccine and post-pandemic recover: Evidence from Bitcoin-cross-asset implied volatility spillover", *Finance Research Letters*, 50: 103289–103296.

60 De Best, R. (2023), "Bitcoin Cash/USD price history up until October09, 2023", *Statista*, 10/10/2023, www.statista.com/statistics/807070/bitcoin-cash-price/, accessed 11/10/2023.

61 Essentially it shows that it is possible to perfectly hedge a European-style put or bought option by buying and selling the underlying commodity at the right time. Thus, the financial risk can be removed.

62 Specifically, options contracts.

63 Makarov, I. & Schoar, A. (2018), "Trading and arbitrage in cryptocurrency markets", *SSRN*, 12/07/2019, https://papers.ssrn.com/sol3/papers.cfm?abstract_id=3171204, accessed 17/02/2020.

64 Some of the analyses related to Ripple and Ethereum in the context of arbitrage spreads between cryptocurrencies.

65 www.businesskorea.co.kr>news>articleView, accessed 14/4/2025.

This type of pattern seems to have continued, although precise statistics are difficult to determine. Generally speaking, prices trade at a premium above the US price elsewhere in the world.

The price deviations seem to have occurred most markedly when there has been a big increase in worldwide demand. Interestingly, though, where there is a large arbitrage spread relative to fiat currencies, cryptocurrencies have narrower price variations between themselves.[66]

It is rational to suppose that as data on such price variations becomes more the recipient of focus by traders, arbitrage trading will start to smooth out these price differentials. This will occur as a result of a party buying in a country with lower Bitcoin prices – and this is currently normally the United States – and selling where the price is higher. This will only make sense if the state where the cryptocurrency is based has no exchange controls, or the profit may become trapped there. It will be interesting to see how long this takes.

2.4 Price variations relative to fiat currencies

Fiat currencies can be put into two categories: those where there are no significant exchange controls and those where there are. In the former case, it would be expected that there would be a smaller price differentiation with respective cryptocurrency prices between two such currencies for the reasons discussed just earlier. However, in the latter case, cryptocurrencies offer the opportunity to change money from one state to another by buying the cryptocurrency inside the state with currency controls and then selling them in a state where there are none. Different cryptocurrency price levels should therefore be expected in this situation, with cryptocurrency prices pulling into line between different fiat currencies. Different price relationships might be anticipated between two cryptocurrencies in separate states both having exchange controls.

2.5 Black–Scholes

The *Black–Scholes formula* is a mathematical model which estimates the price of vanilla options[67] traded on a European style basis (i.e. options that can only be exercised on their final date).[68] What it shows is that the option can be perfectly

66 Ibid note [64], Makarov & Schoar (2018), p. 3.

67 An *option contract* is an arrangement whereby one counterparty contracts to buy, and the other to sell, an asset at a future date at a price agreed now, though in practice the parties just settle up financially on the settlement date rather than trading the underlying commodity. The holder of the contract has to pay a deposit to enter into the contract and then has the right, but not the obligation, to perform. The deposit will be calculated in proportion to the risk to the other party. The holder may forfeit the contract and walk away if the price has moved against them by a greater amount than the value of the deposit, as the counterparty would then keep the deposit. The party who has received the deposit is, however, bound by the arrangement and is obliged to perform. A *vanilla option* is a straightforward one, without the addition of a mathematical formula.

68 As opposed to American ones that can be exercised at any point up until that time. Technically, this is called "continuously revised delta hedging."

hedged by buying and reselling the underlying asset at the right time, and thus, any financial risk is removed.[66] It is therefore possible to determine the right price for the option in the first place. Variations on this model have been created to cover different scenarios, and its existence was the cause of a huge increase in options trading. In the context of cryptocurrencies, it will be interesting to see whether the price movements lend themselves to similar mathematical calculations predicting hedging performance. If so, the possibilities for those utilising cryptocurrency-based options as an investment or for hedging purposes will be huge.

2.6 Cryptoassets

Cryptoasset investors exist in a similar group to cryptocurrency holders, extending from anti-establishment crypto activists and electricity-consuming "miners" to prescient Silicon Valley financiers and investors who got lucky, known as "hodlers".[69] Banking heir Matthew Mellon saw his US$2 million investment in Ripple (XRP) blossom into approximately US$1 billion at the peak, before tragically dying and leaving US$200 million inaccessible as his wallet key codes died with him in May 2018.[70] Others include former child actor Brock Pierce, who went into Bitcoin mining and financing blockchain start-ups; Changpeng Zhao, the owner of Binance, a Bitcoin exchange; and as well as Chris Larsen, Joseph Lubin, Cameron and Tyler Winklevoss, Brian Armstrong, Matthew Roszak, Anthony Di Iorio, Michale Novogratz, Brendan Blumer, Dan Larimer, Valery Vavilov, Charles Hoskinson, Brad Garlinghouse, Barry Silbert, Vitalik Buterin, Tim Draper, and Song Chi-Hyung.[71] Included also in the list are various successful issuers of initial coin offerings (ICOs).[72]

The aforementioned and others would no doubt spur many on, but others could be held back from participating because of the significant risks posed by cryptoasset investments, as well as from powerful cautionary statements from regulators around the world.

The International Organization of Securities Commissions (IOSCO), comprising global securities regulators, recently issued an investors' alert notice to the perceived risks connected with ICOs.[73] Its more notable members include the US Securities and Exchange Commission (SEC), the UK Financial Conduct Authority (FCA), and the European Securities and Markets Authority (ESMA).

69 Ibid note [61], Kauflin (2018).

70 Semenova, L. (2018), "$500 million in ripple lost as billionaire Matthew Mellon dies suddenly", *Madeincrypto*, 31/05/2018, https://madeincrypto.com/500-million-in-ripple-lost-asbillionaire-matthew-mellon-dies-suddenly/, accessed 11/02/2019. Also Cook, J., Field, M. & Chowdhury, H. (2019), "The bitcoin fortune taken to the grave", *Daily Telegraph*, Business Section.

71 Ibid note [49], Ambler, Au-Yeang, Chung, Kauflin, Konrad, Shin & Vardi (2018).

72 Shin, L. (2017), "The emperor's new coins: How initial coin offerings fueled a $100 billion crypto bubble", *Forbes*, 10/07/2017, www.forbes.com/sites/laurashin/2017/07/10/the-emperors-new-coins-how-initial-coin-offerings-fueled-a-100-billion-crypto-bubble, accessed 02/02/2018.

73 IOSCO (2018), "IOSCO board communication on concerns related to initial coin offerings (ICOs)", *IOSCO Media Release*, accessed 18/01/2018.

The IOSCO claims that these coin offerings are not standardised and their legal and regulatory status would depend on the merits of individual ICOs. The IOSCOs regard ICOs/token sales/coin sales as highly speculative investments, where investors could be putting their entire invested capital at risk. Although some operators could be providing legitimate investment opportunities to fund projects or businesses, there is a significant and growing risk coming from the increased targeting of ICOs to retail investors via online distribution channels by entities often located outside an investor's home jurisdiction. These might not be subject to regulation or could be operating illegally[74] and in violation of existing civil and regulatory laws, and in turn, this raises investor protection concerns. There have also been instances of fraud,[75] and as such, investors are cautioned to exercise vigilance when deciding on investing in ICOs.

So far, 2018–23 saw ICO issues raise over US$50 billion.[76] Over 80% of ICO fundraising seems to have seen the proceeds disappear as a result of financial fraud, and half the rest failed. The biggest of them defrauded investors of US$2.6 billion.[77] [78] There also appears to be a correlation between failure rates and the nature of the ICO. Kickstarter projects have a 65% failure rate, venture-backed start-ups 70%, and dot-com tech IPOs 85% over a period of ten years.[79] Nonetheless, such funds held over US$50 billion at the end of 2022,[80] with a smaller sum indirectly exposed to cryptocurrencies through funds or derivatives.[81] It will be interesting to see if this period of expansion continues, given that regulators are starting to treat such offerings as securities (see Chapter 4) and that, as a result, the legal and regulatory overheads are starting to rise. That said, the sales and distribution costs should remain much lower than a traditional share or equity offer.

EOS developed a successful model by releasing its tokens over a 341-day period at a rate of 2 million a day to retain a sense of limited availability and exclusivity in the sale. The total amount raised was US$4.2 billion. Even so, its capacity to raise finance did not leave it with a trouble-free business launch. Nonetheless, the success of this approach to selling the ICOs may well result in imitators.

---

74 Wildau, G. (2017), "China central bank declares initial coin offerings illegal", *Financial Times*, 04/09/2017, www.ft.com/content/3fa8f60a-9156-11e7-a9e6-11d2f0ebb7f0, accessed 02/02/2018.

75 Morris, D. Z. (2017), "The SEC filed fraud charges against 2 'initial coin offerings'", *Fortune*, 01/10/2017, https://fortune.com/2017/10/01/sec-ico-fraud-charges/. See also HM Treasury (2018) "Crypto assets taskforce, final report", *HMSO*, 29/10/2018, at p. 35.

76 Telegram and EOS.

77 AutonomousNext (2018), "#Crypto Utopia: The $20 billion Cambrian explosion of tokenized digital assets, and the emerging infrastructure being built to support them", *AutonomousNext*, p. 3, https://next.autonomous.com/crypto-utopia.

78 Dean, E., "70+ ICO statistics you need to know in 2023", https://icobench.com/stats/ico-statistics/, accessed 26/02/2025.

79 Ibid note [79], AutonomousNext (2018), p. 4.

80 Ibid note [80], Dean at 138.

81 Ibid note [79], AutonomousNext (2018), p. 5.

The two key issues are the obvious explosion in the utilisation of ICOs in certain areas, and one element that has helped facilitate this is the utilisation of discounts in the form of "airdrops". This is the payment of a sign up bonus to the people buying the ICOs, typically of 5–10%. It is rather like a discounted bond issue or, were they permitted, a discounted share issue.[82] Even so, at present they are high risk investments: 34% lose more than half their original price, and 60% have underperformed relative to both Bitcoin and Ether.[83]

As far back as 2015, IOSCO advised that financial regulators from more than 26 countries have issued warnings on ICO risks. The IOSCO's investor alert in 2015 mentioned that investors should be cautious and carefully research before investing.[84] The investors' alert on the perceived risks of cryptoassets merits close scrutiny, given the range of risks associated with Bitcoin, despite ICOs falling behind on the fintech curve earlier. This is exacerbated by the absence of a clear legal framework, as the systems have emerged too quickly for the legal and regulatory systems to stay in front. The state of affairs which De Filippi and Wright refer to as the *lex cryptographica*[85] is exacerbated by the fact that the peer-to-peer basis on which blockchain operates means that there is not a dominant party or intermediary to impose a code. However, regulators in general and the US SEC have been active in regulating issues within their jurisdiction.

The risk here is to both issuers and investors. There seemed to have been an assumption made in many earlier ICO type issues that if the issue is termed a "token" and the issuing document a "white paper", then the existing securities laws of the state of issuance do not apply. That this is not the case is apparent from the analysis of the securities laws of a number of states analysed later in the book. The attraction to the parties of assuming the issuance takes place outside the securities laws arises from the very high cost of conforming with the prospectus or information memorandum document (a type of advertising brochure which has to comply with strict securities laws and where relevant stock exchange rules). If an issue appears to be in the nature of a share or a bond or an interest in a collective investment scheme, then the starting assumption should be that the home securities regulator will treat it as such.

US SEC Chairman Jay Clayton drew attention to questions raised by investors and market participants on the legal status of cryptoassets, whether they are subject to regulation including those designed to protect investors, whether the products comply with these rules, whether the offering is legal, whether those offering

82 Shares can be issued on a partly paid basis, with the balance to be paid at a later date, but most states have controls on the share buybacks, so discounted shares become a more difficult area. That said, a firm issuing shares has a lot of freedom to set their price, and in the case of a public issue, the underwriters will tend to put downward pressure on the launch price to reduce the risk of having to start buying them.

83 Ibid note [79], AutonomousNext (2018), p. 36.

84 Zhao, W. (2018), "Global securities watchdog warns investors on ICO risks", *Coin Desk*, 19/01/2018, www.coindesk.com/global-securities-watchdog-warns-investors-on-ico-risks, accessed 02/02/2018.

85 De Filippi, P. & Wright, A. (2018), *Blockchain and the law: The rule of code*, Harvard University Press, p. 5.

them are licensed to do so, whether the trading markets are fair, the risk of market price manipulation, market liquidity matters, and theft risks, including hacking.[86] He cautioned that answering the question requires in depth analysis and differs depending on various factors. He offered a general view directed mainly at retail investors and market professionals, such as broker-dealers, exchanges, lawyers, and accountants, whose actions have an impact on retail investors. He highlighted to market investors that the SEC has issued investor alerts, bulletins, and statements in ICO and cryptoasset linked investments, including with respect to the marketing of certain offerings and investments by celebrities and others, but added that, where investors elect to invest in them, to raise questions of concern to them and to demand on clear answers, recognising that these markets span national borders and that significant trading may occur on systems and platforms across other parts of the world. He advised market professionals to review the SEC's various releases and reports on these matters seriously and to pay attention to crucial issues raised, especially those purporting the difference between tokens viewed to be outside the orbit of securities and regulations, and in particular, ICO, with proposed features and marketing efforts that stress the potential for profits based on entrepreneurial or management initiatives but continue to contain the hallmarks of a security under US law and which merit closer attention from those market professionals with gatekeeping function and responsibility, such as securities lawyers, accountants, and consultants.

The European Parliament noted that responses to challenges posed by ICOs and cryptoassets extend from an outright ban by a few on minority, private offerings, and regulatory warnings, as chosen in the EU and the United States.[87] Many others elected to use existing laws to regulate such issues or waited to see how other economies respond to these developments. In November 2017, ESMA issued two statements on ICOs, one pertaining to risks posed by ICOs for investors, and the other on the rules applicable to enterprises partaking in ICOs. In its March 2018 communication on "fintech action plan", the EU directed the European supervisory authorities to evaluate the suitability of the EU regulatory framework pertaining to ICOs and cryptoassets more generally. This was followed by the publication of advice on ICOs and cryptoassets in January 2019 by ESMA that, provided the relevant safeguards are in place, ICOs could offer a useful alternative funding source for blockchain start ups and other innovative businesses facing difficulties or costly to raise capital from conventional funding channels.

86 Clayton, J. (2017), "Statement on cryptocurrencies and initial coin offerings", *SEC Chairman Public Statement*, 11/12/2017, www.iosco.org/library/ico-statements/United%20States%20-%20SEC%20-20Statement%20on%20Cryptocurrencies%20and%20Initial%20Coin%20Offerings%20by%20SEC%20Chairman%20Jay%20Clayton.pdf, accessed 20/12/2023.

87 Delivorias, A. (2021), "Understanding initial coin offerings: A new means of raising funds based on a blockchain", *European Parliamentary Research Service (EPRS) PE696.167*, July 2021, www.europarl.europa.eu/RegData/etudes/BRIE/2021/696167/EPRS_BRI(2021)696167_EN.pdf, accessed 20/12/2023.

ESMA nevertheless drew attention to widespread reports of and concerns over fraudulent ICOs, as well as cybersecurity and other evolving technology risks. Pertaining to existing EU regulation,[88] ESMA noted that prospectus rules should apply to ICOs, that the scope of the directive on prevention of the financial system for the purposes of money laundering should be reviewed to take into account providers of financial services for ICOs, and that EU policymakers should consider the need to have appropriate risk disclosure requirements in place to ensure that consumers are aware of the risks prior to committing funds or cryptoassets. In March 2020, the EU proposed a strategy to support the potential of digital finance reinforced by a package of legislative initiatives, including proposals for regulations on markets in cryptoassets on a pilot regime for market infrastructures based on DLT and on digital operational resilience for the financial sector. In turn, the European Parliament adopted a resolution in October 2020 calling for improving access to capital market finance, especially for SMEs, but insisted that clear and consistent guidance at EU level is needed on the applicability of existing regulatory and prudential processes to cryptoassets that qualify as financial instruments under EU legislation so as to provide regulatory certainty and avoid a non-level playing field, forum shopping, and regulatory arbitrage in the internal market.

The UK Treasury Report drew attention to risks for investors. These extend from high price volatility, hacking risks at cryptoasset exchanges, poor market liquidity contributing to price manipulation risk, use of cryptoassets for moneylending, or cryptoassets' growth risk implications for financial stability. As to whether an ICO is regulated in the UK, much depends on how it is structured and what the token subsequently represents. Where the tokens represent a transferable security such as shares and bonds, the ICO would fall under the regulatory scope of the FCA, requiring the FCA to ensure an appropriate degree of protection for investors as they are consumers for the purposes of the FCA statutory objectives. In contrast, where tokens represent a claim on prospective services or products, they do not amount to transferable securities or other regulated products and, ergo, fall outside the purview of the FCA.

Since then, the Financial Services and Markets Act 2023 has provided a new definition of *cryptoassets* for regulatory purposes to bring them within the financial services' regulatory regime. This is discussed later in **5.2.2**.

Cryptoassets, and, in particular, Bitcoin, have unique investment risks, and these are outlined as follows:[89]

88 Ibid note [89], Delivorias (2021).

89 Investopedia (2018), "Bitcoin", *Investopedia*, www.investopedia.com/terms/b/Bitcoin.asp, accessed 18/02/2018.

2.7 Relevant risks

2.7.1 Regulatory risk

Bitcoin has been associated with black market transactions, money laundering, illicit activities, and tax evasion.[90] Many governments across the world are responding with policies and measures to regulate, restrict, or ban the use and sale of Bitcoin, and some, like China, have already done so.[91] Others, like Japan, require Bitcoin exchanges to maintain minimum capitalisation and follow general anti–money laundering (AML) and know your customer (KYC) procedures resembling those in the banking sector.[92] Yet other countries are initiating their own regulatory approaches, but the lack of uniform regulations covering Bitcoin and other cryptocurrencies could lead to questions over their longevity, liquidity, and universality. Regulatory aspects are discussed at length later in the book.

2.7.2 Security risk

Though until now the Bitcoin platform has not been significantly compromised, Bitcoin exchanges, which are entirely digital, are at risk from hackers, malware, and operational glitches. These have occurred on various occasions, with the more notable ones involving Mt. Gox, a Bitcoin exchange in Japan that was the largest in the world at that time, which had to close down following the theft of millions of dollars of Bitcoin.[93] There was also the 2018 Coincheck case, where some US$530 million worth of coins were stolen,[94] and one report suggests that US$927 million was stolen in hacking attacks in the first nine months of 2018 alone.[95] In 2025, the North Korean government was accused of being behind the hack which stole US$1.5 billion from the Dubai-based exchange Bybit.[96]

---

90 Bloomberg, J. (2017), "Using bitcoin or other cryptocurrency to commit crimes? Law enforcement is onto you", *Forbes*, 28/12/2017, www.forbes.com/sites/jasonbloomberg/2017/12/28/using-Bitcoin-or-other-cryptocurrency-to-commit-crimes-law-enforcement-is-onto-you/#4e623af93bdc, accessed 02/02/2018.

91 Leng, S. (2017), "Why has China declared war on bitcoin and digital currencies?", *South China Morning Post (SCMP)*, 16/09/2017, www.scmp.com/news/china/economy/article/2111456/why-has-china-declared-war-Bitcoin-and-digital-currencies, accessed 02/02/2018.

92 Yagami, K. (2017), "Japan: A forward thinking bitcoin nation", *Forbes*, 02/11/2017, www.forbes.com/sites/outofasia/2017/11/02/japan-a-forward-thinking-Bitcoin-nation/#6608953733a3, accessed 02/02/2018.

93 Harney, A. & Stecklow, S. (2017), "Twice burned-how Mt. Gox's bitcoin customers could lose again", *Reuters*, 16/11/2017, www.reuters.com/investigates/special-report/Bitcoin-gox/, accessed 02/02/2018.

94 Uranaka, T. & Wilson, T. (2018), "Japan raps coincheck, orders broader checks after $530 million cryptocurrency theft", *Reuters*, 29/01/2018, https://de.reuters.com/article/us-japan-cryptocurrency-idUSKBN1FI06S, accessed 02/02/2018.

95 Chavez-Dreyfuss, G. (2018), "Cryptocurrency theft hits nearly $1 billion in first nine months: Report", *Reuters*, 10/10/2018, https://uk.reuters.com/article/uk-crupto-currency-crime/cryptocurrency-theft-hits-nearly-1-billion-in-the-first-nine-months-idUKKCN1MK1JD.

96 Field, M. (2025), "North Korea steals $1.5 billion as it pulls off world's biggest ever heist", *Daily Telegraph*, 27/02/2025.

There are ways to enhance the security features of Bitcoin exchanges, but equally, users could opt for safer ways to store their Bitcoins, such as the option of offline cold wallets. Major global insurers are beginning to offer protection against cryptocurrency theft. They appear willing to solve the daunting challenges this brings rather than miss out on this volatile and loosely regulated, but rapidly growing, business.[97] Guardian Vaults, a leading Australian private vault and safety deposit box operator, now offers a custodial safety deposit box using technology such as biometric hand scanners, facial recognition protocols, and so on. It is seeing a growing customer demand trend for its services.[98]

2.7.3 Insurance risk

Some investments in the United States could be insured via the Securities Investor Protection Corporation, while conventional bank accounts are insured via the Federal Deposit Insurance Corporation, up to a stipulated amount depending on the jurisdiction. Bitcoin exchanges and Bitcoin accounts are generally not insured by any federal or government initiative in the United States, and this appears to be the case in most other economies. Insurance coverage for loss or theft of Bitcoin represents an opportunity and a challenge as cryptocurrencies are purely digital and hold a variable market value. So far, the insurance industry responds to cryptocurrencies rather slowly, with only a few offering insurance covers. These include XL Catlin, Chubb, and Mitsui Sumitomo Insurance. Several others are said to be looking into theft coverage for companies handling cryptocurrencies, such as Bitcoin and Ether, which transact between anonymous parties. The challenge for insurers is how to cover those risks for customers they know little about, who use technology few understand, and a nascent industry lacking troves of data insurers usually rely on in designing and pricing coverage.

2.7.4 Fraud risk

Fraudsters profit from the selling of false coins, a situation that may become more common as Bitcoin users exercise more care when using and safeguarding the use of their private key encryptions. In the United States, for instance, the SEC brought action against an operator of a Bitcoin related Ponzi scheme.[99] The SEC's enforcement division opened dozens of investigations involving ICOs and digital assets, many of which are ongoing. The SEC mentioned that while many of its investigations have focused on fraud, it is also examining cases to

97 Barlyn, S. (2018), "Insurers gingerly test bitcoin business with heist policies", *Reuters*, 01/02/2018, www.reuters.com/article/us-markets-Bitcoin-insurance-insight/insurers-gingerly-test-Bitcoin-business-with-heist-policies-idUSKBN1FL406, accessed 18/02/2018.

98 Redman, J. (2017), "Australian vault provider says securing bitcoin in safety boxes is trending", *Bitcoin*, 05/12/2017, https://news.bitcoin.com/australian-vault-provider-says-securing-bitcoin-in-safety-boxes-is-trending/, accessed 02/02/2018.

99 SEC (2013), "SEC charges Texas man with running bitcoin-denominated Ponzi scheme", *SEC Media Release*, 23/07/2013, www.sec.gov/news/press-release/2013-132, accessed 02/02/2018.

ensure compliance with the registration requirements of US federal securities laws. As such, while companies raised millions of dollars through ICOs prior to mid-2017, these fundraising activities have fallen sharply subsequent to the SEC cautioning that it treats nearly all digital tokens as securities.[100] In August 2024, the SEC prosecuted a number of parties for crypto-related fraud.[101]

Likewise, in the UK, Action Fraud[102] showed that there were 532 reports of cryptoasset fraud in June 2023–September 2024 alone in the UK,[103] and in 2024, the FCA secured convictions against two people for crypto-related fraud.[104]

2.7.5 Market risk

The extreme price volatility of cryptocurrencies presents a serious challenge for most investors and users. Until their applications or uses expand significantly, their price is likely to remain highly speculative and risky. Bitcoin's fate as a currency rests on more individuals and merchants using it for transaction purposes rather than mainly for speculation. Though Bitcoin no longer dominates the cryptocurrency market to the extent that it used to, it still leads the pack, because it appears to benefit from an early mover advantage, brand recognition, and venture capital backup.[105] Even so, technological breakthroughs in the shape of a better digital coin could always present a threat.

2.7.6 Tax risk

There has been a clarification of the tax position regarding cryptocurrencies and assets over recent years. In the United States, they are treated as property, not currency, and are subject to capital gains tax and income tax as appropriate.[106] In the UK, crypto profits are subject to capital gains tax.[107] Also, HMRC's guidance for Bitcoin is that it is not a form of economic activity, and as such,

---

100 Roberts, J. J. (2018), "Cryptocurrency scams are now among the SEC's top enforcement priorities", *Forbes*, 2/11/2018, https://fortune.com/2018/11/02/sec-ico-report-cryptocurrency-scams/, accessed 5/03/2019; SEC, "Annual report 2018: Division of enforcement", *SEC*, 02/11/2018, www.sec.gov/files/enforcement-annual-report-2018.pdf, accessed 05/05/2019.

101 www.sec.gov/securities-topics/crypto-assets#:~:The%Securities%20and%20Exchange%20Commission%20charged%2011%20individuals%20for%20for%20their,including%20in%20the%20United%20States, accessed 27/02/2025.

102 Action Fraud (2018), "Cryptocurrency fraud leads to £2 million worth of losses this summer", *Action Fraud*, 10/08/2018, www.actionfraud.police.uk/alert/2m-lost-to-cryptocurrency-fraud.

103 www.actionfraud.police.uk/cryptocurrency/fraud, accessed 15/05/2025.

104 www.fca.org.uk/news/press-releases/fca-secures-conviction-agsinst-two-individual-fraud, accessed 27/02/2025.

105 Zhao, W. (2018), "Crypto market sets to new high as bitcoin dominance drops to historic low", *Coin Desk*, 02/01/2018, www.coindesk.com/crypto-market-cap-sets-time-high-Bitcoinshare-drops-historic-low, accessed 18/02/2018.

106 www.irs./gov/filing/digital-assets, accessed 15/04/2025.

107 www.gov.uk/guidance/check-if-you-need-to-pay-tax-when-you-sell-cryptoassets, accessed 15/04/2025.

transactions involving it are not subject to value added tax (VAT).[108] This approach of standardising tax treatment with other assets now seems widespread in other countries.

Opinions about the impact this will have on trading are not clear as the technology underpinning them continues to evolve, as business applications expand, and as regulations emerge. One prominent US bank CEO, for example, recently retracted his previous claim that Bitcoin was a fraud and now believes in the technology behind it but remains concerned about how government policies will have an impact on it in the future.[109] More interestingly, the bank's respectable global research unit concludes that cryptocurrencies could one day play a role in the diversification of global bond and equity portfolios.[110] The next chapter evaluates Bitcoin's role as a potential global digital currency.

2.7.7 Legal risk

Perhaps surprisingly, one element that has been neglected is the legal basis on which it is possible to own cryptocurrencies and crypto wallets. The closest existing basis for such legal ownership in common law countries is that of bailment, which traditionally covered leaving an item in store but retaining ownership. The owner can thus withstand a claim against it by the creditors of the warehouse or other locations where the goods are stored. There is a parallel here with crypto wallets which store the cryptocurrency concerned, hopefully securely, by way of a private electronic key.[111] However, it remains a legal grey area as to whether it is possible to have digital bailment of digital products. The long standing English tradition adopted by common law states is that the custom of the marketplace will be applied by the courts, and it is therefore reasonable to assume that the courts would apply the principles of bailment to digital assets.[112]

The alternative possibility in common law jurisdictions is to apply the law of trusts, and in civil law jurisdictions, the law of agency. In the case of applying the law of trusts, the structure would be that the custodian holds the assets for the cryptocurrency owner and holds the legal title to it. The benefits of ownership belong to the owner, who has an equitable title and can claim the assets from the custodian and who also has priority over the custodian's creditors in the event of the custodian's insolvency.[104] In most civil law states, the same structure can be constructed through existing legal principles of agency law.

108 https://www.gov.uk/hmrc-internal-manuals/cryptoassets-manual/crypto45000, accessed 5/08/2025.

109 Kim, T. (2018), "Jamie Dimon says he regrets calling bitcoin a fraud and believes in the technology behind it", *CNBC*, 09/01/2018, www.cnbc.com/2018/01/09/jamie-dimon-sayshe-regrets-calling-Bitcoin-a-fraud.html, accessed 02/02/2018.

110 Loeys, J. & Chang, J. (2018), *Decrypting cryptocurrencies: Technology, applications and challenges*, New York, J.P. Morgan.

111 Micheler, E. & Davies, S. (2018), "The future of money and the impact of fintech and cryptocurrencies", London School of Economics, Speech at Conference, London, 26/11/2018.

112 *Goodwin v Robarts* (1876) 1 App. Cas. 476.104.

The question which then arises is the legal status of the cryptocurrency itself. Is it digital property, with a new legal status, or alternately, would the definition of *chose in action* or *chose in possession* be extended to cover it? The tradition of recognising commercial custom should guarantee that one of the aforementioned options is applied in common law jurisdictions.

In the UK, the Property (Digital Assets) Bill, which at the date of writing is currently proceeding through Parliament, will deal with the matter.

2.7.8 Scale risk

At present, blockchain based systems are slow, taking an average of 40 minutes per Bitcoin transaction, 1 minute 30 seconds for Ethereum, and 1 to 2 seconds for Arbitrum network. Cardano and Solana can be carried out in a fraction of a second. To compete, blockchain based systems are going to have to handle far greater numbers of transactions. As we have already seen, blockchain based transactions grow progressively, and the networks and computers utilising it will thus need far greater capacity than at present to handle it all. In turn, this will require a considerable investment of capital by users, especially at the retail end, where such an increase in costs may be a deterrence to use. It may be possible to resolve this by processing transactions through payment channels which do not require validation by miners[113] or by the development of other approaches which reduce the need for such a vast increase in capacity. At present, this is an area that remains uncertain.

113 Poon, J. & Dryja, T. (2016), "The bitcoin lightning network: Scalable off-chain instant payments", *Lightning Network*, 14/01/2016.

CHAPTER 3

Blockchain and distributed ledger technology

3.1 Introduction

While this text has focused on cryptocurrencies, it is already clear that blockchain has a much wider potential application.[1] Its generic name, "distributed ledger technology", gives a more accurate idea of what the concept is. Essentially, there is a ledger which is distributed on the internet on a peer-to-peer network and runs on the users' computers, not on a central database. It is a purely distributed peer-to-peer system of ledgers that utilises a software unit that consists of an algorithm which negotiates the international content of ordered and connected blocks of data together with cryptographic and security technologies in order to achieve and maintain its integrity.[2]

Or as Vitalik Buterin, the creator of Ethereum, put it:

> [I]t is: a . . . computer that anyone can upload programs to and leave the programs to self-execute, where the current and all the previous states of every program are always publicly visible, and which carries a very strong cryptoeconomically secured guarantee that the programs running on the chain will continue to execute in exactly the way that the blockchain protocol specifies.[3]

The essential concept is not new, it having a history dating back to the start of the 1990s, when Haber and Stornetta created a system of documented time stamps that could not be retrospectively interfered with. Together with Bayer, they then incorporated "Merkle trees" into the design to facilitate this by the successive elements being constructed into a continuing block.[4]

---

1 This is not universally accepted. See, for example, Jon, D. (2018), "Cryptocurrencies: Policy, economics and fairness", in *Systemic Risk Centre Discussion Paper 86*, London School of Economics at p. 14.

2 Drescher, D. (2017), *Blockchain basics*, Frankfurt am Mein, Apress, 2017, p. 35.

3 Buterin, V. (2015), "Visions part 1: The value of blockchain technology", *Ethereum Blog*, 13/05/2015, https://blog.ethereum.org/2015/04/13/visions-part-1-the-value-of-blockchain-technology, See also Borg, J. F. & Schembri, T. (2019), "The regulation of blockchain technology", in Dewey, J. (ed.), *Blockchain and cryptocurrency regulation*, London, Global Legal Insights.

4 Narayanan, A., Bonneau, J., Felten, E., Miller, A. & Goldfeder, S. (2016), *Bitcoin and cryptocurrency technologies: A comprehensive introduction*, Princeton University Press; Haber, S. & Stornetta, W. S. (1991), "How to time stamp a digital document", *Journal of Cryptology*, 3(2): 99–111; Bayer, D., Haber, S. & Stornetta, W. S. (1992), "Improving the efficiency and reliability of digital time stamping", *Sequences*, 2: 329–334.

DOI: 10.4324/9781032667416-3

All blockchains are not the same; indeed, the variety is extensive, and they can be public and permissionless or private and permissioned, and there are also hybrid versions. In the case of the former, anyone can download and use the relevant software and create a new cryptocurrency or asset. This was the original form in which they were created. The latter, on the other hand, are, as their name suggests, run on a private network or intranet. They have normally already been created to carry out a specific function and may operate inside a company or syndicate. By their nature, those using the system are known, and permission must be granted before someone can join. Hybrid blockchains, as their name suggests, combine the two, and as Herian put it,

> data from a closed network can be shielded by a registry layer and moved or released to permissionless blockchains for the purpose of allowing public scrutiny of or prescribed or specified data at a given point in time. The hybrid distinction also includes the option of using ledgers, most likely in permissioned form as an access control medium for other, additional registries or databases in off chain or offline servers and storage infrastructures.[5]

Almost anything could be collected and progressed on DLT; for example, a business transaction can develop from the initial contact, through the negotiations, up to the final contract. If the parties later agree to amend the contract, then this can be added. All set out in a system that allows for no retrospective amendment without the parties' agreement, so the risk of a party seeking to renege by arguing over what had been previously agreed is removed. It thus has great potential for storing government records. Indeed, the claims being made for its potential verge on the surrealistic: As significant for British Society as the creation of the Magna Carta was one suggestion.[6] Others have proposed that it could radically change the manner in which society operates,[7] and a solution to virtually every human problem in existence[8] was another. Even allowing for over enthusiasm, there seem to be reasonable grounds to suppose that blockchain has a potentially important future.

3.2 Encryption

The DLT is open to access by third parties but is also encrypted utilising both public and private keys. Every 10 minutes[9] in the case of Bitcoin, the transac-

---

5 Herian, R. (2019), *Regulating blockchain: Critical perspectives in law and technology*, Routledge, 2019, p. 16.

6 Mulligan, C. (2016), "Applications in government", in Government Office for Science (ed.), *Distributed ledger technology: Beyond blockchain*, A report by the Chief Government Scientific Adviser, p. 65.

7 Wright, A. & De Phillipi, P. (2015), "Decentralised blockchain technology and the rise of lex cryptographica", https://ssrn.com/abstract=2580664.

8 Walch, A. (2016), "The fiduciaries of public blockchains", https://speakerdeck.com/angelawalch/the-fiduciaries-of-public-blockchains.

9 Though in some cases, for example, Ethereum, it is more frequent and can be carried out in a few seconds.

tions are checked, transacted, cleared, and locked into the ledger on a timestamped basis in a link with the preceding transaction. For anyone to interfere with the process, they would need to access and alter the blockchain history, which would be almost impossible at the current level of software development and computer capacity.[10]

This can also operate just as easily on a multilateral basis. For example, most of the population own credit and debit cards, which facilitate paying for goods and services. However, the data which develops in such a system is owned by the company issuing the card. They also charge an annual fee and a percentage of the outstanding amount on the card. It is normally the case that the holders of these cards have a credit line enabling them to spend in excess of their current cash value. A blockchain based payment system would involve the payor and payee dealing directly with each other on the blockchain, with the system showing the payment being made within 10 minutes and the confirmation of transfer of title being returned at the same speed. Credit facilities could still be obtained by users from third parties, but the credit provider would not need to become involved with the process and would no longer own the overall arrangement.

3.3 Overheads

The key point is that there are virtually no overheads in utilising a blockchain-based system for such payments, although, as discussed earlier, costs may start to arise with Bitcoin once no further new coins are issued to miners and it becomes necessary to pay for payments to be verified. All the financial transactions carried out by banks through the SWIFT system or cheque clearing can be carried out directly and at lower cost by the parties to the transaction dealing directly with each other. In addition, a significant part of the world's population, especially in the less developed parts of the world, do not live near a bank branch. The capacity to use mobile access through iPhones and the like opens them up to a much wider range of financial facilities than are currently available to them.

The fundamental development that this involves is that digital assets can be controlled and their availability restricted, thus maximising their potential sale price. Music and films, for example, were originally purchased, but the availability of digital, online versions quickly meant that they could be enjoyed free of charge by the users. New business models evolved which utilised advertising as the income stream, but for product producers in, for example, the music and film industries, the financial loss has been enormous. Blockchain enables the product to be made available again on a controlled basis, meaning that the product itself can be sold, potentially increasing profits. That said, the old digital online system has not gone away, so there will continue to be competition from this source, especially in the form of pirated online material, for the foreseeable future.

10 Tapscott, D. & Tapscott, A. (2018), *Blockchain Revolution*, London, Penguin Random House, pp. 6–7.

Fund managers can also operate DLT systems and reduce costs to the investors through reduced administration costs, fewer intermediaries, and significantly less administration. In addition, the automated, real time process whereby the trades both self clear and settle will reduce them further.[11]

Trade finance is an area where many see great potential,[12] and this was apparent from the feedback to HM Treasury's Cryptoassets Taskforce. The current arrangements involve letters of credit and/or bills of exchange to facilitate payment. There are also time delays, with the majority of letters of credit being initially rejected by banks for failure to be precisely accurate, often on quite trivial points of detail, because of the operation of the relevant law in this area.[13] That said, the vast majority are settled within 48 hours, albeit at some inconvenience to the payee. However, were the payment system for a letter of credit and/or bill of exchange to be constructed on a DLT basis, the money could be released to the vendor at the moment of the delivery of the goods, with the process being self-checking and self-recording. This does now seem to be happening. Recent steps taken by the Monetary Authorities of Hong Kong and Singapore have picked up on this possibility and provide what may be the first of many such steps in creating an international information highway to facilitate trade finance.

The initial design of the respective DLTs is still at a fairly early stage, and questions have been raised[14] regarding the trade off between performance, resilience, and privacy. Performance is still slow at the moment in the context of cryptocurrencies. Transactions can take anything from ten minutes to an hour to go through. In comparison with payment by cash or credit card, this is a significant timeframe and reduces the attractiveness of cryptocurrencies as medium of exchange. Transaction costs for Bitcoin have been assessed as varying between US$0.45 to US$55.[15] The platform being used may also involve extra fees. This compares with no cost for using cash and a nominal, indirect one for using credit or debit cards. That said, for international transactions, the picture changes. The normal banking tool is SWIFT, which, in comparison with cryptocurrencies, is slow and more expensive. There are other cash transfer systems, but the average cost of transferring US$200 is 7.1%, rising to 9.4% in sub-Saharan Africa.[16]

---

11 HM Treasury (2017), *The investment management strategy II*, HM Treasury.

12 Hong Kong Monetary Authority (2017), "Press release – Hong Kong and Singapore launch a joint project on cross-border trade and trade finance platform", *Hong Kong Monetary Authority*, 15/12/2017, www.hkma.gov.hk/eng/news-and-media/press-releases/2017/11/20171115-6/.

13 *United City Merchants v Royal Bank of Canada* [1983] 1 A.C. 168 (HL); *Kvaerner John Brown Ltd v Lear Siegler Services Ltd* [2006] EWCA Civ 1130 and *Balfour Beatty Civil Engineering Ltd v Technical and General Guarantee Co Ltd* [2000] 68 Con. L.R. 108. See also Haynes, A. (2018), *The law relating to international banking*, Professional Publishing, at pp. 260–265.

14 See, for example, Cyproassets Taskforce, final Report, October 2018, p. 26.

15 Danielsson, J. (2018), "Cryptocurrencies: Policy, economics and fairness", Systemic Risk Centre, London School of Economics, Version 1.2, November 2018, p. 20.16.

16 SEC (2017), "Investor bulletin: Initial coin offerings", *Investor Alerts and Bulletins*, 25/07/2017, www.sec.gov/oiea/investor-alerts-and-bulletins/ib_coinofferings, accessed 01/03/2019.

3.4 Security offerings

Companies also raise finance by selling shares which provide a degree of equity in their business to those who will buy them. Now security token offerings can be made on blockchain and can potentially provide a far cheaper way for shares to be issued publicly. This raises the possibility of a greater number of smaller companies going to market to sell shares than at present, thus hugely increasing the size of the share market. Legal issues still arise as share sales normally have to be accompanied by a prospectus, a legal document setting out the finances of the issuing company, the details of the share issue, and what the funds will be used for. These are time-consuming and expensive to produce, requiring extreme care and accuracy because of the criminal and civil legal consequences that can be attracted if they are not. Many security token offerings currently seem to be issued on the assumption that these rules do not apply if the share issue is carried out on an ICO basis, but steps have been taken by regulators to disabuse issuers of this fact. Once those in the marketplace understand this, the costs will rise, but it will still be potentially much cheaper than a standard share issue. Very significant cost savings will still be made, though, from the reduction in investment bank fees, stockbrokers, and sales agents, as the online sales process will hugely reduce the expense of the share issue.

Likewise, a multi-party system such as a bond issue,[17] or ICO, as they are called if the bond exists in the form of an e-currency offering, can all sit on blockchain. Over US$3 billion was raised in this way in 2017. That said, the same legal requirements regarding prospectuses crop up here, and it is clear that market participants have also been cavalier in this context. The company wishing to raise finance, therefore, has to list any prospectus[18] on the blockchain. The lenders can submit payment and receive their title to the debt on the system, and in due course, if they wish to sell title to the debt onto another person, which frequently happens, this will also take place and sit on the blockchain record. Repayment by the borrowing company can also then take place on the same system. In addition, the automated process is much cheaper to operate than the current process, and reconciliation, settlement, and record-keeping are all automated, with all parties sharing identical data.

Shares,[19] bonds, and derivatives can all be traded on such a system and probably will be on a large scale within the next few years.

17 The issue of debt paper, normally by a corporate or government to raised finance at a stated interest rate for a set period.

18 The legal document advertising the details of the bond issue and the company issuing it. Alternately, if the bond is issued in high enough denominations to remove the risk of ordinary members of the public being able to afford them, a simpler and cheaper to produce document, called an "information memorandum", will be issued.

19 Recent tests in the UK by the FCA Sandbox have shown that DLT-based share transfer systems can be set up so that changes of ownership are automatically registered at Companies House.

However, for banks there is one downside, as the existing system requires clearing houses for shares and derivatives. These can take three days to clear trades, even though the trades themselves will usually clear in seconds. This should not be a problem once blockchain based systems take over, as the trades will self clear. The current system does allow participants to engage in multilateral netting. This consists of the parties and the clearing house netting all trades off against each other by each trade being constructed of a sale by the seller to the exchange or clearing house and an immediate sale by the exchange or clearing house to the buyer. As a result, the exchange is a counterparty to each deal, and in the event of a participant becoming insolvent, all the trades that remain outstanding will be offset against each other, thus hugely reducing the amount of money at risk to the other parties involved.[20] The relative ease with which LCH Clearnet was able to cope with the financial consequence of the Lehman Bros collapse is a good example. There were some issues with identifying the clients to whom certain uncleared trades related, and some delays in getting margin payments back to those who required it, but essentially the multilateral netting approach worked well in reducing the total amount of money at risk.

What multilateral netting offers the banks is the opportunity to greatly reduce the amount of capital they have to hold in reserve against the trades they enter into, which is required by the Basel III banking capital requirements which are being applied in all the world's more advanced economies. In addition, reconciliation processes that can be both time consuming and slow can be avoided.[21] No doubt, in due course, amendments to the banking capital rules are likely to be made to move it in line with the financial risks that are left with the banks under a blockchain-based system.

This process would not be without risk, though. While it would significantly reduce costs in that the trading process would no longer need intermediaries, the market could end up in a decentralised financial world where trades were no longer centrally cleared, and such a state of affairs "will simply be a collection of interwoven smart contracts that facilitate the buying and selling of blockchain based assets".[22] This will not offer the same facility as the present exchanges in holding capital against the risk of a participant becoming insolvent, and thus, the risk of a market failure, or at least a localised one based on one collection of interwoven blockchain based contracts, will be much higher.

3.5 Criminal factors

Crucially, blockchain also makes it much more difficult for fraudsters to operate, as they cannot go back later and hide the fraud. Any activity is recorded and

20 Ibid note [13], Haynes (2018), p. 291.

21 Press Release (2017), "ESMA assesses DLT's potential and interactions with EU rules", *European Securities and Markets Authority*, www.esma.europa.eu/sites/default/files/library/esma71-844457584-344_2017_press_release_dlt.pdf.

22 De Philippi, P. & Wright A. (2018), *Blockchain and the law: The rule of code*, Harvard University Press, p. 102.

clears itself, removing the need for traditional audit to verify it. Indeed, given the limited requirements placed on auditors to be "a watchdog, not a bloodhound",[23] in comparison with the inability of the blockchain system to do anything other than record accurately, the future system should be much safer, be automatic, and not require audit fees. "If the (blockchain) ledger says something is true then it is true".[24] That said, to have a checking and regulatory capacity that works properly, both auditors and regulators will need to be granted access rights to the DLT to check.

This makes blockchain and currencies based on it less attractive to criminals. With criminal funds, money laundering, and terrorist finance, there are a multiplicity of ways in which the criminals can hide their identity and the overall transaction. Blockchain records all the details of the trading, and thus the capacity to hide what is going on becomes much more difficult, though there will remain the capacity for the person using the system to do so from behind a false identity. Even so, police, tax authorities, and intelligence services will be able to trace money flows back to their source. That said, some cryptocurrencies, such as Monero and Zcash, are more difficult to police. Monero has an obfuscated public ledger which makes it extremely difficult to trace back. It hides the recipient of the deal and creates a new electronic address and a secret key for them.[25] Zcash[26] has a cryptography based system to guarantee privacy, but with a selective disclosure capacity built in. Its accounts cannot necessarily be traced, and its blockchain does not store information concerning the source and destination of the "money". Thus, for money laundering and disclosure rules, the owner can elect to release information or not.

The other criminal issue is that although criminals may find interfering with the blockchain process to be prohibitively complicated, there is still the possibility that with cryptocurrencies or other items of value based on blockchain, those parties will engage in market manipulation. The other possible way of illegally obtaining money through the new system is to hack people's computers to access their codes, as was discussed earlier.

The regulatory approach has been discussed earlier in the book. What is already apparent is that blockchain-based systems do not fit neatly into existing regulatory structures. Some states have categorised cryptocurrencies differently from each other, and in the United States, money transmission is regulated at the state level, while the impact of the new developments will have an effect both nationally and internationally. The regulators are facing a situation where the two parties to a trade or transaction will be in possession of potentially large amounts of information while the regulators themselves

23 Lopes CJ in *Re Kingston Cotton Mills (No.2)* (1896) 1 Ch. 331.

24 Interview between Austin Hill, Don Tapscott and Alex Tapscott, 22/07/2015. Recorded in Tapscott & Tapscott (2018), p. 76.

25 Fink, M. (2019), *Blockchain regulation and governance in Europe*, Cambridge University Press, 2019, p. 97.

26 A joint development between Israeli and US cryptographers. See Ibid note [22], De Philippi & Wright (2018), p. 67.

will have access to very little. They are also operating against a background of very rapidly changing circumstances, which historically they have not always adapted well to.

Across all these potential activities, and the others that will be created, the new distributed systems will be more resilient than the current centralised systems.[27] This is because having separate copies of data accessible to multiple participants greatly reduces the potential risk of data loss. As the blockchain is developed with an ever increasing number of participants, this becomes more and more the case. A web attacker would need to take control of multiple participants to attack the system, and the longer a distributed ledger has been in use, the greater this number is likely to be: It could be vast. Thus, the system is capable of continuing to perform even if part of it successfully comes under attack, as virtually all the participants will still be able to get direct access to their own data, which will be identical. That said, the Bank of England's testing of a multi-node Ethereum protocol based project warranted further investigation of "scalability, security, privacy, interoperability and sustainability".[28] Even so, most observers see DLT based systems as stronger in these regards than the systems they are starting to replace.

However, now decentralised organisations with illegal intent have been created. Daemon, for example, will enable its anonymous shareholders to manage a market on the dark web. Its aims, amongst other things, are to evade government interference.[29]

There is a further problem in that behaviour that any objective observer would regard as criminal may technically not be so because the wording of the law lags behind the technological developments. For example, the DAO hack arose when US$150 million was invested in Ether by around 11,000 people. The idea was to create a start up fund which would be operated on a democratic basis by the votes of the contributors. Due to a bug in the code, a hacker was able to remove a third of the fund without breaching the criminal law.[30] There was then a democratic vote of the contributors, and 87% of the relatively small number that voted agreed to create a hard fork reversing the effect of the hack.[31] Perhaps surprisingly, some opposed this on what seem to be philosophical grounds, namely, that on principle the blockchain should not be reversed.

27 Cryptoassets Taskforce Final Report, October 2018, p. 22.

28 "FinTech accelerator proof of concept", *Bank of England*, 2016, www.bankofengland.co.uk/-/media/boe/files/fintech/pwc.pdf.

29 Ibid note [22], De Philippi & Wright (2018), p. 145; Butnix, J. P., "Daemon wants to become a decentralized ethereum-based smart darknet market", *The Merkle*, 04/04/2016, https://themerkle.com/daemon-wants-to-become-a-decentralized-ethereum-based-smart-darknet-marketplace/.

30 Ibid note [25], Fink (2019), p. 187; Raskin, M. (2017), "The law and legality of smart contracts", *Georgetown Law and Technology Review*: 305, 335; Werbach, K. & Cornell, N. (2017), "Contracts *ExMachina*", *Duke Law Journal*: 313, 365.

31 Technically, there were two votes, the first on the procedure to be adopted, and the second to reverse the blockchain.

3.6 Downsides

What, then, are the downsides? Energy consumption needs to be considered. The process of running transactions through the secure algorithm[32] consumes a significant amount of energy. That said, there seems to be a huge variation in the estimates that "experts" calculate is utilised.[33] That needs to be offset, though, against the quantity of electricity that would otherwise be consumed by whatever alternative method had been adopted to carry out the transaction.

The greater the resilience built into a system, the more limited the capacity will tend to be, and some of the systems will be designed to cater to huge numbers of users. To maintain privacy, encryptions are used, but there are suggestions that this can reduce performance. That said, in many situations, the use of encryption is a necessary factor to maintain sufficient security, so from the vantage point of the user, this is not going to be a negotiable element. Finally, the resilience of a system can be strengthened by limiting the distribution of data. Unfortunately, this is often not an option, as the common distributed ledger will be a key element of making the system attractive to potential users.

There may prove to be overheads related to coordination once the systems are in widespread use, though this should probably prove considerably less than current systems where parties other than those dealing directly with each other are concerned.[34] As years go by, the complexity of some of the programs may become greater to handle all the data, and security will become a greater concern, especially once computers that can handle mega data become operative.

In addition, there is as yet no standard form of platform for participants to use, although IOSCO is looking into this.[35] It will be simpler to operate a system where there is an international standard, but there is no guarantee that one will emerge. Indeed, some participants may seek a competitive advantage through developing newer systems which have advantages over pre-existing ones.

3.7 The current situation

At the time of writing, the United States leads DLT start-ups,[36] with London having the second highest number of such projects listed, close behind San Francisco. However, the scale of the internet capacity and that of the computers most people use on the system is not capable of carrying a multiplicity of large scale

32 Algorithm 256 (SHA-256).

33 Schneider, N. (2015), "After the bitcoin gold rush", *The New Republic*, 24/02/2015; Kaminska, I. (2014), "Bitcoin's wasted power", *Financial Times*, 05/09/2014; CIA (2012), *The world factbook*, CIA.

34 Ibid note [2], Drescher (2017), p. 13; Stead, C. (2018), *What is cryptocurrency: Your complete guide to blockchain, bitcoin and beyond*, Sydney, Finder, 09/11/2018; Ganne, E. (2018), *Can blockchain evolutionize international trade?* Geneva, WTO, pp. 90–110.

35 "ISO/TC 307 blockchain and distributed ledger technologies", *International Standards Organisation*, 2016, www.iso.org/committee/6266604.html.

36 "State of blockchain 2018 Q2 report", *Coin Desk*, 26/07/18, www.coindesk.com/business/2018/07/25/coindesk-releases-q2-2018-state-of-blockchain-report/.

blockchain transactions: The transactional capacity is not there. It will not be many years before it is, and until then, DLT is likely to develop progressively. Some aspects relevant to its development, such as law and regulation, can be developed fairly quickly. Some areas such as money laundering, market manipulation, and theft will always be with us, but the security DLT provides should render them safer than other methods of financial transfer.

Strictly speaking, the World Trade Organization (WTO) maintains that blockchain represents only one type of DLT, but the term now is commonly employed to refer to them in general. Many would agree that blockchain goes beyond the cryptocurrency hype. Its potential trade related applications are numerous and could probably significantly transform international trade. Some possible deployments of cryptocurrency could include trade finance, customs and certification processes, transportation and logistics, insurance, distribution, intellectual property, and government procurement.[37] Even as the technology unfolds, interesting opportunities appear to enhance efficiencies of numerous processes, so trimming costs in these areas. The technology, though, is not a solution to everything, and this requires carefully weighing the costs and benefits involved. Interestingly, blockchain could help implement the WTO Trade Facilitation Agreement, as well as facilitating business-to-government and government-to-government processes at the national level.

The World Economic Forum has predicted that 10% of global GDP could be stored on blockchain systems.[38] It sees it as akin to the invention of the internet, a system that functions as a general purpose technology. Unfortunately, it remains held back by the limitations of the size of the distributed computer system.

There remain issues to be fully resolved if blockchain is to fulfil its potential: the issues of privacy, security, scalability, costs, hidden centrality, lack of flexibility, and critical mass.[39] Privacy arises because the nature of the blockchain is open so that users can verify ownership and transactions. However, it is possible to limit this, as has been seen with the obfuscated ledger technology used in Monero and the cryptography-based system used for Zcash.

Security is a potential worry with any software system. In the case of blockchain systems, the accounts are cryptographic keys that are accessed through the system. It is safe as long as only the relevant person has access to the cryptographic key. If a third party can access its details, then they can access the system as though they were the other person. The security in the system is so strong that a third party is only likely to access it if they are given it or access records the owner has kept outside the blockchain system. Related to this is the possibility that governments may require computer codes to have trapdoors built

37 Ganne (2018).

38 World Economic Forum (WEF) (2015), "Deep shift: Technological tipping points and societal impact", *WEF*, 09/09/2015, p. 7, www.weforum.org/publications/deep-shift-technology-tipping-points-and-societal-impact/.

39 Ibid note [2], Drescher (2017), p. 206.

into them facilitating analysis, suspension, or disabling.[40] That said, the users cannot be stopped from running the system without it, though this would presumably be illegal. Such an approach by governments would almost certainly lead to a kind of regulatory arbitrage, where systems were based in jurisdictions that did not do so.

The scalability element arises as a result of the security that is built into the system. To stop later users from altering earlier records, the system is constructed of the history of the transactions so far, with each having a hash puzzle added each time a block is added into the system. To retrospectively change this at the current level of software development would be prohibitively time consuming and expensive. The consequence of this is that processing speed and the maximum scale that the systems can currently operate on are limiting factors. This overlaps with the issue of cost, though that needs to be offset against the cost of any alternative system that would have been used by the parties instead. As that would often currently involve the use of third parties, those costs could be considerably higher.

The weak link may be the 51% rule discussed earlier. In a smaller system, it may be possible for someone with considerable software power to achieve 51% control of relevant nodes. The larger a blockchain system becomes, the safer it is from such attacks.

As is apparent elsewhere in this book, the current state of legal and regulatory clarity is extremely low. Where there is any, that in one part of the world often contradicts that in another. It is an area where it is reasonable to expect rapid development. It would appear that the blockchain ecosystem is positive towards effective regulations that would deter nefarious deployment of the technology.

Despite present limitations, blockchain enthusiasts have to be mindful of the potential liability. This raises questions concerning how DLT should be structured, owned, and ultimately regulated. In this respect, consideration should be given as to whether the system is permissioned or permissionless, whether the legal structure is specified in the pertinent agreements, the system's express or implied purpose, the system's consensus mechanism, and the matter of pre-existing relationships between the parties.[41] These features could be treated in law to be one of several legal entities: from a joint venture, or a multi-party contract to a partnership. For instance, the group that designs the code that governs the ledger could be deemed a joint venture, and that this could extend to nodes or even simple users of the ledger depending on the extent of their participation. Conversely, the distributed ledger system could be treated as a multi-party contract where the group that sets up the code design and nodes is

40 De Phillipi, P. & Wright, A. (2018), *Blockchain and the law: The rule of code*, Harvard University Press, p. 181. It could be argued that this would merely be an extension of the current arrangements, whereby some governments impose obligations on those creating codes, for example, the Digital Millennium Copyright Act in the United States.

41 Zetzsche, D. A., Buckley, R. P. & Arner, D. W. (2018), "Blockchain distribute ledgers and liability", *Journal of Digital Banking*, 2(4): 298–310.

under a contractual obligation to maintain the system's security and operations. These potential legal structures could also differ across disparate jurisdictions.

The challenge hinges on the ability of lawmakers to strike a balance between the need for governance and the avoidance of strong state intervention that could terminate the innovation.[42] There is therefore the need to carefully analyse the functional features of various concepts under evaluation, and their implications and risks, to enable the delivery of appropriate and sufficient response to regulatory concerns without over regulation. This is not easy, as blockchain is at an early stage of development, and it is not clear what forms it will evolve into. Technologically, blockchains are also rather limited in that every full node must process each transaction and keep a full copy. This inevitably slows down its utilisation – a problem that will increase as the size of a blockchain grows. Security for users will potentially be at the price of growing inefficiency. That said, there are developments, such as off chain payment channels, arranging for different nodes to store and process only part of the process, carrying out calculations outside the chain, and directed acrylic graphs (DAGs) which do not use a linear blockchain approach.[43] Directed acrylic graphs, or DAGs, allow multiple chains of blocks to co-exist and interconnect. This enables a whole new menu of possible confirmation options, thereby eliminating the need for block times, leading to the unprecedented potential for highly scalable and fast information flow on a completely decentralised network. DAGs are, however, relatively less secure than the classic blockchain, but experts are working hard to transform this concept into a usable, secure, and highly scalable solution.[44] Other approaches will also no doubt emerge.

Accordingly, regulatory intervention should be functional, technology neutral, and premised against regulatory goals and principles.[45] Indeed, like the internet before it, DLT would be subject to regulation from governments around the world.[46]

Finally, blockchain provides potential benefits in terms of improved transparency and reduced transaction costs by the more effective managing of data and streamlining of processes, improving supply chains, enabling tracking and management of intellectual property, improving the reliability and traceability of records, reducing the speed and cost of settlement, facilitating copyright and

---

42 Borg, J. & Schembri, T. (2019), "Blockchain & cryptocurrency regulation 2019: The regulation of blockchain technology", in Dewey, J. (ed.), *Blockchain & cryptocurrency regulation*, London, Global Legal Insights (GLI); Yeoh, P. (2017), "Regulatory issues in blockchain technology", *Journal of Financial Regulation and Compliance*, 25(2): 196–208.

43 Finck, M. (2019), *Blockchain regulation and governance in Europe*, Munich, Max Planck Institute for Innovation and Competition, p. 31.

44 Fantom Foundation (2018), "An introduction to DAG - how they differ from blockchain", *Medium*, 21/06/2018, https://medium.com/fantomfoundation/an-introduction-to-dags-and-how-they-differ-from-blockchains-a6f703462090, accessed 07/02/2020.

45 Ibid note [42], Borg & Schembri (2019).

46 Rodrigues, U. R. (2019), "Law and the blockchain", *Iowa Law Review*, 104(2): 679–730.

patent protection, as well as improving efficiency through automated reporting and smart contracts. Its broader applications are facing various significant challenges. These include, amongst others, the following:[47]

1. Transaction capacity and scalability issues relative to conventional banking payments system.
2. Rising concerns over privacy and security matters. In particular, blockchain design choices frequently lead to inevitable trade-offs needed between performance, privacy, and the degree of decentralisation. Future technical progress hopefully could potentially resolve these.
3. Interoperability challenges between different blockchains, between applications built on the same blockchain, and between blockchain and legacy systems.
4. Rising fears over the theft or loss of private keys. This is best exemplified by the Bitcoin theft of around US$500 from Mt. Gox in 2014.
5. Trade-offs in relation to the governance of blockchains.
6. To achieve wider deployment, the technology needs to be fully accommodated within public policy and legal frameworks, and this suggests the need for clear rules.
7. Competition issues may need attention. This is because as permissioned blockchain network advanced to become essential infrastructure, say in clearing and settlement, competition issues may surface around access.

In 2016, though still in the early days, France installed rules allowing the holding and transfer of non-listed securities via blockchain. Japan also enacted rules requiring the registration of virtual currency exchange business operators. In 2018, the 26 member states in the EU signed a declaration to create the European Blockchain Partnership, as well as co-operating in the setting up of a European Blockchain Services Infrastructure to support the delivery of cross-border digital public services marked by the highest standards of security and privacy.[48] As seen elsewhere in the book, other countries have developed their laws and systems as well.

The advent of blockchain is viewed by some as a revolutionary event moving through the five stages of denial, anger, negotiation, depression, and

47 Madir, J. (2019), "Introduction – what is FinTech?", in Madir, J. (ed.), *FinTech: Law and regulation* (Elgar Financial Law and Practice Series), London, Edward Elgar, 02/09/2019.

48 Digibyte (2018), "European countries join blockchain partnership", *Europa*, 10/04/2018, https://ec.europa.eu/digital-single-market/en/news/european-countries-join-blockchain-partnership, accessed 12/11/2019.

eventually, acceptance.[49] At its commencement, Bitcoin was largely ignored as an internet based "geek" money without mainstream interest or a future. Then anger came as a result of it being used for transactions by terrorists, money launderers, and drug dealers. Next, even though Bitcoin was deemed unsavoury, the blockchain technology (DLT) underpinning it is viewed positively, and hence the negotiation phase. The technology went into a depression phase in 2017, but beliefs and passion for this returned strongly in 2018, with many quarters rallying behind its wider applications in financial services and beyond. Indeed, DLT along with other exponential technologies,[50] like the Internet of Things (IoT), 3D, edge computing, robotics, and artificial intelligence, have become the symbols of the Fourth Industrial Revolution,[51] as they transform business and public processes to be many times faster, better, and cheaper.

In the meantime, *DeFi* refers to the emerging alternative or complementary infrastructure to the existing centralised financial system, layered on public blockchains. This employs smart contracts to replicate existing financial services in a more open, inclusive, transparent, and efficient way, including the generation of novel financial services enabled by the underlying blockchain technology, like autonomous liquidity pools, decentralised stablecoins, and flash loans. Contemporary research suggests DeFi may provide solutions to some of the key problems inherent in the centralised financial system, namely, centralised control, limited access, inefficiency, lack of interoperability, and opacity.[52] Additionally, there are risks like fraud, volatility, and usability to consider, including regulatory uncertainty, leading to barriers towards widespread adoption of the DeFi applications.

The decentralised property of DeFi leads to an independence from large financial institutions, overall reducing the costs of transactions. This can also enhance the overall trust in the system. Hence, the increased efficiency and trust are the main benefits of DeFi, where smart contracts hold the custody, with no fund manager needing to be trusted, such as found to be abused in the past. As the efficiency of transactions grows, this turns business models that were not viable in a centralised finance into feasible kinds.[53]

Thus, DeFi substitutes CeFi's trusted central counterparties with smart contracts that are theoretically capable of fulfilling central counterparty tasks,

---

49 Mignon, V. (2019), "Blockchain-perspectives and challenges", in Kraus, D., Obrist, T. & Hari, O. (eds.), *Blockchains, smart contracts decentralised autonomous organizations and the law*, London, Edward Elgar, 2019.

50 Ismail, S., Malone, M. S. & Van Geest, Y. (2019), *Exponential organizations*, New York, Diversion Books.

51 World Economic Forum (2019), "Globalization4.0: Shaping a global architecture in the age of the fourth industrial revolution", WEF Annual Meeting, 22–25/01/2019, Overview, www3.weforum.org/docs/WEF_AM19_Meeting_Overview.pdf, accessed 12/11/2019.

52 Khan, A. & Sandner, P. (2024), "DeFi: An overview of use cases and a status quo analysis of the ecosystem", in Cronqvist, H. & Pely, D. J. (eds.), *The Elgar companion to decentralized finance, digital assets, and blockchain technologies*, Cheltenham, Edward Elgar.

53 Ibid note [52], Khan & Sandner (2024); Cronqvist, H. & Pely, D. J. (eds.) (2024), *The Elgar companion to decentralized finance, digital assets, and blockchain technologies*, Cheltenham, Edward Elgar.

including as custody, escrow agents, and clearing and settlement. In turn, such methods provide a considerably reduced counterparty risk to render transactions more efficient overall. Within the context of the present low interest rates environment, the different DeFi protocols offer comparably high yields. The present high yields for depositors are attributed to the high demand of liquidity in the protocols.[54] Further, DeFi enables anyone to assume various roles within the ecosystem, like providing liquidity to pools or participating in the governance of protocols that is not possible in centralised finance, thereby unfolding the opportunity to generate further income.[55] Aside from participating in the DeFi ecosystem with different potential roles, DeFi's openness enables innovativeness through its open source code base.

In the absence of many restrictions, opportunities for unleashing new financial services abound, where ideas can be coded without one needing to be a coder, meaning the potential for combining certain parts to generate smart contracts to serve as a financial service. It pays, though, to be alert to technical and regulatory risks associated with DeFi applications. Other risks include usability risks and risks linked to human errors, infrastructural risks, and centralisation risks.

Indeed, significant developments have advanced in financial services through cryptos, specifically Bitcoin, towards the application of blockchain technology compared to other sectors. It is estimated that by 2025, 10% of global gross domestic product (GDP) will be on the blockchain. Some 80% of prior research on blockchain, though, focused on cryptos, and the balanced 20% on other sectors.[56] Research findings suggest that blockchain technology takes significant roles in promoting trust, enhancing social cohesion, facilitating funds transfers, initial public offers, global commerce, and extinguishing intermediaries, with the result of greater efficiency.[57]

Unsurprisingly, there is concurrently exponential growth in the application of blockchain across other spaces, like healthcare, IoT, cloud computing, and smart contracts.[58] The implementation of blockchain technology in transportation and accommodation like "Arcade City" is challenging the present Uber business model by enabling commuters to transact directly with taxi drivers.[59] Nevertheless, blockchain may not be entirely immutable, as nodes with superior computing power may do anything from changing the blocks to manipulating transaction.[60] Also, full adoption of blockchain technology may impose significant risks to banks extending from cyberattacks to loss of financial and

54 Ibid note [52], Khan & Sandner (2024).
55 Ibid note [52], Khan & Sandner (2024).
56 Witts, J. O. (2024), "The role of blockchain technology and cryptocurrencies in the digital economy", *Journal of Advanced Management Science*, 12(1): 47–51.
57 Ibid note [52], Khan & Sandner (2024).
58 Ibid note [52], Khan & Sandner (2024).
59 Ibid note [52], Khan & Sandner (2024).
60 Notomoro (2024), "16 disadvantages of blockchain: Limitations and challenges", *Webisoft Blog*, 13/02/2024, https://webisoft-com.webpkgcache.com/doc/-/s/webisoft.com/articles/disadvantages-of-blockchain/, accessed 19/07/2024.

non-financial data and capital investments for early adopters migrating from legacy systems.[61] Still, blockchain technology is becoming more common in other data based applications, including supply chain management, energy internet, building information management (BIM), and the IoT.[62] It is therefore not only a disruptive technology but also a foundational technology that enables progress or applications in a range of problem domains. Blockchain participants in general are continually addressing challenges linked with the technology, ranging from data integrity, privacy, and vulnerability to malware, and limited scalability, including legal and regulatory limitations.[63] There is a thorough need for more public education on the technology, its vast economic potentials, and its unique challenges, as the phenomenon is relatively new and complex that only relatively small numbers of potential users understand and embrace.

---

61 Biswas, S. (2024), "Disadvantages of blockchain technology", *Cleartax*, 08/06/2024, https://cleartax.in/s/disadvantages-of-blockchain, accessed 19/07/2024.

62 Wasiq, M. et al. (2023), "Adoption and applications of blockchain technology in marketing", *Sustainability*, 15(4): 3279–3298.

63 Panda, S. K. et al. (eds.) (2021), *Blockchain technology applications and challenges*, Cham, Springer.

CHAPTER 4

A digital global currency

4.1 Introduction

When releasing his famous Bitcoin white paper, Satoshi Nakamoto announced that he had developed a new electronic cash system that was fully peer-to-peer, with no trusted third party. In effect, Nakamoto introduced a system of online exchange to enable two parties to exchange tokens of value without divulging vulnerable information about themselves or their financial accounts. The idea was to operate outside of the conventional banking structure and allow people to send digital money directly to each other – peer-to-peer (P2P), as the notion of middleman free commerce is known – and where no banks or credit cards are needed and no payment processors or other "trusted" third parties are involved.[1] This, in essence, is digital cash.

Whether Bitcoin could evolve as digital cash as intended or take different directions is explored in the context of the following five scenarios.[2]

4.2 The case against

Mainstream economists, most central banks, and most regulators recognise that money has three main characteristics: as a unit of account, a medium of exchange, and a store of value. For Bitcoin and other cryptocurrencies to achieve these, they need broad based support from consumers and businesses. Despite being in existence for a number of years, it is still an open question whether cryptocurrency usage has reached a critical mass or is still held back by insufficient users, lack of sellers accepting it, and insufficient reason to hold it due to price volatility.

Those critical of cryptocurrency point to extreme price volatility,[3] which inhibits its function as a medium of exchange or store of value. It is not entirely convenient to buy a cup of coffee with Bitcoin even when some merchants are willing to accept them, as most items are priced in fiat currency, like the US dollar. The quick and deep price changes within minutes could mean profit or loss

1 Vigna, P. & Casey, M. J. (2015), *Cryptocurrency: How bitcoin and digital money are challenging the global economic order*, London, The Bodley Head.

2 Ibid note [1], Vigna & Casey (2015).

3 Periaky, A., Artigas, J. C., Hewitt, A. & Reade, J. (2018), "Cryptocurrencies are no substitute for gold", World Gold Council White Paper, 25/01/2018.

DOI: 10.4324/9781032667416-4

being exaggerated in terms of fiat currency value, unless some kind of financial solution is available to cut down these swings. Research suggests that Bitcoin is mostly held for speculative rather than for transaction purposes, and thus, most current holders are less concerned at its utility to buy goods and services.

As the speculative element is very strong, Bitcoin as a store of value could be compared to gold or other precious commodities. Bitcoin dwarfs gold and other precious commodities in terms of the extent of price swings. Gold, by comparison, is less volatile, has a more liquid market, trades in an established regulatory framework, and has a well understood role in investment portfolios and little overlap with Bitcoin on many sources of demand and supply. These characteristics underpin gold's function as a mainstream financial asset that will probably continue to resonate in the new digital world.[4] Mainstream analysts generally support the contention that Bitcoin's extreme price volatility and relatively lower usage as a medium of exchange disqualify Bitcoin's claim as a potential global digital currency, at least for the moment.[5]

As alluded to earlier, to succeed, Bitcoin needs to facilitate transactions, be a store of value, become increasingly important in modern monetary system, and be the lender of last resort in providing liquidity to financial institutions in times of crises.[6] Seashells, cigarettes, silver, and gold have, in the past, operated as money; on many occasions, are scarce real assets with value to their users; and are available in small units to facilitate easy transactions.[7] Hardly any economy uses these as money anymore. Instead, the world has migrated to the use of fiat money, or a currency with no intrinsic value. They are paper printed by governments with quantities amplified by the financial system and are valuable or sought after because governments guarantee them and want taxes to be paid in them. Fiat currency issued by central banks is superior to money based on real assets, such as gold as it could be adjusted to better serve economies instead of being constrained by the production of a natural resource. In comparison, the volume of cryptocurrency, including Bitcoin, like a natural resource, cannot be adjusted.

There have been past occasions when governments have abused fiat money and printed too much, as exemplified by the stagflation of the 1970s or the immediate years following the 2008 global financial crisis. In extreme cases, the hyperinflation of Germany in the 1920s and 30s, coupled with that of Zimbabwe

4 Ibid note [3], Periaky, Artigas, Hewitt & Reade (2018).

5 Montag, A. (2017), "Kevin O'Leary explain one big thing people don't understand about bitcoin (but need to)", *CNBC*, 07/12/2017, www.cnbc.com/2017/12/07/kevin-oleary-bitcoin-is-anasset-not-a-currency.html, accessed 02/02/2018.

6 Danielsson, J. (2018), "Why cryptocurrencies don't make sense", *World Economic Forum (WEF)*, 15/02/2018, www.weforum.oeg/agenda/2018/02/why-cryptocurrencies-dont-make-sense, accessed 18/02/2018.

7 Ferguson, N. (2012), *The ascent of money: A financial history of the world*, 4th edition, London, Penguin Books.

in recent years and Venezuela today, shows how extreme this can get. There are therefore problems associated with fiat money as well, depending on the role of central banks as stewards of money.

For now, Bitcoin is far less useful for commercial transactions.[8] With cash, transactions are costless, anonymous, and immediate, while electronic transactions are very cheap and also immediate for most amounts. In contrast, Bitcoin transactions could require an hour or more at a cost of at least US$25 and are not fully anonymous. There are now other cryptocurrencies promising greater efficiency, privacy, and speed. Still, it takes time to locate businesses or entities willing to accept Bitcoin, and probably considerably longer for other cryptocurrencies. The largest amount that could be transacted by cryptocurrencies are dwarfed by the scale of transactions in fiat currency.

As a store of value, neither cryptocurrencies nor fiat money has any intrinsic value. Their utilisation is based on belief, faith, credibility, and the expectation that the money would retain its value over time. In the case of fiat money, most central banks are committed to keeping its value stable at a decreasing rate of 2% annually, and most have been able at keeping their tracking errors small for sustained periods. Cryptocurrencies, including Bitcoin, are less successful in this regard, with values doubling or halving sometimes in a matter of hours. Thus, most holders hold cryptocurrencies, including Bitcoin, for speculative reasons.

This leaves the "lender of last resort" issue. Central banks as lenders of last resort have been seen as essential ever since Walter Bagehot's 1873 analysis of the 1866 crisis. It was used more recently during the 2007 global financial crisis and could be needed again in the future. There appears at this stage of cryptocurrency evolution no real sign of any such equivalent facility. The three points taken together suggest that cryptocurrencies are less useful than existing fiat money.[9]

4.3 The evolution of Bitcoin

With its low cost, high speed, and decentralised network, Bitcoin could become the first cryptocurrency to start to function as money. In the digital world, simplicity and cost savings are close to essential benefits. Many people believe that Bitcoin would gradually achieve the three essential features of modern day money and so be as heavily utilised as the US dollar. It is argued that despite some public image issues and regulatory constraints, the ecosystem is not entirely unaccommodating for Bitcoin to flourish. Innovation friendly countries such as Switzerland, Singapore, the UK, and Canada are fostering hubs of innovation to give the technology underpinning Bitcoin a strong forward momentum. In

8 Ibid note [6], Danielsson (2018).
9 Ibid note [6], Danielsson (2018).

the United States, thoughtful federal regulators are leaving space for innovation despite the controversy regarding the New York Department of Financial Services BitLicense concept. Various large and small emerging economies have not been too slow to participate in the evolution of Bitcoin as a global digital currency, especially for their large unbanked population, such as can be found in India, Africa, and Indonesia.[10]

It is therefore likely that Bitcoin will continue to evolve, whereas blockchain, which underpins it, is increasingly adopted by a variety of institutions and businesses as it has a far wider range of uses.

From a legal perspective, cryptocurrencies could be regarded as negotiable, performing an essential function of money through judicially recognised mercantile usage in the UK.[11] The judiciary's view of this is, however, based on the mercantile situation in the 19th century and before the emergence of digital currency. An indication of the current judicial view on the matter could come from the outcome of forthcoming cases, where decisions would have to be made on the status of Bitcoin.[12] However, there have been recent cases[13] that have recognised cryptocurrencies as property in the context of people having been defrauded of cryptocurrency or an ICO, although the precise type of property they represent remains unclear.

Further, with regards to the UK, a Bank of England research report argues that whether digital currency could be considered to be money rests on the extent to which it serves as a store of value, a medium of exchange, and a unit of account. On the basis of this, at its present stage of evolution, cryptocurrencies have not yet reached that status.[14] The UK's position on the status of digital currency could be shaped differently if the country were ever to opt for the use of a central bank issued digital currency. Researchers at the Bank of England suggest significant benefits from central bank digital currency, such as an increase of as much as 3% in GDP and improved stability when stabilising inflation and reducing the risk of "boom and bust", but they caution that further research is

10 Carrick, J. (2016), "Bitcoin as a complement to emerging market currencies", *Emerging Markets Finance and Trade*, 52(10): 2321–2334.

11 The House of Lords upheld he decision in *Goodwin v Robarts* (1875) L.R. 10 Exch. 337, Exchequer Chamber and approved in the *ratio decidendi* of the decision: (1876) 1 App. Cas. 476; Clarke, M. A., Hooley, R. J. A., Muday, R. J. C., Sealey, L. S., Tettenborn, A. M. & Tuners, P. G. (2017), *Commercial law: Text cases and materials*, 5th edition, Oxford, Oxford University Press.

12 Falvey, D. (2018), "Cryptocurrency latest: 'Unprecedented' bitcoin legal battles BAFFLE top regulation lawyers", *Daily Express*, 15/02/2018, www.express.co.uk/finance/city/919207/cryptocurrency-news-bitcoin-legal-battle-regulation-litecoin-rille-etherium, accessed 18/02/2018.

13 *D'Aloia v Persons unknown and others* [2022] EWHC 1723 (Ch), Ion Science Ltd v Persons Unknown [2020] Commercial Court (unreported), *Tulip Trading Ltd v Bitcoin Association for BSV and others* [2023] EWCA Civ 83, *Piroozzadeh v Persons Unknown and others* [2023] EWHC 1024 (Ch), *Mooij v Persons unknown* [2021] EWHC (Unreported).

14 Ali, R., Barrdear, J., Clews, R. & Southgate, J. (2014), "The economics of digital currencies", *Bank of England Quarterly Bulletin*, Q3.

required.[15] As matters stand, the Bank of England has no immediate plans to issue one.[16]

The *Spinoza* case,[18] a US example from the jurisdiction of Florida, took the view that Bitcoin is property, not a currency, as it did not meet the definition of a "payment instrument". A "payment instrument" includes a cheque, draft, warrant, money order, travellers' cheques, electronic instrument, or other instrument, payment of money, or monetary value, whether or not negotiable.[19] The court's finding that Espinoza did not engage in the sale of a payment instrument is puzzling.[20] While Florida's money transmitter law does not define "money", many US state laws define "money" as a medium of exchange issued by a government, implying that Bitcoin is not "money" under state law. Decentralised digital currencies such as Bitcoin commonly fall within the definition of "monetary value". This is almost universally defined as medium of exchange whether or not redeemable in currency.

While "monetary value" is listed within Florida's definition of a "payment instrument", the circuit court moved past this analysis, focusing instead on determining whether Bitcoin is "money". Therefore, instead of considering whether Bitcoin could be something of monetary value, the court held that cryptocurrencies are not currently included in the statutory definition of a "payment instrument", nor does Bitcoin fit into one of the defined categories listed. The court went on further to state that even though it was not an expert in economics, it is very clear, even to someone with limited knowledge in the area, that Bitcoin has a long way to go before it is the equivalent of money.[21] The Florida circuit court's decision would eventually have to follow the opinions of its federal circuit and other superior federal courts.

An equivalent decision was also reached in one federal case, drawing from "funds" as defined in 18 USC s. 1960,[22] while in an earlier federal case,[23] the court concluded that in light of the consensus as to the ordinary meaning of "funds" for the purposes of s. 1960, it means "pecuniary resources which are generally accepted as a medium of exchange or a mean of payment". Applying this definition, the court held that it is clear that Bitcoins are funds within the meaning of that term. Two other subsequent federal cases also reached the conclusion that Bitcoin is a digital currency.[24] Differing opinions on Bitcoin will continue as it evolves or until the involvement of the US Supreme Court or when US Congress passes legislation that defines Bitcoin for legal purposes.

15 Barrdear, J. & Kumhof, M. (2016), "The macroeconomics of central bank issued digital currencies", Bank of England Working Paper No. 605, 18/07/2016, www.bankofengland.co.uk/working-paper/2016/the-macroeconomics-of-central-bank-issued-digital-currencies, accessed 02/02/2018.

16 Buntix, J. P. (2018), "Bank of England cancels plans to issue digital currency", *The Merkle*, 8/01/2018, https://thebitcoin.pub/t/bank-of-england-cancels-plans-to-issue-a-digital-currency/22289, accessed 2/02/2018; Carney M., "The Future of Money", Speech at the Scottish Economics Conference, Edinburgh University, 2 March 2018, https://www.bankofenglandco.uk/-/media/boe/files/speech/2018/the-future-of-money-speech-by-mark-carney, accessed 05/08/2015.

For the moment, US Federal regulators, such as the SEC, maintain that US federal securities law may apply to cryptocurrencies,[17] depending on the circumstances, and in particular because of the "*Howey* test"[18] created by the Supreme Court as a means of determining whether certain transactions qualify as investment contracts or securities.[19] The *Howey* test comprises a four-part question. These ask whether there was an investment of money, whether this occurs in a common enterprise, whether it is undertaken with the expectation of profit, and whether any such profit arises from the managerial initiatives of others.

The SEC's investigative report on DAO's international coin offering (ICO) concludes that the DAO tokens issued constituted a security or stock and should therefore be regulated under existing securities laws.[20] The SEC report advises that whether or not a particular transaction involves the offer and sale of security regardless of the terminology used will depend on the facts and circumstances, including the economic realities of the transaction.

The CFTC appears to have no intention of interfering with cryptocurrencies or blockchain, though that would no doubt change were derivatives structured in relation to cryptocurrencies or cryptoassets to emerge at a significant level. The CFTC envisions a future not only with Bitcoin and blockchain in it but also with them having a transformative effect, and it has stated that it has no intention of standing in the way of such innovation. It adds that until the US Congress chooses to act, it calls upon the investment community and advocacy community around digital currencies to create some kind of self-regulatory organisation to develop standards around cyber policy and insider trading ethics code of conduct.[21]

While the SEC and bank regulators supervise specific institutions and discrete activities, and state regulators have jurisdiction in their respective jurisdictions over money transmission, the CFTC is the only federal regulator of cryptocurrency markets. In terms of CFTC regulation, cryptocurrencies such as Bitcoin are treated as a commodity under the Commodity Exchange Act, over which the SEC does not enjoy direct oversight. The CFTC has wide jurisdiction over derivatives markets, including futures in digital currencies, but only limited jurisdiction over spot markets, where participants buy and sell virtual currencies for prompt delivery.

The CFTC has previously announced that the Chicago Mercantile Exchange Inc. (CME) and the Chicago Board Options Exchange (CBOE) Futures Exchange

17 The SEC ruling specifically related to Ethereum, but the principle is worded in a manner which suggests that it is generally applicable to cryptocurrencies.

18 *SEC v W J Howey* Co. 328, US 293.

19 Churchhouse, T. (2017), "Is a cryptocurrency like a stock? This is what the SEC says . . .", *Stansberry Pacific Research*, 28/07/2017, https://stansberrypacific.com/asia-wealth-investment-daily/cryptocurrency-like-stock-sec-rules/, accessed 02/02/2018.

20 SEC (2017), "Report of an investigation pursuant to section 21(a) of the securities exchange act 1934: The DAO", SEC Release No. 81, 207, 25/07/2017.

21 Terzo, G. (2018), "CFTC's Quintenz 'bitcoin and blockchain are transformative'", *CCN*, 07/02/2018, www.ccn.com/cftc-quintenz-bitcoin-blockchain-transformative, accessed 18/02/2018.

(CFE) had been given the regulatory green light to list Bitcoin futures.[22] This is a significant step in allowing mainstream investors to buy and sell the highly volatile cryptocurrency. Both had also agreed to operate under a self-certified regime for their upcoming contracts. These future exchanges are also required to monitor for potential market manipulation and market dislocations, such as rapid price changes and trading outages. The announcement led to an immediate surge in Bitcoin prices, as market participants hope that with the availability of Bitcoin futures through these futures exchanges, more institutional investors' funds would flow into the Bitcoin space to raise its profile as an asset class.[23]

The IRS virtual currency guidance treats virtual currency as property for US federal tax purposes, and that general rules for property transactions would apply.[24] The IRS has defined *Bitcoin* as a convertible digital currency that functions as a medium of exchange and operates like a real currency but does not have legal tender status in any jurisdiction. In December 2024, the US Treasury and IRS issued regulations requiring brokers rather than individual asset holders to report gross proceeds of sale on digital assets.[25]

The US Federal Reserve regards cryptocurrencies as highly speculative assets and not a stable source of value.[26] They Feds noted that Bitcoin remains a very small part of the overall payment system and that it did not have the authority to regulate cryptocurrencies.[27] Its regulatory powers extend only to those banking institutions that they already supervise. It does not play any regulatory role with respect to cryptocurrencies, other than ensuring that banking organisations that they do supervise are attentive, that they are appropriately managing any interactions they have with participants in that market and appropriately monitoring anti-money laundering and Bank Secrecy Act responsibilities that apply. The US Federal Reserve does not differentiate between decentralised currencies, like Bitcoin, which are neither issued nor given any value by any particular jurisdiction, and digital currencies issued by governments themselves.

Though central banks are exploring the option of creating their own centralised digital currencies constituted as legal tender, the Federal Reserve has no

22 Stafford, P. (2017), "US regulator gives green light for bitcoin futures trading: CME, CBOE and Cantor pass hurdle in preparing derivatives on volatile cryptocurrency", *Financial Times*, 02/12/2017.

23 Shen, L. (2017), "Bitcoin futures are about to be a thing and it's sent prices soaring", *Fortune*, 01/12/2017.

24 Internal Revenue Service (IRS), "IRS virtual currency guidance: Virtual currency is treated as property for US federal tax purposes: General rules for property transactions apply", IR-201436, 25/03/2014, www.irs.gov/businesses/small-businesses-self-employed/virtual-currencies, accessed 02/02/2018.

25 Specifically by filing Form 1099.

26 Buck, J. (2017), "US fed chair speaks out on bitcoin and national crypto", *Coin Telegraph*, 15/12/2017, www.cointelegraph.com/news/us-fed-chair-speaks-out-on-bitcoin-and-national-crypto, accessed 02/02/2018.

27 Melloy, J. (2017), "Fed chief Yellen says bitcoin is a 'highly speculative assets'", *CNBC*, 13/12/2017, www.cnbc.com/2017/12/13/fed-chief-yellen-says-bitcoin-is-a-highly-speculative-asset.html, accessed 02/02/2018.

current agenda of launching a digital dollar,[28] even as Venezuela, Catalonia, Russia, and Dubai have announced plans in this direction.[36] The United States' tentative conclusions are that there are limited benefits and limited needs from introducing central bank issued digital currency that are counterweighed by other concerns.[37] China has issued a state-backed cryptocurrency, the e-CNY, which is currently undergoing trials across a number of cities. Since 2021, however, China has banned crypto. Although it is permitted in Hong Kong. This is discussed later in the book.

The Financial Crimes Enforcement Network (FinCEN) of the US Department of the Treasury clarified the differences between currency and cryptocurrency. Its guidance defines *cryptocurrency* as a medium of exchange that operates like a currency in some environments but does not have all the attributes of a real currency. It also differentiated between specific entities and persons involved in cryptocurrency transactions in an initiative to clarify which Bitcoin participants could be defined as a money transmitter, but as alluded to earlier, this contributed to a fluid interpretation in several federal cases.

It is unsurprising that Bitcoin, characterised by peer-to-peer transfers, relative anonymity, encryption, and the absence of an administrative clearing house, is the cryptocurrency of appeal for those engaged in tax evasion and other illegal activities.[29] The potential for misuse goes well beyond this. With tax consequences associated with using Bitcoin having been settled in many jurisdictions, the focus is now likely to shift to whether taxpayers are properly reporting their gains when disposing of Bitcoins, at least in those jurisdictions where such profits are taxable.

It is right for central banks and other financial authorities to warn users that they are at risk of losing their money if the currency suddenly devalues. It is also a fact that cryptocurrencies could be used for illicit purposes, such as drug dealing, tax evasion, and money laundering. Equally, in many respects, they are not too far removed from current forms of conventional money.[30] In the unlikely event that the US dollar were to lose its status as a world reserve currency, its value would also probably drop dramatically. Illicit activities, such as drug smuggling, tax evasion and money laundering, fraudulent Ponzi schemes, and other illegal activities are also associated with fiat currencies and in larger amounts at both offshore and onshore financial centres. Linking these common deficiencies of fiat currencies to cryptocurrencies is not helpful.[31] Satoshi Nakamoto's vision of Bitcoin evolving into a global digital currency might be realisable.

---

28 Ibid note [27], Melloy (2017).

29 Larson, J. (2016), "Implications of bitcoin not being actual currency: The Espinoza case", *ABA Tax Times*, 36(1): 1–10, 18/11/2016.

30 Bjerg, O. (2016), "How is bitcoin money?", *Theory, Culture and Society*, 33(1): 53–72.

31 Ibid note [30], Bjerg (2016).

4.4 Beyond currency functions

Another scenario that could evolve involves cryptocurrencies assuming a vital role inside the national and global infrastructure of financial systems, but in the background, with fiat currencies as economies' main units of accounts and mediums of exchange. This would imply that cryptocurrency protocols and blockchain-based systems for confirming transactions could replace the cumbersome payment system currently run by banks, credit card companies, payment processors, and foreign exchange traders. Eventually, some of these would disappear into oblivion, leaving others to apply cryptocurrency technology for their own business-to-business (B2B) transactions. Owing to real-time conversion into fiat currencies after each transaction, businesses and end users' customers would continue to quote prices and pay money in the same currencies as in the past.

Were Bitcoin to become the top choice in this situation, its value as a currency or equivalent equity in the ecosystem would rise significantly, as it would be consistently in demand. Alternative cryptocurrencies might, however, challenge this assumption. For instance, Ripple Lab's system, designed to facilitate international transfers in fiat currencies and other units of value, simultaneously eliminating all intermediary steps which currently make money transmission expensive, could be one such candidate. Those not keen on Ripple could take up Stellar, Ripple's notable clone.

Then there is Ethereum, a decentralised platform for applications running exactly as programmed without any chance of fraud, censorship, or third-party interference. These apps run on a custom built blockchain, a hugely powerful shared global infrastructure that could move value around and represent the ownership of property. This could enable developers to create markets, store registries of debts or promises, or move funds in accordance with prior established instructions, such as wills or futures contracts. All such activities could be facilitated without a middleman or counterparty risk, hence eliminating unnecessary costs.

Important Ethereum based platforms include Cardano, EOS, Neo, and Qtum, with respective market capitalisation as of mid-February 2025 of US$21.370 billion, US$30.24 billion, US$621 billion, and US$256 billion.[32] Other competing alternatives include Realcoin, an altcoin (see Section **4.7.1** for an explanation of *altcoins*) layered upon the Bitcoin blockchain that is transparently backed by auditable reserves of dollar-based assets. This transforms altcoins into a proxy for a fiat currency and an instrument by which people could simply transfer money to one another without Bitcoin's exchange risks. Uphold (formerly Bitreserve) is a cloud based financial services platform which facilitates users in converting deposits to their bank and credit card accounts and to retrieve them

32 Chatrrvedi, S. (2018), "Our final ethereum killers review-QTUM", *Daily Fintech*, 19/02/2018, https://dailyFintech.com/2018/02/19/our-final-ethereum-killers-review-qtum/, accessed 20/02/2018.

later. Then there are tokens from ICOs, where another currency or corporation goes crypto. Russia is said to be considering the crypto-rouble after Venezuela's apparent success with its Petro. Camera Company Kodak pivoted to Kodak-Coins, while Long Island Iced Tea Corporation started mining Bitcoins. Liberal US cities like Berkeley in California became the first to develop its own digital currency for buying municipal bonds.[33]

Despite these competitive cryptocurrencies on the horizon, and despite falling from its highly dominant position of over 90% of market at the beginning of its journey to 56% at the start of 2025, Bitcoin enjoys the advantage of being the first cryptocurrency to emerge publicly, with brand recognition and a generally reliable reputation. Bitcoin's future as the internet native currency[34] could continue to flourish, at least in the short term, as the preferred unit of exchange for online commerce.

On the other hand, one global US investment bank thinks most, if not all, cryptocurrencies would be likely to reduce in value to zero, since they have no intrinsic value.[35] This was echoed by Stefan Hofrichter, Alliance Global's Head of Economic Strategy. In his view, Bitcoin's intrinsic value must be zero or worthless, and that a Bitcoin bubble will inevitably arise at some point. It remains to be seen whether the large decline in price in 2018 is a prelude to this. As of early summer 2025, this does not appear to be the case.

Counterarguments contend that groundbreaking technology and collaborations with established business could replace the current 'fear of missing out' syndrome.[36] Other potential blockchain applications could compensate for scope limitations in cryptocurrencies in places where databases are employed, such as supply chains, medical records, and logistics. This suggests why industry behemoths like Disney, Amazon, and IBM have moved into proprietary blockchain. Bitcoin in particular is still by far the safest cryptocurrency. Its limitations as an effective currency exist because of its relative slowness and cost, which could be solved with the onset of the Lightning Network. This is a protocol that generates an off-chain system by forming a network of payment channels that could be accessed by involved entities independent of the wider blockchain. This latch on to Bitcoin's blockchain is designed to solve scalability, speed, and cost issues by

33 Holder, S. (2018), "To fund the resistance, Berkley turns to cryptocurrency", *City Lab*, 12/02/2018, www.citylab.com/equity/2018/02/berkeley-crypto/552884/, accessed 18/02/2018.

34 Popper, B. (2014), "Meet the man building for Fort Knox of bitcoin", *The Verge*, 11/01/2014, www.theverge.com/2014/8/29/6082195/the-fort-knox-of-bitcoin-xapo-wences-casares, accessed 02/02/2018.

35 Kharpal, A. (2018), "Most cryptocurrencies will crash to zero Goldman Sachs say", *CNBC*, 07/02/2018, www.cnbc.com/2018/02/07/most-cryptocurrencies-will-crash-to-zero-goldman-sachssays.html, accessed 07/02/2018.

36 Goss, S. (2017), "Commentary: Yes bitcoin may be a bubble, but not for the reason you think", *Fortune*, 04/12/2017, https://fortune.com/2017/12/04/bitcoin-value-today-bubble-burst/, accessed 02/02/2018.

lifting transactions off the main network onto a private system among users of the underlying payment channel.[37]

However, the key issue in the background is that governments are not going to unilaterally abandon their powers to issue sovereign currencies, and so fiat currencies will persist as key pillars in the financial system alongside cryptocurrencies. This also means that concerns that the rising use of cryptocurrencies induces deflation are likely to be off the mark.[38]

4.5 The multi-coin world

Given that blockchain could enable the attachment of a digital value to anything, it is possible that the global economy could end up with everything having its own currency. This would be a world where digitised claims to assets would be created via the technology behind the blockchain. This refers to the smart property notion[39] where all property is assigned a digital ownership token and a tradable title. These could be divided into various coin denominations required to facilitate easy exchange with other digitised asset claims. Such digital coins or tokens could be traded between each other through interlinked blockchain based exchanges that would fairly and transparently formulate universally recognised prices.

Such a multi-asset global digital exchange would not need a common currency at all. It would operate as a sophisticated kind of barter, where its divisibility and flexibility overcome the original limitations found in the raw version. A coin-based economy such as this would allow goods and services to be transacted without needing the medium of exchange provided by fiat currencies. Where such a market is allowed to flourish, there would be little need for central banks and a centralised interest rate to operate, as tradable items would be priced against each other. The system could thus become more efficient as digital coins are exchanged in seconds without moving physical goods, in the absence of minimum transaction sizes, and without large fees penalising smaller transactions. A global marketplace for all asset classes and instruments could emerge, levelling the playing field between users. Big companies with big brand names with large-scale operations might not be favoured, as in an electronic barter society, individuals and small groups could compete with them at no loss in efficiency, thus igniting a wave of innovation and wealth creation.[40]

37 Upson, S. (2019), "The lightning network could make bitcoin faster and cheaper", *Wired*, 19/01/2019, www.wired.com/story/the-lightning-network-could-make-bitcoin-faster-and-cheaper/, accessed 02/02/2018.

38 Buntix, J. P. (2017), "Cryptocurrency inflation vs deflation", *The Merkle*, 25/04/2017, https://themerkle.com/cryptocurrency-inflation-vs-deflation/, accessed 2/02/2018.

39 Bursell, M. (2017), "What is a blockchain smart contract?" *Open Source*, 11/12/2017, www.opensource.com/article/17/12/whats-blockchain-smart-contract, accessed 02/02/2018.

40 Olsen, R. & Mulchandani, S. (2017), "Blockchain will help society: Blockchain will become the notary of choice for these traditional financial assets, but there is something more exciting afoot", *B W Business World*, 08/09/2017.

This digital barter economy[41] could avoid the economic distortions that lead to the 2007 global financial crisis, where prices, and especially wages, had been unable to find their natural levels, and where central banks had to intervene with interest rates to locate desirable economic balances, but which inevitably gave rise to new distortions, leading to ongoing economic problems. The scenario under discussion potentially implies a much less crisis prone economy, which is the vision of most free market fundamentalists.[42]

This vision of a cryptocurrency based digital barter economy could, however, face significant obstacles along the way. These include the logistical complexity of a global exchange system to provide market based valuations for an infinite range of digitised assets, and the unlikely happening for a world of entirely free floating prices because of almost insurmountable political barriers. Some elements of a digital barter economy are more likely to appear when digitised assets and blockchain exchanges become much more widely used.

4.6 Digital fiat currencies

Global consumer payments are still primarily carried out in cash, and over 2 billion of those are at the bottom of the pyramid in terms of size because of the inaccessibility to financial services for those in some parts of the world. Globally, the use of cash has a cost for societies in terms of printing, distribution, and destruction. Digital fiat currencies issued by central banks offer interoperable instruments, instant settlements, and robust system security, but it would also mean sovereign denomination and greater accountability for central banks.

Cryptocurrencies' deflationary attributes, backed by its 21-million-capped supply, differ crucially from the inflationary tendencies of digital currencies and, in particular, digital fiat currencies. Knowing the limited supply of Bitcoin and its eventual potential values prompts people to save Bitcoins to simultaneously strengthen its purchasing power. In contrast, in the world of digital fiat currencies, central banks could, and often do, create more money through quantitative easing and bank bailouts that could lead to strong inflation that erodes purchasing power. Cryptocurrency supporters drawing on this crucial difference believe that this could lead to more financial freedom for everyone, while those on the other side of the fence stoke fears of financial insecurity, bubbles, and frauds.

Finally, the internet has empowered a lot of ordinary people and many small businesses to drive the sharing and collaborative economy, and perhaps soon a digital barter economy that cryptocurrencies such as Bitcoin envision. This is a pure form of information technology. At its heart is the decentralised Bitcoin network and its public ledger, the blockchain, which represents a new manner for dealing with information. This involves extracting information concerning

41 Hastreiter, N. (2017), "The future of cash free barter economy for business", *Future of Everything*, October 2017, www.futureofeverything.io/future-cash-free-barter-economy-business/, accessed 02/02/2018.

42 Ibid note [40], Olsen & Mulchandandi (2017).

monetary transactions and economic exchanges, but outside the hands of monopolist institutions, to lead to a decentralised mechanism for society to evaluate the validity of that information.[43]

In this sense, cryptocurrencies could claim to be among the latest in a long line of technological developments that are perceived to have the potential to shift powers from centralised elites back to the common people. Yet there are those who would use it to advance all kinds of illicit activities, but these Bitcoin anarchists could be relegated to minor participations when Bitcoin technology and applications overcome their present constraints and policymakers provide the enabling environment for cryptocurrencies' innovations to flourish. They could well end up amounting to less than the stateless third party, less utopian dream of its most ardent supporters.[44] However, the financial world would have a different kind of discipline imposed on it, and were costs to come down dramatically, then commerce and economic activity could grow along digital lines, further expanding its impact.

Cryptocurrencies are backed by mathematics and only resemble the characteristics of money in terms of a unit of account, a store of value, and a medium of exchange. It is also based on a decentralised P2P network that uniquely differentiates it from other virtual currencies. It is also worthwhile recalling that the 1899 English case of *Moss v Hancock*[54] defined *money* to be that which passes freely from hand to hand throughout the community in the final discharge of debts, and also being accepted equally without reference to the character or credit of the person who offered it and, concurrently, without the intention of the person who received it to consume it.

Neither the US Coinage Act nor the UK Bank of England Act 1833, or any regulation in both jurisdictions, state as such that the actual process must involve payment in cash. Thus, the judicial interpretation is complemented by the economic perspective of money as anything that is widely accepted in payment for goods and services, used as a medium of exchange and articulated as the standard unit wherein prices and debts are calibrated.

Cryptocurrencies are therefore virtual currencies, that is, a kind of unregulated digital money issued and generally controlled by its developers and used and accepted among members of a particular virtual community. Money in closed "in-game-only schemes", with no link to the real economy or fiat currency; schemes with a unidirectional flow, whereupon the currency could initially be acquired with a fiat currency but not convertible back to it, such as Facebook credits; or schemes with a bidirectional flow, allowing conversion in both directions, such as frequent flyer miles, are not truly virtual currencies. Money in such schemes exists in the form of an account balance rather than distinct identifiable items. These are less regarded as cryptocurrencies but more as a variant of e-money.

43 Ibid note [1], Vigna & Casey (2015).
44 Ibid note [1], Vigna & Casey (2015); 54 [1899] 2 Q.B. 111.

At least in the EU, e-money are characterised, firstly, by electronic storage; secondly, by issuance upon receipt of funds; and thirdly, by acceptance as a means of payment by a legal or natural person other than the issuer. Bitcoin and similar cryptocurrencies, as such, are not deemed as e-money as they do not comply with the second criterion. They do, however, share two of the characteristics of e-money. They are also not issued in or linked to a sovereign currency, not the liability of any entity, and not backed by any authority. Bitcoin and other cryptocurrencies operate along the lines of retail payment systems, except that non-banks rather than financial intermediaries are almost exclusively involved in the payment process.

The Bitcoin system enables users to exchange online credit for goods and services from retailers, contractors, and online trading intermediaries that accept Bitcoin for payments. Competing currency systems are not altogether new, as local, unregulated, community currencies came into being long before the digital age. The virtual currency system has positive features when it contributes to financial innovation and provides additional payment alternatives to consumers. Nevertheless, they also generate risks for their users in the absence of regulation.

Though cryptocurrencies resemble the key characteristics of currency, they also have the characteristics of a commodity of other property. As such, their legal treatment varies from jurisdiction to jurisdiction, and regulators within the same jurisdiction could also take differing approaches relative to the regulatory context under review. For example, New York actively regulates entities doing business and allows virtual currencies into the state's banking system, whereas in the UK such trading remains largely unregulated. China currently prohibits cryptocurrencies but has not been entirely effective, as the ban was immediately followed by a large increase in the number of people accessing virtual currency systems on Hong Kong websites. For now, there appears to be no existing legal framework addressing the unique features and functionality of cryptocurrencies, although, as is seen later in the book, China is developing a state-backed cryptocurrency.

Regulators are struggling with the option of prohibiting cryptocurrencies or isolating them from the regulated financial system. Concerns over their legal status and regulation arise because they have the potential to be used in illegal activities outside the reach of law enforcement and their extreme price volatility could hurt ill-informed investors. Importantly, they are complicated and complex financial instruments, as they have features enabling them to function as a commodity, as demonstrated by a self-imposed scarcity limit of 21 million Bitcoins and the extreme volatility of its value, and as security in the form of ICOs. Economic blocs such as the G20 and international or supranational regulators such as the International Monetary Fund (IMF) are planning consensus building forums to address the issue.

In part, this struggle is the result of the disparate nature of cryptocurrencies. The most thorough categorisation of them would seem to be the following breakdown.[45] Many cryptocurrencies will have more than one of these characteristics.

4.7 Different types of cryptoassets

4.7.1 Altcoins

These are crypto coins that are alternatives to Bitcoin and are a variant of it. They are created using either Bitcoin's open sourced protocol, with the underlying codes being changed, resulting to a fork in the original blockchain, or they are the result of a separate blockchain and a protocol that supports them.[46] There are currently a number using the same hashing algorithms as Bitcoin, others using a script algorithm, and a third category using other innovative algorithms. All altcoins have their own independent blockchain. The result of this is that their features are different.

4.7.2 Asset-backed tokens

These represent a claim on an underlying asset and are effectively a modern version of the certificates issued by medieval goldsmiths. Those not wishing to risk carrying their gold around could deposit it at a goldsmith's in return for a certificate. This could be used to pay for goods or services, and a later owner could cash it in for the gold.[47] Put simply, they are IOUs and, unlike some other types of cryptocurrency, are rooted in something of real value, and the range that exists on the current market is very wide.[48] It is worth flagging up at this point the difference between tokens and coins. Coins that are part of an e-currency can be used to buy things, for example, tokens. The token itself can only be used, however, within the ecosystem of the blockchain concerned.[49]

45 Crypto Utopia (2018), "The $20 billion Cambrian explosion of tokenized digital assets, and the emerging infrastructure being built to support them", *AutonomousNext*, p. 79, https://next.autonomous.com/crypto-utopia.

46 Aziz, "Coins vs tokens: What's the difference", *Master the Crypto*, www.masterthecrypto.com/differences-between-cryptocurrency-coins-and-tokens, accessed 14/02/2019.

47 Lewis, A. (2015), "A gentle introduction to digital tokens", *BitsonBlocks*, 28/09/2015, https://bitsonblocks.net/2015/09/28/gentle-introduction-digital-tokens/, accessed 14/02/2019.

48 Midlifecroesus (2018), "Midlifecroesus", 23/02/2018, https://midlifecroesus.com/2018/02/what-is-an-asset-backed-token/, accessed 14/02/2019.

49 Bonpay (2018), "What is the difference between coins and tokens", *Medium*, 13/03/2018, https://medium.com/@bonpay/what-is-the-difference-between-coins-and-tokens-6cedff311c31, accessed 14/02/2019.

4.7.3 Blockchain native tokens

These are tokens that are implemented on the blockchain at the protocol level. The investors will normally have had no prior involvement with each other and are a disparate group. They are an integral part of its consensus mechanism and necessary to operate the blockchain.[50]

4.7.4 Commodity tokens

Rather like a hybrid of security tokens for commodities and futures contracts, these have been mainly used so far for natural assets, such as carbon.[51] It still remains a market in its very early stages, and it remains to be seen whether or not it will develop significantly.

4.7.5 Crypto fiat currencies

Discussed elsewhere in the book, these are crypto versions of existing currencies. For reasons of financial desperation, it was the Government of Venezuela that first expressed an interest in the idea, with China considering it more recently. Russia has also discussed it, while the UK has made clear they are not considering it at the moment. It will be an interesting idea to watch. The governor of the Bank of England (BoE), though open to the idea of a central bank digital currency (CBDC), stressed that any such adoption would not happen while the BoE maintains that cryptocurrencies do not currently constitute money.[52] The BoE's recently released staff working paper suggests that there is no reason to believe that introducing a crypto pound could have a negative impact on private credit or on total liquidity provision to an economy.

At this juncture, recent developments suggest taking note of potential digital currencies issued by central banks. Various central banks from Canada, Ireland, Norway, to Switzerland and others are now considering the viability of these and are investigating their logistical and technical details. It has been argued that the progress of digital commerce could ultimately make the benefits seem overwhelming, and it would be strategically competitive to stay ahead of the curve instead of trying to catch up at the eleventh hour.[53]

For now, the Federal Reserve Bank in the United States nevertheless is not taking this position. The US Federal Reserve maintains that even though a crypto dollar might be able to overcome some of the special vulnerabilities that

50 www.blockchainhub.net, accessed 14/02/2019.

51 Tapscott, D. & Tapscott, A. (2018), *Blockchain revolution*, Penguin Random House, p. xxxvi.

52 Wood, A. (2018), "Bank of England Governor: Open to the idea of a central bank digital currency", *Coin Telegraph*, 26/05/2018, https://cointelegraph.com/news/bank-of-england-governor-open-to-the-idea-of-a-central-bank-digital-currency, accessed 05/03/2019.

53 Bordo, M. D. & Levin, A. T. (2017), "Central bank digital money and the future of monetary policy", National Bureau of Economic Research (NBER), Working Paper Series 23, 711, August 2017.

cryptocurrencies encounter, they, too, have significant challenges pertaining to cybersecurity, money laundering, and the retail financial system.[54] A more positive stance is taken by the International Monetary Fund (IMF), as reflected by its call for central banks around the world to turn their fiat currencies digital.[55]

4.7.6 dApp tokens

These are tokens that are implemented at the application level on top of the blockchain. They are part of the app's incentive mechanism and are tracked on an underlying blockchain to which they are not integral. They must have four key ingredients to be a distributed application token:

- The source code of the e-application must be open to everyone.
- It must use a blockchain type of cryptography.
- It must operate itself on crypto tokens or digital assets.
- It must generate tokens and have an inbuilt consensus mechanism.[56]

Effectively, they facilitate access to the blockchain for which the users will pay transaction fees.[57]

4.7.7 Hybrid tokens

These are hybridised usage and work tokens.

4.7.8 Security token offerings (STOs)

These are intended as passive investments in the issuing entity or in an asset which it owns. Unlike ICOs, they grant a share in the profits, and unlike equity tokens, they do not grant part ownership of the company. They may go up in value and are saleable. They can be seen as a subset of security tokens (see later text).

---

54 Brainard, L. (2018), "Cryptocurrencies, digital currencies and distributed ledger technologies: What are we learning?", Paper presented by Lael Brainard, Member Board of Governors of the Federal Reserve System at the Decoding Digital Currency Conference, San Francisco, CA, 15/05/2018; Kumhoff, M. & Noone, C. (2018), "Central bank digital currencies: Design principles and balance sheet implications", BoE Staff Working Paper No. 725, May 2018.

55 Lagarde, C. (2018), "Winds of change: The case for the new digital currency", Paper presented by Christine Lagarde, IMF Managing Director at the Singapore Fintech Festival, 14/11/2018; Mancini-Griffoli, T., Soledad, M., Martinez, P., Agur, I., Ari, A., Kiff, J., Popescu, A. & Rochon, C. (2018), "Casting light on central bank digital currency", IMF Staff Discussion Note 2018SDN/18/08.

56 Agrawal, H. (2019), "What are DApps (decentralized applications)? The beginner's guide", *Coinsutra*, 06/09/2019, https://coinsutra.com/dapps-decentralized-applications, accessed 03/06/2019.

57 Warren, W. (2017), "The difference between app coins and protocol tokens", *0x Blog*, 02/02/2017, https://blog.0xproject.com/the-difference-between-app-coins-and-protocol-tokens7281a428348c, accessed 14/02/2019.

4.7.9 *Network tokens*

These are designed to be used within a specific system or network rather than as a general currency. Every token in the network is convertible with each other. This can be useful for creating loyalty programmes or as tokens to take part in a game. They reduce the risk of fraud and increase functionality because unlike, say, a credit card, the functionality is limited to each token, not transferred across all transactions on the same credit card.

4.7.10 *Network value tokens*

As their name suggests, these are tokens whose value is measured by the development of a network. They are communication protocols for a local area network on which they operate by way of a string of workstations.

4.7.11 *Non-native protocol tokens*

Tokens that are implemented in a cryptoeconomic protocol at the top of the blockchain. Again, they are an integral part of the blockchain's protocol consensus mechanism. It is, however, tracked on an underlying blockchain to which it is not integral.

4.7.12 *Pure cryptocurrencies*

These are both a medium of exchange and a store of value. There is no central authority, and they do not represent part ownership of anything. Effectively, they are a type of money, even if not legally categorised as such in most places.

4.7.13 *Usage tokens*

These function as an access key to a digital service. Beyond that, the holders do not acquire any special rights. If the demand for the service is high and the number of tokens limited, then the token itself can acquire a high value.[58]

4.7.14 *Utility tokens*

These offer the holders access to a utility, normally within a digital ledger system. They do not function as a currency but enable the holder to act as an investor in a future service or product, though their real value can be hard to assess. Purchase tokens might have been a better name.

58 www.blockchain.hub.net, accessed 14/02/2019.

4.7.15 Work tokens

These provide a right to contribute to the system by doing work in return for some type of reward. The work might be done on the blockchain or at a smart contract level. Rewards can be given for recommendations or building up a work profile on the system.[70]

The IMF in particular views cryptocurrency payments as immediate, safe, cheap, and potentially semi-autonomous and, from this perspective, urges central banks to consider issuing digital assets so that they can retain a sure footing in payments. The IMF nevertheless cautions central banks to consider their particular country circumstances, giving special attention to the risks and relative merits of alternative solutions. The Bank for International Settlements (BIS) cautioned that central banks eyeing a general purpose CBDC as an alternative to cash would need to ensure the fulfilment of anti-money laundering and counter-terrorism financing (AML/CTF) requirements, simultaneously satisfying the public policy requirements of other supervisory tax regimes.[59] A recent BIS survey[60] suggests that most central banks appeared to have clarified the challenges of launching a CBDC but are yet unconvinced that the benefits would outweigh the costs. Central banks from advanced and emerging economies are moving at different speeds. This could generate a potential risk for spillover effects across borders. However, the BIS survey evidence suggested that central banks are proceeding cautiously, collaborating, and sharing the outcomes of their work. This implies that the world will have to wait to use a CBDC.

4.8 Blockchain applications beyond cryptoassets

4.8.1 Blockchain transformative powers

Cryptoassets' wide following in May 2024 was led by Bitcoin with US$1.4 trillion market capitalisation; Ethereum with market cap of US$454.4 billion; Tether with market cap of US$111.3 billion; Binance Coin (BNB) with market cap of US$90.3 billion; Solana (SOL) with market cap of US$80.8 billion; US Dollar Coin (USDC) with market cap of US$33.2 billion; XRP (XRP) with market cap of US$30 billion; Dogecoin (DOGE) with market cap of US$24.1 billion;

59 BIS (2018), "Central bank digital currencies", *BIS Paper*, March 2018; Carstens, A. (2024), "Central bank: Embracing change", Speech by Augustin Carstens, Bis General Manager at the People's Bank of China, Beijing, 22/04/2024, www.bis.org/speeches/sp240522.htm, accessed 23/05/2024. Here, it is argued that when the winds of change blow, reinforcing the walls on which trust in money is built and digital revolution are both needed that necessitates central banks to think afresh about the potential opportunities to build windmills that leverage technology for improving the financial system; Auer, R. et al. (2024), "Rise of central bank digital currencies: Update as of 1 March 2024", www.bis.org/publ/work880_updates_mar2024.pdf, accessed 22/05/2024; Nili, C. & Walicezek, S. (2024), "Modernizing financial markets with wholesale central bank digital currency (wCBDC)", *World Economic Forum (WEF)/Accenture*, April 2024, www.weforum.org/publications/modernizing-financial-markets-with-wcbdc/, accessed 22/05/2024.

60 Barotini, C. & Holden, H. (2019), "Proceed with caution: A survey on central bank digital currency", *BIS Papers*, 101, January 2019.

Toncoin (TON) with market cap of US$22.2 billion; and Caedano (ADA) with market cap of US$17.8 billion.[61]

It is to be noted that while some cryptoassets function like currencies, others are deployed to develop infrastructure. Blockchain applications beyond cryptoassets are evolving steadily, drawing on blockchain's extensive capabilities and transformative powers by substituting the trust economy with an authentication economy.[62] This is because data on a blockchain is innately legitimate, where, as a distributed record, multiple parties or all computers on the network have an identical copy, and where all the records are linked in a manner that not a single party is the sole holder of the record, and therefore no party can disrupt the record, as that will involve tampering simultaneously every copy of the record located everywhere. As the data are verified and linked together, transactions can be completed instantaneously, eliminating delays and processing fees. In this sense, blockchains eliminate all middlemen or intermediaries between the transacting parties or between buyers and sellers.

4.8.2 Blockchain features

The features of blockchain include the following:[63]

- *Transparency*. Every participant enjoys equal access to all records, resulting in the democratisation of information.
- *Absence of preferential authority or hierarchical structure as associated with centralised systems.*
- *Decentralised.* Absence of a single point of potential failure, where no single location or party can disrupt the network because of incompetency or malicious intent.
- *Absence of collusion.* Being decentralised makes it very difficult for manipulation to take place.
- *Immutability*. Upon creation, a record cannot be deleted, duplicated, or altered.

61 Adams, M. & Dammeyer, L. (2024), "Top 10 cryptocurrencies of May 2024", *Forbes Advisor*, 21/05/2024, www.forbes.com/advisor/investing/cryptocurrency/top-10-cryptocurrencies/, accessed 23/05/2024.

62 Tripathi, G. et al. (2023), "A comprehensive review of blockchain technology: Underlying principles and historical background with future challenges", *Decision Analytics Journal*, 9: 1–21; Minsker, M. (2018), "The transformative power of blockchain", *Cornell Business*, 29/08/2018, https://business.cornell.edu/hub/2018/08/29/the-transformative-power-of-blockchain/, accessed 20/12/2023; Schacklford, S. J. & Myers, S. (2017), "Block-by-block: Leveraging the power of blockchain technology to build trust and promote cyber peace", *The Yale Journal of Law & Technology*, 19: 335–388.

63 Barney, N. et al. (2023), "Blockchain", *Tech Target*, October 2023, www.techtarget.com/searchcio/definition/blockchain, accessed 20/12/2023; Tyagi, N. et al. (2020), "A framework for blockchain technology including features", in Hassanien, A. E. et al. (eds.), *Emerging technologies in data mining and information security*, Proceedings of IEMIS 2020, vol. 1, Singapore, Springer.

- *Open-source software*. Meaning, that it is not only seeable and auditable by any party but also only altered through consensus, implying the absence of autocracy.
- *Limitless appending to existing records*. Thereby providing information endlessly and seamlessly.
- *Incredible speed for completion of transactions between parties.*
- *Relatively lower transaction costs*. This makes it widely affordable and accessible, thereby contributing to inclusiveness.
- *Anonymity*. The flexibility of engaging with the use of blockchain while maintaining privacy.

In short, blockchain is a specialised database where data is stored on individual, independent computers that exist in all locations all over the planet, thereby making the blockchain network distributed as it comprises computers that are not all in one location. Blockchain, though, is also decentralised, without single points of failure, where every computer can access all the information on the blockchain, and where there is no central entity controlling any particular blockchain interaction but kept on track by cryptography and computer software.

4.8.3 Blockchain applications

These continue to evolve, drawing on the major benefits of blockchain, which include that it and its implementation technology are public, where each participating entity possesses an updated and complete record of the transactions and the associated blocks, and where as such the data remains unaltered, as any changes will be publicly verifiable, but also where the data in the blocks are encrypted by a private key and therefore cannot be interpreted by everyone.[64] The other major benefit is that the blockchain technology is decentralised, with no single device storing the data, comprising transactions and the associated blocks, but instead is distributed among the participants throughout the network supporting the blockchain, but where transactions are not subject to approval of any single authority or have to adhere to specific rules that involve substantial trust to reach a consensus.[65]

Meanwhile, although the internet is contributing immensely to almost every sphere of modern digital life, it is deficient in terms of the lack of security and privacy, especially when it concerns fintech and e-commerce. Blockchain offers a mechanism for peer-to-peer (P2P) transactions without needing any new intermediary, such as banks, as blockchain to equivalent cryptoasset techniques neither need to trust each other nor do need an intermediator, because the trust is manifested within the decentralised network system itself. Cryptocurrencies such as Bitcoin are just an exemplary use of the blockchain, as the blockchain

64 Miraz, M. H. & Ali, M. (2018), "Applications of blockchain technology beyond cryptocurrency", *Annals of Emerging Technologies in Computing (AETiC)*, 2(1): 1–6.

65 Ibid note [64], Miraz & Ali (2018).

technology is viewed as a novel revolution in the sphere of computing enabling limitless applications of storing and verifying legal documents.[66] Blockchain merits recognition as the "World Wide Ledger" that enables many new applications beyond verifying transactions, such as in smart deeds and decentralised and/or autonomous organisations/government services.[67]

In the cloud space, the history of the creation of any cloud data object and the subsequent operations performed thereupon is recorded by the data structure mechanism of "data provenance", a kind of cloud metadata. It is viewed as important to provide the strongest security to the data provenance to ensure its data privacy, forensics, and accountability. A fully decentralised, blockchain-based trusted cloud data provenance architecture, ProveChain, has already been proposed.[68] The adoption of blockchain in a cloud environment can provide strong protection against records being altered, thereby enabling enhanced transparency, including data accountability, which will also increase the availability, trustworthiness, privacy, and eventually, value of the provenance data itself.[69]

In the IoT ecosystem, most of the communication is in the form of machine-to-machine (M2M) interactions.[70] As such, establishing trust among the participating machines represents a formidable challenge that IoT technology has not widely addressed. This could be achieved by using blockchain to monitor billions of devices linked to the IoT ecosystems to enable enhanced and coordinated transaction processing to increase reliability by axing the single point of failure (SPF). The cryptographic algorithms used for the encryption of the block data, including the hashing techniques, should be able to provide better security, but their need for more processing power the present IoT devices might not be able to provide. Thus, blockchain can act as a catalyst to enable enhanced scalability, security, and privacy.[71]

The use of blockchain could eventually overhaul the digital economy.[72] The primary and initial concern of blockchain involves ensuring and maintaining

66 Ibid note [64], Miraz & Ali (2018).

67 Tapscott, D. & Tapscott, A. (2016), *Blockchain revolution: How the technology behind bitcoin is changing money, business and the world*, New York, Penguin Publishing Group.

68 Liang, X. P. et al. (2017), "ProveChain", in *Proceedings of the 17th IEEE/ACM International symposium on cluster, cloud and grid computing (CCGrid '17), Madrid Spain, 14–17/05/2017*, pp. 468–477, https://dl.acm.org/citation.cfm?id=3101176&CFID=994896989&CFTOKEN=44228545, accessed 20/12/2023.

69 Ibid note [64], Miraz & Ali (2018).

70 Miraz, M. H. et al. (2015), "A review on internet of things (IoT), internet of everything (IoE) and internet of nano things (IoNT)", in *Proceedings of the fifth international IEEE conference on internet technologies and applications (ITA 15), Wrexham, UK*, pp. 219–224, http://ieeexplore.ieee.org/xpl/articleDetails.jsp?arnumber=7317398, accessed 20/12/2023; Miraz, M. H. et al. (2018), "Internet of nano-things, things and everything: Future growth trends", *Future Internet*, 10(8): 1–28.

71 Miraz, M. H. & Ali, M. (2018), "Blockchain enabled enhanced IoT ecosystem security", in *Proceedings of the first international conference on emerging technologies in computing 2018 (iCETiC) London, 23/08/2018*, pp. 38–46, https://doi.org/10.1007/978-3-319-95450-9_3, accessed 20/12/2023.

72 Underwood, S. (2016), "Blockchain beyond bitcoin", *Communications of the ACM*, 59(11): 15–17.

trust. Blockchain can be applied to collect chronological and sequence information of transactions, as it could be treated as an enormous, networked timestamping machine. This is reflected in NASDAQ's deployment of Linq blockchain to record private securities transactions.[73] Also, the Depository Trust & Clearing Corporation (DTCC) in the United States is working with IBM, Axoni, and R3 to implement financial settlement services such as post-trade matters and swaps.[74] Regulators are also watching blockchain's ability to provide secure, private, traceable, real-time monitoring of transactions.[75]

Where an enterprise has critical data that it intends to share, a package of existing database, cloud, and identity management technologies would probably be sufficient for its requirements, but where it seeks to have its data immutable and auditable, blockchain, then, could be suitable. Blockchain, beyond its application in the cryptocurrency space, can be used in the following:[76]

- *Healthcare*. Applications of blockchain in this sector could involve the management of electronic health records, such as to authenticate patients and health providers and to enable the sharing of electronic health records (EHRs).[77] Here, the records are held on a system hosted by the provider, but the existence of the record is published on the blockchain. The patient will be able to use the blockchain to authorise who may have access to that record. This could, however, be inhibited in the United States by federal laws, such as the Health Insurance Portability and Accountability Act 1996 or the Health Information Technology for Economic and Clinical Heath Act 2009, and elsewhere by health record privacy laws.
- *Identity management*. Here, a user has a private key to validate transactions made with their public key, thereby making sure that only those with the private key are able to execute transactions. This resolves the double-spend problem, as the transactions are published so other users can validate the contract. This kind of identity management requires

73 Das, S. (2021), "NASDAQ launches Linq, a private blockchain-powered trading platform", *CCN*, 04/03/2021, www.ccn.com/nasdaq-launches-linq-a-private-blockchain-powered-trading-platform/, accessed 20/12/2023.

74 Axoni (2017), "DTCC selects IBM, Axoni and R3 to develop distributed ledger solution for derivatives processing", *Axoni*, 09/01/2017, https://axoni.com/press/dtcc-selects-ibm-axoni-and-r3-to-develop-distributed-ledger-solution-for-derivatives-processing/, accessed 20/12/2023.

75 Ibid note [64], Miraz & Ali (2018); Tiwari, H. (2019), "Blockchain research beyond cryptocurrencies", *IEEE Communications Standards Magazine*, 3(4): 21–25.

76 Jaikaran, C. (2018), "Congressional hearing on beyond bitcoin: Emerging applications for blockchain technology", *Statement of Chris Jaikaran, Analyst in Cybersecurity Policy Before Committee on Science, Space and Technology Subcommittee on Oversight & Subcommittee on Research and Technology U.S. House of Representative*, 14/02/2018, Congressional Research Service (CRS) TE10025, https://crsreports.congress.gov/product/pdf/TE/TE10025, accessed 20/12/2023.

77 Ekblaw, A. et al. (2016), "A case study for blockchain in healthcare", www.healthit.gov/sites/defult/files/5-56_blockchainchallengee_mitwhitepaper.pdf, accessed 20/12/2023.

a computing device and an internet connection. Private entities might be able to require users to maintain a compatible device for their blockchains and the internet connection to execute a transaction on the blockchain. On the other hand, entities such as those in the public sector might encounter difficulties in moving a blockchain that only identity management approaches, as some of their customer base may lack the computing elements necessary to execute the transaction.

- *Provenance*. This refers to the ability to know the chronology of an item to ensure that users are legitimate consumers and thus to enable the transfer of property, rights, or goods without needing clearance from a third party intermediary. Here, users publish on the blockchain that they have rights to an asset, and such users' claims are thus verified and governed by the rules of that blockchain. It can thus be used for transactions such as land transfer, physical chattels, and digital images.
- *Smart contracts*. Traditional contracts signify an agreement between parties that upon execution of particular conditions, a transfer of assets or rights will occur. Smart contracts codify these attributes in codes to enable machines to validate that these conditions are fulfilled and initiate the transfer of assets. Other than the parties partaking in the transaction, other users of the blockchain platform may provide computational resources needed to process or validate the contractual transaction, thereby gaining a stake in the transaction or contributing to the verification of the transaction on the ledger. Ethereum is an illustration of a smart contracts platform. Here, users build their smart contracts and pay fees so that other users contribute computational resources to enable the smart contracts and validate the transactions.[78] Some banks have found blockchain underlying the digital sector provides opportunity for banks to respond to margin compression across financial services, such as the offer of digital services for tokenised funds.[79]
- *Supply chain*. The management of physical and digital goods on blockchain is similar to smart contract application. In this application, goods are tagged with a digital value (such as a scannable code for physical goods or tracker for digital goods), and as it passes from one entity to the next, that entity accepts it and then transfers it to another using its public–private key. These transactions are added to the blockchain

78 Huang, Y. & Wang, B. (2021), "Research and application of smart contract based on Ethereum blockchain", *Journal of Physics Conference Series*, 1748(4): 042016–042023, https://doi.org/10.1088/1742-6596/1748/4/042016, accessed 20/12/2023.

79 Ghosh, S. (2024), "Deutsche bank says blockchain can help weather margin pressure: German lender is latest to enter Singapore's project Guardian. Bank testing a platform offering services for tokenized funds", *Bloomberg*, 29/05/2024, www.bloomberg.com/news/articles/2024-05-28/deutsche-bank-says-blockchains-can-help-weather-margin-pressure#:~:text=The%20blockchain%20technology%20underlying%20the,according%20to%20Deutsche%20Bank%20AG, accessed 30/05/2024.

to enable participants to monitor the disposition of the goods from creation through distribution to retail and potentially to the end users.[80] However, this system will only allow for accountability regarding which party has control of the real-world item at which point. Considering that the item itself does not contain traceable code, it must be affixed with a tracker, like a scannable code or a sensor, which enables its tracking. Parties with bad intentions in the supply chain could still manipulate the item, alter trackers, or adulterate items in the chain that may not be logged on the blockchain.

An example of a supply chain management on a blockchain platform used in the tracking of blockchain technology is deployed in business sectors such as the food and vehicle industries, in smart devices, and in precious mineral transactions.[81], [82] There are thus extensive commercial applications for blockchain technology as it enables both the public and private sectors to operate at high speed, with greater safety, at lower cost, and with enhanced transparency. Blockchain allows consumers to avoid the credit card infrastructure to transfer money directly to merchants, thereby enjoying cost savings, while businesses and individuals can transfer money globally in seconds virtually free of charge. Corporate finance and foreign trade enjoy cost benefit, too, as transfers using blockchain occur in real time, eliminating foreign currency exchange rate risk. Through the use of blockchain, currencies can be exchanged within seconds at comparatively little cost, resulting in huge savings in both money and time. Other examples include blockchain enabled smart contracts; complex agreements in finance, manufacturing, and real estate; and in expediting payments for those engaged in music, content creation.

All these can be executed with enhanced transparency, efficiency, safety, and compliance, thereby protecting buyers from the risk that sellers are unable to deliver on their promises. Those needing to rely on micropayments from millions of people lacking bank accounts to run their global business can rely on digital money enabled by blockchain as, unlike currency, digital money can be fractionalised into bits, bytes, ones, and zeros that small buyers can easily access and partake in the huge e-commerce globally using cell phones and through integration with Internet of Things (IoT).[83]

80 Fefer, R. F. (2019), "Blockchain and international trade", Congressional Research Services (CRS) 7-5700 25/06/19, https://sgp.fas.org/crs/row/IF10810.pdf, accessed 20/12/2023.

81 Lewis, B. (2018), "Blockchain to track Congo's cobalt from mine to mobile", *Reuters*, 02/02/2018, www.reuters.com/article/us-mining-blockchain-cobalt/blockchain-to-track-congos-cobalt-from-mine-to-mobile-idUSKBN1FM0Y2, accessed 20/12/2023.

82 Arora, P. & Makani, R. (2022), "Blockchain technology and its applications: A systematic review of the literature", *Proceedings of the International Conference on Innovative Computing & Communication (CICC) 2022*, https://papers.ssrn.com/sol3/papers.cfm?abstract_id=4121824, accessed 20/12/2023.

83 Edelman, R. (2022), *The truth about crypto*, New York, Simon & Schuster.

It is to be noted that, combined with AI and robotics, IoT is facilitating major initiatives in automation. In this era of autonomy, crypto, blockchain, and smart contracts allow for automated financial transactions to unleash an economy where autonomous, permissionless software can optimise, make real-time decisions, and move capital 24/7. Large-scale financial opportunities are thus opened up via smart contract platforms. A good illustration of this is decentralised finance (DeFi). *DeFi* are smart contracts that reside on a blockchain, not controlled by any central authority and not easily exposed to manipulation risk.[84] The best business cases for DeFi are collateralised lending and collateralised borrowing. Via smart contracts platforms, developers are using blockchain technology to create DeFi platforms that enable market participants to borrow and lend funds, speculate on price movements on assets applying derivatives, trade cryptoassets, insure against risks, and earn interest in savings accounts.[85]

There is, as such, no central authority to report to. It is, in effect, a radical, novel manner of undertaking business, as DeFi operates through a public blockchain that is accessible to anyone with an internet connection. It culminates in a level playing field, where the supply side allows investors to create new kinds of capital, with investors infusing collateral into the system through smart contracts.

It is also possible to print a new form of currency known as stablecoins, and on the demand front, investors can use that digital money to provide the first formation of capital that lends money back to investors and developers for investment purposes,[86] and conventional banks are starting to prioritise digital assets. Notable illustrations of these include the following:[87]

- Wells Fargo partnering with NYDIG to offer Bitcoin investments to their clientele
- JPMorgan Chase partnering with DBS Singapore's DBS Group and Temasek to form a blockchain payments platform to facilitate cross-border payments, trade, and foreign exchange settlement in the new digital era
- Bank of New York Mellon designing a digital custody platform for transferring, safekeeping, and issuing digital assets
- Cryptocurrency platform Mastercard and Gemini offering a credit card that provides real-time crypto rewards on purchases made with various cryptocurrencies
- Commerzabank, Isbank, and LBBW becoming the first banks to execute a commercial cross-border transaction through Marco Polo, a blockchain-enabled trade finance network

84 Ryan, J. & Diorio, J. (2023), *Crypto decrypted*, Hoboken, NJ, Wiley & Sons.
85 Ibid note [84], Ryan & Diorio (2023).
86 Ibid note [84], Ryan & Diorio (2023).
87 Ibid note [84], Ryan & Diorio (2023).

- Binance, a leading international exchange, operating a US$100 million accelerator fund to support blockchain ecosystem building
- A blockchain supported exchange traded fund (ETF) referred to as the iShares Blockchain and Tech ETF (IBLC) having been designed to open multiple avenues of opportunities for BlackRock, the world's largest asset management firm

In relation to IBLC, through this initiative, BlackRock seeks to assist crypto enthusiasts in gaining much needed exposure to this fast-growing market without needing for them to own digital assets for the purpose. ETFs combine features of both mutual funds and stocks. Like mutual funds, ETFs offer investors an interest in a professionally managed, diversified portfolio of investments, but unlike mutual funds, ETF shares trade like stocks on exchanges, with prices fluctuating throughout the day based on market demand.[88]

The product is designed as a unified cluster comprising 42 distinct holders contributing therein, where the largest single share of 11.45% of the ETF funds is held by US-based Coinbase. Other significant holders are renowned BTC miners Marathon Digital Holdings with 11.19% share, and Riot Blockchain Inc. having 10.42% of the total share, and whereas at July 2025 the ETF claims a potential 9.15% US$ cash status. In conjunction with this, a BlackRock report highlights the new core market areas currently undergoing rapid permanent changes that underpin the strong belief of the firm in crypto growth.

The rise in crypto operations accelerated the need for launching crypto ETFs that provide better exposure to the industry for the users. Since listing in January 2023, BlackRock's iShares Bitcoin Trust has become the world's largest cryptocurrency, accounting for about US$20 billion in total assets. Its ETF is said to hold US$19.68 billion of tokens, overtaking Grayscale Trust's US$19.65 billion.[89] On 10 January 2024, the SEC approved 11 Bitcoin ETFs. Bitcoin, the leading cryptocurrency, has a present market cap of about US$900 billion but has seen volatile swings throughout its 15-year history.[90]

Digital assets evolved as the internet evolved from Web 1.0 to Web 3.0. Web 1.0, the early internet, comprised mainly static websites from the early 1990s through to about 2004, illustrating a period of predominantly consumer engagement. This subsequently evolved into Web 2.0 from 2004 to today,

88 Abner, D. J. (2016), *The ETF handbook: How to value and trade exchange traded funds*, New York, John Wiley & Sons.

89 McGee, S. (2024), "BlackRock's ETF becomes largest bitcoin fund in the world, Bloomberg news reports", *Reuters*, 29/05/2024, https://ca.investing.com/news/stock-market-news/blackrocks-etf-becomes-largest-bitcoin-fund-in-world-bloomberg-news-reports-3432172?utm_source=google&utm_medium=cpc&utm_campaign=18959642585&utm_content=696197994210&utm_term=dsa-1463805041937_&GL_Ad_ID=696197994210&GL_Campaign_ID=18959642585&ISP=1&npl=1&af_adset_id=144433385715&gad_source=1&gclid=EAIaIQobChMI4azx3rXNhgM-VaI5LBR1G_gjXEAAYAyAAEgIuhPD_BwE, accessed 09/06/2024.

90 Ibid note [90], McGee (2024).

illustrating an era of business consolidation. Importantly, this was a period when consumers gave up their data freely to conglomerates in the service of convenience. However, Web 3.0 could be perceived as decentralised internet, where all parties interact but where data is owned and shared at the individual level, peer-to-peer.[91] It is a World Wide Web that is built incorporating blockchain technologies and is essentially decentralised, with all the benefits therein.[92] It is further contended that whereas legacy internet forces creators to create content with costs, Web 3.0 will equip creators to produce content they can own and monetise, and with this, the prospects for the creator would look better.[93]

The static informative features of Web 1.0 thus advanced into the interactive experience that Web 2.0 could provide. Web 3.0 is already operating and involves an integrated experience where computers become capable of understanding and cataloguing data in ways equivalent to humans.[94] This resulted in a World Wide Web warehouse where any format of data could be shared and understood by any device over any network. Web 3.0 transforms the ways users interact with devices and networks, particularly regarding how businesses apply data gathered to operate their businesses. This is especially useful in the marketing and selling of products and services.[95]

Global digital platform corporations (GDPCs) such as Meta, Google, and others monetise profitably from data stored and recombined and from other data business users, including private individuals, and also acquire insights regarding the opportunities arising from Web 3.0 technologies.[96] These GDPCS would, however, need to be mindful of the risks associated with Web 3.0 applications, particularly pertaining to data privacy concerns.[97] Other than antitrust laws and other-sector-focused online niches for minors, health, transport services, and others, the United States, unlike the EU and the UK, does not as yet have a federal legislation for dealing with GDPC's excesses in the digital markets on various online harm.[98] As matters currently stand, it is probable that the UK and the EU will have laws, albeit contentious ones, for dealing with data accessibility and various kinds of online harm. The position is relatively less clear for the United States, given the heavy partisan politics dominating the issue, as well as the governing influence of the US Constitution, particularly pertaining

91 Ibid note [84], Ryan & Diorio (2023).

92 Edelman, G. (2021), "The father of Web3 want you to trust less: Gavin Wood who coined the term Web3 in 2014 believes decentralized technologies are the only hope of preserving liberal democracies", *Wired*, 29/11/21, www.wired.com/story/web3-gavin-wood-interview/, accessed 20/12/2023.

93 Ibid note [84], Ryan & Diorio (2023).

94 Yeoh, P. (2023), "Data management in the world wide web: Innovations, dominance, and regulatory risks", *Journal of Business Law*, 4: 253–288.

95 Ibid note [95], Yeoh (2023).

96 Ibid note [95], Yeoh (2023).

97 Ibid note [95], Yeoh (2023).

98 Ibid note [95], Yeoh (2023).

to free speech and the overwhelming free enterprise beliefs and practices in US society.[99] Blockchain applications here and in general, though, raised several concerns with regards to matters of data portability, key security, user collusion and control, user savviness and safety, and including business legal and technical aspects.[100]

99 Ibid note [95], Yeoh (2023).

100 Panda, S. K. et al. (eds.) (2021), *Blockchain technology: Applications and challenges*, Cham, Springer.

CHAPTER 5

Global cryptoassets hubs

5.1 Introduction

The cryptoassets industry is a subset of the larger fintech digital space. Some cryptoassets hubs with large scale activity, such as Canada, Singapore, and Hong Kong (SAR), are boosted by the presence of users from other nationals barred from using cryptoassets because of bans in their countries of origin. In the case of Hong Kong, notably nationals from China. Some cryptoassets hubs with apparently low cryptoasset utilisations are due to inhospitable cryptoasset ecosystems, such as India. Active cryptoassets hubs such as those found in advanced Western economies are due to the strong pursuits of liberalism even though they have the most advanced and powerful banking systems in the world, as strongly exemplified in the United States, UK, and various continental European economies. Countries with relatively less developed banking systems, such as those in the African continent, leap straight to cryptoassets and other subsets of the fintech space because of the need to provide financial inclusiveness to large tracts of their populations. Multilateral financial institutions, such as the IMF in particular, support cryptocurrencies and other fintech subsets to help foster financial inclusiveness in emerging economies where there are many less well-off.

Forming a precise view of where the heaviest use of cryptoassets occur is not easy, as many crypto entities and platforms will not share users' data for various reasons, including data protection laws or the fact that some wallet providers prevent the gathering of location-based data. Combining available public resources with others available from private sources could offer a crude estimate of where most crypto activity is occurring.[1] An indication of activity could be gleaned from local Bitcoin volumes and P2P exchange platforms connecting users across 249 countries. High-volume growth has been seen in emerging Asian economies, such as China, India, Thailand, and Malaysia; Latin American states, such as Brazil, Chile, Colombia, Mexico, and Venezuela; African and Middle Eastern states, such as Kenya, Nigeria, Saudi Arabia, Tanzania, and Turkey; and Eastern European states, such as Russia and Ukraine.[2]

1 Hileman, G. & Rauchs, M. (2017), *Global cryptocurrency benchmarking study*, Cambridge, Cambridge Centre for Alternative Finance.
2 Ibid note [1], Hileman & Rauchs (2017).

DOI: 10.4324/9781032667416-5

The geographical distribution of cryptocurrency ATMs including Bitcoin in a recent global cryptocurrency benchmarking study suggests that some 94% of all publicly known ATMs are based in North America and Europe, with the United States and Canada having a total share of 59% and 15%, respectively, of all ATMs; Africa, the Middle East, and Latin America have less than 1% of worldwide cryptocurrency ATMs.[3] Coinmap hosts some 9,000 known merchants across the globe that entertain cryptocurrencies, suggesting that significant concentrations of merchants could be seen in North America and Europe. Some activity could also be observed in the Asia–Pacific belt, with concentrations in Australia, Japan, and South Korea; Latin America, with concentrations in Brazil and Argentina; and Africa and the Middle East, notably in Kenya, South Africa, and Israel.[4]

An analysis of Bitcoin full nodes suggests that the United States has the highest number of full node operators of all economies. User data analysis suggests that nearly 40% of cryptocurrency users are based in the Asia–Pacific, followed by Europe at 27%, with the US share notably low and inconsistent with the data alluded to earlier.[5] The data provided are from a very limited number of wallet providers and payment platforms and exclude users from exchanges as well as mining pools. All in all, it would appear that cryptocurrencies' adoption is most advanced in the United States and Europe, but numbers are growing in other jurisdictions, like those in the emerging economies of Asia, Latin America, and the Middle East.[6]

The geographical distribution of study participants further suggests that Europe accounted for 29% of the study participation rate. Exchanges, wallets, payments, and mining there, respectively, accounted for 37%, 42%, 33%, and 13%.[7] The United States accounted for 27% of the participation rate. Exchanges, wallets, payments, and mining there, respectively, accounted for 18%, 39%, 19%, and 33%. Asia–Pacific accounted for 36% of the study participation rate. Exchanges, wallets, payments, and mining there respectively accounted for 27%, 19%, 33%, and 50%. Latin America accounted for 6% of the study participation rate. Exchanges, wallets, payments, and mining there respectively accounted for 14%, 0%, 11%, and 4%. Africa and the Middle East accounted for 2% of the study participation rate. Exchanges, wallets, payments, and mining there respectively accounted for 4%, 0%, 4%, and 0%.

The third edition of the Global Cryptoasset Benchmarking Study generated the following findings:[8]

---

3 Ibid note [1], Hileman & Rauchs (2017).

4 Ibid note [1], Hileman & Rauchs (2017).

5 Ibid note [1], Hileman & Rauchs (2017).

6 Ibid note [1], Hileman & Rauchs (2017).

7 Ibid note [1], Hileman & Rauchs (2017).

8 Blandin, A. et al. (2020), *3rd global crypto asset benchmarking study*, Cambridge, Cambridge Centre for Alternative Finance.

1. Full-time equivalent (FTE) growth slowed a lot subsequent to the late 2017 market frenzy across all market segments' reported year-on-year growth of 21% in 2019, down from 57% in 2018. Growth in industry wide FTE employment declined by 36% between 2017 and 2019, while the median firm reported 75% downward change in employment growth. The difference in the industry level and firm-level employment growth data, reflecting the rise of large enterprises within each industry group that dominates the total change in employment, suggests that a few large participants are dominating the industry.
2. Significant differences arise when comparing the cost structure of US and Chinese hashers, where capital expenditures, mainly of mining equipment purchases, account up to 56% of US hashers' costs, compared to 31% for Chinese ones. This suggests that Chinese hashers have a competitive edge in the purchase of mining machines, explained mostly by the concentration of hardware manufacturers in China, leading to a shorter supply chain; easier business conduct, such as language, working culture, and local connections; and the absence of international shipping fees and import tariffs. Along with this, the study reported that some 52% of ASIC manufacturers' total sales went to Chinese hashers in 2019. Some 58% of hashers reported receiving support from governments mainly in the form of locally focused support, such as electricity subsidy for users within a region.
3. Along with the 2018 findings, new survey data shows that, in terms of volumes and numbers, off-chain transactions continue to be dominated by fiat cryptoassets trades and vice versa. This suggests that users mainly interact with "gateway" service providers like exchanges to enter and exit the cryptoasset ecosystem. Usage seems to vary with the geographic location of the service provider.
4. The updated estimate of the number of cryptoassets users shows an aggregate of some 101 million unique users across 191 million accounts opened at service providers as of the third quarter of 2020.
5. Some 40% of surveyed enterprises are licensed or in the process of getting a license, and these are sited mainly in Europe. Nonetheless, the remaining firms should not be viewed as the share of entities undertaking unregulated activities or evading regulations, as some surveyed service providers are undertaking activities that do not, as yet, require any authorisation process. While almost all customer accounts at European and US service providers are subject to KYC/AML obligations, this is the case only for some 50% of accounts at Middle East and Africa based service providers. The proportion of cryptoasset only firms that did not undertake any KYC verification at all slipped from 48% to 13% between 2018 and 2020, mainly arising

from the progressive harmonisation KYC/AML standards across jurisdictions, such as initiated by the FATF.

6. Irrespective of their location or size, the vast majority of surveyed cryptoasset service providers maintain cryptoasset funds in cold storage, or some 90%. To a lesser degree, they make use of multi-signature approaches to secure their cold and hot storage systems.
7. The decoupling of duties between custody, clearing, and settlement responsibilities appears to be underway and could lead to greater resemblance with conventional financial market infrastructure. For example, some 45% of respondents show using a third party, primarily crypto native custodians, as part of their cold storage system. Nonetheless, further intertwining with the conventional financial system depends on enhanced compliance with international standards, like those laid out by the FATF. Survey data found that cryptoassets service providers legally incorporated in a jurisdiction member of FATF that is more likely to serve conventional institutional investors. More risky and experimental innovations like those in the DeFi space are envisaged to emerge in the near future.

The global cryptoasset market size was estimated at US$1.1 billion in 2023. This is expected to reach US$3 billion in 2032, growing at a CAGR of 11.18%.[9] The factors driving the applications of the cryptoasset market extend from peer-to-peer payment, retail, trading, and remittance to e-commerce. The United States, the EU, and the Asia–Pacific are leading the cryptoasset markets.

Cryptocurrency ICOs[10] also emerged as a popular and effective crowdfunding method for both start-ups and established companies seeking to raise further capital. This drives further the publicity attaching to cryptoassets.[11] The rapid pace of development in the cryptocurrencies' sector in terms of technology, applications, and economics has, in turn, attracted the attention of governments, international financial regulators, and analysts. The surge in investments in cryptocurrency and assets, coupled with the incidences of theft and the perceived linkage with money laundering, tax evasion, and drug transactions, has ushered in disparate national attitudes towards cryptocurrencies. Cryptocurrencies and blockchain applications have also been touted by developmental experts as a viable instrument for helping the large underbanked populations in many

---

9 Introspective Market Research (IMR) (2024), "The cryptocurrency market research report 2024–2032", *IMR*, 19/06/2024, https://markets.financialcontent.com/stocks/article/abnewswire-2024-6-19-cryptocurrency-market-is-projected-to-reach-usd-30-billion-2032-growing-at-a-rate-of-411-to-forecast-2024-2032-according-to-introspective-market-research, accessed 03/07/2024.

10 Cadigan, T. N., Frank, J. & Chin, K. (2017), "This is what you get when you invest in an initial coin offering", *Business Insider*, 09/11/2017, www.businessinsider.com/ico-initial-coin-offering-explained-bitcoin-ethereum-2017-11?r=US&IR=T, accessed 02/02/2018.

11 Hackett, R. & Wieczner, J. (2017), "How high can bitcoin's price go in 2018?" *Fortune*, 21/12/2017, https://fortune.com/2017/12/21/bitcoin-price-value-prediction-bubble/, accessed 02/02/2018.

emerging economies by enabling their access to finance which has been previously restricted in the more conventional forms of financing.[12]

The ten cities in the world with the strongest Bitcoin presence are San Francisco (USA), Vancouver (Canada), Amsterdam (the Netherlands), Ljubljana (Slovenia), Tel Aviv (Israel), Zurich (Switzerland), Tampa (USA), Buenos Aires (Argentina), New York (USA), and London (UK). The identification is based on the number of Bitcoin merchants in each city, the number of Bitcoin ATMs, and the population size relative to Bitcoin activity.[13]

Not many governments could openly be seen to be very hospitable towards cryptocurrencies because of the controversies surrounding them. Also, no one is really sure of their eventual economic and technological potentials, despite the fact that they have been around for a number of years. As a result, most governments assume a cautious stance. So rather than analysing which economies are more hospitable to cryptocurrencies, it could be more pragmatic to differentiate economies in terms of their tolerance levels towards this asset class. For the purpose of this chapter, economies with a relatively higher level of tolerance will be spotlighted. These are referred to as Bitcoin friendly economies in other research initiatives.[14] They refer to countries where the underpinning technology is being tested and applied with increasingly rapid momentum.[15] Advanced Western economies in this category include the United States, the UK, Canada, Australia, and the continental European economies of Germany, Switzerland, and Estonia. Asian economies under this category include Japan, South Korea, and Singapore. The reasons behind the surging interest in cryptoassets in each of these are examined in what follows.

5.2 Advanced Western economies

5.2.1 The United States

The United States unsurprisingly hosts the highest concentration of cryptocurrency users and Bitcoin trading volumes in the world.[16] The country has been home to crowdfunding technology at the cutting edge of digital currency from the beginning.[17] Spurred by the dynamism and innovative spirit of Silicon Valley

12 Dale, O. (2017), "How Bitcoin & cryptocurrencies are helping developing countries", *Blockonomi*, 24/12/2017, www.blockonomi.com/cryptocurrencies-developing-countries, accessed 02/02/2018.

13 Blystone, D. (2018), "10 cities leading bitcoin adoption", *Investopedia*, updated 19/09/2019, www.investopedia.com/articles/forex/042415/10-cities-leading-Bitcoin-adoption.asp, accessed 02/02/2018.

14 Dedi, D. (2017), "Top 10 most crypto-friendly countries", *Crypto Slate*, 16/09/2017, www.cryptoslate.com/top-10-most-crypto-friendly-countries, accessed 02/02/2018.

15 Scott, A. (2016), "These are the world's top 10 bitcoin-friendly countries", *Bitcoin*, 29/03/2016, www.bitcoin.com/worlds-top-10-bitcoin-friendly-countries/, accessed 02/02/2018.

16 Hileman, G. & Rauchs, M. (2017), *Global cryptocurrency benchmarking study*, Cambridge, Cambridge Centre for Alternative Finance.

17 Pipikaite, A. & Grover, V. (2018), "US needs to lead digital currency revolution, or other nations will", *The Hill* 08/01/2018, https://thehill.com/blogs/pundits-blog/finance/313224-us-needsto-lead-digital-currency-revolution-or-other-nations-will, accessed 02/02/2018.

as well as New York's fintech prowess, the United States is home to numerous cryptocurrency and blockchain related start-ups and the highest number of Bitcoin ATMs in the world.[18] Eleven of the biggest names in the cryptocurrencies space are US based or US inspired. They are, namely, Brian Armstrong of Coinbase, Vitalik Buterin of Ethereum, Juthica Chou of Ledger X, Jack Dorsey of Square, Terry Duffy of the CME Group, Charlie Lee of Litecoin, Naval Ravikant of MetaStable and CoinList, Elizabeth Rossiello of BitPesa, Barry Silbert of Digital Currency Group, Balaji Srinivasan of Earn.com, and Elizabeth Stark of Lightning Labs. In addition, there are many other smaller companies in the United States still fighting for recognition.

Many economies look toward the United States for guidance and inspiration pertaining to the technology underpinning cryptocurrencies as well as the laws and regulations surrounding them, not only from Washington, DC, but also from states better known for fintech innovations, such as California, New York, and New Hampshire. It is therefore unsurprising for the United States to serve as the testing ground for cryptocurrency regulation and direction.[19]

At the federal level in the United States, interests on cryptoassets have been at the SEC, the Commodity Futures Trading Commission (CFTC), the Federal Trade Commission (FTC) and the Treasury through the Internal Revenue Service (IRS), the Office of the Comptroller of the Currency (OCC), and the Financial Crimes Enforcement Network (FinCEN). Despite decent levels of engagement by these agencies, not much rulemaking has taken place. Responding to the mushrooming of cryptoassets in the mainstream economy, US policymakers (Congress) commencing in 2022 initiated a range of legislation to offer clarity to this unfolding sector.[20]

These include the Responsible Financial Innovation Act (RFIA), constructed to provide regulatory clarity for agencies tasked with supervising digital asset markets; the proposed Stablecoin Trust Act 2022, which authorises three options for the issuance of payment stablecoins; the Digital Commodities Consumer Protection Act 2022 (DCCPA), authorising the CFTC to regulate digital commodity platforms and digital commodity trading; and the Digital Trading Clarity Act 2022, which provides that a digital asset not subject to a determination by the SEC or a federal court and listed through an intermediary that satisfies particular requirements related to custody, disclosure, and other investor protection would not be considered a security. The RFIA provides a strong, tailored regulatory framework for stablecoins and integrates digital assets into existing

18 Roberts, D. (2017), "The 11 biggest names in cryptocurrency right now", *YahooFinance*, 30/11/2017, https://finance.yahoo.com/news/11-biggest-names-cryptocurrency-2017-110033921.html?guccounter=1, accessed 02/02/2018.

19 McKenna, F. (2017), "Here's how the U.S. and the world regulate bitcoin and other cryptocurrencies", *MarketWatch*, 28/12/2017, www.marketwatch.com/story/heres-how-the-us-and-theworld-are-regulating-bitcoin-and-cryptocurrency-2017-12-18, accessed 02/02/2018.

20 Dewey, J. N. & Patel, S. (2024), "Country chapter: USA", in Dewey, J. N. (ed.), *Blockchain & cryptocurrency laws and regulations 2024*, 6th edition, London, Global Legal Insights (GLI).

tax and banking laws, besides boosting innovations in digital assets.[21] The July 2023 updated version of the RFIA provides enhanced consumer protection amidst a flurry of bankruptcies among blockchain companies and stakeholders. This was soon followed by the proposed Responsible Financial Innovation Act (McHenry–Thompson Bill). This proposed a strong, tailored regulatory framework for stablecoins and integrated digital assets into existing tax and banking laws, besides boosting innovations in digital assets[22] and digital asset derivatives into the existing US regulatory framework, mainly that of the SEC and the CFTC, instead of a standalone framework.[23]

Various US states have proposed or passed laws that have an impact on cryptoassets and the blockchain technology, with some trying to promote the technology by passing favourable regulations exempting cryptoassets from state securities laws and/or money transmission statutes. Such states hope to leverage investment in the technology to boost local economies and improve public services, such as illustrated in the state of Wyoming, which became the first US state to allow for the creation of crypto focused, special purpose depository bank that can act in both a custodial and fiduciary capacity, thereby enabling businesses to hold digital assets safely and legally.[24] Wyoming also passed legislation targeted at easing the formation of decentralised autonomous organisations (DAOs), via the DAO Supplemental Bill, by recognising them as a kind of limited liability company. This further enables the state to issue the United States' first government issued stablecoin fully backed by reserves of US dollars. In contrast, increasing numbers of US states are making it more difficult for blockchain enterprises to operate within their borders by requiring money transmitter licenses and/or the need to strictly adhere to state blue sky securities laws. Florida and the District of Columbia amended their transmitter regulations to include virtual currencies/cryptoassets besides requiring certain intermediaries to have a state issued license.[25]

There appears to be no uniform definition of cryptocurrency, virtual currency, digital assets, digital tokens, or cryptoassets. Nevertheless, the Uniform Law Commission and the American Law Institute (ALI) amended the Uniform Commercial Code to include Article 12, which defines and governs digital assets specifically. The new Article includes virtual currencies in its definition of "controllable electronic records".[26] Several states have adopted the amendment, while other jurisdictions endeavour to formulate a detailed definition for the asset class, but most have opted for wider, more technology agnostic definitions and are thus better placed to regulate as and when the technology evolves.

The Biden presidency released an executive order outlining a way to address risks arising from the growth of digital assets and blockchain technology while

21 Ibid note [20], Dewey & Patel (2024).
22 Ibid note [20], Dewey & Patel (2024).
23 Ibid note [20], Dewey & Patel (2024).
24 Ibid note [20], Dewey & Patel (2024).
25 Ibid note [20], Dewey & Patel (2024).
26 Ibid note [20], Dewey & Patel (2024).

supporting responsible innovation. It highlights six key priorities, namely, consumer and investor protection, financial stability, illicit finance, US leadership in the global financial system and economic competitiveness, financial inclusion, and responsible innovation. To expedite implementation of these key priorities, the Order called for various reports, studies, and including reports from the Treasury on the future of money and potential impacts of a central bank digital currency, as well as policy decisions around consumer protection and financial inclusion matters. It also calls for the Financial Stability Oversight Council to produce a report on financial stability risks and regulatory gaps.[27]

The White House also released a fact sheet structured to provide a comprehensive framework for regulating digital assets based on inputs from various US government agencies and departments. The framework authorises regulators such as SEC and the CFTC to continue coordinating initiatives to enforce law in the industry and to share data on consumer complaints in the space, while the Treasury will take an active role in working with financial institutions to help identify and mitigate cyber risks via data sharing and analysis, besides being tasked with working with regulators to ensure that crypto enterprises have regulatory guidance. The fact sheet also mentions a potential US CBDC, mentioning many potential benefits in technology, the economy, security, and individual liberty.[28]

An entire 35 page chapter on digital asset that provides a degree of criticism of cryptoassets is included for the first time in the 2023 Economic Report of the President, reflecting an apparent shift from the approach of the Biden presidency voiced in the executive order. The report mentions that cryptoassets do not currently provide widespread economic benefits, apart from claiming that cryptoassets are mainly a speculative investment vehicle and not a viable alternative to fiat currency. It does acknowledge, however, that some cryptoassets are here to stay and that much of the activity in the cryptoasset space is covered by present regulations.[29]

Cryptoasset sales are regulated only where the sales constitute the sale of a security under state or federal laws or is treated as money transmission under state law or conduct otherwise making the person a services business (MSB) under federal law.[30] Additionally, futures, options, swaps, and other derivative contracts making reference to the price of a cryptoasset that constitutes a commodity are subject to regulation by the CFTC under the Commodity Exchange Act (CEA).[31] Further, the CFTC oversees engagements in market manipulation pertaining to those cryptoassets viewed as commodities. The CFTC, for example, initiated a civil enforcement action in the United States in the Southern District of New York charging Avaham Eisenberg with unlawfully misappropriating

27 Ibid note [20], Dewey & Patel (2024).
28 Ibid note [20], Dewey & Patel (2024).
29 Ibid note [20], Dewey & Patel (2024).
30 Ibid note [20], Dewey & Patel (2024).
31 Ibid note [20], Dewey & Patel (2024).

over US$110 million in digital assets from Mango Markets, a purported decentralised digital asset exchange, via "oracle manipulation in the CFTC's maiden enforcement action for a fraudulent or manipulative scheme involving trading on an assumed decentralized digital asset platform".[32]

In general, the SEC oversees the issuance or resale of any token or other digital asset that constitutes a "security". This includes "an investment contract defined by the US Supreme Court as an investment of money in a common enterprise with a reasonable expectation of profits to be derived from the entrepreneurial or managerial initiatives of others".[33] The SEC and the courts, when deliberating whether a token or other digital asset are investment contracts, consider the substance rather than their form. The US Supreme Court takes the position that the reach of the securities legislation does not stop with the obvious and commonplace. This means that novel, uncommon, or irregular devices, whatever they appear to be, can also be recached were it is proved as a matter of fact that these were widely offered or dealt in under terms or courses of dealings establishing their character in commerce as investment contracts or as any interest or instrument commonly known as a security.[34] The purpose of Congress in enacting the securities laws was to regulate investments in whatever form they are made and by whatever name they are addressed as.[35] The SEC has been clear that even if a token issued in an initial coin offering (ICO) has "utility", the token will still be treated as a security that is regulated under securities laws, where it complies with the Howey test elements.[36]

The SEC's enforcement actions included those against Telegram in October 2019, alleging that the company has raised US$1.7 billion via the sale of 2.9 billion GRAMS (the company's native cryptoasset) to finance its business. A federal district court entered a final judgement against Kik Interactive Inc. pertaining to Kik's unregistered offering of "Kin" tokens in 2017, which the SEC argued breached US securities laws. The SEC filed an action in the Southern District of New York (SDNY) against Ripple Labs Inc., charging that it raised over US$1.3 billion via an ongoing unregistered digital asset securities offering in December 2020. The complaint alleged that Ripple raised funds commencing in 2013 via the sale of the XRP digital coin in an unregistered securities offering to investors in the United States. In 13 July 2023, the court issued an order granting in part, and denying in part, cross motions for summary judgement filed by both parties, maintaining that under the Howey test, unregistered sales of XRP to retail investors on digital asset exchanges did not constitute an offer and sale of cryptoasset securities under US securities laws, while the sales of XRP to institutional investors were prohibited offers and sales. The court ruled that programmatic sales of XRP to retail investors on digital asset exchanges did not

32 Ibid note [20], Dewey & Patel (2024).

33 *SEC v W.J. Howey Co.*, 328 U.S. 293, 301 (1946).

34 *SEC v. C. M. Joiner Leasing Corp.*, 329 U.S. 344, 351 (1943).

35 *Reves v. Ernst & Young*, 494 U.S. 56, 61 (1990).

36 SEC Written Testimony to the US Senate Banking Committee 06/02/18, www.banking.senate.gov/download/clayton-testimony-2-6-18pdf, accessed 20/12/2023.

constitute the offer and sale of securities as these sales were blind bid/ask transactions, where retail investors could not have known whether their payments of money went to Ripples or another unaffiliated intermediary. Sales of XRP to institutional investors, though, did constitute the offer and sale of securities, as institutional investors would have acquired XRP with the expectation that they would derive profits from Ripple's initiatives, and Ripple led institutional investors to believe it would employ the capital accessed from its institutional sales to improve the market for XRP and develop uses for the XRP ledger, leading to the enhanced valuation of XRP.[37]

The SEC charged Singapore based Terraform Labs (Terraform) with breaching SEC registration and anti-fraud provisions by orchestrating a multi-billion cryptoasset securities fraud involving tokens that the SEC maintained were security based swaps designed to pay returns by mirroring stock prices of US companies and Terra USD (UST), an algorithmic stablecoin that supposedly maintained the US dollar peg by being interchangeable for LUNA coin, another of the cryptoasset securities issued by Terraform. In denying Terraform's dismissal, the court rejected to consider the categorisation of sales employed in the Ripple case. The rulings in the Telegram, Kik, and Ripples proceedings make it very hard to consummate most token-generating events involving persons. Many issuers have elected to exclude US persons from token offerings and have instead opted to limit sales to non-US persons.[38]

A likely impediment standing in the way of integrating conventional securities laws revolves around the transfer of securities, and the idea of a P2P network aiming to function without intermediaries is that, as of this date, only a handful of security tokens are actively trading on licensed securities exchange or alternative trading systems (ATS) platforms approved by the SEC. For tokens to be constituted as a security, the requirement is that the persons involved need to be a broker-dealer licensed with the SEC and a member of the Financial Industry Regulatory Authority (FINRA). This is to facilitate the sale of securities or to act as market maker or otherwise constitute a dealer in the asset and where the asset can only trade on a licensed securities exchange or ATS. To address this, the SEC has proposed amendments to Rule 3b-16 and the "exchange" and "dealer" terms in January 2022. Here, *exchanges* are defined in terms of buyers and sellers with trading interest as opposed to orders. Exchanges include organisations, associations, or groups of persons that simply make available, rather than use, established non-discretionary methods that allow for interaction and agreement on the term of trades and include also those organisations, associations, or groups of persons that merely provide communication protocols.[39]

37 Ibid note [20], Dewey & Patel (2024).

38 Ibid note [20], Dewey & Patel (2024).

39 SEC (2022), "Amendments regarding the definition of alternative trading systems (ATSs) that trade U.S. Treasury and agency securities, national market system (NMS) stocks, and other securities: A proposed rule by the SEC", *Federal Register*, 18/03/2022, www.federalregister.gov/documents/2022/03/18/2022-01975/amendments-regarding-the-definition-of-exchange-and-alternative-trading-systems-atss-that-trade-us, accessed 20/12/2023.

These amendments are said to clear potentially serious barriers to decentralised finance (DeFi).

Additional to including proprietary traders in equities, fixed income, and other conventional financial assets, this proposal may result in a dealer registration requirement for automated market makers and other liquidity providers in the cryptoasset and DeFi area. An increasing number of entities and software developers in the crypto and DeFi turf could also become subject to the SEC's broker-dealer framework, including registering in SEC and FINRA membership. For example, Prometheum Ember Capital LLC (Prometheum) received approval on 17 May 2023 from FINRA to operate as a maiden special-purpose broker-dealer (SPBD) and qualified custodian for digital assets in the United States. The SPBD deals with the lack of investor protection in the digital assets turf by offering retail and institutional investors an opportunity to custody their digital assets with a SEC registered SPBD and a FINRA member.[40] Related to this development is SEC's insider trading charges against a former Coinbase product manager and others for perpetrating a scheme to transact ahead of multiple announcements pertaining to particular cryptoassets that would be made available for trading on the Coinbase platform.[41] The case was settled on 30 May 2023.[42] This SEC complaint stimulated strong criticism from a CFTC commissioner over the alleged categorisation of utility tokens and certain tokens relating to DAOs as securities. The tension between the SEC and CFCT over this matter culminated in the updating of the RFIA in July 2023, aiming to structure a clearer regulatory framework for which cryptoassets are securities or commodities. The CFTC under the RFIA enjoys exclusive jurisdiction over crypto tokens that qualify as ancillary assets, but not the security that constitutes an investment contract. An ancillary asset must not offer the holder any financial rights in a business, such as to debt or equity, liquidation, or interest, or dividend payments.[43]

However, where the average daily total value of transactions in the ancillary assets go beyond a particular threshold, and where the issuer engaged in entrepreneurial or managerial initiatives that principally determined the value of the ancillary asset, the issuer would be required to submit detailed disclosures to the SEC. Similarly, the McHenry–Thompson Bill provides the CFTC primary jurisdiction over the digital asset markets but details a process for market participants and regulators to follow in allocating oversight of digital assets between

40 Mack, W. et al. (2023), "FINRA approves Peometheum Ember Capital LLC as special purpose broker-dealer for digital assets", *Greenberg Traurig Law*, 28/06/2023, www.gtlawfinancialservicesobserver.com/2023/06/finra-approves-prometheum-ember-capital-llc-to-operate-as-special-purpose-broker-dealer-for-digital-assets/, accessed 20/12/2023.

41 SEC (2022), "SEC charges former coinbase manager, two others in crypto asset insider trading action", *SEC Press Release* 21/07/2022, www.sec.gov/newsroom/press-releases/2022-127, accessed 20/12/2023.

42 Melinek, J. (2023), "SEC settles with former coinbase employee over insider trading charges", *Tech Crunch*, 30/05/2023, https://techcrunch.com/2023/05/30/sec-settles-with-former-coinbase-employee-over-insider-trading-charges/, accessed 20/12/2023.

43 Ibid note [20], Dewey & Patel (2024).

the CFTC and the SEC. A *digital asset* is categorised as a digital commodity and regulated by the CFTC where a blockchain network to which a digital asset relates is both functional and certified as decentralised. Any person related to the network's development, or not, may certify an asset's status as a digital commodity.[44]

Networks are presumed to be decentralised, unless the SEC objects with reasons provided. The SEC regulates restricted digital assets that are digital assets held by the issuer of the digital assets or affiliates before the networks to which the assets relate are functional and certified as decentralised, as well as digital assets held by persons other than issuers or affiliates before the networks to which the assets relate are functional and certified as decentralised, unless the digital assets are distributed via an end user distribution or acquired on a CFTC-regulated exchange.[45] Congress could feel a sense of urgency should the Courts rule against the SEC in other cases, as they did in Terraform, to enact statutes to resolve legal ambiguities between the CFCT and the SEC or other administrative agencies.[46]

The Bank Secrecy Act (BSA) empowers the Financial Crimes Enforcement Network (FinCEN)[47] to regulate money service businesses (MSBs). FinCEN issued guidance on 18 March 2013 stating that a virtual currency exchange and an administrator of centralised repository of virtual currency empowered to both issue and redeem the virtual currency would be treated as MSBs.[48] An MSB that is money transmitter has to undertake a comprehensive risk evaluation of its exposure to money laundering and implement an anti–money laundering (AML) initiative based on such risk evaluation. FinCEN regulations require MSBs to develop, implement, and maintain a written procedure that is reasonably designed to prevent the MSB from being employed to facilitate money laundering and the financing of terrorist activities. Such an AML system must include written policies, procedures, and internal controls reasonably designed to ensure ongoing compliance; designate an individual compliance executive responsible for ensuring day to day compliance with the reporting system and BSA requirements; provide training for suitable personnel, which particularly includes training in the detection of suspicious transactions; and provide for independent review to monitor and maintain an adequate system.[49] US persons are prohibited from doing business with foreign nationals included on the Specially Designated Nationals and Blocked Persons List (SDN List) of the Treasury's Office of Foreign Assets Control (OFAC). OFAC provides an

44 Ibid note [20], Dewey & Patel (2024).
45 Ibid note [20], Dewey & Patel (2024).
46 Ibid note [20], Dewey & Patel (2024).
47 FinCEN was established in April 1990 by Treasury Order Number 106–108.
48 FinCEN (2013), "Application of FinCEN's regulations to persons administering, exchanging or using virtual currencies", *FIN-2013-G001*, 18/03/2013, www.fincen.gov/resources/statutes-regulations/guidance/application-fincens-regulations-persons-administering, accessed 20/12/2023.
49 Ibid note [48], FinCEN (2013).

updated and searchable version of its SDN List.[50] The OFAC requires all US citizens to freeze the assets of individuals and companies who are engaging in transactions with economies that are subject to US economic sanctions, particular companies and entities that act as agents for such economies, particular individuals that act as agents for such nations, and particular individuals that act as agents for such economies. In this regard, it is vital to have a compliance system in place to avoid or mitigate receiving civil and criminal penalties from OFAC for non-compliance.[51] Some controversies arose as to whether stablecoin issuers and dealers are money transmitters and need to adhere to BSA's AML laws.[52]

State laws on money transmission vary widely but could be categorised into money transmission, issuing and/or selling payment instruments, or issuing and/or selling stored value. In general, state money transmission laws apply to any entity that is located either in the state or outside of the state, including in a foreign jurisdiction, but transacts business with residents of the state.[53] A practical answer to the redundancy of procuring state licenses is by becoming a New York limited purpose company, as this kind of trust company charter exempts the company from many states' money transmission laws and requirements, besides providing the ability to undertake a wide range of custody and fiduciary services pertaining to cryptoassets. Wyoming and Nevada have since followed New York in allowing the use of special purpose depository institutions.

Decentralised finance (DeFi), or the permissionless, decentralised version of conventional financial instruments, with the focus on exchanging assets, lending and borrowing, and designing synthetic assets, provides further stress to AML laws. Uniswap, for example, is a decentralised exchange made up of four smart contracts hosted on the Ethereum blockchain and a public open source, front end client. This eventually enables those with internet connections to trade many Ethereum native tokens with other users of the application. Uniswap's open-source nature means it does not have a customer identification vetting process, and indeed, bypassing AML laws is cited as a key Uniswap foundational

50 OFAC (2024), "Sanctions list search", https://sanctionssearch.ofac.treas.gov/, accessed 09/07/2024.

51 OFAC (2009), "Economic sanctions enforcement guidelines", *OFAC*, 09/11/2009, https://ofac.treasury.gov/recent-actions/20091109, accessed 20/12/2023.

52 Kimpel, S. H. (2019), "FinCEN director discusses virtual currency reporting trends", *Hunton Andrews Kurth*, 18/12/2019, www.huntonak.com/blockchain-legal-resource/fincen-director-discusses-virtual-currency-reporting-trends, accessed 20/12/2023; Cleary Gottlieb (CG) (2018), "U.S. regulators continue scrutiny of virtual currencies and ICOs", *CG*, 15/03/2018, www.clearygottlieb.com/-/media/files/alert-memos-2018/us-regulators-continue-scrutiny-of-virtual-currencies-and-icos.pdf, accessed 20/12/2023.

53 CSBS (2024), "Money transmission modernization act (MTMA)", *Conference of State Bank Supervisors (CSBS)*, 22/04/2024, www.csbs.org/csbs-money-transmission-modernization-act-mtma, accessed 09/07/2024; Cooley (2023), "Model money transmission modernization act: 12 states take action", *Cooley*, 12/09/2023, www.cooley.com/news/insight/2023/2023-09-12-model-money-transmission-modernization-act-12-states-take-action, accessed 20/12/2023.

value within the crypto community.[54] Some US$620 billion of transactions are said to have taken place in 2022 using the Uniswap protocol. It has been reported that since September 2021, the SEC had initiated investigating Uniswap Labs and its Uniswap protocol, and again in 2024.[55] With the need for better regulation becoming clearer, authorities could commence exploring new routes of regulation. They could resort to completely novel approaches, such as embedded supervision, a kind of regulation built into the protocol itself. When implemented, the affirmative reporting obligations of money services businesses (MSBs) under the BSA could perhaps be written into DeFi protocols themselves such that particular transactions are automatically reported to relevant state authorities.[56] This form of approach could generate benefits, like being low-cost, transparent, and where properly implemented, inescapable, and become a reality than existing presently in theory.

Cryptoassets services, whether decentralised or not, have to at least make efforts to implement controls to prevent bad actors from abusing them. This adds Tornado to the SDN List, with 38 unique crypto addresses included as identifiers. Tornado Cash, a popular crypto mixer, repeatedly failed to impose effective controls designed to prevent it from being used to launder funds for fraudulent cyber actors on a regular basis. This eventually prompted OFAC to sanction it in August 2022, specifically with regard to Tornado's role in laundering US$455 million of cryptos siphoned from Axie Infinity's Ronin Bridge Protocol by North Korea–affiliated hacking Lazarus Group. This suggests that decentralised protocols may be subject to some of the compliance obligations to which centralised services are held.[57] OFAC, in November 2022, settled with Kraken, a crypto exchange, for suspected breach of OFAC sanctions against Iran,[58] while a year later, it announced settlement of charges against Poloniex, a virtual currency exchange, whereby Poloniex agreed to pay US$7591,630 for processing transactions amounting to US$15,335, 349 between January 2014 and

54 Garnett, A. G. (2023), "Uniswap (UNI): What it is, pos and cons, FAQs", *Investopedia*, 22/08/23, www.investopedia.com/uniswap-uni-definition-5217463#:~:text=Uniswap%20is%20a%20decentralized%20exchange,whose%20symbol%20is%20(UNI), accessed 20/12/2023.

55 Ligon, C. (2024), "DEFi exchange Uniswap receives enforcement notice from the SEC: Uniswap's Hayden Adams took to X on Wednesday to say that the exchange is 'ready to fight' after receiving notice that the regulator is planning an enforcement action", *Coin Desk*, 10/04/2024, www.coindesk.com/policy/2024/04/10/defi-exchange-uniswap-receives-enforcement-notice-from-the-sec/, accessed 10/07/2024; Kim, J. (2021), "Regulation of decentralized systems: A study of Uniswap", *Harvard Journal of Law & Technology*, 35(1): 335–366.

56 Auer, R. (2019), "Embedded supervision: How to build regulation into blockchain finance", Bank for International Settlements (BIS) Working Paper No. 811, www.bis.org/publ/work811.pdf, accessed 20/12/2023.

57 US Treasury (2022), "U.S. Treasury sanctions notorious virtual currency mixer Tornado cash", *US Treasury Press Release*, 08/08/2022, https://home.treasury.gov/news/press-releases/jy0916, accessed 20/12/2023.

58 OFAC (2022), "Settlement agreement between U.S. Department of the Treasury's Office of Foreign Assets Control and Payward, Inc. ('Kraken')", *OFAC*, 28/11/2022, https://ofac.treasury.gov/recent-actions/20221128, accessed 20/12/2023.

November 2019 in suspected breaches of US economic sanctions against Syria, Sudan, Iran, Cuba, and Crimea.[59]

An indicator of organic demand for cryptos in the United States is the large population and number of Bitcoin users in the country. This is reflected by the steady growth in Bitcoin trading volume since 2013, as confirmed by the progress achieved by LocalBitcoins,[60] the major P2P Bitcoin trading service in the country. Some 38% of US workers said in a February 2023 EY survey that blockchain technology is widely employed within their businesses, while 44% said that the technology would be widely employed within 3 years, and 18% reported the technology was still more than 3 years from being widely employed within their businesses. Increased adoption requires an understanding of how the technology works and the benefits it provides across industries, including financial services, retail, advertising and marketing, and digital health.[61]

The US Inland Revenue Service (IRS) announced in March 2014 that cryptos, like Bitcoin, will be taxed by the agency as "property" and not currency.[62] In 2024, some 10 years later, the IRS issued further guidance as part of a wider initiative to assist taxpayers and to enforce tax laws in the rapidly transforming niche. Two new tranches of guidance were issued for taxpayers engaged in transaction involving cryptos. These include Revenue Ruling 2019–24, which supplements IRS Notice 2014–21.[63] In this regard, the IRS is actively addressing potential non-compliance in this space via various initiatives, extending from taxpayer education to audits, to criminal investigations. Specifically, the IRS published guidance pertaining to the treatment of cryptos staking rewards. The IRS clarifies that when taxpayers stake cryptos and receive validation rewards, the fair market value of the rewards must be included in the taxpayers' gross income for the taxable year when the taxpayer gains control over the rewards, meaning, once that taxpayer gains the ability to sell, exchange, or dispose of the received units.[64]

---

59 OFAC (2023), "Settlement agreement between U.S. Department of the Treasury's Office of Foreign Assets Control and Poloniex, LLC", *OFAC*, 01/05/2023, https://ofac.treasury.gov/recent-actions/20230501_33#:~:text=05%2F01%2F2023-,The%20U.S.%20Department%20of%20the%20Treasury's%20Office%20of%20Foreign%20Assets,Iran%2C%20Sudan%2C%20and%20Syria, accessed 20/12/2023.

60 Haig, S. (2017), "Local bitcoins markets set record trading volume", *Bitcoin*, 03/12/2017, https://news.bitcoin.com/localbitcoins-markets-set-record-trading-volume/, accessed 02/02/2018.

61 Feger, A. (2023), "Blockchain technology: What it is, benefits, and its cross-industry applications", *Marketer*, 19/10/2023, www.emarketer.com/insights/blockchain-technology-applications-use-cases/, accessed 20/12/2023.

62 IRS (2014), "IRS notice 2014–21", *IRS Guidance*, 25/03/2014, www.irs.gov/pub/irs-drop/n-14-21.pdf, accessed 20/12/2023.

63 IRS (2024), "Virtual currency: IRS issues additional guidance on tax treatment and reminds taxpayers of reporting obligations", *IRS*, 05/01/2024, www.irs.gov/newsroom/virtual-currency-irs-issues-additional-guidance-on-tax-treatment-and-reminds-taxpayers-of-reporting-obligations, accessed 10/07/2024.

64 KPMG (2023), "Rev. Rul.2023–14: Cryptocurrency rewards included in income when taxpayer gains dominion and control over rewards", *KPMG*, 31/07/2023, https://kpmg.com/us/en/home/insights/2023/07/tnf-rev-rul-2023-14-cryptocurrency-rewards-included-in-income-when-

Also, earlier in November 2021, the Infrastructure Investment and Jobs Act (IIJA) was signed into law that will require digital asset brokers to report to the IRS digital asset transactions exceeding US$10,000.[65] The IRS defines "broker" widely, such that it could subject parties that are peripheral to digital asset transactions, including crypto miners, software developers, and parties validating crypto transactions or selling cryptoasset storage devices, to the reporting and compliance requirements of the IIJA. Taxpayers have also been advised that those failing to report transactions involving cryptos, or reporting them incorrectly, may, when appropriate, be liable for tax, penalties, and interest and, in certain cases, could be subject to criminal prosecution.

To help guide the development of the so called "Fourth Industrial Revolution" (4IR) enabling technologies like fintech, blockchain, and cryptos within US borders, Arizona, along with various other US member states, adopted regulatory sandbox modelled after those earlier initiated in the UK. Here in the designated US states, the law grants regulatory relief for innovators in those sectors seeking to launch novel products for marketing within the respective US states.[66] Under this initiative, businesses could be able to test their products for 2 years and host as many as 10,000 customers before needing to apply for formal licenses. With regards to ownership and licensing requirements, cryptoassets fund managers that invest in cryptoassets futures contracts (in contrast to spot transactions in these items) are required to register as commodity trading advisers (CTAs) and commodity pool operators (CPOs) with the CFTC and the National Futures Association (NFA), or to satisfy an exemption. Cryptoassets hedge fund managers that use leverage or margin will also need to register with the CFTC and NFA.[67] The CFTC exercised this jurisdiction in its action against BFXNA Inc. in 2016.[68] The CFTC charged 14 entities for failing to register as futures commission merchants (FCMs) or, else, making false and misleading claims of having CFTC registration and NFA membership in September 2021.[69]

Extinguishing industry wide perception that DeFi participants are immune to regulatory scrutiny, the US District Court of the Northern District of California

taxpayer-gains-dominion-and-control-over-rewards.html#:~:text=2023%2D14%20%5BPDF%20 92%20KB,in%20the%20tax%20year%20in, accessed 20/12/2023.

65 Whitehouse (2021), "Fact sheet: The bipartisan infrastructure deal", *Whitehouse Briefing*, 06/11/2021, www.whitehouse.gov/briefing-room/statements-releases/2021/11/06/fact-sheet-the-bipartisan-infrastructure-deal/, accessed 20/12/2023.

66 Greater Phoenix Economic Council (GPEC) (2021), "Things to know about Arizona's Fintech sandbox", *GPEC*, 10/07/2021, www.gpec.org/blog/things-to-know-about-arizonas-fintech-sandbox/, accessed 20/12/2023.

67 Capital Fund Law Group (CLFG) (2023), "CFTC regulation of crypto-asset funds", *CLFG*, 23/04/2023, www.capitalfundlaw.com/blog/cftcregulationcryptofunds, accessed 20/12/2023.

68 CFTC (2016), "CFTC orders bitcoin exchange bitinex to pay USD75,000 for offering illegal off-exchange financed retail commodity transactions and failing to register as a futures commission merchant", CFTC Release No. 7380-16, 02/06/2016, www.cftc.gov/PressRoom/PressReleases/7380-16, accessed 20/12/2023.

69 CFTC (2021), "CFTC charges 14 entities for failing to register as FCMs or falsely claiming to be registered", CFTC Release No. 8434-21, 29/09/2021, www.cftc.gov/PressRoom/PressReleases/8434-21, accessed 20/12/2023.

held that Ooki DAO is a "person" under the Commodity Exchange Act (CEA) and, therefore, can be held liable for violations of the law when engaging in unlawful leveraged and margined retail commodity transactions, including soliciting and accepting orders for leveraged or margined retail transactions with customers and accepting money or property to margin these transactions. The legislation assigns liability to "any person" who takes particular actions and defines "person" to include individuals, associations, partnerships, corporations, and trusts. Th CFTC was found by the court to have sufficiently pleaded facts demonstrating that Ooki DAO is an unincorporated association.[70]

More guidance on the classifying of individual cryptoassets as securities or commodities is needed, and pending the availability of such clarities, the probability of many cryptoassets being treated as securities is high. As such, it is prudent for cryptoassets funds that invest in anything other than Bitcoin or Ether and other clearly commodity coins to comply with the Investment Company Act of 1940 (Company Act) and the Investment Advisers Act of 1940 (Advisers Act), including state investment adviser laws that impose regulations on investment funds that invest in securities pre-emptively.[71] Further, irrespective of whether a start-up crypto fund manager is required to register as a CPO/CTA with the CFTC under the Commodities Act or register or seek exemption from the SEC as an investment adviser or investment company, every crypto fund manager will be subject to the fraud provisions of the CFTC and/or the SEC.[72] The CFTC charged Nicholas Gelfman and Gelfman Blueprint Inc. with fraudulent solicitation in September 2017, its maiden anti-fraud enforcement action against Bitcoin.[73] Meanwhile, the Office of the Comptroller of the Currency (OCC) in July 2020 confirmed that national banks and savings associations can offer custody services for cryptos.[74] Simultaneously, they can also offer related services like cryptoassets–fiat exchange, transaction settlements, trade execution, valuation, tax services, and reporting. This initiative supplements a mosaic of state regulation and guidance that motivated presently only a few national banks and financial services companies to adopt cryptoassets. Acknowledging that underlying keys are essentially irreplaceable if lost, the OCC is strongly of the view that banks could be part of a solution by providing more secure storage services compared to present choices.[75]

---

70 Boniel, M. (2023), "From code to consequences: CFTC obtains default judgment against Ooki DAO for commodity exchange act violations", *Prokauer*, 20/07/2023, www.blockchainandthelaw.com/2023/07/from-code-to-consequence-cftc-obtains-default-judgment-against-ooki-dao-for-commodity-exchange-act-violations/, accessed 20/12/2023.

71 Ibid note [20], Dewey & Patel (2024).

72 Ibid note [20], Dewey & Patel (2024).

73 CFTC (2017), "CFTC charges Nicholas Gelfman and Gelfman Blueprint, Inc. with fraudulent solicitation, misappropriation, and issuing false account statements in bitcoin Ponzi scheme", CFTC Release No. 7614-17, 21/09/2017, www.cftc.gov/PressRoom/PressReleases/7614-17, accessed 20/12/2023.

74 OCC (2020), "Federally chartered banks and thrifts may provide custody services for crypto assets", OCC News Release 2020-98, 22/07/2020, www.occ.gov/news-issuances/news-releases/2020/nr-occ-2020-98.html, accessed 20/12/2023.

75 Ibid note [74], OCC (2020).

While the federal government examines the feasibility of crypto mining at the national level from the perspective of energy impacts,[76] US states have also been active in regulating crypto mining that would require comprehensive generic environmental impact review and effectively suspend all blockchain mining operations operating on carbon-based power sources[77] or provide tax exemptions[78] for the sale of certain crypto mining equipment and machinery. This legislation and some studies reflect policymakers' concerns over the environmental and energy impacts of cryptoassets mining operations.

5.2.2 The United Kingdom

The UK is competing successfully with the United States and Singapore as a leading international fintech hub that includes cryptocurrency innovations. More recently, the UK has collaborated with Singapore through the annual UK–Singapore Financial Dialogue, the 9th of which was held on 8 May 2024 in Singapore. In these annual dialogues, both economies discuss collaboration opportunities in priority niches, like sustainable finance and fintech, and innovation and exchange perspectives on recent developments in non-bank financial intermediation (NBFI), as well as including initiatives to improve cross-border payment connectivity. Other matters deliberated on include AI, UK's final proposals for financial services regulatory regime for cryptoassets, CBDC, and tokenisation to the financial ecosystem, from broadened investor access to investment products simplifying distribution and trading of such products digitally.[79] Also, based on recent investment data, London appears to be Europe's leading fintech hub.[80] US$14.6 billion was invested in UK financial technology companies in 2022, dropping to US$5.8 billion in 2023. The country has an active cryptocurrency community, numerous Bitcoin and blockchain related start ups and Bitcoin BTMs (BTM, or Bytom, is a blockchain project launched to develop a protocol to facilitate the standardised storing of different cryptocurrencies on a blockchain system) to qualify as a Bitcoin friendly destination. The country's

76 US House of Representatives (2022), "Cleaning up cryptocurrency: The energy impacts of blockchains", *House of Representatives Committee on Energy and Commerce's Subcommittee on Oversight and Investigations Hearing*, 20/01/2022, https://docs.house.gov/Committee/Calendar/ByEvent.aspx?EventId=114332, accessed 20/12/2023.

77 New York State Senate Bill S6486D, June 2022, www.nysenate.gov/legislation/bills/2021/S6486, accessed 20/12/2023.

78 Oklahoma Senate Bill 590, 2022, www.oklegislature.gov/BillInfo.aspx?Bill=SB590&amp%3BSession=2022, accessed 20/12/2023.

79 Monetary Authority of Singapore (MAS) (2024), "UK and Singapore strengthen collaboration in sustainable finance and FinTech", *MAS*, 08/05/2024, www.mas.gov.sg/news/media-releases/2024/uk-and-singapore-strengthen-collaboration-in-sustainable-finance-and-fintech, accessed 16/07/2024.

80 London Partners (2017), "London is Europe's number one fintech hub for global investors", *London Partners Press Release*, 19/10/2017, https://media.londonandpartners.com/news/londonis-europe-s-number-one-fintech-hub-for-global-investors, accessed 02/02/2018.

central bank sees new payment solutions as inevitable.[81] The UK is preparing itself for large-scale digital currency adoption in the future.

The Bank of England is closely looking at Bitcoin technology as the candidate to improve the country's monetary system. Mark Carney, the then Bank of England's governor, conceded that the cryptocurrency's underlying blockchain technology may still prove useful due to its decentralised nature.[82] As a senior member of the Financial Stability Board, Carney regularly took the position that though cryptoassets do not presently pose serious risk to the financial system, it still warrants close monitoring owing to the inherent risk of cryptoassets. He surprised the crypto community in September 2019 at Jackson Hole in the United States with the suggestion that central bankers could develop a network of national digital currencies to create a new basket managed synthetic hegemonic digital currency. It has been argued, though, that his proposal should be treated as a thought exercise to inspire conversation around solutions to the risky imbalances brought about by the current system's dependence on the dollar as the world's reserve currency. This and any other solutions are likely to be politically and technically difficult. Still, there are views that rather than contemplating a whole new global currency, central bankers should seriously consider developing digital currency interoperability.[83]

The UK's Financial Services and Markets Act 2023 determines that cryptocurrencies are now specified as investments for the purposes of Financial Conduct Authority regulation. It states that *cryptocurrencies* are

> any cryptographically secured digital representation of value or contractual rights that-
>
> a. can be transferred, stored or traded electronically, and
> b. that uses technology supporting the recording or storage of data (which may include distributed ledger technology).[84]

This is a wide definition, designed to cover the range of products now on the market in this area. The definition would seem to cover a range of cryptocurrencies and assets, namely, utility tokens, payment tokens, security tokens, and stablecoins.

---

81 Sagone, R. (2017), "Results of the Bank of England/ripple proof of concept published today", *Ripple*, 10/07/2017, https://ripple.com/insights/results-of-the-bank-of-englandripple-proofof-concept-published-today/, accessed 02/02/2018.

82 Carney, M. (2018), "The future of money", *Governor of the Bank of England Speech at the inaugural Scottish Economics Conference*, Edinburgh University, 02/03/2018, www.bankofengland.co.uk/-/media/boe/files/speech/2018/the-future-of-money-speech-by-mark-carney, accessed 08/06/2018.

83 Casey, M. J. (2019), "A Crypto fix for a broken international monetary system", *Coin Desk*, 02/09/2019, www.coindesk.com/a-crypto-fix-for-a-broken-international-monetary-system, accessed 09/09/2019.

84 S. 69 of the Financial Services and Markets Act 2023 which introduces the definition of "cryptoassets" into section 417 of the Financial Services and Markets Act 2000.

The 2023 Act also brings cryptoassets under the designated activities regime (DAR), which brings those issues connected with financial products sold or marketed in the UK under the remit of the FCA.[85] In the words of the FCA:

> Some activities currently regulated under retained EU law are not "regulated activities" under the Financial Services and Markets Act 2000 and may be carried out by non-financial services entities or persons without needing to be authorised by us.[86]

The DAR framework enables the Treasury to "designate" activities and to confer rulemaking, supervisory, and enforcement powers on us over these activities. Our rulemaking under the DAR will apply in relation to the designated activity, but not the other unrelated activities of the person carrying on the designated activity. The DAR does not require authorisation, and designated activities can be done by both authorised and unauthorised persons.

One area of cryptoassets treated differently from the rest is related to stablecoins. These are crypto coins whose value relates to an underlying group of assets, and therefore, they should be considerably more stable in value than other cryptocurrencies. Again, a legal definition is provided. The Act states that they are

> a digital representation of value or rights, whether or not cryptographically secured that:
>
> - can be used for settlement of payment obligations,
> - can be transferred, stored or traded electronically, and
> - uses technology supporting the recording or storage of data (which may include distributed ledger technology).[87]

The reason that stablecoins have a separate definition is that the Financial Services and Markets Act 2023 provides HM Treasury with the power to regulate them separately in the future.[88] They are also categorised as one of the payment systems over which the Bank of England has regulatory oversight.[89] This means that they will also come under the regulatory oversight of the Payment Systems Regulator.

The UK taxation authority generally treats Bitcoin as private money. Accordingly, VAT is imposed in the usual way from suppliers of any goods sold in exchange for Bitcoin or other cryptocurrencies, with the value being assessed in

85 This is a much wider area than cryptoassets, including derivatives, short-selling, securitisation, and benchmarks, although crypto-based derivative contracts would be caught under the first of these.

86 www.fca.org.uk/firms/repeal-replacement-retained-eu-law. Repeal and replacement of assimilated law. Last updated 22/03/2024.

87 Sch 6(4) Financial Services and Markets Act 2023 inserting s.182 (4A) in the Banking Act 2009.

88 S.23 Financial Services and Markets Act 2023.

89 S.22 Financial Services and Markets Act 2023.

sterling at the time of the transaction.[90] Bitcoin is therefore likened to a "foreign currency" for most purposes, including value added tax. Bitcoin miners are not subject to VAT, as the act of mining is not classed as an economic activity, nor would VAT be added to Bitcoin when it is used as a currency for goods or services. Much like the United States, profitability outcomes from cryptocurrencies transactions are subject to applicable capital gains tax in the UK. Though not a legal tender, Bitcoin is not prohibited for use in the UK.

For now, there are at least 11 Bitcoin start-ups in the UK meriting attention according to a recent Accenture fintech study. This, together with other fintech support systems, makes the UK the centre of European cryptocurrency space as they appear to be at the cutting edge of blockchain technology that underpins much of the cryptoasset space.[91] Importantly, on 13 March 2024, the London Stock Exchange (LSE) announced its decision to accept applications for the admission of exchange traded notes (ETNs) backed by Bitcoin and Ether. This will open up a fresh avenue for professional investors by providing them with opportunities to partake into the rapidly evolving world of cryptos. The LSE further released its plan to begin accepting applications in the second quarter of 2024. The criteria, though, for the proposed notes are strict, with the exchange stressing the importance of non-leverage and the necessity for the underlying cryptos to be at least 90% held in an offline depository wallet or equivalent cold storage arrangements.[92]

Compared to the new EU Markets in Cryptoassets Regulation (MICAR),[93] the UK seeks to adopt a phased approach so as to bring cryptos within the existing regulatory framework for advertising financial products designed by the FSMA, supplemented by the Regulated Activities Order.[94] The government initially launched legislation to bring "qualifying cryptoassets" into the scope of the existing financial promotions regime under the Financial Promotion Order (FPO).[95] The Financial Services and Markets Act 2000 (Financial Promotions) Order 2005[96] sets out the various exemptions to the financial promotion prohibition under section 21 of FSMA 2000. The proposed scope of crypto activity that would be regulated would be broad and includes issuance activities; payment activities; exchange activities; investment and risk management activities;

90 HM Revenue & Customs (2014), "Revenue and customs brief 9 (2014): Bitcoin and other cryptocurrencies", *HMRC*, 03/03/2014, www.gov.uk/government/publications/revenue-and-customs-brief-9-2014-bitcoin-and-other-cryptocurrencies, accessed 02/02/2018.

91 Ali, B. (2017), "11 bitcoin start-ups from London you need to know in 2017", *Tech Flier*, 10/08/2017, www.techflier.com/2017/08/10/11-bitcoin-startups-from-london-you-need-to-know-about-in-2017/, accessed 02/02/2018.

92 Chhetri, V. (2024), "London stock exchange opens doors to crypto", *Tech Funding News (TFN)*, 13/03/2024, https://techfundingnews.com/london-stock-exchange-opens-doors-to-crypto-top-crypto-vcs-for-2024/, accessed 16/07/2024.

93 EY (2023), "The new EU markets in crypto-assets regulation (MICAR)", *EY*, 21/06/23, www.ey.com/en_gr/tax/tax-alerts/the-new-eu-market-in-crypto-assets-regulation, accessed 20/12/2023.

94 SI 2001/544 as amended.

95 LexisNexis (2024), "Financial Promotions Order (2005) as amended", www.lexisnexis.co.uk/legal/glossary/financial-promotion-order-fpo, accessed 17/07/2024.

96 SI 2005/1529 as amended.

lending, borrowing, and leverage activities; safeguarding and/or administration (custody) activities; and validation and governance activities. In the case of the more nascent niche of the market, the UK will actively seek consultations to inform future policy development that will continue to strategically evaluate developments in the market to ascertain future stages of work, taking into account the views of consumers, the industry, and its regulators.[97]

Trading of cryptos in the UK is subject to sales regulations comprising the financial promotions regime, the prospectus regulations and consumer protection, and online/distance selling legislation.[98] The Money Laundering Regulations 2017[99] (MLRs) imposed a general duty on crypto business enterprises to maintain appropriate risk-based policies and procedures to prevent occurrences where their systems might be employed for money laundering or terrorist financing. These MLRS transposed provisions of the Fourth[100] and Fifth[101] Money Laundering Directives into UK laws. In scope, crypto businesses are envisaged to have been complying with the MLRs since 10 January 2020. Businesses undertaking the transfer of money by way of business, including money transmitters and money services, businesses that are not subject to an exemption from registration, are supervised by the FCA under the payment systems regulators (PSR) and electronic money regulations (EMRs).[102] These regulations seek to ensure the security and efficiency of payment services and e-money issuance within the UK. Such money transmission businesses are subject to regular audits and compliance verifications by the FCA to ensure that they adhere to regulatory requirements pertaining to money laundering supervision, such as customer due diligence, recordkeeping, and the reporting of suspicious activities. The FCA may decide that particular kinds of cryptos trigger the regulatory perimeter under the EMR where they constitute e-money tokens, such as fiat-backed stablecoins that are employed for payments, and the payment service regulation (PSR) when facilitating regulated payment services, like the provision of wallet services for stablecoins.[103] Finally, the FCA Innovation Hub uses several initiatives to provide direct support to innovative enterprises that are aiming to launch into the market. These include CryptoSprint Events, TechSprints, the Global Financial Innovation Network (GFIN), the Digital Sandbox, and the regulatory sandbox.[104] Some of these have been adopted, adapted, or replicated in advanced and emerging economies across the world.

---

97 Kerrigan et al. "Blockchain and Cryptocurrency Laws and Regulations 2025 – United Kingdom", *Global Legal Insights*. https://www.globallegalinsights.com/practice-areas/blockchain-cryptocurrency-laws-and-regulations/united-kiongdom/, accessed 5/08/2025.

98 Ibid note [97], Kerrigan et al. (2024).

99 SI 2017/692 as amended.

100 Fourth Money Laundering Directive (EU) (2015/849).

101 Fifth Money Laundering (EU) Directive (EU) (2018/843).

102 FCA (2024), "PSR and FCA launch joint call for information on big tech and digital wallets", *FCA*, 15/07/2024, www.fca.org.uk/news/press-releases/psr-fca-launch-joint-call-information-big-tech-digital-wallets, accessed 17/07/2024.

103 Ibid note [97], Kerrigan et al. (2024).

104 Ibid note [97], Kerrigan et al. (2024).

5.2.3 Canada

Canada is generally perceived as a cryptocurrency host country. Various Bitcoin ventures and numerous ATMs have sprung up in Canada. It has two internationally known Bitcoin hubs, one in Toronto, and the other in Vancouver. This has resulted in cryptocurrency communities arguing that the country has the potential to become the Silicon Valley for Bitcoin, especially when Bitcoin miners now outlawed in China have taken domains there.[105] The Canadian central bank is looking into cryptocurrency regulation, but in the meantime, anti–money laundering and counter-terrorism laws are applicable. The central bank considers the blockchain technology behind Bitcoin a true piece of genius, but Bitcoin trading a form of gambling.[106]

The country hosts a thriving cryptocurrency community. Decentral, its first leading blockchain start-up, makes Jaxx Cryptocurrency Wallet and hosts Toronto's first Bitcoin ATM. As early as May 2017, the Vanbex Group has raised US$365,474 to finance the development of blockchain based products, including Etherparty, the company's easy-to-use smart contract creator.[107] Many businesses and retail outlets in Canada are also accepting Bitcoins, including KFC Canada and Subway.[108] In August 2017, Impak Coin became the first Canadian-approved cryptocurrency. This means that Montreal based Impak Finance could go ahead with the public sale of its digital Impak Coin money. These aside, Canada has the potential to become a prime destination for Bitcoin mining because of a long list of benefits, including a stable government and cheap electricity, which is helpful for Bitcoin mining.[109] For the wider crypto market, rising adoption rates, strong performance, and positive regulatory tailwinds suggest a reasonable basis for optimism in Canada.[110]

5.2.4 Australia

The country is a key fintech hub within the Asia–Pacific region. Initially unappealing for Bitcoin start-ups because of heavy taxation and unreported bank

105 Freeman, S. (2014), "Will Canada become 'the silicon valley of bitcoins'", *Huffington Post*, 28/01/2014, www.huffingtonpost.ca/2014/01/28/bitcoin-canada_n_4676044.html?guccounter=1, accessed 02/02/2018.

106 Tso, K. & Kharpal, A. (2018), "Bitcoin is 'gambling' and regulations are needed, Canada central bank head says", *CNBC*, 25/01/2018, www.cnbc.com/2018/01/25/bitcoin-trading-is-gambling-canada-central-bank-governor.html, accessed 02/02/2018.

107 Vanbex (2017), "Vanbex group raises C$500,000 in first seed round", *PRNewswire*, 30/05/2017, www.prnewswire.co.uk/news-releases/vanbex-group-raises-c500000-in-first-seed-round- 625422734.html, accessed 02/02/2018.

108 Chokun, J. (2018), "Who accepts bitcoin as payment? List of companies, stored, shops", *99 Bitcoins*, 14/01/2018, https://99bitcoins.com/bitcoin/who-accepts/, accessed 02/02/2018.

109 Vomiero, J. (2018), "Why Canada is poised to become prime destination for bitcoin mining", *GlobalNews*, 21/01/2018, www.globalnews.ca/news/3978151/canada-Bitcoin-mining-prime-destination, accessed 02/02/2018.

110 KPMG (2023), "Rosing cryptoasset adoption in Canada", https://kpmg.com/ca/en/home/insights/2024/04/rising-cryptoasset-adoption-in-canada.html, accessed 20/12/2023.

account freezes, there has been a turnaround since the recent Double Taxation Relief legislation.[111] Through this new legislation, Australians are no longer charged goods and service tax (GST)[112] on purchases of digital currency, allowing it to be treated the same way as physical money for GST purposes. This law change is widely seen as making it easier for new, innovative digital currency business to operate so as to boost jobs and wages in the country.

There are now some 18 cryptocurrency start ups in the country. These include ACX, a Bitcoin exchange platform; Bata, a cryptocurrency platform; Bit Trade Australia; and Bitcoin Australia, which buys and sells Bitcoins on customers' behalf.[113]

There are two major factors driving cryptocurrency start-ups away from the country, as well as causing the Australian Bitcoin exchange market to fall significantly behind growing markets like South Korea and Japan. These are the termination of Bitcoin banking services by leading Australian banks and the double taxation of Bitcoin trading in Australia.[114] Positive sentiments towards cryptocurrency technology are driven by the Austrian Securities Exchange's (ASX) willingness to trial distributed technology in its operation,[115] as well as by the Australia Post[116] to use this technology to store digital identities and other improvements to strengthen its services.

Subsequent to its earlier regulatory guidance for ICOs, the Australian Securities and Investments Commission (ASIC) provided further guidance detailing the legal obligations for cryptocurrency firms under the country's Corporations Act (CA), the ASIC Act (AA), and other laws.[117] These regulatory requirements seek to maintain the integrity of the country's financial market and ensure consumer protection. The ASIC guidance explained that ICOs and cryptoassets in many situations are financial products that are regulated under the CA. This means that a firm issuing a token that falls within the definition of a *financial product*, like an interest in a managed investment scheme or a security, these laws would apply, including the requirement to hold an Australian financial services (AFS) license. More recently, ASIC Commissioner Alan Kirkland has

111 Higgins, S. (2017), "Bitcoin 'double taxation' relief bill introduced in Australia", *Coin Desk*, 18/09/2017, www.coindesk.com/bitcoin-double-taxation-relief-bill-introduced-australia, accessed 02/02/2018.

112 This is a goods and services tax normally assessed at 10% of value.

113 Finder (2018), "Complete list of Australian cryptocurrency start-ups", *Finder*, 07/02/2018, www.finder.com.au/australian-cryptocurrency-startups, accessed 18/02/2018.

114 Young, J. (2017), "Australia will recognize bitcoin as money and protect bitcoin businesses, no taxes", *Coin Telegraph*, 11/05/2017, https://cointelegraph.com/news/australia-will-recognize-bitcoin-as-money-and-protect-bitcoin-businesses-no-taxes, accessed 02/02/2018.

115 Mathes, S. & Irrera, A. (2017), "Australia's ASX selects blockchain to cut costs", *Reuters*, 07/12/2017, https://uk.reuters.com/article/us-asx-blockchain/australias-asx-selects-blockchain-tocut-costs-idUKKBN1E037R, accessed 18/02/2018.

116 Bhunia, P. (2017), "Australia post exploring blockchain technology to secure food products supply chain", *OpenGovernmentAsia*, 06/06/2017, www.opengovasia.com/australia-post-exploring-blockchain-technology-to-secure-food-products-supply-chain/, accessed 02/02/2018.

117 Australian Securities & Investments Commission (2019), "Digital transformation: Initial coin offerings and crypto-assets", *ASIC*, 30/05/2019, https://asic.gov.au/regulatory-resources/digital-transformation/initial-coin-offerings-and-crypto-assets/, accessed 02/06/2019.

made clear that Australia will promote financial innovation in this area subject to it being handled with appropriate regard for consumers, investors, and market integrity.[118]

These laws are extended to those giving advice, dealing, or providing other intermediary services for crypto-based financial products. Further, cryptocurrency wallet and custody service providers are required to ensure that they hold the suitable custodial and depository authorisations. The said laws also bound cryptocurrency miners when assisting the clearing and settlement of tokens that are financial products. The applicable rules, including the holding of an Australian market license, also apply to cryptocurrency exchanges and trading platforms. In turn, cryptocurrency payment and merchant service providers are required to apply for an AFS license when involved in providing a non-cash payment facility. Additionally, with regards to ICOs and cryptoassets that are not financial products, promoters must ensure that they do not partake in misleading or deceptive conduct or statements. ASIC Commissioner John Price[119] stressed that Australian laws would also apply even when the ICOs or cryptoassets are sold or promoted to Australians from offshore and that issuers of ICOs, cryptoassets, and their advisers should not assume the deployment of these structures implies that main consumer protections under Australian laws do not apply or could be disregarded.

Australia remains a neutral and stable jurisdiction for cryptos.[120] This has facilitated significant growth, powered initially by the government's approach for new and innovative services and products in the fintech space. The pace of growth, though, has moderated in recent years, owing to headwinds from lower global economic growth, turbulent crypto business closures, enhanced regulatory enforcement, and the country's relative inactions in advancing crypto policy and legislation. Clarity pertaining to the application of Australian regulatory regimes to the sector has been iterative.

5.2.5 Germany

Germany, the EU's anchor economy, generally provides favourable government policies for cryptocurrencies, especially in activities connected with developing blockchain solutions. Bitcoin is recognised by the German Finance Ministry as a "unit of account"; meaning, it can be employed for tax and trading purposes in the country.[121] Unlike other European destinations that classify Bitcoin as e-money or a foreign currency, Germany's Finance Ministry specifies Bitcoin

118 Kirkland, A. (2024), "Crypto and digital assets: Policy, regulation and innovation", Speech to The Brief – Open Forum, 20/03/2024, https://asic.gov.au/about-asic/news-centre/speeches/crypto-and-digital-assets-policy-regulation-and innovation, accessed 17/04/2025.

119 Ibid note [117], ASIC (2019).

120 Reeves, P. et al. (2024), "Australia" in Dewey, J. N. (ed.), *Blockchain and cryptocurrency laws and regulations 2024*, London, Global Legal Insights.

121 Clinch, M. (2013), "Bitcoin recognized by Germany as 'private money'", *CNBC*, 19/08/2013, www.cnbc.com/id/100971898, accessed 02/02/2018.

as a financial instrument under German banking rules, more closely resembling "private money"[122] that can be applied in multilateral clearing circles. This appears to be in support of Friedrich August von Hayek's scheme[123] to nationalise money so as to provide competition in the production of money. Bitcoin represents the first step in this direction.

The new ruling suggests that German authorities are preparing regulations on how to tax Bitcoin transactions. The legal classification of Bitcoin means that commercial profits arising from using the currency might be taxable. For now, though, Bitcoin held for a year or more is exempted from the 25% tax on profits achieved up to €1,000. Being legal in Germany, Bitcoin has had an impact on its value, due to the perceived legitimacy given to it by such government recognition. Germany is also home to one of the biggest Bitcoin marketplaces in the world. The country has also recently finalised plans to introduce Ethereum, the second most valuable cryptocurrency trading, into the platform. Germany persists as a top ten crypto-hospitable jurisdiction.[124]

5.2.6 The Netherlands

The Netherlands calls Arnhem its Bitcoin city, with over 100 merchants.[125] The place has been touted as the place where those with Bitcoin can used it to get most things their owners need, from petrol, accommodation, and bicycles to dental services. This means that within the Bitcoin City in Arnhem, Bitcoin is just like any fiat currency, a store of value and medium of exchange. As people engage in economic interaction using Bitcoins, a consciousness is generated within the general public that cryptocurrencies can function in a similar way to fiat currencies. Bitcoin for now does not fall under any identified regulation, but because of the growing risks and, in particular, the growing frauds linked to ICOs, the Dutch Finance Minister says the country is researching on the possibilities for a tighter rein on Bitcoin in the country.[126]

---

122 McElroy, W. (2017), "The Satoshi revolution – chapter 1: How and why government outlawed private money (part 2)", *Bitcoin*, 07/10/2017, https://news.bitcoin.com/the-satoshi-revolution-chapter-2-how-and-why-government-outlawed-private-money/-, accessed 02/02/2018.

123 Von Hayek, F. A. (1977), *Denationalisation of money: The argument refined (an analysis of the theory and practice of concurrent currencies series)*, London, The Institute of Economic Affairs.

124 B2B Broker (2024), "Top ten crypto friendly countries for your business in 2024", *B2B Broker*, 01/07/2024, https://b2broker.com/news/top-10-crypto-friendly-countries-for-your-business-in-2024/, accessed 18/07/2024.

125 Scott, A. (2016), "How 'bitcoin city' Arnhem signed up its 100th merchant, Burger King", *Bitcoin*, 20/02/2016, https://news.bitcoin.com/bitcoin-city-arnhem-signed-100th-merchant-burger-king/, accessed 02/02/2018; Juskalian, R. (2015), "A weekend in bitcoin city: Arnhem, the Netherlands: Is it possible to live 48 hours on nothing but bitcoin?", *MIT Technology Review*, 26/01/2015, www.technologyreview.com/s/534011/a-weekend-in-bitcoin-city-arnhem-the-netherlands/, accessed 02/02/2018.

126 de Witte, S. (2018), "Watchdog AFM and minister of finance plea for a ban on bitcoin in the Netherlands", *Start-Up Delta*, 04/02/2018, www.startupdelta.org/watchdog-afm-and-ministerof-finance-plea-for-a-ban, accessed 18/02/2018.

Numerous start-ups, from Bitcoin ATMs to a Bitcoin embassy, have sprung up in the country. The generally hospitable Bitcoin climate has fostered vibrant Bitcoin communities across the country that host regular conferences and other events.

The country's largest banks, ABN Ambro and ING, have also been increasingly looking at Bitcoin and blockchain to improve on their own technology and costs and to transform to agile businesses. The idea is to self-disrupt their status quo to avoid being swamped by newly emerging fintechs.[127]

Globally known BitPay set up their European headquarters in Amsterdam, where the business could support over 7,000 merchants in Europe. It has the eventual mission of serving more than 30,000 merchants in Europe.[128] BitPay enables merchants to accept Bitcoin payments from customers while receiving bank deposit settlements in their local currency, without price volatility or direct Bitcoin integration. The service provider claims that by accepting Bitcoin through BitPay, merchants gain access to a payment network and a new customer base as global as the internet, but without the fees, country by country integrations costs, and fraud risks of traditional online payment methods. Netherlands is acknowledged for its positive attitude toward crypto and is also generally recognised as one of the 16 most crypto-friendly countries in 2024.[129]

5.2.7 Finland

This is the home of Nokia,[130] once renowned globally but is now looking to exert its former glories through a strategic review action plan. Like its Scandinavian brethren, the country is also at the forefront of technological innovation.

The Finnish Central Board of Taxes has deemed Bitcoin as a category of financial services, thereby exempting it and Bitcoin purchases from value added tax. It announced that Bitcoin does not meet the definition of a currency or even an electronic payment form in Finland, and as such, the country's central bank has instead decided to categorise the software as a commodity.[131] Relative to its

---

127 Petkovic, S. & Sinha, A. (2017), "Ideation to realization: How Dutch banks are harnessing blockchain", *Coin Desk*, 04/09/2017, www.coindesk.com/ideation-realization-dutch-bank-harness-blockchain, accessed 02/02/2018.

128 Gallippi, T. (2016), "BitPay opens European headquarters in Amsterdam", *BitPay*, 02/02/2014, https://bitpay.com/blog/bitpay-opens-european-headquarters-in-amsterdam/, accessed 02/02/2018.

129 Sarkauskaite, Z. (2024), "The 16 most crypto-friendly countries in 2024", *Swiss Money*, 08/03/2024, https://swissmoney.com/most-crypto-friendly-countries/, accessed 18/07/2024.

130 Schroeder, P., Finkle, J. & McCool, G. (2018), "Nokia starts review of digital health business, cuts jobs in Finland" *Reuters*, 15/02/2018, https://uk.reuters.com/article/uk-nokia-strategy/nokia-starts-review-of-digital-health-business-cuts-jobs-in-finland-idUKKCN1FZ12C, accessed 18/02/2018.

131 Hajdarbegovic, N. (2014), "Finland classifies bitcoin as VAT-exempt financial services", *Coin Desk*, 19/11/2014, www.coindesk.com/finland-classifies-bitcoin-vat-exempt-financial- service, accessed 02/02/2018.

small population of 5.5 million, there are 21 Bitcoin ATMs in Finland, including 6 in its capital of Helsinki.[132]

Finland is also home to exchanges like FinCCX,[133] Bittiraha,[134] and leading global P2P Bitcoin exchange LocalBitcoins. Interestingly, the most expensive Bitcoin sale for a luxury vehicle happened in 2016 at Helsinki, involving a Tesla vehicle, for over €140,000.[135] The country recognises cryptos to be an increasingly popular investment product, with the Finnish Supervision Authority (the FIN-FSA) taking a cautious view on cryptoassets and investments and reminding consumers of that their investments may not be protected. Nevertheless, the ownership and trading crypto is not prohibited, while the government supports the work to drive digital transformation of financial services in the European market by the EU.[136]

5.2.8 Denmark

This is a very advanced economy in terms of living standards and technology. It is also at the forefront of the journey towards digital currency so as to eliminate the use of cash altogether.[137] The Danish central bank is unenthusiastic about cryptocurrencies due to price volatility and, whilst following the idea of a central bank digital currency, remains wary.[138]

Denmark is home to various Bitcoin start-ups and exchanges, like the CCEDK, which has grown to be a prolific innovator in the crypto space with recent releases of Bitcoin 3.0 technology.[139] CCEDK's CEO, Ronny Boesing, stressed that the company's mission is to bring Bitcoin into mainstream acceptance in a responsible way.[140] A recent joint survey undertaken by EY and crypto research firm K33 Research suggests a rising trend in cryptoasset ownerships

132 Coin ATM Radar (2018), "Bitcoin ATMs in Finland", www.coinatmradar.com/country/72/Bitcoin-atm-finland, accessed 02/02/2018.

133 Coinalert (2015), "Finland bitcoin exchange FinCCX now accepts Euros and stopped USD", *Coinalert*, 20/05/2015, http://coinalert.eu/2015024124-Finland+Bitcoin+Exchange+FinCCX+Now+Accepts+Euros+and+Stopped+USD.html, accessed 02/02/2018.

134 Barrier, E. (2013), "Finland gets its first bitcoin ATM", *Coin Telegraph*, 19/12/2013, https://cointelegraph.com/news/finland_gets_its_first_bitcoin_atm, accessed 02/02/2018.

135 Redman, J. (2016), "€140,000 tesla bought for bitcoin in Finland", *Bitcoin*, 23/01/2016, https://news.bitcoin.com/e14000-tesla-bought-bitcoin-finland/, accessed 02/02/2018.

136 Kumpulainen, E. et al. (2023), "Finland", in *Navigating the global crypto landscape with PwC: 2024 outlook*, www.pwc.com/gx/en/industries/financial-services/assets/navigating-the-global-crypto-landscape-with-PwC-2024.pdf, accessed 18/07/2024.

137 Lyon, N. (2016), "Norway, Sweden and Denmark say 'no' to cash", *Coin Telegraph*, 25/01/2016, https://cointelegraph.com/news/cash-electronic-money-scandinavia, accessed 02/02/2018.

138 www.nationalbanken.dk./en/what-we-do/safe-and-efficient-payments/money-in-the-future-new-digital-opportunities, accessed 17/04/2025.

139 Snook, C. J. (2017), "As bitcoin passes $11,000 regulators are accelerating the adoption of blockchain 3.0 technology", *Inc.*, 29/11/2017, www.inc.com/chris-j-snook/as-bitcoin-passes-11000-regulators-are-accelerating-adoption-of-blockchain-30-technology.html, accessed 02/02/2018.

140 Thomas, C. (2015), "A conversation with Ronny Boesing, founder of CCEDK", *Coin Report*, 02/12/2015, https://coinreport.net/conversation-ronny-boesing-founder-ccedk/, accessed 02/02/2018; Ibid note [137], Lyon (2016).

among Danish younger adults, or some 7% of the Danish population. Comparatively, Denmark stands out to its Nordic peers, with crypto ownership being twice as common for the 30s to 40s cohort of the population, and with over 70% of Danish crypto owners attracted by the rising prices after 2019, thereby enabling crypto to reach mainstream during Covid. The same survey also highlights a strong future trajectory, demonstrating more than 900,000 Danes, or some 20% of Denmark's adult population, could own cryptos within the next decade.[141] Noting the positive reception and quick adaptation to cryptos among young adult Danes, there are expectations for a potential threefold increase over the next decade. This sends an unmistakable signal of a diversified investment culture to institutional investors and regulators at a time where EU's Markets in Crypto Assets Regulation (MiCAR) is entering into force.[142] Responding to this development, the Danish Financial Supervisory Authority (DFSA) is said to be planning to abolish non-custodial Bitcoin wallets to strengthen the regulation of crypto platform activities. Here, the DFSA stressed the need to supervise "interface providers" and mobile application developers to comply with the Markets in Crypto-Asset Regulation (MiCAR).[143]

5.2.9 Sweden

Like Denmark, Sweden is also on a mission to become a largely cashless society.[63] The Swedish Financial Supervisory Authority has legitimised Bitcoin a means of payment,[144] and this could well spur the growth of the cryptocurrency industry in the country.

Sweden is home to various Bitcoin start-ups, including the Safello Bitcoin exchange[145] and Stockholm-based KnCMiner,[146] a well-known hardware developer that has been generating cutting-edge ASIC miners since 2013. The LocalBitcoins volume in Sweden also reflects continued surge

141 Nordic Fintech Magazine (NFM) (2024), "Crypto reached mainstream in Denmark during Covid: 90000 owners predicted within a decade", *NFM*, 12/04/2024, https://nordicfintechmagazine.com/crypto-reached-mainstream-in-denmark-during-covid-900-000-owners-predicted-within-a-decade/, accessed 18/07/2024.

142 Ibid note [141], NFM (2024).

143 Binance (2024), "Denmark's financial regulator plans to strengthen supervision of crypto platforms", *Binance*, 02/07/2024, www.binance.com/en/square/post/2024-07-02-denmark-s-financial-regulator-plans-to-strengthen-supervision-of-crypto-platforms-10256353500114, accessed 28/07/2024.

144 John, U. (2017), "Countries that love, use and understand bitcoin", *Politics & Society*, 01/12/2017, https://thebitcoin.pub/t/countries-that-love-use-and-understand-bitcoin-money-bag/18083, accessed 02/02/2018.

145 Kallgren, J. (2014), "Swedish exchange safello aims to be 'CoinBase for Europe'", *Coin Desk*, 03/04/2014, www.coindesk.com/safello-introduces-europe-wide-bitcoin-trading, accessed 02/02/2018.

146 Higgins, S. (2017), "The Swedish telecom that bought KnC is now mining bitcoin", *Coin Desk*, 08/02/2017, www.coindesk.com/swedish-telecom-knc-mining-bitcoin, accessed 02/02/2018; Smolaks, M. (2015), "KnC miner to build fourth Bitcoin facility in Sweden", *Data Center Dynamics*, 14/12/2015, www.datacenterknowledge.com/archives/2015/12/14/bitcoin-mining-data-center-update, accessed 02/02/2018.

in cryptocurrency demand.[147] The Swedish Financial Supervisory Authority (SFSA), reflecting Swedish policy towards cryptos, has indicated that, in general, cryptoassets are not suitable for consumer investments, owing to their speculative nature. The Swedish Consumer Agency reinforced this view when stating that cryptos are an investment niche prone to fraud, including their links to misleading and aggressive marketing activities. Also, a government appointed special investigator, in a December 2020 report, stated that cryptos entail risks for financial stability and that it is vital that cryptos are subject to an appropriate regulatory framework proportionate to the specific risks that cryptos could pose to the financial and monetary systems as a whole, and that to the extent feasible, new rules should be based on principles set at global levels.[148]

There is presently no specific regulation directed at cryptos, but effective from 1 January 2020, a legal or natural person that undertakes business in Sweden from a physical entity as a branch, an agent, or a Swedish company in the jurisdiction, including professional operations comprising the management of, or trading in, virtual currency, has to register with the Finansinspektionen. Such registrants with the CFOA must comply with the Swedish Anti–Money Laundering and Financial Terrorism Act. Also, as to whether a crypto constitutes a "virtual currency", this has to be decided on a case by case basis. Though the CFOA does not define a *virtual currency*, it is deemed to have the equivalent meaning as set out in the 5th Anti–Money Laundering Directive. Further, depending on the design of the cryptoasset, it may fall within the scope of the Electronic Money Act or the Financial Trading Act.

5.2.10 Estonia

This small Baltic former Soviet nation of 1.3 million people is globally known for its tech-friendly government and, in particular, for its digitisation processes said to save the state some 2% of its GDP annually in salaries and expenses.[149] This is unsurprising, given that it has a significant technology-savvy population in the workforce. The government seems willing to implement blockchain initiatives[150] for healthcare and banking services. These are guided by competitive governance,[151] meaning unrestrictive borderless innovation, so as not to miss out on the global innovation competition.

147 Haig, S. (2017), "Sweden sees record trading volume as MP Sundin joins bitcoin exchange BTCX", *Bitcoin*, 09/06/2017, https://news.bitcoin.com/sweden-sees-record-trading-volume-asmp-sundin-joins-bitcoin-exchange-btcx/, accessed 02/02/2018.

148 Bergsten, A. et al. (2024), "Sweden", in Dewey, J. N. (ed.), *Blockchain & cryptocurrency laws and regulations 2024*, London, Global Legal Insights (GLI).

149 Heller, N. (2017), "Estonia, the digital republic", *The New Yorker*, 18 & 25/12/2017, https://www.newyorker.com/magazine/2017/12/18/estonia-the-digital-republic, accessed 24/01/2020.

150 Galeon, D. (2017), "Estonia's plans to build a digital nation using blockchain are taking shape", *Futurism*, 29/12/2017, www.futurism.com/estonias-plans-build-digital-nation-using-blockchain-taking-shape/, accessed 02/02/2018.

151 Ibid note [150], Heller (2017).

These measures together facilitate its citizens to become "e-Residents".[152] This gives Estonian citizens and businesses digital authentication. This is an ambitious project in technological statecraft that includes all members of the government and alters citizens' daily lives. Government services such as legislation, voting, education, justice, healthcare, banking, taxes, policing, and so on have been digitally linked across one platform to wire up the nation.[153] The country is one of the first to apply a blockchain-based e-voting service which also enables people to become shareholders of NASDAQ's Tallinn Stock Exchange. It is also among the first economies in the world to go into robotics[154] in a big way.

Better known globally as the birthplace of Skype,[155] Estonia now hosts many Bitcoin ATMs and start-ups, like Paxful, a global P2P buying and selling service for Bitcoin. Reinforced by one of the highest internet penetration rates in the world, the country is well poised to be a location where cryptocurrencies communities can feel welcome.[156] Along with these, this EU member state has the lowest business tax rate in the EU and is fast becoming known for liberal regulations around technological research.

Nevertheless, a major banking scandal in Estonia[157] recently may restrain the state's cryptoasset initiatives. The scandal has tarnished the reputation of the tiny state that has marketed itself as a digital hub, offering electronic residency cards to foreigners, including Pope Francis. Subsequent to the scandal, European regulators are more actively looking into the regulatory aspects of digital banking, including those involving cryptoassets. This is unfortunate, as the incident involved a branch of a large bank from Denmark, an entity outside of Estonia. Still, Estonia is generally perceived to be a crypto-hospitable jurisdiction. This is attributed to the jurisdiction being one of the first economies to embrace and actively promote its use, establishing a licensing system to/for crypto businesses marked by clarity end efficiency, being widely known as a cashless society that is supported by a well-developed digital infrastructure supporting crypto adoption, apart from being widely known for its promotion of blockchain start-ups and an ecosystem that fosters a thriving crypto community.[158]

---

152 Hammersley, B. (2017), "Concerned about Brexit? Why not become an e-resident of Estonia", *Wired*, 27/03/2017, www.wired.co.uk/article/estonia-e-resident, accessed 02/02/2018.

153 OECD (2017), *OECD public governance reviews- Estonia: Towards a single government approach*, Paris, OECD.

154 Pettit, H. (2017), "Are robots more than just 'personal property'? Estonia works toward giving AI legal status", *Mail Online*, 10/10/2017, www.dailymail.co.uk/sciencetech/article-4965922/Estonia-working-giving-robots-AI-legal-status.html, accessed 02/02/2018.

155 Walt, V. (2017), "Is this tiny European nation a preview of our tech future?", *Fortune*, 27/04/2017, https://fortune.com/2017/04/27/estonia-digital-life-tech-startups/, accessed 02/02/2018.

156 Master, C. (2017), "Bitcoin in the Baltics: Estonia leads crypto-friendly region", *Coinspectator*, 12/10/2017, https://coinspectator.com/news/86099/bitcoin-in-the-baltic-estonia-leads-thecrypto-friendly-region, accessed 02/02/2018.

157 O'Donnell, J. (2019), "Estonia warns of risks in wake of money laundering scandal", *Reuters*, 24/06/2019, www.reuters.com/article/us-moneylaundering-estonia/estonia-warns-of-risksin-wake-of-money-laundering-scandal-idUSKCN1TP1VS, accessed 24/06/2019.

158 Ibid note [129], Sarkauskaite (2024).

5.3 Advanced Asian economies

Other than those advanced Western economies discussed earlier, advanced economies in Asia, like Japan, South Korea, and Singapore, are also known for relatively high levels of cryptoasset and blockchain technology activities. These will now be explored.

5.3.1 Japan

Two countries not on the list of Bitcoin-friendly economies or places where people are actively using Bitcoin merit some attention here as those states have no official policy obstructing it. First, there is Japan, which, although now is no longer the commercial capital of Asia, is fast evolving as the region's cryptocurrencies hub.[159]

As China and South Korea take steps to discourage Bitcoin-related activities, Japan has been provided with the opportunity to become the breeding ground for the growth of cryptocurrency, including Bitcoin trading, in Asia. Japan's Payment Services Act 2009 (as amended)[160] provides a framework that makes it legal to use cryptocurrencies for payment services. China dominated Bitcoin mining for some years, until the present government policy compelled many Chinese Bitcoin miners to move their operations elsewhere. In contrast, Japan has the lion's share of cryptocurrency trading/exchange activities, where the region is concerned for some years now, and still does. Japan's FSA, the country's financial regulator, has approved four new cryptocurrency exchanges,[161] as well as cryptocurrencies that could be traded on these platforms.

Given the support from the Japanese government, cryptocurrency operations are thriving, and it is envisaged that, in the immediate years, many ICOs could even opt to host their issuance campaigns in the country. Leveraging the reticence and ambivalence of many economies with respect to cryptocurrencies, Japan is positioning itself to become a major global player in the market. Japan's case appears to suggest that, for the infant industry to thrive, it needs a supportive ecosystem and well balanced regulation. Japanese authorities acted swiftly when Coincheck, a large cryptocurrency exchange in Japan, lost some US$530 million through hacking.[162] Authorities quickly raided Coincheck's office and

159 Pal, R. (2017), "Countries approving cryptocurrencies", *Hacker Noon*, 19/21/2017, www.hackernoon.com/countries-approving-cryptocurrencies-d1fb7fefa261, accessed 20/02/2018.

160 Global Legal Monitor (2016), "Japan: Bitcoin to be regulated", *Global Legal Monitor*, 04/11/2016, www.loc.gov/law/foreign-news/article/japan-bitcoin-to-be-regulated/, accessed 02/02/2018.

161 Althauser, J. (2017), "Japanese financial regulator legalizes four new cryptocurrency exchanges", *Coin Telegraph*, 04/12/2017, https://go2co.in/news/japanese-financial-regulator-legalizes-four-new-cryptocurrency-exchanges/amp, accessed 02/02/2018.

162 Uranaka, T. & Wilson, T. (2018), "Japan raps Coincheck, orders broader checks after $530 million cryptocurrency theft", *Reuters*, 29/01/2018, www.reuters.com/article/us-japan-cryptocurrency/japan-raps-coincheck-orders-broader-checks-after-530-million-cryptocurrency-theft-idUSKBN1FI06S, accessed 18/02/2018.

started investigating all cryptocurrency exchanges in the country for security gaps. They ordered Coincheck to raise its operating standards.[163]

Japan, therefore, continues to fascinate the world with its ability to maintain traditions while modernising. The Japanese habitually appear to prefer to transact in cash for their daily needs, yet when it comes to digital currency, the country is able to embrace it at the same time. According to Yuko Kawai, the fintech head of the Bank of Japan, cash is still predominantly used.[164] The value of physical currency in circulation was the highest among major nations according to the report by the Bank for International Settlements.[165] About 76% of consumer activity was settled in cash in 2021. Under present circumstances, it is not easy for cryptocurrency to become a major means of settlement. Still, Japan, like most economies, is keen to make available fintech services like Bitcoin for tourists and other people visiting the country. This is why Japan hosts many facilities convenient for cryptocurrencies users.

Japan revised its Payment Services Act to tighten cryptocurrency regulation so as to promote user protection; to more robustly regulate crypto derivatives trading; to mitigate industry risks, such as exchange hacks; and to establish a more transparent regulatory framework for the new asset class. The amendments further establish a legal name change for cryptocurrencies as cryptoassets that were previously identified as virtual currencies in the country. Additionally, the amendments provide for more robust legislation for crypto margin trading, limiting leverage to two to four times the initial deposit. Through its position as the G20 chair for 2019,[166] Japan sought to promote its framework as the global benchmark for regulating the sector. It accordingly prepared a handbook for the June 2019 G20 meeting in Osaka that each G20 country could use for regulations that include measures to prevent the outflow of virtual currency.

Thus, Japan is a major player in the cryptoassets market, with a mature and advanced approach and, since 2017, has recognised Bitcoin as a legal currency supported by clear regulations for crypto exchanges and driven by best practices driven by the self-regulated Japan Virtual Currency Exchange Association (JVCEA).[167] Japan is generally perceived as a cryptoasset-hospitable jurisdiction. This is attributed to its clear and comprehensive regulations; the recognition of cryptos as legal assets; its existing financial institutions entering the crypto space, adding to further legitimacy; regulatory focus on boosting innovation

163 Shane, D. (2018), "$530 million cryptocurrency heist may be biggest ever", *CNN*, 29/01/2018, https://money.cnn.com/2018/01/29/technology/coincheck-cryptocurrency-exchange-hack-japan/index.html, accessed 20/02/2018.

164 Fujioka, T. & Kidaka, M. (2018), "Japan's central bank Sees no need to mint a digital currency", *Bloomberg*, 29/01/2018, www.bloomberg.com/news/articles/2018-01-28/japanese-don-t-need-digital-currency-as-they-love-cash-boj-says, accessed 20/02/2018.

165 Bank for International Settlements (BIS) (2017), *Statistics on payment, clearing and settlement systems in the CPMI countries*, Basel, BIS.

166 Helms, K. (2019), "Japan to provide G20 with solution for crypto regulation", *Bitcoin.com*, 23/04/2019, https://news.bitcoin.com/japan-g20-cryptocurrency-regulation/, accessed 02/06/2019.

167 Ibid note [129], Sarkauskaite (2024).

within a controlled framework; and having one of the most active and mature crypto trading markets globally.[168]

5.3.2 South Korea

The rhetoric over the South Korean government's displeasure of Bitcoin's links to money laundering and other illicit activities, plus the country's concerns over the extreme investment risk, appears to suggest that cryptocurrency has no place in Korean society.[169] This is evidently not the case when the cryptocurrency space in the country is looked at more closely.

South Korea has a technology space that is conducive for cryptocurrency development. It has a technology adaptive population that is quick to adapt. Its younger generation sees cryptocurrencies as a way to better life. When a minister recently mentioned that regulators were preparing legislation to halt cryptocurrency trading, global Bitcoin prices temporarily plummeted. A public petition to the country's president attracted overwhelming support such that the heavy internet traffic briefly crashed the president's website. This "online uprising" led to the president's office announcing that the minster's idea was a mere proposal under consideration.[170] The recent talk of Bitcoin banning and so on arises from the government's fear of the political disputes of being held accountable for doing nothing when Bitcoin investment risks and Bitcoin frauds seem to be common in many parts of the world, including its closely watched neighbour, China. Calm returned to the crypto community recently with the announcement of regulation over crypto exchanges.

South Korea is home to global technology titans like Samsung and LG. It also has one of the highest smartphone penetration and mobile payment rates in the world. As the country seeks to find ways to regulate cryptocurrencies without restricting the technology innovations that underpin them, various related startups have already arrived. This includes Korbit,[171] a secure and comprehensive Bitcoin exchange that also focuses on remittances and cross-border payments. Coinplug,[172] another South Korean Bitcoin exchange platform, enables people to buy Bitcoins at 7-Eleven stores across the country. A friendly climate is

168 Ibid note [129], Sarkauskaite (2024).

169 Kim, C. & Kim, D. (2018), "South Korea inspects six banks over virtual currency services to clients", *Reuters*, 08/01/2018, www.reuters.com/. . . southkorea-Bitcoin/south-korea-inspects-sixbanks-over-vir, accessed 02/02/2018.

170 Kim, C. & Yang, H. Y. (2018), "Uproar over crackdown on cryptocurrencies divides South Korea", *Reuters*, 12/01/2018, www.reuters.com/article/us-southkorea-bitcoin/uproar-over-crackdown-on-cryptocurrencies-divides-south-korea-idUSKBN1F10YG, accessed 02/02/2018.

171 Young, J. (2017), "South Korea's largest bitcoin exchanges ready for strict regulations", *Coin Telegraph*, 14/12/2017, https://cointelegraph.com/news/south-korean-financial-authorities-plan-to-regulate-bitcoin-exchanges-soon, accessed 02/02/2018.

172 Helms, K. (2017), "South Korea's coinplug launches new exchange and begins trading bitcoin cash", *Bitcoin*, 03/09/2017, https://news.bitcoin.com/south-koreas-coinplug-launches-new-exchange-trading-bitcoin-cash/, accessed 02/02/2018.

provided for the local Bitcoin community, while the country is also a regular host of Bitcoin conferences.

South Korea is the third largest market, after Japan and the United States, accounting for about 20% of all Bitcoin trading.[173] However, concerns over Bitcoin are growing, at least as far as the government is concerned. These concerns are most profound across Asia, where cryptocurrency is also illegal in Kyrgyzstan, Bangladesh, and Nepal. China, which at one time accounted 90% of all Bitcoin trading, banned ICOs in September 2017 and began to crack down on exchanges and Bitcoin mining. The Bank of Japan in particular cited the dangers of speculative investing in Bitcoin. The Reserve Bank of India articulated concerns over tax evasion and other abuses and has been looking into ways to outlaw Bitcoin as a payment mechanism. Indonesia acted against ICOs, and Malaysia and Singapore have warned speculative investors of the risks of losing their money in cryptocurrencies' investments and in badly designed ICOs.[174]

There are, nevertheless, legitimate concerns about crypto and crypto-related frauds in Asia, where South Korea is located. In one case, South Korean police ended a US$200 million cryptocurrency Ponzi scheme named MiningMax and the Bitcoin exchange BitKRX that claimed to be a legitimate venture created by the Korean Exchange. The latter was subsequently revealed to be fraudulent.[94] Such incidents prompted the case for more Bitcoin regulation, but others claim that the country usually struggles with the acceptance of new technologies that could infringe on some of the major vested interests, and it is suspected that Bitcoin would be no different.

What differentiates South Korea from the rest of the Bitcoin adoptee states in Asia is the existential threat posed by North Korea.[175] For example, Youbit[176] became insolvent in December 2017 after losing one-fifth of its clients' holdings from hacking. North Korean hackers are believed to be behind the attacks on four South Korean Bitcoin exchanges in the summer of 2017. The North Korean regime is believed also to have begun Bitcoin mining in May 2017 and is likely to use what it mines or steals to circumvent present UN sanctions against the country. Despite such problems, shutting down Bitcoin exchanges or other equivalent actions to slow down Bitcoin adoption in South Korea is not viewed as a good economic decision by the country's population. Rather, what is needed for the country is for these various Bitcoin challenges to be managed by the right

173 Das, S. (2017), "$250 million ethereum mining scam? Korean prosecutors file charges", *CCN*, 22/12/2017, www.ccn.com/250-million-ethereum-mining-scam-korean-prosecutors-file-charges/, accessed 02/02/2018.

174 Volodzko, D. J. (2018), "Why is South Korea suddenly terrified of Bitcoin?", *South China Morning Post*, 01/01/2018, www.scmp.com/week-asia/business/article/2126189/why-south-korea-suddenly-terrified-bitcoin, accessed 02/02/2018.

175 Ibid note [175], Volodzko (2018).

176 Castor, A. (2017), "After second hack this year, South Korean exchange Youbit closes down", *Bitcoinmagazine*, 19/12/2017, https://bitcoinmagazine.com/articles/after-second-hack-year-southkorean-exchange-youbit-closes-down, accessed 02/02/2018.

balance of regulation and support.[177] Widely known for early adoption of new technologies, South Korea embraced micropayments and digital tokens as early as 1996. With the early familiarity with cryptos as a common asset and payment method, many young Koreans have successfully traded cryptos to make money. The country follows through with the enactment of the Virtual Asset User Protection Act on 18 July 2023 that safeguards crypto investors, regulates the jurisdiction's virtual asset market, and tackles unfair trading practices and introduces critical protections, marking a milestone in industry regulation.[178] The legislation took effect from 19 July 2024.

5.3.3 Singapore

Alongside Hong Kong (SAR), Taiwan, South Korea, and Japan, Singapore is an economic powerhouse despite being a small island economy. Through good political governance, world class education, world class financial system, and generally innovative and pragmatic economic and industrial policies and strategies, Singapore was brought to the attention of the world in Michael Porter's *The Competitive Advantage of Nations* in the 1990s.[179] The island city state generally fights shy of such publicity, but many multilateral institutions and many economies continue to speak positively of Singapore. With a small population of some 5.6 million, Singapore had GDP per capita averaging US$24,547 from 1960 to 2018, rising from a record low of US$3,503 to US$58,247.[180] It continues to progress, drawing mostly on its generally stable political and legal system, as well as its forward looking and pragmatic economic and industrial policies. In particular, it boasts one of the best and most secure financial systems in the world, where its three largest domestic banks have carved out a sound global reputation for innovation, safety, and financial stability.

In the face of growing competition from regional and other economies, Singapore is pushing forward its greater participation in the global fintech industry, including the cryptoasset industry subset and inclusive of the underpinning blockchain technology. Singapore already functions in a similar way to Hong Kong as a regional financial hub and now aspires to be the crypto hub of Asia.[181] In this, the island state enjoys a relative advantage in that when compared to its brethren in the region or even much of the rest of the world, the regulators in Singapore are relatively better informed and more transparent about their thinking on blockchain and cryptoassets. Relative to the regulatory uncertainties in much

177 Ibid note [175], Volodko (2018), citing the view of Business Administration Professor Yoo Bying-Joon of Seoul National University.

178 Coin Market Cap (CMC) (2024), "Crypto regulations in South Korea 2024", *CMC*, 01/07/2024, https://coinmarketcap.com/community/articles/6683a30d9acdf5622941992c/, accessed 20/12/2023.

179 Porter, M. (1990), *The competitive advantage of nations*, New York, The Free Press.

180 Trading Economics (2018), "Singapore GDP per capita", *Trading Economics*, https://tradingeconomics.com/singapore/gdp-per-capita.

181 Yang, J. (2018), "Singapore is the crypto sandbox that Asia needs", *TechCrunch*, 22/09/2018, https://techcrunch.com/2018/09/22/singapore-is-the-crypto-sandbox-that-asia-needs/, accessed 26/09/2019.

of Asia and even some advanced economies like the United States, the Monetary Authority of Singapore (MAS) has already released its guidance on digital token offering that shows the application of securities laws to digital token offerings and issuances.[182] This is not a new approach, as the young nation, since its birth, has been pioneering economic and regulatory standards in Asia.

In respect of the crypto space, Singapore has successfully launched a "Token Day" marking the tenth anniversary of cryptocurrency, showing the potential for crypto addition across the island state.[183] Some 30 retailers in Singapore, during a 19-day period, then accepted cryptocurrency as payments. This led to increased discussion over the emergence of cryptocurrencies as an alternative for settling payments. Singapore was among the first economies to commence regulating the employment of digital currencies in 2014, imposing taxation on earnings.[184]

In late November 2018, the MAS finalised its regulatory framework to safeguard cryptocurrencies against counter-terrorism financing and to bolster cybersecurity. Via the Payments Services Act 2019 (PSA), the MAS requires crypto payment service providers to be licensed. Prior to this, crypto exchanges were an unregulated industry.[104] The PSA has therefore laid the foundations for absorbing blockchain into the securities framework and payment systems. This accelerated blockchain-based partnerships and investments that would eventually further the progress of the cryptocurrency asset class. In Singapore, ICOs set the trend, followed by blockchain, whereas in other economies blockchain adoption came after cryptocurrency.[105]

MAS has also issued a retail investor's guide to digital assets, last updated on 26 May 2020, contrasting its earlier lukewarm position out of fear of their volatility. This might be the signal that Singapore is preparing for cryptocurrency's entry into mainstream payment solutions. MAS has also more recently announced the widening of its regulatory regime for payment providers to bring designated cryptocurrencies under its jurisdiction.[106] These initiatives have already attracted various high-profile exchanges to domicile in Singapore, while numerous innovative crypto-based ventures have also sprung up.

Branded as the fintech capital of Asia, Singapore boasts a landscape that has become increasingly favourable for cryptocurrencies and a magnet for large inflows of funds into crypto and blockchain technologies, especially with its closest competitor, Hong Kong, facing serious political problems. Hence, the envisaged influx of crypto exchanges into Singapore[185] is expected to make the island economy the crypto and blockchain capital in the region and perhaps the

182 Ibid note [182], Yang (2018).

183 Deogawanka, S. (2019), "Is Singapore on the way to embracing cryptocurrency as part of the financial system?", *ASEANToday*, 15/01/2019, www.aseantoday.com/2019/01/is-singapore-on-theway-to-embracing-cryptocurrency-as-part-of-the-financial-system/, accessed 18/02/2019.

184 Ibid note [184], Deogawanka (2019).

185 Cox, D. (2019), "Binance CEO hails Singapore's crypto-friendly jurisdiction on its 54th birthday", *CryptoNewsZ*, www.cryptonewsz.com/binance-ceo-hails-singapores-crypto-friendlyjurisdiction-on-its-54th-birthday/35933/, accessed 08/09/2019.

world. Singapore's reputation as a respectable global hub for financial innovation is recently boosted by remarks of Tim Berners-Lee, the creator of the World Wide Web, that the island state can lead the way when it comes to developing law with technology.[186] The city state has positioned itself as a leading jurisdiction for cryptos and innovation through the offers of tax exemptions for specific digital tokens and clear tax structures for investors and businesses.[187] Singapore is generally perceived as a hospitable jurisdiction for crypto activities, owing to its clear and relatively flexible regulatory framework for the crypto industry, with the Monetary Authority of Singapore (MAS) taking a forward-thinking approach that encourages innovations and collaborations in cryptos, and positive initiatives, like the Sandbox, which allows businesses to test and develop innovative crypto solutions.[188]

5.3.4 China and India

The world's two biggest populations, China and India, both exceeding 1.3 billion people, are both in Asia. Over the last two decades, both have had large and robust growing economies, though lately China has had to contend with a trade war with the United States and with some serious domestic economic challenges, while India has also seen significant economic problems. On the geopolitical front, China has to grapple with political challenges in the South China Sea, whereas India has issues with Pakistan over Kashmir.

Both China and India are growing in GDP terms relatively better than most other economies, but unlike them, their very large population bases mean that their GDP per capita puts them as emerging middle income economies. Both have relatively respectable banking systems supported by relatively well-managed monetary policies. However, large tracts of their populations are without access to banking services, for various reasons. To date, China has addressed this problem through the use of fintechs in impressive fashion, while India is also doing the same, though relatively less impressively.

Both economies are hostile towards cryptoassets even though they are highly supportive of other fintech subsets. China, being a Communist authoritarian regime, is unable to condone the crypto industry, as the decentralisation and democratisation principles behind the industry do not synchronise with its political practices. India, on the other hand, is highly concerned over the use of cryptoassets for illicit activities, notably the corruption risk that is high on its national agenda.

The People's Bank of China, the country's central monetary and regulatory authority, has stated that it would block access to all domestic and foreign

186 Khan, A. (2019), "Singapore can be role model for how technology, law can develop, says Tim Berners-Lee", *ChannelNewsAsia (CNA)*, 05/09/2019, www.channelnewsasia.com/news/singapore/singapore-can-be-role-model-for-how-technology-law-can-develop-11877308, accessed 06/09/2019.

187 Ibid note [129], Sarkauskaite (2024).

188 Ibid note [129], Sarkauskaite (2024).

cryptocurrency exchanges and ICO websites.[189] It is the country's aim to clamp down on all cryptocurrency trading with a ban on foreign/offshore exchanges/ platforms. Over the past few years, it has been issuing regular advisories and implementing initiative to deter the use of cryptocurrency in the country.

Together with the latest move, these could completely eliminate cryptocurrency trading and mining activities in the world's most populous and second largest economy.[190] Still, this does not necessarily mean that crypto activities are altogether dead in the country, as it is an open secret that many of its population engaged with these through various means, including via virtual private networks through Hong Kong and via Canada and other places where Bitcoin mining is concentrated. For example, the country's Tron or TRX token pioneer, Justine Sun, paid US$4.7 million for lunch with Warren Buffett.[191]

Regulatory authorities have conceded that recent attempts to stamp out digital currencies by shutting down domestic exchanges have failed to completely eradicate crypto trading, as ICOs and virtual currency trading did not completely recede subsequent to the country's official ban on cryptocurrencies and the closure of domestic virtual currency exchanges, with many people turning to overseas platforms to continue transacting in virtual currencies. China's regulatory authorities are perturbed that oversea transactions and regulatory evasion have resumed, with many risks fuelled by illegal issuance, and even fraud and pyramid selling.[192]

The tough stance taken by the authorities, aside from its authoritarian agenda, was also prompted by the frenzy among retail investors that led to huge price volatility and various reports of major frauds that could potentially have led to social unrest. China, though, takes a less tough stance on the use of blockchain beyond cryptocurrencies. More recently, China's central bank said it is developing its own digital currency as if in response to the IMF's positive stance on central bank digital currency.[193] China is unlikely to be alone in this, as Sweden's Riksbank is another central bank looking into the idea.[194] India, on the other hand, opposes the greater use of cryptoassets for different reasons. The country has struggled over many decades to curb corruption in the country. It also struggled to provide banking services access to large tracts of its rural population.

---

189 Seth, S. (2019), "Is bitcoin banned in China", *Investopedia*, 25/06/2019, www.investopedia.com/news/Bitcoin-banned-china/, accessed 28/06/2019.

190 Ibid note [190], Seth (2019).

191 Ablan, J. (2019), "Crypto pioneer Justin Sun pays $4.7 million for lunch with Warren Buffett", *Reuters*, 04/06/2019, www.reuters.com/article/buffett-lunch/crypto-pioneer-justin-sun-pays4-57-million-for-lunch-with-warren-buffett-idUSL2N23A0V4, accessed 18/06/2019.

192 Xie, Y. (2018), "China to stamp out cryptocurrency trading completely with ban on foreign platforms", *South China Morning Post*, 05/02/2018, www.scmp.com/business/banking-finance/article/2132009/china-stamp-out-cryptocurrency-trading-completely-ban, accessed 19/09/2018.

193 Browne, R. (2019), "China's central ban says it's close to releasing its own digital currency", *CNBC*, 12/08/2019, www.cnbc.com/2019/08/12/china-central-bank-close-to-releasing-digital-currency-pboc-official.html, accessed 19/08/2019.

194 Browne, R. (2018), "People in Sweden barely use cash- and that's sounding alarming bells for the country's central bank", *CNBC*, 03/05/2018, www.cnbc.com/2018/05/03/sweden-cashlessfuture-sounds-alarm-bells-for-the-central-bank.html, accessed 19/08/2019.

To deal with both problems, India first launched its AADHAR policy, which is the world's largest biometric system. The AADHAR journey began in 2009. This is a unique 12-digit number provided to each and every registered Indian resident. The 12-digit number houses biometric details, address, DOB, and all major details of an individual. Some 1.19 billion or 93% of India's population have already been registered.[195]

AADHAR enables digitalisation and centralisation of data. It will be linked to bank accounts. This is by no means a modest achievement, but it seems to violate privacy issues that are of vital importance elsewhere in other democracies.[196] India also launched its demonetisation move in 2016. It managed to withdraw the two largest banknotes that accounted for 86% of cash transactions from circulation in the country. The idea was to break the grip of corruption and black money (or money from gains unreported to the tax authorities).[197] Both are a rampant and persistent scourge in India. Since then, the tax base in India has gone up, while some cash transactions have gone down and motivations to try out digital payments were induced, as seen by the spike in mobile wallets. These suggest some progress in terms of financial maturity and financial sophistication. Still, some 94% of other asset classes were not impacted by the move.

More importantly, however, cash that has a cost to society is gradually being replaced by a variety of alternatives, like digital, electronic credit cards that provide some kind of paper trail of payment transactions.[198] As digital currency has a relatively lower transparency and is associated with various kinds of money laundering and related illicit activities, India, having done much to curb these kinds of activities, inevitably view these negatively. In April 2018, the Reserve Bank of India (RBI), the country's central bank, issued a notice to Indian banks, telling them to stop dealing with any cryptocurrency businesses, but peer-to-peer trading of virtual currencies remains legal in India.[199] The Internet and Mobile Association of India (IAMAI), though, has challenged RBI's directive in the Supreme Court of India.[200]

A government panel has more recently issued a recommendation to ban all cryptocurrencies created by non-sovereigns or entirely private enterprises. The panel recommended that anyone found dealing with digital currencies of any

195 Prabhu, J. R. (2018), "AADHAR-India's digital identity and world's largest biometric system", *Medium*, 20/10/2018, https://medium.com/@jairamrprabhu/aadhar-indias-digital-identity-and-world-s-largest-biometric-system-9ce81ebb4b8b, accessed 19/08/2019.

196 Ibid note [196], Prabhu (2018).

197 Chakravorti, B. (2018), "When India killed off cash overnight", *Harvard Business Review*, 27/08/2018, https://hbr.org/ideacast/2018/06/when-india-killed-off-cash-overnight.html, accessed 28/08/2019.

198 Ibid note [198], Chakravorti (2018).

199 Perez, Y. B. (2019), "Indian government ban on 'non-sovereign' cryptocurrency would see holders jailed for up to 10 years", *TheNextWeb*, 05/09/2019, https://thenextweb.com/hardfork/2019/07/22/indian-government-ban-cryptocurrency-jail-10-years/, accessed 08/09/2019.

200 The Economic Times (2019), "IAMAI says RBI has no authority to ban cryptocurrencies", *The Economic Times*, 14/08/2019, https://m.economictimes.com/news/economy/policy/iamai-says-rbi-has-no-authority-to-ban-cryptocurrencies/articleshow/70677612.cms, accessed 08/09/2019.

kind could face up to 10 years in jail as well as hefty fines.[201] The panel argued that all these private cryptocurrencies have no underlying intrinsic value and lack all the attributes of fiats, as they have no fixed nominal value and could act neither as any store of value nor as medium of exchange. The panel, while largely critical of decentralised currencies, is supportive of the possibility of a state-issued digital currency in the country. It also views decentralised ledger technology as an important and innovative technology that could play vital roles in ushering in the digital age and has even called for specific legislations to promote and regulate the use of blockchain in financial and related domains.

Thus, both China and India oppose the use of cryptoassets, but from different perspectives. Both, though, are generally positive towards central bank digital currency, as well as blockchain technology. While China and India discourage their citizens from participating in crypto activities, they see strong adoption. The Atlantic Council (AC) that monitors crypto regulation in 60 economies evaluated their impact, drawing on data from Chainalysis, the leading crypto tracking firm. The AC found that whole or partial bans are weakly correlated with reducing participation, with 33 nations legalising holding cryptoassets and 27 generally or partially banning them.[202] Also, the world's two most populous economies, namely, China and India, have strong crypto niches, despite their inhospitable policies towards the crypto industry.[203] Chainalysis estimated US$86.4 billion in peer-to-peer transactions in China over 12 months through June 2023, and with the country having one of the largest numbers of people owning cryptos in the world.[204] Most important businesses in the crypto space are said to be rooted in China. Beijing-based Bitmain is a distant leader in the manufacture of Bitcoin mining equipment, with what Nvidia is to AI, Bitmain is to Bitcoin.[205] Further, three of the largest cryptoasset exchanges in the world, namely, Binance, HTX (formerly Huobi), and OKX, originated in China.[206] India's banking authority in 2018 banned banks from supporting cryptoassets trading and investing, but the court reversed the decision in 2020, when more citizens entered the market.[207] In 2025, India imposed taxes on traders taxing 30% on profits from any trade and a 1% transaction tax on most of them. Amidst Coinbase's exit from the Terra stablecoin fallout, at the end of 2023, regulators drove multiple exchanges out of the jurisdiction.[208] Still, Chainalysis ranked India highest in grassroots adoption in 2023.[209] Thus, while India lacks major

201 Ibid note [200], Perez (2019).
202 Dale, B. (2024), "India, China's regulation of crypto 'weakly correlated with participation'", *Axios*, 19/07/2024, www.axios.com/2024/07/18/india-china-crypto-regulation-participation, accessed 19/07/2024.
203 Ibid note [203], Dale (2024).
204 Ibid note [203], Dale (2024).
205 Ibid note [203], Dale (2024).
206 Ibid note [203], Dale (2024).
207 Ibid note [203], Dale (2024).
208 Ibid note [203], Dale (2024).
209 Ibid note [203], Dale (2024).

crypto firms with global reach like China, it may have the largest addressable market, despite its government's ambivalence.[210]

5.4 Offshore Financial Centres (OFCs)

OFCs became highly controversial all over the world subsequent to the unofficial release of the Panama[211] and Paradise Papers.[212] Both suggested serious problems with various OFCs operating because of the implications that various well known politicians, royalties, businesses, and high-profile celebrities could be involved in storing unaccounted for savings/funds in exotic OFCs. More significantly, so could criminals. Subsequent to the revelations, various national and global financial regulators began probing the named beneficiaries or holders of all these accounts.

Various reports also alleged money laundering and related illicit activities through the deployments of various kinds of cryptoassets in these offshore accounts. Many of the named OFCs were condemned for helping to condone such activities. National regulators, led by the United States, and international global multilateral institutions, such as the OECD and the EU, launched probes into the named OFCs. The regulators threatened to blacklist some of these OFCs, and the EU has, in effect, done so already. In response, and to avoid being blacklisted, some OFCs have come out with various initiatives to deal with the sins of cryptoassets. Attention is drawn to two of these OFCs, namely, the Cayman Islands and the Isle of Man.

The Cayman Islands seem to adopt a fairly flexible regulatory environment for cryptocurrencies and blockchain technology. Though there are no specific laws dealing with cryptocurrencies, there are laws that are, in certain respects, applicable. Among these are the Securities Investment Business Law (Revised) 2015, the Anti–Money Laundering Laws and Regulations 2017, the Revised 2010 Money Services Law, and the Electronic Transactions Law (Revised) 2003. The Cayman Islands legal community are of the opinion that more specific legislation will eventually appear. For the time being, it seems that the regulators and lawmakers in the jurisdiction are keen to avoid rushing through any laws before the pitfalls of blockchain technology, cryptocurrencies, and ICOs are properly understood.[213] The Cayman Islands are pitching blockchain entities from across the world to locate in the Cayman Enterprise City, which is a special economic zone targeting technology-related entities.

---

210 Ibid note [203], Dale (2024).

211 Zaidi, S. H., Wang, X.-Y., Ahamd, S., Tan, X. P. & Meng, Q. (2017), "Panama papers and the dilemma of global financial transparency", *International Journal of Modern Research in Management (IJMRM)*, 1(1): 18–35.

212 Berglez, P. & Gearing, A. (2018), "The Panama and paradise papers: The rise of the global fourth estate", *International Journal of Communication*, 12: 4537–4592.

213 Humphries, C. A. & Smith, J. (2018), "Cayman Islands: Initial coin offerings (ICO) in the Cayman Islands", *Mondaq*, 19/02/2018, www.mondaq.com/caymanislands/x/667952/Commodities+Derivatives+Stock+Exchanges/Initial+Coin+Offerings+ICO+In+The+Cayman+Islands, accessed 25/03/2018.

The Isle of Man is a UK Crown Dependency that has a robust online gambling industry and a burgeoning financial sector. Many businesses there accept Bitcoin as payments alongside its national fiat.[214] This jurisdiction was an early adopter of law to regulate cryptocurrencies within its borders. It amended its Proceeds of Crime Act 2015 to absorb virtual currency businesses within its regulated sector as a designated business.[215] The said legislative amendment meant that those seeking to offer ICOs within the confines of its AML laws will be required to use KYC practices.[216] Such businesses would be overseen by the Isle of Man FSA to ensure compliance.

The Isle of Man differentiates between digital, virtual, convertible, and non-convertible virtual currencies.[217] Also, the FSA has stated that it will not register an applicant where the ICO provides tokens that do not offer any benefit to the purchaser other than the token itself, because such features are generally considered by the FSA to pose an unacceptable high risk that the money raised from the ICO could be used for unanticipated and illegal purposes besides giving risk to consumers.[218] More recently, the Isle of Man has amended its online gambling laws to enable operators to accept virtual currencies.[219]

Finally, revelations from the Panama and Paradise Papers suggest that the tentacles of OFCs as tax havens are far bigger and more central to the world economy than previously thought, and that the biggest havens are located not where previously thought. These tax havens collectively cost governments between US$500 billion and US$600 billion annually in lost corporate tax revenues through legal and not so legal means.[220] Of this, US$200 billion was accounted for by low-income economies, a relatively larger loss as a percentage of GDP than that for the advanced economies. Trillions were also stashed away by individuals in these often-obscure tax havens.[221] *Tax haven* definitions vary, but they are commonly characterised by two key words: "escape" from financial regulations, disclosure, criminal liability, and more, and "elsewhere", implying offshore and across borders.[222] It has now been

214 Milmo, C. (2016), "Bitcoin: How the Isle of Man is leading a cryptocurrency revolution", *Independent*, 03/01/2016.

215 Isle of Man FSA (2018a), "Questions & answers in respect of persons seeking to launch an initial coin offering in or from the Island", *Isle of Man FSA*, 05/10/2018, www.iomfsa.im/media/2365/icoguidanceforapplicants.pdf, accessed 21/05/2018.

216 Ibid note [216], Isle of Man FSA (2018a).

217 Isle of Man FSA (2018b), "Virtual currency business: Sector specific AML/CFT guidance notes", https://tile.loc.gov/storage-services/service/ll/llglrd/2018298387/2018298387.pdf.

218 Ibid note [218], Isle of Man FSA (2018b).

219 Online Gambling (Amendments) Regulations 2016, SD 2016/0341, reg. 11(1)-(2), www.gov.im/media/1354648/online-gambling-amendments-regulations-2016.pdf, accessed 28/08/2019.

220 Cobham, A. & Jansky, P. (2018), "Global distribution of revenue loss from corporate tax avoidance: Re-estimation and country results", *Journal of International Development*, 30(2): 206–232.

221 Henry, J. S. (2016), "Taxing tax havens", *Foreign Affairs*, 12/04/2016.

222 Shaxson, N. (2019), "The billions attracted by tax havens do harm to sending and receiving nations alike", *Finance & Development*, 7–10, September 2019.

argued that, tax losses aside, free capital flows across borders carry risks, including the danger of financial instability in emerging market economies. Of surprise to many in the world, the Corporate Tax Haven Index[223] identified the British Virgin Islands, Bermuda, and the Cayman Islands as the top three in the world. These are all British Overseas Territories, and they are followed closely by the Netherlands, Switzerland, Luxembourg, Jersey (British Dependency), the Bahamas, and Hong Kong. In turn, the Financial Secrecy Index[224] ranks Switzerland, the United States, and the Cayman Islands as the top three jurisdictions for private wealth. They are followed by Hong Kong, Singapore, Luxembourg, Germany, Taiwan, United Arab Emirates (Dubai), Guernsey, Lebanon, Panama, Japan, Netherlands, Thailand, the British Virgin Islands, Bahrain, Jersey, the Bahamas, Malta, Canada, Macau, UK, Cyprus, France, Ireland, China, and Russia.

Subsequent to the 2008 global financial crisis and the Panama and Paradise Papers revelation, the OECD suggested that the use of tax havens for illicit purposes posed serious risks and increased pressure for multilateral entities to act to reduce the risk. The OECD took this further with the Common Reporting Standard (CRS)[225] and the base erosion and profit shifting (BEPS)[226] initiative targeted at multinationals. Resolving working problems associated with these two initiatives led to gradual global acceptance of four best practices. These are the automatic exchange of financial information across borders, public registers of beneficial ownership of financial assets, country by country reporting, and a unitary tax with formula apportionment.

Subsequent to 2008, when the United States found Swiss bankers assisting US citizens to evade tax, the US Department of Justice (DOJ) targeted Swiss bankers and banks that led to major concessions on banking secrecy.[227] This initiative suggests that any effective international responses need to include strong sanctions against the private enablers, like solicitors and accountants, particularly when they facilitate tax evasion.

---

223 Mansour, M. B. (2019), "New ranking reveals corporate tax havens behind breakdown of corporate tax system; toll of UK's tax war exposed", *TaxJusticeNetwork*, 28/05/2019, www.taxjustice.net/2019/05/28/new-ranking-reveals-corporate-tax-havens-behind-breakdown-of-global-corporate-tax-system-toll-of-uks-tax-war-exposed/, accessed 08/08/2019.

224 VIDC, "Financial secrecy index 2018", www.attac.at/fileadmin/dateien/Presse/FSI_2018/Schattenfinanzindex_Ranking.pdf; Cobham, A., Jansky, P. & Meinzer, M. (2015), "The financial secrecy index: Shedding new light on the geography of secrecy", Center for Global Development Working Paper 404, May 2015, pp. 1–28.

225 OECD (2018), *Standard for automatic exchange of financial information in tax matters- implementation Handbook*, 2nd edition, Paris, OECD, www.oecd.org/tax/exchange-of-tax-information/implementation-handbook-standard-for-automatic-exchange-of-financial-information-in-tax-matters.pdf, accessed 08/08/2019.

226 OECD (2013), *Action plan on base erosion and profit shifting*, Paris, OECD, www.oecd.org/ctp/BEPSActionPlan.pdf, accessed 08/08/2019.

227 Lengwiler, Y. & Salijihaj, A. (2018), "The U.S. program for Swiss banks: What determined the penalties", *Swiss Journal of Economics and Statistics*, 154(1): 23–35.

More recent research by the BIS and the IMF[228] suggests a risk from the financialisation of economies where financial services, instead of serving businesses, become overly dominant.[229] Indeed, financial flows looking for secrecy or fleeing corporate taxes are precisely the type that would exacerbate this. It is also why many global regulators are worried about the anonymity and secrecy that cryptoassets can provide to users with assets to conceal.[230] Indeed, as tax havens come under closer international regulatory probing, cryptoassets offer, in many respects, a near-perfect alternative to tax evaders. As such, it is reasonable to envisage that as the market volume of cryptoassets increased, as they have over the past decade, so would the tax avoidance associated with it.

5.5 Comparative note

Alternative financing forms, such as crowdfunding, developed quickly subsequent to the 2008 global financial crash. People and small businesses in particular were perturbed by the excesses of financialisation. Private money such as cryptocurrencies became the next order of business in the financial space. The United States and the UK and major continental European economies took the lead in the mushrooming of cryptoassets hubs. It is still surprising to many people, as all these advanced Western economies all boast having the best and most powerful banking systems in the world.

It would be unsurprising, though, for three major reasons. First, the widening financial gaps between the haves (meaning the powerful big corporations and other financial elites) and the have nots (meaning the small businesses and the working people) identified the need to do something for the latter. Second, the latter argued for fairer and easier access to financial resources under more democratic means. Third, the squeeze-and-seize pressures from the said financial crisis induced many to question the infallibility of the monetary system controlled and managed by central authorities. These were said to be the main reasons behind the rise of the fintech space and its cryptoasset subset. The quest for private currency away from the sole controls of the government, together with the technological talents found in these advanced economies, helped usher in the world of cryptoassets.

Then the use of cryptoassets spread quickly to much of the rest of the world, given the interconnectedness of global financial systems and,

228 Cecchetti, S. G. & Kharroubi, E. (2015), "Why does financial sector growth crowd out real economic growth?", BIS Working Papers No. 490, February 2015, pp. 1–31, www.bis.org/publ/work490.pdf, accessed 08/08/2019; Arcand, J.-L., Enrico, M. & Panizza, U. (2012), "Too much finance?", IMF Working Paper WP/12/161, June 2012, pp. 1–50, www.imf.org/external/pubs/ft/wp/2012/wp12161.pdf, accessed 08/08/2019.

229 Smith, Y. (2015), "IMF paper finds that too much finance is bad for growth", *Naked Capitalism*, 20/05/2015, www.nakedcapitalism.com/2015/05/imf-paper-finds-that-too-much-finance-is-bad-for-growth.html, accessed 08/08/2019.

230 Marian, O. (2013), "Are cryptocurrencies super tax havens?", *Michigan Law Review First Impressions*, 112(1–2): 38–48.

importantly, the cross-border features of blockchain and cryptoassets. While the advanced Western economies saw the use of cryptoassets as part of its more mature democratisation system and, to some degree, inclusive participation by the disadvantaged, the reality is that cryptoassets are more fondly embraced by millennials, those with some secrets to shelter, those with nefarious intentions, and those simply with the greed for exponential profits. Taken together, they have the effect of propagating the deployment of cryptoassets across other parts of the world, but especially in many of the more affluent as well as the very large economies in Asia, respectively, Japan, South Korea, India, and China.

As highlighted earlier, the levels of cryptoasset activity are not necessarily linked to the kind of official attitude towards the use of cryptoassets. So while China bans the use of cryptoassets, many of their nationals engaged with them via private virtual networks into other economies more tolerant towards the use of these assets. Thus, a low official incidence of cryptoasset usage does not necessarily suggest low utilisation by the nationals in their respective jurisdictions, while high incidence could be attributed to utilisation by nationals beyond a designated jurisdiction. This thus marks out the cross-border nature of virtual currencies, and the reason the FATF tightened its rules against the risk of money laundering via the use of these kinds of virtual currencies.

The way and the pace upon which cryptoassets hubs proliferate is therefore the outcome of the financial system and nature of particular economies concerned. Globally, there are some concerns that the race to be premier fintech or cryptoassets hubs could, at some point, lead to enhanced risks to the stability of the global financial system. This is a reasonable view, given that various businesses and national economies have exploited the more favourable attitudes towards the use of blockchain technology rather than the use of cryptocurrencies when, in reality, they could be more involved with the propagation of the blockchain technology to promote the greater use of virtual currencies. The debate and controversies will likely continue unabated as long as there is the motivation to look for an alternative global virtual currency. This could further mean that such activities would gather momentum in tax havens even though lately some have provided laws and rules against the use of cryptoassets for illicit purposes. For those crypto businesses looking for the right jurisdiction for incorporation and operational base, this is not a trivial matter, and they need to examine particularly the regulatory maturity of operations' costs, the availability of talent pools, as well as the global reputation of the jurisdiction.[231] The next chapter will look at how national financial regulators grapple with the risks and dangers of cryptoassets.

231 PwC (2023), "Navigating the global crypto landscape with PwC: 2024 outlook", *PwC*, 07/12/2023, www.pwc.com/gx/en/industries/financial-services/assets/navigating-the-global-crypto-landscape-with-PwC-2024.pdf, accessed 20/12/2023.

CHAPTER 6

Cryptoasset policies of international bodies

6.1 Introduction

This chapter goes beyond the emerging national-based regulatory initiatives to multilateral regulatory approaches. It covers those focusing on economic advancement and anti–money laundering concerns, such as the G20 economies and the OECD, those whose role includes focusing on fintechs and techfins, such as the BIS and the IMF; those focusing on capital markets, such as the IOSCO; and those focusing on anti–money laundering, such as the FATF.

6.2 G20 economies

The G20, or Group of Twenty, was formed in 1999. It is an international forum represented by the governments and central bank governors of Argentina, Australia, Brazil, Canada, China, France, Germany, India, Indonesia, Italy, Japan, Mexico, the Republic of Korea, the Russian Federation, Saudi Arabia, South Africa, Turkey, the UK, the United States, and the EU as represented by the European Commission (EC) and the European Central Bank (ECB). The G20 engages in policies and actions to promote international financial stability, hosts leaders' summits, and has, in recent years, extended to cover forums involving finance and foreign ministers. The G20 economies together account for about 85% of the world's gross domestic product (GDP), 75% of world trade, and some two-thirds of the world's population.

Cryptoassets, and especially Bitcoin, have attracted the attention of the G20. They have expressed concerns over the potential spillover of risks into the economies of the existing international financial system. G20 member nations, driven mainly by France and Germany, made joint proposals to regulate cryptoassets at the March 2018 summit of the G20. These two advanced economies provided a joint Franco–German analysis of the relevant risks and included proposals for regulatory interventions. Arising from this development, arguments have been raised that there could be a link between the evolution of cryptoasset regulations and the 80% decline in Bitcoin prices from its peak of U$20,000 in mid-December 2017 to the end of 2018.[1]

1 Rivet, M., Le Guernigou, Y, Thomas, L. & Rose, M. (2018), "France, Germany to make joint Bitcoin regulation proposal at G20 summit", *Reuters*, 19/01/2018, https://uk.reuters.com/article/

DOI: 10.4324/9781032667416-6

The Franco–German initiative was supported by the United States, which did not then see cryptoassets as a serious threat to financial market stability and is more concerned over their deployment in money laundering and other illegal activities.[2] The United States already has a functioning cryptoasset working group dedicated to the investigation of the market to ensure that these are not being misused. The US Senate Banking Committee started meeting on 11 February 2025 with regard to the topic as part of a process of clarifying the legal and regulatory position on Crypto. President Trump's stated enthusiasm for the area will no doubt have an impact, but as of May 2025, it remains unclear as to how specifically this will operate. By comparison, the UK Select Committee Hearings have already made their recommendations pertaining to UK's regulatory stand on cryptoassets.[3]

The G20 communique issued on 28–29 June 2019 at the Osaka, Japan, summit stated that, whilst recognising that cryptoassets do not presently pose threats to global financial stability, they would nonetheless closely monitor their developments and remain vigilant to existing and emerging risks and have also requested standard-setting bodies like the FSB to advise on further multilateral responses as needed.[4] The G20 have also reaffirmed their commitment to applying the FATF Standards to cryptoassets and related providers for anti–money laundering and the countering of terrorism financing. The Virtual Asset Service Providers Summit (V20) held simultaneously in Osaka announced that a group of national trade associations representing virtual asset service providers signed a memorandum of understanding (MOU) for establishing an association that would assist in setting mechanisms to engage with government agencies and the FATF to ensure that their best interests are understood and appreciated at international forums. The G7 economies, comprising the world's most powerful economies (but excluding China and Russia, for political reasons), have examined the risks posed by cryptoassets since 2015. The G7 would, together with the G20, address the policy implications of cryptoassets, and in particular Facebook's Libra, as these could have an impact on the financial sovereignty of national economies.[5] Eventually, Facebook (now Meta) wound down the Libra (rebranded as "Diem") idea. This failed venture has since been treated as a case

us-global-bitcoin-france-germany/france-germany-to-make-joint-bitcoin-regulation-proposal-at-g20-summit-idUKKBN1F728X, accessed 02/02/2018.

2 Skolimowski, P. (2018), "Coeure urges G-20 to discuss regulating Bitcoin at March Meeting", *Bloomberg*, 26/01/2018, www.bloomberg.com/news/articles/2018-01-26/coeure-urges- g-20-to-discuss-regulating-bitcoin-at-march-summit, accessed 02/02/2018.

3 HM Treasury/FCA/Bank of England (October 2018), *Cryptoassets Taskforce: Final Report*, London, HM Treasury, https://assets.publishing.service.gov.uk/government/uploads/system/uploads/attachment_data/file/752070/cryptoassets_taskforce_final_report_final_web.pdf, accessed 02/11/2018.

4 G20 (2019), "Full text of the G20 Osaka leaders' declaration", *G20 Communique*, 29/06/2019, www.japantimes.co.jp/news/2019/06/29/national/full-text-g20-osaka-leaders-declaration/, accessed 02/07/2019.

5 Helms, K. (2019), "G7 agrees on crypto action plan spurred by Facebook's Libra", *Bitcoin.com*, 24/08/2019, https://news.Bitcoin.com/g7-agrees-cryptocurrency-action-plan-facebooks-libra/, accessed 26/08/2019.

of big tech hubris and a warning to those who might aspire to repeat the idea. An unintended effect, though, has been the development of a custom programming language, Move, to write smart contracts on the proposed blockchain, and thus, while the originally conceived cryptoasset proposal came to an end, Move lives on.[6] At the global level, G20 finance ministers and central bank governors (FMCBG) eventually adopted the new cryptoassets' regulatory roadmap that suggests a step away from an outright ban, focusing instead on proactive and collaborative oversight, as demonstrated in the IMF and FSB synthesis paper at the behest of the G20 presidency, chaired by India at that time.[7]

The IMF/FSB paper initiated advanced policy and regulatory recommendations to identify and respond to macroeconomic and financial stability risks linked to cryptoassets, including considerations and guidance for macroeconomic, legal, and financial integrity of implications to monetary and fiscal policies, as well as regulatory and supervisory recommendations and standards for dealing with crucial matters to do with financial integrity, financial stability, market integrity, investor protection, and prudential and other risks arising from the use and abuse of cryptoasset applications, such as seen in the collapse of FTX and other scandals. FSB's cryptoasset July 2023 roadmap comprised interlinked recommendations for the regulation, supervision, and oversight of crypto activities; and updated recommendations for global stablecoin, including its expectations for national authorities to ensure global stablecoin workings are supported by well structured comprehensive governance and risk supervision, systems, processes for gathering, storing, and effective protection of data.

6.3 The Organisation for Economic Co-operation and Development (OECD)

The OECD's mission is to promote policies that would improve the economic and social well-being of people around the world. It provides a forum by which governments can collaborate to share experiences and seek solutions to common problems. It works with governments to understand the underlying forces that drive economic, social, and environmental change. The OECD measures productivity and global flows of trade and investments. It also analyses and compares data to predict future trends.

The OECD sets international standards on a wide menu of matters, extending from agriculture and tax to the safety of chemicals. It also examines issues that directly impact on everyone's daily life, such as how much people pay in taxes and social security and how much leisure time they can have. The OECD's current agenda includes restoring confidence in markets and the institutions that

---

6 Morales, J. (2024), "Life after Libra: How Facebook's failed cryptocurrency kicked of a Web3 movement", *CCN*, 13/07/2024, www.ccn.com/news/crypto/libra-facebook-cryptocurrency-move-web3-language/, accessed 18/08/24

7 Comply Advantage (2024), "G20 finance ministers adopt new cryptoassets regulatory roadmap", *Comply Advantage*, 08/02/2024, https://complyadvantage.com/insights/g20-finance-ministers-adopt-new-cryptoassets-regulatory-roadmap/, accessed 18/07/24

make them function, re-establishing healthy public finance as a basis for future sustainable economic growth, and fostering new sources of growth through innovation, environmentally friendly green growth strategies, and the development of emerging economies.[8] Hence cryptocurrency and blockchain technology attracted the OECD's attention.

One OECD paper suggested the following:[9]

1. The 2008 global financial crisis prompted extensive erosion of trust in all categories of financial services that move towards greater positivity and towards deployment of alternative exponential technologies associated with industry.
2. Pertaining to the application of the Blockchain technology in the design of virtual or cryptocurrency, the OECD maintains that this would not undermine the ability and power of central banks in relation to monetary policy.
3. The OECD, nevertheless, raised concerns over consumer welfare protection and bank secrecy priorities. In particular, attention is drawn to Bitcoin's valuation and price volatility challenges, including electronic thefts, contracts failures, and so on, that could lead to large losses for consumers, with ultimate negative impact costs to taxpayers. The cryptocurrency's anonymity characteristic arguably facilitates money laundering and tax evasion that could snowball into significant public concerns.
4. Blockchain, as an innovative technology, going beyond its use in Bitcoin as a virtual currency could transform the core trust element in financial transactions. The blockchain, or decentralised ledger technology (DLT), enjoys the ability to shift to execute transactions without needing to rely on a trusted intermediary, thereby making the migration towards trustless transactions. This could lead to transaction cost reductions, particularly heralding healthy competition to incumbent financial services firms.
5. Importantly, the general aims of national and global policy considerations should involve encouraging technologies that foster healthy competition in the payments system (especially in mobile payments), as well as ensuring the proper use of cryptocurrencies.

Overall, various generic policy issues need to be explored.[10] Should there be a general ban on any form of the use of cryptocurrencies in the clearing system between banks and the central banks, there needs to be suitable systems and processes in place to ensure that the monetary system is not undermined.

8 OECD (2018), "About the OECD", *OECD*, www.oecd.org, accessed 02/02/2018.

9 Blundell-Wignall, A. (2014), "The Bitcoin question: Currency versus Trust-less transfer technology", *OECD Working Papers on Finance, Insurance and Private Pensions No. 37.*

10 Ibid note [9], Blundell-Wignall (2014).

Finally, should there be some form of agreement for best practice registration that permits consumer protection, tax, and anti–money laundering authorities to verify the owner's identity, the general aim of the policy should be to encourage technologies that improve competition in the payments system and to ensure that cryptocurrency use includes the revelation of the user's identity so as to avoid the darker aspects of Bitcoin use and to meet minimum requirements for consumer protection. The crypto community in general did not fully endorse the OECD's main suggestions.[11] Bans and prohibitions on cryptocurrencies in the interbank clearing system are likely to prove totally ineffective. A ban would enhance global awareness of cryptocurrencies, inspiring alternative and parallel clearing systems, and as a consequence, this could potentially end up harming the usefulness of existing clearing systems.

The technology supporting the Bitcoin network is distributed and decentralised for the reason that it had to be immune to plenary power shutdown and strong enough to sustain an attack from outside computational powers. The Bitcoin unit provides the incentive for maintaining the security and integrity of the blockchain, which makes it inseparable.

Cryptocurrency exchanges could be treated as financial institutions when exchange endpoints interface with national currencies and not merchants. Physical cash transactions do not typically demand owner identity verification, but when cryptocurrency exchanges are involved, the operating jurisdiction defines the required conditions around getting in and out of national fiat currency. These best practices registration could be conducted on an opt in basis.

With respect to balance sheet and income statement reporting for networks, market competition could demand exchange solvency and reporting of financial status. In response to the suggestion that mandatory capital should be held by exchanges in the form of legal tender, the Global Policy Counsel at the Bitcoin Foundation suggested that consumer protection may differ in the future, as the assumption of government regulation providing sophisticated commercial oversight becomes challenged. Cryptographic proof of reserves could deliver a responsible public audit of exchange assets as Bitcoin's cryptography based public ledger allows an organisation to prove control of Bitcoin assets without disclosing private information about consumer or account holders. Multi-signature transactions are a second innovation that might assist with consumer protection. They allow any combination of consumers and business entities to exercise control over a Bitcoin-based asset. Such innovations and others forthcoming would tend to render consumer oversight of Bitcoin businesses easier and government oversight a less important part of the mix. Consumers could be better placed to apply their own monitoring and, in the best case, to enjoy cryptographic proof that they are being properly served.

Requesting gold backing for Bitcoin suggests a gold backed Bitcoin that would lead to centralisation in the manner of specific reserves and would

11 Matonis, J. (2014), "Why the OECD needs to do its homework on Bitcoin", *Coin Desk*, 01/07/2014, www.coindesk.com/oecd-needs-homework-bitcoin, accessed 02/02/2018.

irreparably damage the incentive structure for securing the distributed blockchain, which precludes the process of new Bitcoin issuance. The sovereign power to collect taxes and declare legal tender imbues a currency with ultimate value, but it is still based on a state-sanctioned illusion. The question of political control over the monetary system is the greatest litmus test for discovering those that seek control over others. In practice, it would be cloaked in terms such as *full employment*, *price stability*, *temporary stimulus*, *quantitative easing*, and *economic growth*, but manipulation of money supply serves only to favour the issuers of that particular monetary unit. Here, Bitcoin is the primary value unit and requires backing from neither state sanction nor gold. It is freedom in the monetary standard untouched by the politicising process. At some level, money requires a leap of faith. The belief in gold requires this, too, as the non-monetary value assigned to gold is arguably no more than 5% of its market price. This, however, is also what makes Bitcoin the ultimate social money, because for its value, it merely requires others to accept it, not the law.[12] Money is already the most viral thing on earth, and the network effects exponentially reinforce that.

It is further argued that governments could no longer maintain a monopoly position over money because an alternative exists, and that alternative does not rely on legal tender status for its legitimacy. It relies on global acceptance of the mathematics behind the protocol for its market based legitimacy. Such arguments have their roots in the Hayek notion of private currency.[13]

A subsequent OECD cryptocurrency analysis undertaken in the context of disruptive innovation in financial services teased out various issues.[14] The OECD treats virtual currencies as stores of value that can be traded between users. While Bitcoin is the best known, there are more than a hundred others. The ECB estimated the combined value of cryptocurrencies around the world at about €3.3 billion as of February 2015. Trades of currency occur over currency exchanges on the internet, often with the exchanges of cryptocurrency used as payment for real-world goods. Cryptocurrencies have limited issuance, and they use digital techniques for securing the transactions. On the one hand, this provides confirmation of the ownership of each coin keeping track of the entire history of ownership in a blockchain to ensure that one unit of virtual currency cannot be sold multiple times by one owner. On the other hand, they do not necessarily identify the trader's full identity publicly.

Unlike nationally issued fiat currencies, cryptocurrencies are not backed by the full faith and credit of national governments, nor are they governed by a regulation that restricts activities such as legally preventing the sudden introduction

12 Matonis, J. (2013), "The fiat emperor has no clothes", *Forbes*, 18/04/2013, www.forbes.com/sites/jonmatonis/2013/04/18/the-fiat-emperor-has-no-clothes/#40af66f26e9e, accessed 02/02/2018.

13 Ferrara, P. (2013), "Rethinking money: The rise of Hayek's private competing currencies", *Forbes*, 01/03/2013, http://www.forbes.com/sites//peterferrara/2013/03/01/rethinking-money-the-rise-of-heyeks-private-competing-currencies/, accessed 05/08/2025.

14 Emmis, S. (2015), "Hearing on disruptive innovation in the financial sector-note by the (OECD) secretariat", *OECD Secretariat Working Paper Party No. 20 on Competition and Regulation Paper*, 26/10/2015.

of more currency. Provided the expectations of purchasers that others would accept the virtual currency as a store of value, they might be willing to purchase it. Cryptocurrencies differ from these in the ease with which they could be transformed back into legal tender currency, mainly through exchanges and trading platforms performing this conversion. They are alternatives to cash and other fiat currencies and are smaller and more secure than paper currencies. Cryptocurrency owners have the potential to achieve profits both from the float and from issuing initial currency to themselves.

As a consequence of the apparent anonymity of transactions, some users of cryptocurrencies misused them for improper and illicit activities, such as money laundering and a transfer of value for illegal goods. In response, some governments have taken measures that effectively rules out their use as currencies. These suggest a clear and implied possibility of governments' declaring cryptocurrencies to be illegal, though at present this is not the general direction of travel. The focus on them as mechanisms for fraudulent transactions could be attributed to a perceived high frequency of improper motives behind their use. This, in turn, is the consequence of the apparent anonymity built into the system. Arguably, cash functions as a more anonymous way of transferring value than virtual currencies. The ownership string of a cryptocurrency is public, but not the actual owner's name and address. Where that name and address are, in some stages, identified by law enforcers, the latter have a powerful instrument to track entire chains of value in manners that cash would never enable. Hence, the arguments against cryptocurrency anonymity could be much weaker than comparable arguments against cash.

Governments worry that virtual currencies could substantially supplant the fiat currency they issue, as it could put at risks central banks' abilities to conduct monetary policy, while the seigniorage from issuing currency could be reduced. However, it has been argued that cryptocurrencies cannot undermine the ability of central banks to conduct monetary policy, as long as taxes are paid in legal tender, that, in turn, necessitates that banks be able to clear with the government's bank or central banks. Supplanting does not appear to be a significant risk for now, as the level of public trust in virtual currencies is limited. Nonetheless, to the extent that a regulator is empowered to regulate virtual currencies in the future, it is debatable whether central banks should be given the role to regulate cryptocurrencies, or whether other bodies with less direct financial interest in the regulator outcome could be more apt. Central banks and finance ministries might have interests to maintain seigniorage, but they also have a counterbalancing experience with the oversight of money.

Undoubtedly, the risks from using cryptocurrencies are real. Exchanges could be breached, as has already happened in a few cases recently. For cryptocurrencies to succeed and grow, rules would be needed, providing clear guidelines on registration and KYC rules. Their repudiation as a currency, as has happened in China, Germany, France, South Korea, and Thailand, would clearly make operating cryptocurrencies as a virtual currency a challenge. Even where they are permitted, only an estimated 3 out of 10,000 merchants accept them.

Where competition between cryptocurrencies is encouraged, a clear identification of them as currencies would be needed. The UK, for instance, for now exempts them from VAT, thus treating them in and of themselves as currencies and not as goods and services. Simultaneously, the UK requires cryptocurrencies to provide mechanisms to prevent money laundering. Australia treats them as currencies, while the US IRS issued guidance treating them as property, and the US CFTC treats them as a commodity.

To the extent possible, regulations should ensure that a level playing field exists between banks and P2P lenders, but that the relevant regulations should be proportionate to the perceived risks and needs. Only time will confirm whether such a regulatory approach will yield clear benefits or allow pent up risks to develop. Regulation alone might not generate the desired result if not complemented by sufficient information, awareness, and education for investors, issuers, users, or borrowers.

The OECD 2019 Global Blockchain Policy Forum (OECD GBPF) highlighted the helpfulness for policymakers and pertinent stakeholders to fully understand what blockchain is and where its applications can add value, and hence the importance of the education aspects of blockchain. The OECD GBPF reinforces the need for a collaborative, multi-stakeholder policy approach that protects both the rights of citizens and the flow of innovations. By extension, such collaborations need to embrace the borderless nature of blockchain itself, implying that governments and innovators globally should share data pertaining to the outcomes of pilots, regulatory sandboxes, and other excursions into DLT applications. Instead of exacerbating inequality and environmental issues, the OECD GBPF advocated the tapping of blockchain technology for the advancement of sustainable development and human rights. These are particularly evident where financial inclusion and supply chain due diligence are concerned.

It merits noting that the EU's European System of Accounts 2010 contains a section on "borderline cases", which requires the inclusion and reporting of the so called illegal trade in its respective members' GDP. This working paper contended that even when a cryptocurrency is not declared illegal, discussing the possibility that it could be made so might undermine its value.[15]

The OECD's special adviser, Joseph Weinberg, commented positively on the quality of due diligence undertaken by cryptocurrency exchanges with regards to KYC/AML compliance. He added that most crypto exchanges processing fiat to crypto transactions are very compliant, and in some cases, even more so than banks. He cited a recent review that stated that Australian banks make potential customers go through a less stringent due diligence process than crypto exchanges, while for crypto exchanges, the challenge lies in how little formal guidelines there are from regulators, and as a consequence, most of the industries have been engaging in self compliance in the absence of clear procedures

15 Cohen, B. (2015), "OECD: Simply 'Discussing' Bitcoin illegality is mutually damaging", *Coin Telegraph*, 03/01/2015, www.cointelegraph.com/news/oecd-discussing-possible-Bitcoin-illegality-is-mutually-damaging, accessed 02/02/2018.

and, as a consequence, overregulate themselves to err on the safe side.[16] This phenomenon of strict self regulation, coupled with a rather vague regulatory feedback, is not unique to Australia as it is being observed around the world, notably in China and South Korea. Not many businesses wish to operate in a legal grey area; thus, the lack of clear regulation has led many cryptocurrency exchanges to over-regulate themselves to err on the side of caution and to show their commitment to legitimate operations.[17]

The OECD has now started looking at the accounting implications, starting at the meeting of the Working Party on Financial Statistics on 3 November 2018.[18] They have also called for a global ICO regulation, stressing the high risks and asking for a standardised set of regulations to avoid money laundering. This appears to be happening anyway, as evidenced by the 5th EU Anti-laundering Directive.

The OECD's further insights on ICOs suggest that ICOs, by their nature, are not the optimal solution for every venture.[19] For instance, blockchain enabled products/services have a higher opportunity of benefiting from an ICO offering. Specifically, ICOs are especially beneficial for products/services underpinned by networks.

The OECD is of the view that clarity in the regulatory and supervisory framework could be a good stepping stone to the safer deployment of token issuance for financing purposes. These could include standardised disclosure requirements and expanded investor protection for retail investors, together with enhanced awareness of risks by retail investors that could fortify their informed participation in such financing.[20] In the context of unique risks posed by cryptoassets, as highlighted by the FBI,[21] AML/CTF requirements on ICO issuance are of particular importance.

The OECD is presently working on cryptoassets and the applications of DLT in financial services, and its Committee on Financial Markets released a report looking at the potential benefits from the deployment of regulated ICOs for small business capital formation, the issuing and trading of tokens, tokenomics, limitations in ICO designs, together with the risks to which investors subscribing to ICO offerings and SMEs issuing tokens are exposed to. Insights were also generated on the potential of ICOs as mainstream financing instruments

16 Munro, A. (2018), "OECD advisor: Cryptocurrency exchanges are over-regulating themselves", *Finder*, 28/02/2018, www.finder.com.au/oecd-advisor-cryptocurrency-exchanges-are-over- regulating-themselves, accessed 03/03/2018.

17 Ibid note [16], Munro (2018).

18 OECD (2018), "Joint meeting of the Working Party on Financial Statistics and the Working Party on National Accounts", *OECD COM/SDD/DAF/A(2018)*, 2, 03/11/2018, www.oecd.org/officialdocuments/publicdisplaydocumentpdf/?cote=COM/SDD/DAF/A(2018)2& docLanguage=En, accessed 07/02/2020. 18 Ibid note [1], Helms (2020).

19 Nassr, I. K. (2019), "Initial coin offerings (ICOs) for SME financing", *OECD*, January 2019, www.oecd.org/finance/ICOs-for-SME-Financing.pdf, accessed 05/03/2019.

20 Ibid note [19], Nassr (2019).

21 Ibid note [19], Nassr (2019).

for SMEs, regardless of project types or business models used by the business.[22] This latest OECD report on cryptoassets called for clarity and proportionality in the regulatory and supervisory framework applied to ICOs. The 2nd annual OECD Blockchain Policy Forum, held on 12–13 September 2019, included high-level discussion on these issues, as well as the outcome of the OECD study on tokenisation of assets. This was combined with a consideration of the possible proliferation that such mechanisms would have on financial markets, as well as an analysis of the benefits and risks of stablecoins.[23]

The preceding suggests that a delicate balance is needed when developing regulatory and supervisory requirements that would not deprive the ICO mechanism of its speed and cost benefits in relation to smaller size offerings. In this respect, a proportional application of regulatory requirements such as those deployed in small public equity offerings merits positive consideration.[24] Co-operation at the global level is needed, given the global nature of ICO issuing and cross-border trading. This would prevent regulatory arbitrage and enable ICOs to achieve their potential for the funding of blockchain-based SMEs while protecting investors appropriately.

The OECD has recently reaffirmed[25] the Crypto-Asset Reporting Framework (CARF) and a set of amendments to the Common Reporting Standard (CRS), together with the associated commentaries and exchange of information frameworks, collectively known as the International Standards for Automatic Exchange of Information in Tax Matters (AEOI). These were adopted earlier on 15 July 2014 and revised on 8 June 2023.[26]

6.4 The International Monetary Fund (IMF)

The IMF recognises both the benefits and perils of cryptocurrencies. It said that regulatory responses to cryptocurrencies are still at an early phase because they are difficult to regulate, as they cut across the responsibilities of different agencies at the national level and function on a global scale.[27] Many cryptoassets are seen to be opaque and operate outside of the conventional financial system, making it difficult to monitor their operations. The IMF raised several issues.[28] Cryptocurrencies are digital representations of value, issued by private developers and denominated in their own unit of account. They can be obtained, stored, accessed, and transacted electronically. The expression "cryptocurrencies"

22 OECD (2019), *Initial coin offerings (ICOs) for SME financing*, Paris, OECD.

23 FSB (2019), "Crypto-assets: Work underway, regulatory approaches and potential gaps", *FSB*, 31/05/2019, www.fsb.org/wp-content/uploads/P310519.pdf, accessed 02/07/2019.

24 Ruggeieri, N. (2019), "Making a list and checking it twice: The FBI highlights key features in SCO scams", *Eth News*, 20/02/2019, www.ethnews.com/making-a-list-and-checking-it-twicethe-fbi-highoights-key, accessed 05/03/2019.

25 CTPA/CFA (2022) 16 and CPTA/CFA (2023) 5

26 OECD/LEGAL/0407, http://legalinstruments.oecd.org/, accessed 18/07/2023

27 He, D., et al. (2016), "Virtual currencies and beyond: Initial considerations", *IMF Staff Discussion Note SDN/16/03/012016*.

28 Ibid note [27], He et al. (2016).

covers a broad range of currencies, from simple IOUs of issuers, like mobile coupons, to airline miles, cryptocurrencies, and those backed by gold.[29] Cryptocurrencies are used interchangeably with cryptoassets, and vice versa, in most mainstream policy and research papers. The ECB, the European Banking Authority (EBA), the ESMA, the World Bank, the IMF, and the FATF classify cryptocurrencies as a subset of virtual or digital currencies or a form of unregulated digital money, while the Bank for International Settlements qualifies cryptocurrencies as digital currencies or digital currency schemes characterised by asset with value, use of distributed ledgers and not operated by any particular institution. There is thus no generally accepted definition of cryptocurrencies in the regulatory domain other than those provided by the World Bank and the FATF, while most policymakers avoid defining the term and treat cryptocurrencies as a kind of virtual or digital currencies. The FATF and the World Bank, as alluded to earlier though, provided more precise definitions. Some mainstream legal scholars have defined a cryptocurrency as

> a digital representation of value that (i) is intended to constitute a peer-to-peer (P2P) alternative to a government-issued legal tender, (ii) is used as a general-purpose medium of exchange (independent of any central bank), (iii) is secured by a mechanisms known as cryptography and (iv) can be converted into legal tender and vice-versa.[30]

Still, for reasons mentioned earlier they too prefer to use the terms cryptocurrencies, digital currencies and cryptoassets interchangeably. Much therefore depends on the ultimate direction of the research and the disciplinary perspective used. As digital representation of value, cryptocurrencies fall within the wider category of digital currencies but differentiated from the others such as e-money, a digital payment system for and denominated in fiat currency as cryptocurrencies are not denominated in fiat currency and have their own unit of account.

Non-convertible cryptoassets (or closed system ones) function exclusively within self-contained environments where the exchange of cryptocurrencies with fiat currencies or other virtual ones, or their use in payment for goods and services outside of the virtual domain, is significantly restricted.[31] Convertible cryptocurrencies, or open schemes, facilitate their exchange with fiat currency or other cryptos and for the payment of goods and services in the real economy. Interaction levels between convertible cryptocurrencies and the real economy are more extensive than in closed schemes. They can function via centralised,

29 Houben, R. & Snyers, A. (2018), "Cryptocurrencies and blockchain: Legal context and implications for financial crime, money laundering and tax evasion", *European Parliament Study PE 619.024*, July 2018, www.europarl.europa.eu/cmsdata/150761/TAX3%20Study%20on%20cryptocurrencies%20and%20blockchain.pdf, accessed 01/02/2019.

30 www.fatf-gafi.org/en/topics.virtual-assets.html, accessed 04/05/2025

31 FATF (2014), "Virtual currencies: Key definitions and potential AML/CTF risks", *FATF Report*, July 2014, www.fatf-gafi.org/media/fatf/documents/reports/Virtual-currency-key-definitions-and-potential-aml-cft-risks.pdf, accessed 02/03/2019.

decentralised or hybrid models. Cryptocurrency schemes include their issuance and redeemability, mechanisms to implement and enforce internal rules on the use and circulation of the currency, and the payments and settlement process. Each of these could be managed by a trusted agency and private party or in decentralised among participants. Hybrid schemes exist where some functions are undertaken by a central authority with others distributed among market participants.

The IMF argues that decentralised schemes employ techniques from cryptography for their operations and thus it is appropriate to call them "cryptocurrencies". In decentralised schemes there is no central party such as a central bank administering the system or issuing them. These systems could allow for the issuance of a limited or unlimited number of currency units. Most cryptocurrencies are pseudo anonymous, where the transactions are publicly recorded but users are known only by their virtual currency addresses, which cannot be traced back to the users' real world identities. They are as such more transparent than cash but more anonymous than other kinds of online payment. Cryptocurrencies challenge the standard concept of fiat currencies. The latter are backed by the creditworthiness of the central bank and the government. The value of privately issued virtual currencies have historically been supported by the private issuers' credibility and commodity reserves. The value of cryptocurrencies, however, does not enjoy backing from any sources and derive their value solely from the expectation that others would also value and use them.

When deliberating on the role of cryptoassets as money, questions arise as to whether they satisfy the legal definition of money and fulfil all the economic roles of money such as store of value, medium of exchange and unit of account? Questions are also raised as to how they compare to other privately issued monies that existed historically and whether they qualify as substitutes for fiat currencies when used more widely. Both historic and economic theory seem to support a monetary regime with public provisions of currency over a competitive private system. The historical track record of containing inflation is mixed across both public and private systems, but public systems appear to function when there is a systemic liquidity shortage at the time of a financial crisis and the need arises for a lender of last resort.

Cryptocurrencies fall short of the legal concept of currency or money.[32] The legal notion of currency is associated with the power of the sovereign to establish a legal framework providing for central issuance of banknotes and coins. This being the case, the value and credibility of a sovereign currency are intrinsically linked with the ability of the state to support that currency. It is also based on the power of the state to regulate the monetary system. The concept of money as a legal matter is wider than the concept of currency, as it includes not

32 Carney, M. (2018), "The future of money", *Mark Carney, Governor Bank of England, Speech Delivered at the inaugural Scottish Economics Conference Edinburgh University*, 02/03/2018, www.bankofengland.co.uk/-/media/boe/files/speech/2018/the-future-of-money-speech-by-markcarney, accessed 08/03/2018.

only banknotes and coins but also instruments such as demand deposits. While money could be created by private parties like banks as well as central banks, it must be generally denominated in a currency issued by a sovereign authority and must be intended to serve as a generally accepted medium of exchange within that state.

For now, the IMF and others argue that cryptoassets do not completely fulfil the three economic roles associated with money. Their high price volatility limits their ability to serve as a reliable store of value and their use as a medium of exchange is restricted by the small size and limited acceptance network of those who will accept them. There appears to be little evidence that cryptocurrencies are used as independent units of account. Rather than measuring the value of goods and services directly they instead represent the value in fiat currency based on the cryptocurrencies' exchange rate. Retailers quote prices in fiat currency, with the price in cryptocurrency based on the exchange rate at a particular point in time.

Along with other developments in financial technology, distributed ledger modalities could herald important structural shifts in the financial industry.[33] In play already are growing numbers of blockchain-based financial services provided by non-bank start-ups, while some e-commerce firms are actively exploring the technology. Simultaneously, large global banks are also participating. Large technological changes have historically led to significant adjustments in market shares, with new firms often gaining at the expense of established ones. At the minimum, the internal structure and staffing of conventional financial intermediaries is likely to focus on technology skills.

Cryptoassets are a relatively novel phenomenon and have surfaced in the absence of effective regulation.[34] This led to their potential benefits, like low transaction fees and processing time, but has left unaddressed the risks they pose. These risks are most serious with respect to cryptocurrencies but are not limited to them. Risks fall into a continuum, with immediate and pressing concerns about financial integrity pertaining to money laundering and terrorism financing (AML/CTF), consumer protection, tax evasion and the regulation of capital movements. Concerns about financial stability or the implications of monetary policy are less immediate, but would require further analysis and monitoring. The growing interest in blockchain technology, separate from a cryptoassets scheme, a priori raises fewer policy concerns as the technology could be used in a closed system administered by regulated financial institutions.

33 Garg, G., Vudayagiri, Pillai, S. G. & Sharma, R. (2017), "Top 10 trends in payments 2018: What you need to know", *Capgemini Paper*, October 2017, www.capgemini.com/wp-content/uploads/2017/12/payments-trends_2018.pdf, accessed 12/12/2018.

34 IOSCO (2019), "Issues, risks and regulatory considerations relating to crypto-asset trading platforms", *IOSCO Consultation Report CRO2/2019*, May 2019, www.iosco.org/library/pubdocs/pdf/IOSCOPD627.pdf, accessed 03/06/2019.

The effective regulation of cryptocurrencies poses unique challenges in various ways.[35] They posed a definitional challenge to regulators as they combined properties of currencies, commodities and payment systems. Their classification as one or the other could have implications for their legal and regulatory treatments, such as determining which national agencies should regulate them. The disparity of treatment within and among jurisdictions may hamper coordination and could lead to inconsistencies. Cryptocurrency schemes are difficult to monitor too due to their opaque nature by design. The transactional reach of virtual currencies complicate regulation as national regulators may find it difficult to enforce laws and regulations in a virtual online environment. Questions swirl around who to regulate because of their decentralised nature: individual users or other participants within the system.

Different regulatory responses have surfaced to address the risks posed by this new technology, while paying attention to the policy priorities of each jurisdiction.[36] Policymakers often seek to find the balance between solving the risks and vulnerabilities posed by virtual currencies, while not stifling innovation. Some economies ban their use; others address particular risks pertaining to financial integrity, tax evasion and consumer protection, in particular by amending or clarifying the interpretations of existing laws and regulations; and yet others by issuing consumer warnings. Various jurisdictions have yet to take a formal position. When deliberating on who to regulate, national authorities have mostly targeted cryptocurrency market participants and financial institutions interacting with them. The interface between cryptocurrencies and the wider economy would often go through a virtual currency exchange or other relevant service provider. Also, because of the limited size of the cryptoasset network, virtual currency users would at some point need to "cash out", meaning converting their cryptocurrency into fiat currency. Taking cognisance of these practices and features of the current market, regulators have targeted the gatekeepers by regulating cryptoasset market participants providing an interface with the wider economy, such as cryptocurrency exchanges, and by restricting the ability of regulated entities like banks to interact with cryptocurrencies and their market participants.

The effectiveness of emerging regulatory initiatives would depend on how the cryptoasset market evolves. Their more widespread use might warrant a more comprehensive regulatory response. For instance, where the system operates more on a P2P basis, regulating cryptoasset gatekeepers might be inadequate. In this respect, a few regulators have gone further and are regulating a wider range of virtual cryptoasset market participants, such as wallet service providers

35 Poskriakov, F., Chiriaeva, M., Cavin, C. & Staehelin, L. (2019), "Cryptocurrency compliances and risks: A European KYC/AML perspective", in Dewey, J. (ed.), *Blockchain & cryptocurrency regulation*, London, Global Legal Insights, pp. 162–173.

36 Blandin, A., Cloots, A. S., Hussain, H., Rauchs, M., Saleuddin, Allen, J. G., Zhang, B. & Cloud, K. (2019), *Global cryptoasset regulatory landscape study*, Cambridge, Cambridge Centre for Alternative Finance (CCAF).

operating entirely within the system. The evolving nature of the technology requires regulation to be flexible to adapt to the evolving circumstances.

Regulatory responses are also being adopted at the global level. These tend to focus on achieving consensus on the potential benefits and risks of virtual currencies and seeking areas for future co-operation. Some have provided forums to discuss cryptocurrency matters and have contributed to the issuance of reports, guidance, and manuals in their areas of expertise. The FATF has contributed the AML/CTF standard setter,[37] while the UN Office on Drugs and Crime (UNODC) focuses on the prevention and law enforcement response to the money laundering risks they pose.[38] The Committee on Payments and Market Infrastructures (CPMI)[39] reviews the implications of cryptocurrencies as a means of exchange and distributed ledger technologies for central banks. Others contributing to the dialogues and debate include the OECD, the EBA, and the Commonwealth Secretariat.

More initiatives could be taken at the international level to facilitate the development of suitable policy responses. With experience, developing international standards and best practices could be considered to provide guidance on the most suitable regulatory responses in different fields to promote harmonisation across jurisdictions. These standards could also offer frameworks for co-operation and coordination across economies over questions such as the sharing of information and the investigation and prosecution of cross border offences.[40] Specific risks are attached to cryptocurrencies pertaining to financial integrity, consumer protection, tax evasion and treatment, enforcement of exchange controls, financial stability, and monetary policy.

Financial integrity, i.e., the anonymity and cross border reach of cryptocurrencies raises genuine concerns from a financial integrity perspective.[41] These vulnerabilities are not merely theoretical but are exploited in practice. Cryptocurrencies are frequently the currency of choice in cyber related criminal activity. Bitcoin was used in Silk Road, a dark web market place for illegal goods that was eventually shut down by US law enforcement authorities in 2013. Applying AML/CTF controls to cryptocurrency transactions can help to prevent such abuses. The FATF, the international standard setter for AML/CTF, has provided

37 FATF (2019), "FATF report to the G20 Leaders' Summit", *FATF Report*, June 2019, www.fatf-gafi.org/media/fatf/content/images/G20-June-2019.pdf, accessed 03/07/2019.

38 UNODC (2017), "The global programme against money laundering, proceeds of crime and the financing of terrorism 2011–2017", *UNODC Report GLOU40Global*, 02/10/2017, www.unodc.org/documents/evaluation/indepth-evaluations/2017/GLOU40_GPML_Mid-Term_In-Depth_Evaluation_Final_Report_October_2017.pdf, accessed 08/10/2018.

39 CPMI (2018), "Cryptocurrencies: Looking beyond the hype", *BIS Annual Economic Report 2018 91–114*, 17/06/2018, www.bis.org/publ/arpdf/ar2018e5.htm, accessed 08/10/2018.

40 Helms, K. (2019), "G20 leaders issue declaration on cryptoassets-a look at their commitments", *G20 Osaka Summit 2019 Communique*, Bitcoin, 01/07/2019, https://news.bitcoin.com/g20-leaders-declaration-crypto-assets-commitments/, accessed 11/08/2019.

41 Katarzyna, C. (2019), "Cryptocurrencies: Opportunities, risks and challenges for anti-corruption compliance systems", *OECD Paper Presented at OECD Conference Centre Paris 20–21st March 2019*, www.oecd.org/corruption/integrity-forum/academic-papers/Ciupa-Katarzyna-cryptocurrencies.pdf, accessed 23/06/2019.

some guidance on the application of the AML/CTF standards to virtual currencies. Their stance reflects the current knowledge of the money laundering/terrorism funding (ML/TF) risks but might eventually need to be expanded to other virtual currency network participants, such as wallet service providers and payment processors, operating entirely within the system. Such entities could be treated as covered entities required to implement the preventive AML/CTF measures.

Enforcement would remain challenging despite dealing with these changes. In decentralised virtual currency schemes, law enforcement may not have a counterparty like a central administrator to deal with for investigative purposes and to implement freezing and seizing orders on funds held in virtual currencies. It is thus difficult for regulators to take enforcement actions like the freezing of assets and the seizure and confiscation of illicit assets in such circumstances. FATF guidance has helped to clarify the suitable responses to the ML/TF risks generated by cryptocurrencies, but different jurisdictions have taken different approaches to regulating them. The United States, Germany, UK and Canada have acted to clarify the applicability of existing AML/CTF obligations to certain cryptocurrency businesses, usually finding that their administrators and exchanges fall within covered entities for the purpose of AML/CTF preventive measures. Other jurisdictions usually do not, while China bars interaction between virtual currency businesses and the formal banking sector.

The regulatory uncertainty and lack of transparency in virtual currencies generates significant consumer vulnerability. Such risks could be in relation to cryptocurrency systems, virtual currency intermediaries and service providers, scams, or those risks related to the irreversibility of transactions. Policy responses focus on increasing awareness[42] of users and investors about these risks and clarifying the scope of relevant legislation.

Cryptocurrencies have high potential to be used as a vehicle for tax evasion,[43] more so where participants need not disclose their identity, transactions are P2P and can occur across borders. To the extent that they are performing as store of value or a medium of exchange they raise potential tax implications. A key issue concerns whether they should be treated as a form of non-monetary property or as a form of currency. The former could pertain to capital gains or losses and the latter foreign exchange gains or losses. Additional issues include the tax treatment of newly created cryptocurrencies obtained through mining as against acquiring already ones that already exist, and the VAT and sales tax treatment

42 Securities and Exchange Commission (SEC) (2018), "Investor alert: Ponzi schemes using virtual currencies", *SECPu.No.153(7/13)*, www.sec.gov/investor/alerts/ia_virtualcurrencies.pdf, accessed 10/03/2019.

43 Hardy, P. D., Went, A. M. & Pierson, S. (2019), "IRS highlights international efforts to tackle cryptocurrency abuse, money laundering and tax evasion", *Ballard Spahr LLP*, 09/12/2019, www.moneylaunderingnews.com/2019/12/irs-ci-highlights-international-efforts-to-tackle- cryptocurrency-abuse-money-laundering-and-tax-evasion/, accessed 07/02/2020.

of transactions they involve.[44] Greater international consistency should be promoted in these and related areas. Record keeping requirements for virtual currencies could be substantial and may reduce their appeal in everyday use.

Cryptocurrencies may also be used to circumvent exchange and capital requirements as reported in the media, notably in China, Venezuela, Cyprus, Greece, North Korea and possibly other jurisdictions too.[45] Cryptocurrencies have arguably as yet to enter the mainstream financial system to pose significant systemic financial risks as per present positions of various national and global regulators. They have, however, cautioned that as cryptocurrencies achieve larger scale use and greater interconnectedness with other parts of the financial system especially via the mobile payments landscape, various financial risks could arise.[46] However, their potentially larger scale use and greater interconnectedness with other parts of the financial sector could in due course give rise to significant systemic financial risks.[47] Cryptocurrency users face payment system risks such as operational risk, credit risk, liquidity risks and legal risk.[48] Cryptocurrencies and blockchains are also vulnerable to cryptographic risks. Under a tail risks scenario, some schemes or blockchains could become too big, too interconnected to fail, and could also be difficult to resolve.

Regulatory responses to financial stability concerns are still at the nascent stage. These raise a number of challenges for policymakers and regulators at both the national and international levels. Questions at the national level revolve around whether some cryptocurrency intermediaries could replace the functions of a bank, requiring them to be regulated in a similar fashion, or whether cryptocurrencies in virtual currency wallets should be considered as deposits protected by deposit insurance schemes.[49] At the international level, given the cross border nature of virtual currency networks, questions arise as to who should oversee the cryptocurrency and asset markets and others using the blockchain technology in payment, settlement and other activities.[50] While internationally agreed regulatory principles and co-operation among national authorities would

44 HM Revenue & Customs (HMRC) (2018), "Tax on cryptoassets", *HMRC*, 19/12/2018, www.gov.uk/government/publications/tax-on-cryptoassets, accessed 21/02/2019.

45 Redman, J. (2019), "Venezuelan government accused of using bitcoin to bypass US sanctions", *Bitcoin.com*, 25/07/2019, https://news.Bitcoin.com/venezuelan-government-accused-of-using-Bitcoin-to-bypass-us-sanctions/, accessed 27/07/2019.

46 Ibid note [40], Helms (2019).

47 Inman, P. & Monaghan, A. (2019), "Facebook's Libra cryptocurrency 'poses risks to global banking'", *The Guardian*, 23/06/2019, www.theguardian.com/technology/2019/jun/23/facebook-libra-cryptocurrency-poses-risks-to-global-banking, accessed 25/06/2019.

48 Thackeray, J. (2018), "Breaking down the inherent risks of cryptocurrencies", *academia.edu*, www.academia.edu/37252500/Breaking_down_the_inherent_risks_of_Cryptocurrency, accessed 18/01/2019.

49 Library of Congress (2019), "Regulation of cryptocurrency around the world", www.loc.gov/law/help/cryptocurrency/world-survey.php, accessed 18/09/2019.

50 Silva, D. (2017), "Cryptocurrencies: International regulation and uniformization of practices", *United Nations Commission on International Trade Law (UNCITRAL) Paper*, www.uncitral.org/pdf/english/congress/Papers_for_Congress/29-DOLES_SILVA-Cryptocurrencies_and_International_Regulation.pdf, accessed 19/01/2019.

be beneficial, the appropriate framework for such co-operation remains to be defined.

Cryptocurrencies do not currently have significant implications for monetary policy, but some concerns could arise where they become more widely used. By design, cryptocurrencies such as Bitcoin have limited inflationary risks unlike other private currencies that came before it. That said, current systems lack other critical features that stable monetary regimes would typically be expected to provide. These include guarding against the risk of structural deflation, flexibility to respond to temporary shocks to money demand, and the capacity to function as a lender of last resort (LOLR).[51] Moreover, the near fixed supply of cryptocurrencies could lead to deflation in the same manner as gold standard. In general, in an economy with a high share of cryptocurrencies the ability of monetary policy to manage the business cycle could be diminished. Importantly, they would be unable to replace the LOLR function of central banks. Experience and economic theory suggest that a public agency is needed to solve the externalities and coordination failures that arise in such cases. In the absence of regulatory measures and other interventions, cryptocurrencies would be more readily adopted in countries with less credible monetary policies.

Cryptocurrencies are still rapidly evolving and the future landscape remains difficult to predict. They offer benefits and perils. The development of effective regulatory responses are still at an early phase. National authorities' potential regulatory responses should be commensurate to the risks without stifling innovation; adapt to the challenges emerging in the cryptocurrency landscape; have design approaches that take into account the novel business models inherent in such schemes; and address not only market conduct issues such as AML/CTF and fraud but also the financial adequacy of relevant intermediaries. They should also provide due consideration to the degree of integration between the conventional financial system and the cryptocurrency market. In respect of the last issue, regulators should consider whether to prohibit any interaction between the financial institutions and the virtual currency markets, allow a certain level of integration, or allow full integration.[52]

Much more could be done at the international level to help develop an effective international framework for the regulation of cryptocurrencies. International bodies have a role to play in strengthening the international community's understanding them more broadly. More work could be done to study their evolution and their potential impact on the conventional banking and payments system to understand the risks they pose and to identify the most effective regulatory responses taking into view national circumstances. As experience is gained, consideration could be given to developing standards and best practices

51 Claeys, G., Demertzis, M. & Efstathiou, K. (2018), "Cryptocurrencies and monetary policy: Monetary dialogue", *European Parliament Paper PE619.018*, June2018, www.europarl.europa.eu/cmsdata/150000/BRUEGEL_FINAL%20publication.pdf, accessed 28/07/2018.

52 Peprah, W. K., Afriyie, A. O., Abandoh-Sam, J. A. & Afriyie, E. O. (2018), "Dollarization 2.0 a cryptocurrency: Impact on traditional banks and fiat currency", *International Journal of Academic Research in Business and Social Sciences*, 8(6): 341–349.

to provide guidance on the most suitable regulatory responses to different virtual currency schemes.

An important agenda is the need to involve ongoing monitoring and analysis of the way in which cryptocurrencies are evolving and the policy challenges that they pose.[53] Further insights are needed as to how virtual currency schemes and their underlying distributed ledger technologies change existing business models in financial services and the kind of risks that could evolve from such developments. This could arise through the use of digital learning technologies in the mainstream financial system giving rise to new specific risks necessitating regulatory responses and what potential implications cryptocurrency schemes could have for IMF and other multilateral financial institutions in the future.

While cryptocurrencies have potential benefits such as payment efficiency, the IMF argues that their losses go beyond losses for individual investors. They can pose considerable risk as potential vehicles for money laundering, terrorist financing, tax evasion and fraud. The IMF has evolved since its inception into a lender of last resort (LOLR) for indebted nations and its views on currencies still carry special weight. In mid-January 2018, IMF spokesman Gerry Rice called for global coordination on cryptocurrencies as it warned of the risks from surging prices.[54] Rice added that when asset prices go up quickly risks can accumulate, especially if market participants are borrowing money to buy and hence the importance of people being aware of the risks and taking the necessary risk management measures.

On 29 September 2017, IMF's then Managing Director Christine Lagarde advocated a balanced approach on cryptocurrency regulation.[55] She advised that they may give traditional government issued currencies a run for their money and hence it was not wise to ignore them. She stressed further that cryptocurrencies could bring potential disruption and cautioned that central banks and financial services need to pay close attention to the technology. Lagarde also suggested that cryptocurrencies posed little or no challenge to the existing order of fiat currencies and central banks. This is a consequence of them being too volatile, too risky, too energy intensive and the underlying technology not yet scalable, while many are too opaque for regulators and some have even been hacked. Such challenges could also be addressed over time as a repetition of the dot-com decade.[56] Also, cryptocurrencies have the potential to become more stable, provide better payment services, or more effective new models of

53 Ibid note [40], Helms (2019).

54 Hagan, S. & Mayeda, A. (2018), "IMF calls for global talks on cryptocurrencies" *Bloomberg*, 18/01/2018, www.bloomberg.com/news/articles/2018-01-18/imf-calls-for-global-talks-on-digitalfx-as-Bitcoin-whipsaws, accessed 23/02/2018.

55 Sundararajan, S. (2018), "IMF calls for international cooperation on crypto", *Coin Desk*, 22/01/2018, www.coindesk.com/imf-calls-for-international-cooperation-on-cryptocurrencies, accessed 02/02/2018.

56 Lagarde, C. (2017), "Central banking and fintech – A brave new world", *Speech by Christine Lagarde, the IMF Managing Director at Bank of Engl and Conference London*, 29/09/2017, www.imf.org/en/News/Articles/2017/09/28/sp092917-central-banking-and-fintech-a-brave-newworld, accessed 02/02/2018.

financial intermediation. In the face of such possible potential, the best response by central bankers is to continue running an effective monetary policy, whilst being open to fresh ideas and new demands as economies evolve.

More lately, Lagarde has called for a different approach in dealing with the challenges posed by cryptocurrencies. She opines that IMF needs to "fight fire with fire", meaning she seeks to use blockchain analysis to track cryptocurrency users' behaviour.[57] In so doing, the IMF could address any concerns regarding money laundering and tax evasion. This initiative when implemented could bring more legitimacy to cryptocurrencies as a whole. She argued that those having shared interests in maintaining safe online transactions need to be able to communicate seamlessly. Technologies enabling instant global transactions could be applied to create registries of standards and verify customer information along with digital signatures. More effective employment of data by governments could also help free up resources for priority needs and reduce tax evasion, including evasion related to cross border transactions. She appears to be leaning towards using AI, biometrics and cryptography. Bitcoin supporters immediately seized this as evidence of IMF supporting Bitcoin as a form of money.

To make things smoother, dialogues are needed between experienced regulators and those regulators just beginning to tackle fintech, between policymakers, investors and financial services firms, and between economies. As the focus of regulation widens from national entities to borderless activities, from local bank branch to quantum encrypted global transactions, reaching across borders would be critical and crucial. The IMF with a global membership of 189 economies is the ideal platform for these dialogues.[58] It fits within the IMF's remit as being a focal point for economic and financial stability and the safety of the world's global payments and financial infrastructure.

One IMF position was Christine Lagarde's suggestion on 13 November 2018 that governments should create their own cryptocurrencies to avoid the existing ones becoming a vehicle for fraudsters and money launderers.[59] This does not seem entirely rational, whilst national currencies created as cryptocurrencies would have a more stable value than the existing cryptocurrencies it would not necessarily deter fraudsters and launderers. Neither would necessarily wish to hold the currency for a long period to satisfy their illegal activities and in the case of those wishing to engage in market manipulation of cryptocurrencies or of investments priced in relation to them, the more stable national cryptocurrencies would be less attractive. Likewise, those holding cryptocurrency as an investment asset are likely to see the existing ones as offering more opportunity.

57 Lagarde, C. (2018), "Addressing the dark side of the crypto world" *IMF Blog*, 13/03/2018, https://blogs.imf.org/2018/03/13/addressing-the-dark-side-of-the-crypto-world/, accessed 21/03/2018.

58 Ibid note [57], Lagarde (2017).

59 Inman, P. (2018), "IMF says governments could set up their own cryptocurrencies", *The Guardian*, 14/11/2018, www://guardian.com/business/2018/nov/14/imf-says-governments-shouod-set-up-their-own-cryptocurrencies, accessed 02/03/2019.

The IMF has also shown recent concerns that the rapid increase in the holding and use of cryptocurrencies could create vulnerabilities in the world's financial system.[60] Specifically, in the IMF's Global Stability Report of September 2018:

> Despite its potential benefits, our knowledge of its potential risks and how they might play out is still developing. Increased cybersecurity risks pose challenges for financial institutions, financial infrastructure and supervisors. These developments should act as a reminder that the financial system is permanently evolving, and regulators and supervisors must remain vigilant to this evolution and be ready to act if needed.[61]

Put in a wider context, in the words of CEO Brad Garlinghouse, the IMF has also vowed to continue "devoting attention to blockchain and cryptocurrency".[62] "[B]ut we think it is difficult to talk about blockchain without considering it in the light of the other new technologies that are forming part of the fintech debate". It is clear from other comments that these are taken to include artificial intelligence and cryptoassets.[63] The IMF's recent fintech policy paper, suggests further work on international dimensions of data policy frameworks, and evaluations of new international standards by standard setting bodies including cryptoassets, mobile money service, and P2P lending.[64] Thus, further developments in the IMF's views are awaited.

IMF research suggests that the sheer volume of Bitcoin transactions both on and outside the blockchain, as well as their pseudonymous nature complicate the examination of cross border flows facilitated by Bitcoin. The IMF study suggests that cross border on chain transactions are, on average much bigger than off chain transactions.[65] Off chain data further suggests that an increase in a Bitcoin based measure of the parallel rate premium is associated with higher outflows. Such findings aligned with other studies[66] suggesting that the circumvention of capital flow restrictions. Accordingly, the IMF drew attention to

---

60 Hasan, S. (2018), "How the IMF and central banks are taking on cryptocurrencies", *Trtworld*, 16/11/2018, www.trtworld.com/magazine/how-the-imf-and-central-banks-are-takingon-cryptocurrencies, accessed 02/03/2019.

61 International Monetary Fund (2018), "Global financial stability report April 2018: A bumpy road ahead", April 2018, www.imf.org/en/Publications/GFSR/Issues/2018/09/25/Global-Financial-Stability-Report, accessed 02/03/2019.

62 Speaking at Singapore Fintech 2018.

63 Suberg, W. (2018), "IMF vows to continue 'Devoting Attention' to blockchain, cryptocurrency in fintech drive", *Coin Telegraph*, 13/11/2018, www.cointelegraph.com/new/imf-vows-to-continue-devoting–attention-to-blockchain-cryptocurrency, accessed 02/03/2019.

64 Adrian, T. & Mancini-Griffoli, T. (2019), "The rise of digital money", *IMFFintechNote/2019/01*, 01/07/2019, www.imf.org/~/media/Files/Publications/FTN063/2019/English/FTNEA2019001.ashx, accessed 22/08/2019; IMF (2019), "Fintech: The experience so far", *IMF*, 17/05/2019, www.imf.org/~/media/Files/Publications/PP/2019/PPEA2019024.ashx, accessed 02/07/2019.

65 Cerutti, E. M. et al. (2024), "A primer on Bitcoin cross-border flows: measurement and drivers", *IMF Working Papers* 24(085): 1–43.

66 Von Lucker, G. et al. (2024), "Crypto as a marketplace for capital flight", *IMF Working Paper forthcoming*; von Luckner, G. et al. (2023), "Decrypting new age international capital flows", *Journal of Monetary Economics*, 138: 104–122; Hu, M. et al. (2021), "Evading capital controls via cryptocurrencies: evidence from the blockchain", *SSRN Paper*, https://papers.ssrn.com/sol3/papers.cfm?abstract_id=3956933, accessed 20/1/2023

policymakers seeking to manage capital flows to ensure that capital flow management regulations include cryptos.[67] Also, from a structural perspective, it is helpful to deal with the underlying imbalances that manifest in exchange rate pressures, since the adoption of cryptos would represent just symptoms of these.

The IMF study further illuminates that economies with relatively large capital inflows tend to have lower Bitcoin inflows and vice versa.[68] Additionally, Bitcoin cross-border flows respond differently than capital flows to conventional drivers. It appears that on chain flows are negatively correlated with wider appreciations events, but in contrast to capital flows, they react positively to changes in the market volatility index (VIX).[69] As capital flows and Bitcoin cross-border flows are not directly comparable to methodological differences, IMF research conjectures that Bitcoin cross-border flows at this juncture have not replaced existing capital flows. Therefore, capital flows persist as the most vital quantitative channel for the transmission of global spikes in risk aversion and/or flight to safety triggers. Still, crypto markets are transforming rapidly. The authorisation of spot Bitcoin ETFs in the United States more recently suggests that Bitcoin may increasingly be adopted, even if indirectly, by more mainstream financial operators. Indeed, this and other potential future Bitcoin developments could result in the response of Bitcoin cross-border flows resembling conventional capital flows, especially when the average user base for both kinds of assets inch closer to complicate policy responses.[70] The IMF research acknowledges that their datasets do not capture the entire universe of Bitcoin cross border transactions, and that improvements in the measurement of flows and identification of the residency both for on-chain and off-chain cross-border flows are solutions for gaining deeper insights of Bitcoin cross-border dynamics and for examining the need for and designing sufficient policy responses in the future.[71]

6.5 The Financial Stability Board (FSB)

The FSB is an international body that monitors and makes recommendations concerning the global financial system. Significant economies, international financial institutions, standard-setting and other bodies, and the G20 are represented in the FSB. The FSB promotes international financial stability. It does this by coordinating national financial authorities and international standard-setting bodies as they collaborate toward developing strong regulatory, supervisory, and other financial sector policies. The FSB fosters a level playing field by encouraging coherent implementation of these policies across sectors and jurisdictions.[72]

67 Ibid note [65], Cerutti et al. (2024).
68 Ibid note [65], Cerutti et al. (2024)
69 Antoshin, S. et al. (2018), "Volatility strikes back", *IMF 03/05/18*, www.imf.org/en/Blogs/Articles/2018/05/03/volatility-strikes-back, accessed 20/12/23
70 Ibid note [65], Cerutti et al. (2024)
71 Ibid note [65], Cerutti et al. (2024)
72 FSB (2018), "About the FSB", *FSB*, www.fsb.org/about/, accessed 03/03/2018.

Specifically, the FSB assesses vulnerabilities having an impact on global financial systems. It promotes coordination and information exchange among authorities responsible for financial stability, monitors and advises on market developments and their implications for regulatory policy, monitors and advises best practice in meeting regulatory standards, undertakes joint strategic reviews of the international standards-setting bodies, and coordinates their respective policy development work to address gaps in a timely, coordinated fashion. The FSB also sets out guidelines for establishing and supporting supervisory challenges, supports contingency planning for cross-border crisis management, collaborates with the IMF to conduct early warning exercises, and promotes member jurisdictions' implementation of agreed commitments, standards, and policy recommendations.[73]

With the emergence of fintech activities, including cryptocurrencies, there would be both opportunities and risks to financial stability that policymakers, regulators, supervisors, and overseers could consider.[74] This is important, as many fintech innovations have not been tested through a full financial circle and decisions taken in this early stage could set important precedents. The FSB in this context advises policymakers to continue assessing the adequacy of their regulatory frameworks as the adoption of fintech increases, with the aim of reaping the benefits while mitigating risks. The FSB has been mandated during the German G20 presidency to build on the monitoring to date and identify supervisory and regulatory issues of fintech meriting authorities' attention from a financial stability viewpoint.[75]

Currently, any evaluation of the financial stability implications of fintech is challenging, given the limited availability of official and privately disclosed data.[76] It would be important to account for materiality and risks when evaluating new areas such as fintech. In this regard, it is necessary to understand how business models of start-ups, incumbents, and the market structure are evolving.

The FSB has developed a framework that defines the scope of fintech activities and their potential gains and risks to financial stability.[67] This is to draw out the supervisory and regulatory issues of fintech. The analysis focuses on conceivable benefits and risks, as most fintech activities for now are small relative to the overall financial system. Still, international bodies and national authorities should consider accounting for fintech in their existing risk assessments and regulatory frameworks. There are clear benefits for greater international co-operation, given the commonalities and global dimensions of many fintech activities. This is important when mitigating risks of fragmentation or divergence in regulatory frameworks that could impede the development and

73 Ibid note [72], FSB (2018).

74 FSB (2017), "Financial stability implications from Fintech: Supervisory and regulatory issues that merit authorities' attention", *FSB Working Paper*, 27/07/2017, www.fsb.org/wp-content/uploads/R270617.pdf, accessed 02/02/2018.

75 Van Hulst, N. (2017), "Germany's successful G20 presidency", *OECD Insights*, 13/07/2017, http://oecdinsights.org/2017/07/13/germanys-successful-g20-presidency/, accessed 18/08/2017.

76 Ibid note [74], FSB (2017). 67 Ibid note [74], FSB (2017).

diffusion of beneficial innovations in financial services and limit the effectiveness of initiatives to promote financial stability.[77]

Back in 2017, drawing from the prevailing view, the FSB concluded that there were no compelling financial stability risks from emerging fintech innovations. Ten issues, however, merit the authorities' attention, of which three are seen as priorities for international co-operation.[69] They believed that resolving these is important to the promotion of financial stability, fostering responsible innovation and preventing any derailment of authorities' initiatives to achieve a more inclusive financial system. Though many of these issues are not new, they could be accentuated, given the speed of growth of fintech, new kinds of interconnectedness, and increased dependencies on third-party service providers. The issues identified are building blocks for ensuring a strong, sustainable, and resilient financial system as innovations in financial services evolve and are adopted. The ten issues were as follows:[70]

1. Authorities should determine whether current oversight frameworks from important third-party service providers are appropriate and, in particular, if financial institutions rely on the same third-party service providers. This may entail greater coordination globally across financial authorities and with non-traditional partners.
2. Recent reports of significant and successful cyberattacks underscore the difficulties of mitigating cyber risks.
3. While there are currently no compelling signs of macro financial risks materialising, experience shows that they can emerge quickly if left unchecked. Authorities should consider developing their own capacity to access existing and new sources of information. The seven items featured next cover other issues that were thought to merit authorities' attention.
4. Innovations in cross-border lending, trading, and payment transactions, including via smart contracts, as these raise questions about the cross-jurisdictional compatibility of national legal frameworks.
5. Giving attention to governance and disclosure frameworks for big data analytics.
6. The issue of assessing the regulatory perimeter and updating it on a timely basis.
7. The issue of shared learning with a diverse set of private sector parties.
8. The growing importance of fintech activities and the interconnections across the financial system may lead authorities to consider developing further their lines of communication to ensure preparedness.
9. Supervisors and regulators should consider placing greater emphasis on ensuring they have adequate resources and skill sets to deal with fintech.

77 Ibid note [67], FSB (2017). 69 Ibid note [67], FSB (2017). 70 Ibid note [67], FSB (2017).

10. Relevant authorities should analyse the potential implications of virtual currencies for monetary policy, financial stability, and the global monetary system, including the use of virtual currencies for illegal activities and cyberattacks.

The FSB framework applies to particular fintech activities, including wholesale payment innovations, digital currencies, AI, and so on, to assess potential benefits and risks to financial stability. The lack of data and information poses constraints to assessing the significance of the financial stability implications of fintech. The gathering of data in industry and academic associations on specific fintech activities on a voluntary basis is at a nascent stage. The nature of information needed by regulators and supervisors may be different. The five key observations on possible implications for fintech stability include considerations over the complementarities and trade-offs between financial stability, competition, consumer investors protection, and financial inclusion.

The degree to which regulators will respond to fintech activities may be a function of whether current regulatory frameworks cover emerging risks. Macro financial issues related to systemic importance are embedded in the FSB policy framework for addressing systemically important financial institutions (SIFIs), while some micro financial risks of certain fintech activities may be within the FSB policy framework for strengthening oversight and regulation of shadow banking activities. The FSB's stock take of regulatory approaches to fintech finds that a majority of jurisdictions surveyed have already taken or plan to take regulatory measures to respond to fintech activities. In general, the policy objectives pursued are mostly consumer and investor protection, market integrity, financial inclusion, and promoting innovation or competition. Interestingly, financial stability was often not cited as an objective for recent or planned regulatory reforms with respect to fintech.

In 2017, the FSB's position was affected by events unfolding over the previous two years. In October 2018, they published a report, "Cypro-asset markets: Potential channels for future financial stability implications",[78] where they expressed concern at the risks cryptocurrencies posed, which they balanced against the potential advantages that blockchain could bring. The risks they were concerned about were:

- Risks to consumers and market protection (This was subcategorised as made up of market liquidity, volatility, leverage, and technological and operational risk.)
- Market integrity
- Sanctions evasion
- Fraud

78 FSB (2018), "Crypto-asset markets: Potential channels for future financial stability implications", *FSB Paper*, 10/10/2018, www.fsb.org/wp-content/uploads/P101018.pdf, accessed 11/10/2018.

- Tax evasion
- Circumventing capital controls

The FSB's then chairperson, Randal Quarles, commented at the BIS special governors' meeting in Hong Kong in February 2019 that "developments like the emergence of cryptoassets may challenge any framework". Quarles went on to suggest what further needs to be done.[79] As the FSB continues to assess that cryptoassets do not pose material risks to global financial stability, it nevertheless acknowledges that these products raise various further policy issues beyond financial stability. The FSB takes the position that vigilant monitoring remains justified, especially as a variety of new products and services appear to be under development. Thus, a further monitoring note was submitted to its Standing Committee on the Assessment of Vulnerabilities (SCAV) in September 2019 incorporating developments in stablecoins and tokenisation.[80] In general, the FSB enjoys the opportunity to have an impact on the financial policies of influential economic blocs like the G20. Thus far, it has submitted three reports to the G20 Finance Ministers and Central Bank Governors meetings. The first provided a directory of cryptoassets regulators; the second detailed standard-setting focuses on the financial stability and regulatory and governance implications of decentralised financial technologies.[81]

On 17 July 2023, the FSB issued its global regulatory framework for cryptoasset activities so as to promote the comprehensiveness and international consistency of regulatory and supervisory approaches.[82] This is in direct response to the intrinsic volatility and structural vulnerabilities of cryptoassets and related market participants witnessed in the events of 2022 to 2023. Such events demonstrated the failure of a key service provider in the cryptoasset ecosystem that can rapidly transmit risks to other parts of that ecosystem.[83] They have also shown that if linkages to conventional finance were to grow further, spillovers from cryptoasset markets into the wide financial system could increase. The G20 mandated the FSB to coordinate the delivery of an effective regulatory, supervisory, and oversight framework for cryptoassets. The recommendations that followed focused on addressing risks to financial stability but do not cover

79 Quarles, R. K. (2019), "Ideas for order: Charting a course for the financial stability board", *Remarks by Randal K. Charles, Chair FSB at BIS Special Governors Meeting*, Hong Kong, 10/02/2019, www.moodysanalytics.com/regulatory-news/feb-10-19-fsb-chair-randal-quarles-speaks-about-the-upcoming-work-of-fsb, accessed 03/03/2019.

80 FSB (2019), "Cryptoassets: Work underway, regulatory approaches and potential gaps", *FSB*, 31/05/2019, www.fsb.org/2019/05/crypto-assets-work-underway-regulatory-approaches-and-potential-gaps/, accessed 02/07/2019.

81 Helms, K. (2019), "G20 leaders issue declaration on crypto assets- A look at their commitments", *Bitcoin*. 01/07/2019, https://news.bitcoin.com/g20-leaders-declaration-crypto-assets-commitments/, accessed 07/02/2020.

82 FSB (2023), "FSB global regulatory framework for crypto-asset activities", *FSB*, 17/07/2023, www.fsb.org/wp-content/uploads/P170723-1.pdf, accessed 20/12/23

83 FSB (2023), "FSB finalizes global regulatory framework for crypto-asset activities", *FSB Press Release*, 17/07/2023, www.fsb.org/2023/07/fsb-finalises-global-regulatory-framework-for-crypto-asset-activities/, accessed 20/12/2023

all specific risk categories linked to cryptoasset activities.[84] Central Bank Digital Currencies (CBDCs) treated as digitalised central bank liabilities are not subject to the recommendations as made.[85] In this regard, the FSB collaborates closely with sectoral standard-setting bodies (SSBs) and international organisations to ensure that the in progress co-operative works pertaining to the monitoring and regulation of crypto activities and markets are coordinated, mutually supportive, and complementary.[86] Thus, the global framework includes a shared work plan that the FSB and SSBs have developed for 2023 and beyond. By this method, they would continue to coordinate work under their respective mandates to promote the development of a comprehensive and coherent global regulatory framework, including through the provision of more targeted guidance by the SSBs, monitoring, and public reporting.[87]

6.6 The Bank for International Settlements (BIS)

The BIS is an international financial organisation owned by its 60-member central banks, representing countries that together make up about 95% of the world's GDP.[88] Its mission is to serve central banks in their pursuit of monetary and financial stability, to foster international co-operation in those areas, and to act as a bank for central banks. The BIS pursues its mission by fostering discussion and facilitating co-operation among central banks, supporting dialogues with other authorities promoting financial stability, undertaking research and policy analysis on issues of relevance for monetary and financial stability, acting as a prime counterparty for central banks in their financial transactions, and serving as an agent or trustee in connection with international financial operations.[89] The BIS does not think for now that cryptocurrencies can substitute for some forms of money; it claims to be seeing the fraudulent behaviour that brought down other private currencies starting to appear in the Bitcoin space.

The BIS mentions the following flaws of cryptocurrencies: modern day clipping and culling takes the form of forks, a kind of spin off where developers clone the relevant cryptocurrency's software, then release it with a new name and a new coin after tinkering with the algorithm's parameter. The objective often is to capitalise on the public's familiarity with the cryptocurrency to make a profit. Forks can fork again, and more could occur. Such modern-day clippings could dilute the value of existing ones to the extent that such cryptocurrencies have little, if any, economic value at all.[90]

---

84 Ibid note [83], FSB (2023)

85 Ibid note [83], FSB (2023)

86 Ibid note [83], FSB (2023)

87 Ibid note [83]; FSB (2023)

88 Hayes, A. (2022), "Bank for international settlements: Overview, history", *Investopedia*, 12/08/2022, www.investopedia.com/terms/b/bis.asp, accessed 20/12/2023

89 Ibid note [88], Hayes (2022)

90 Carsens, A. (2018), "Money in the digital age: What role for central banks?", *Lecture by Augustin Carstens, BIS General Manager at the House of Finance Goethe University*, Frankfurt, 06/02/2018

Cryptocurrencies are not the liability of any individual or institution, nor are they backed by any authority. Governance weaknesses[91] such as the concentration of their ownership could make them even less trustworthy. To use them often means to resort to intermediaries such as cryptocurrency exchanges which users have to trust. Often, they piggyback on similar institutional infrastructure serving the overall financial system and on the trust it provides. This reflects the challenge to set up their own trust in the face of cyberattacks, loss of customers' funds, limits on transferring funds, and inadequate market integrity. Novel technology such as Bitcoin blockchain does not necessarily equate with better technology or better economics. Bitcoin's volatility renders it a poor means of payment and an unwise way to store value. Few use it for payments or less, even as a unit of account.

To the extent that they are used, Bitcoins and other cryptocurrencies appear more attractive to those seeking to make transactions in the black or illegal economy rather than in everyday transactions. This is unsurprising, since individuals who evade taxes or launder money are those willing to adapt to Bitcoin's volatility. Central bank experiments show that, in practice, the distributed ledger technology–based systems are very expensive to run and much less efficient to operate than conventional payment and settlement systems. Electricity used in Bitcoin mining is estimated to equal to Singapore's daily electricity consumption, thereby making it socially wasteful and environmentally undesirable.[92]

The preceding suggests that the current fascination with cryptocurrencies seems to have more to do with a speculative mania than any use as a form of electronic payment, other than for illicit activities. It is unsurprising that authorities are accordingly inching closer to clamping them down to mitigate the risks related to virtual currencies. There is a strong case for policy intervention. These assets, according to many securities markets and regulatory and supervisory agencies, can raise concerns related to consumer and investor protection. Relevant authorities have a duty to educate and protect investors and consumers and to be alert to act. There are, moreover, further concerns relating to tax evasion, money laundering, and criminal finance. Authorities should welcome or even promote innovation, but they also concurrently have a duty to ensure that technological advances are not applied to legitimise profits from illegal pursuits.

Central banks acting on their own and/or in coordination with other financial authorities, such as bank regulators and supervisors, ministries of finance, tax agencies, and financial intelligence units, may also need to respond, given their roles in providing money services and the safeguarding of money's real value. Working with commercial banks, authorities have a part to play in policing the digital frontier. Commercial banks operate in the front line as they provide the

91 Nagarajan, M. (2018), "An analysis of cryptocurrency governance", *Joseph Wharton Scholars*, https://repository.upenn.edu/joseph_wharton_scholars/51/, accessed 19/01/2019.

92 Küfeoğlu, S. & Ozkuran, M. A. (2019), "Energy consumption Bitcoin mining", *Cambridge Working Papers in Economics No. 1948*, 04/06/2019, www.researchgate.net/publication/333564703_Energy_Consumption_of_Bitcoin_Mining, accessed 05/06/2019.

real liquidity that keeps exchanges going and interacting with customers, which means authorities need to watch with concerns those banks offering Bitcoin ATMs. Central banks also need to safeguard payment systems. To date, cryptocurrencies are not functional as a means of payment and are essentially trading apps that link users to conventional bank accounts. Where the only business case is used for illegal transactions, central banks cannot allow such tokens to rely on much of the same institutional infrastructure serving the overall financial system and freeload on the trust that it provides.[93]

Authorities should apply the same principles that the Basel process has held on to for years to provide a level playing field to all participants in financial markets, banks, and non-banks alike, besides simultaneously fostering innovative, secure, and competitive markets. This means ensuring the same high standards that money transfer and payment service providers have to comply with are also met by Bitcoin-type exchanges. It further implies ensuring that legitimate banking and payment services are only offered to those exchanges and products meeting these high standards. A further justification for financial authorities to intervene is the need to ensure financial stability. There are suggestions that, given cryptocurrencies' small size and limited interconnectedness, concerns about them have not reached a systemic level, but if authorities do not act pre-emptively, they could become more interconnected with the main financial system and eventually become a threat to financial stability.[94]

Importantly, the spectacular rise of cryptocurrencies should not divert attention from the important role central banks play as stewards of public trust. Private digital tokens masquerading as currencies must not be allowed to subvert this trust. History has shown there simply is no substitute. Central banks nevertheless are embracing new technologies as appropriate. Fintech and techfin with reference to established technology platforms venturing into financial services are changing financial services deliveries in many economies, especially in payments in emerging economies, such as Kenya and China. Even as these produce the possibility of non-banks introducing money-like instruments and raise a familiar set of regulatory questions, they do offer the potential for many benefits.

Overall, while cryptocurrencies may pretend to be currencies, they fail the basic textbook definitions. Most would agree that they do not function as a unit of account, while their volatile valuations make them unsafe to rely on as a common means of payment and stable store of value. Importantly, given their many fragilities, cryptocurrencies are unlikely to satisfy the requirement of trust to make them suitable forms of money. It is not invariably the case that new technologies improve lives and economies. Central banks have the obligation to intervene when it is needed.[95] After all, cryptocurrencies piggyback on the

93 Chiu, J. & Koeppl, T. V. (2018), "The economics of cryptocurrencies", *Bank of Canada/ Queen's University Working Paper.*

94 Heald, J. (2018), "Regulating virtual currency risk", *Review of Banking & Financial Law*, 37: 567–578.

95 Carstens, A. (2018), "Money in the digital age: what role for central banks?", *Lecture by Augustin Carstens, General Manager BIS at House of Finance Goethe University Frankfurt*,

institutional infrastructure serving the wider financial system, thereby gaining a semblance of legitimacy from their links to it. This is clearly central banking territory. It further suggests that central banks and financial authorities need to focus foremost on the ties linking virtual currencies to real currencies to ensure a non-parasitic relationship and, second, with reference to the level playing field principle of same risk, same regulation, with no exceptions.

The BIS's view on cryptocurrencies and, in particular, Bitcoin drew extensive financial media attention, especially coming a day after the ECB's chief's description of Bitcoin as a very risky and entirely speculative asset. Media reporting focuses on BIS's call for a clampdown on Bitcoin to stop them piggybacking on mainstream institutions and becoming a threat to financial stability.[96]

Additional BIS revelations suggest that Bitcoin counterfeiting through double spending attacks is inherently profitable. Further, the transaction market is unable to generate a sufficient level of "mining" income through fees as users freeride on the fees of other transactions in a block and in the subsequent blockchain. Newly minted cryptocurrencies, known as block rewards, instead accounted for the bulk of mining income to date. These two constraints would imply that liquidity could fall significantly as these block rewards are phased out. Preliminary estimates suggest that, at the moment, block rewards are zero. It would require a significant time delay before a Bitcoin payment is final compared with other payment methods, unless new technologies were available to expedite payment finality. Lightning Network second layer solutions could assist, but the only fundamental remedy would require departing from proof of work, and this would likely need some kind of social coordination or institutionalisation.

In a recent publication on the matter, "Proceeding with caution – a survey on central bank digital currency",[97] the BIS shows that 70% of central banks are studying cryptocurrencies, but very few have issued them. At some point, this may change. Agustin Carstens, BIS Chief, subsequent to previously issuing statements and reports strongly critical of cryptocurrencies, has conceded that central banks would probably soon need to issue their own digital currencies.[98] He recently stated that BIS is supporting global central bank initiatives to research and develop digital currencies based on national fiat currencies.

06/02/2018, www.bis.org/speeches/sp180206.pdf, accessed 10/11/2018.

96 Arnold, M. (2018), "Head of BIS calls for clampdown on Bitcoin: Cryptocurrency has lost more than half its value since start of 2018", *Financial Times*, 06/02/2018, www.ft.com/content/78bf5612-0b1a-11e8-839d-41ca06376bf2, accessed 03/03/2018; Bosley, C. & Speciale, A. (2018), "BIS chief sees 'Strong Case' for cryptocurrency intervention", *Bloomberg*, 06/02/2018, www.bloomberg.com/news/articles/2018-02-06/bis-chief-sees-strong-case-for-intervening-on-cryptocurrencies, accessed 03/03/2018.

97 Barontini, C. & Holden, H. (2019), "Proceeding with caution – a survey on central bank digital currency", *BIS Paper No 101*, 08/01/2019, www.bis.org/publ/bppdf/bispap101.htm, accessed 02/01/2020.

98 Palmer, D. (2019), "BIS chief: Central Bank may issues digital currencies 'Sooner Than We Think'", *Coin Desk*, 01/07/2019, www.coindesk.com/central-banks-may-issue-digital-currencies-sooner-than-we-think-bis-chief, accessed 02/07/2019.

Importantly, regulators need to ensure a level playing field between big technology companies and banks, taking into account big technology's wide customer base, access to information, and broad ranging business models. The BIS chief added that the simple way to regulate such cryptocurrency networks is to start addressing immediate and very obvious money laundering concerns.[85] The latter concern was echoed by the US Treasury Secretary.[99] Importantly, the Group of Central Bank Governors and Heads of Supervision (GHOS), the oversight body of the Basel Committee on Banking Supervision, at its 13 May 2024 meeting, agreed to defer implementation of the Committee's prudential standard[100] for banks' cryptoassets exposures by 1 year to 1 January 2026.[101]

In December 2022, the Basel Committee on Banking Supervision (BCBS) articulated its rules on the prudential treatment of cryptoasset exposures. Based on these rules, unbacked cryptoassets and stablecoins with ineffective stabilisation mechanisms will be subject to a conservative prudential treatment. Banks have to classify cryptoassets on an ongoing basis into group 1 and group 2.[102] Group 1 cryptoassets have to meet a set of classification conditions. Assets in this group include tokenised conventional assets that bear the equivalent level of credit and market risks as the non-tokenised form of the asset (or 1a assets) and cryptoassets with effective stabilisation mechanism, linking the value to one or more conventional assets (stablecoins, or 1b assets). The capital requirements for group 1 assets generally adhere to the present Basel framework.[103] However, an infrastructure risk add-on to risk-weighted assets may be applicable where weaknesses are identified in the underlying exposure upon which the cryptoassets are based. Group 1 stablecoins have to also satisfy a redemption risk test and additional supervision/regulation requirements that are likely to evolve in the future. The BCBS announced in December 2023 that it will consult on potential revisions pertaining to the criteria for stablecoins to receive a preferential "group 1b" regulatory treatment, and on various technical amendments to help boost a consistent understanding of the standard.[104]

Group 2 cryptoassets do not satisfy the classification conditions for group 1 and are subject to a new conservative capital treatment. Such assets include unbacked cryptoassets, algorithmic stablecoins, and assets relying on protocols to maintain their values.[105] A further hedging recognition criterion maps the

99 De, N. (2019), "US Treasury Secretary Mnuchin is 'not comfortable' with Facebook's Libra", *Coin Desk*, 15/07/2019, www.coindesk.com/us-treasury-secretary-mnuchin-is-not-comfortable-with-facebooks-libra, accessed 16/07/2019.

100 BIS (2022), "Prudential treatment of cryptoasset exposures", *BIS December 2022*, www.bis.org/bcbs/publ/d545.htm, accessed 20/12/23

101 BIS (2024), "Governors and Heads of Supervision reiterate commitment to Base III implementation and provide update on cryotoasset standard", *BIS*, 13/05/2024, www.bis.org/press/p240513a.htm, accessed 18/07/24

102 BCBS (2022), "Prudential treatment of cryptoasset exposures", *BIS*, December 2022, www.bis.org/bcbs/publ/d545.htm, accessed 20/12/2023

103 Ibid note [102], BCBS (2022)

104 Ibid note [102], BCBS (2022)

105 Ibid note [102], BCBS (2022)

conditions for those group 2 assets where a limited degree of hedging can be recognised (2a) and where hedging is not recognised (2b).[106] Banks' aggregate exposure to group 2 assets must not go beyond the 2% threshold of the tier 1 capital and should not generally be lower than 1%.[107] Exposures under the 1% threshold will be risk-weighted according to whether the assets do or do not meet the hedging recognition criteria for group 2a assets. Banks exceeding the 1% limit expectation have to apply group 2b capital treatment (1,250% risk weight) to the amount by which the limit is breached.[108] Where a 2% limit is exceeded, the whole of group 2 exposures is subject to the group 2b capital treatment. Also, further additional operational risk, liquidity, leverage ratio and large exposure, supervisory review, and disclosure requirements apply to both groups.[109]

6.7 The International Organization of Securities Commissions (IOSCO)

The IOSCO website describes it as the international body that brings together the world's securities regulators and is recognised as the global standard setter for securities and their regulation. IOSCO develops, implements, and promotes adherence to international recognised standards for securities regulations. It collaborates extensively with the G20 and the FSB on the global regulatory reform agenda. IOSCO's total membership regulates more than 95% of the world's securities markets in more than 115 jurisdictions. Securities regulators in emerging markets account for 75% of its ordinary membership.

IOSCO's objective and principles of securities trading are endorsed by the G20 and FSB as the relevant standards in this area. They represent the overarching core principles guiding it in the development and implementation of internationally recognised and consistent standards of regulation, oversight, and enforcement. They are the basis for the evaluation of the securities sector for the Financial Sector Assessment Programs (FSAPs) of the IMF and the World Bank.

Through providing high quality technical assistance, education, training, and research to its members and other regulators, IOSCO seeks to build sound global capital markets and a robust global regulatory framework. IOSCO members agree to co-operate in developing, implementing, and promoting adherence to internationally recognised and consistent standards of regulation. These include oversight and enforcement to protect investors; maintain fair, efficient, and transparent markets; and seek to address systemic risks. They also agree to exchange information at both global and regional levels on their respective experiences so as to assist the development of markets, strengthen market infrastructure, and implement suitable regulations.

106 Ibid note [102], BCBS (2022)
107 Ibid note [102], BCBS (2022)
108 Ibid note [102], BCBS (2022)
109 Ibid note [102], BCBS (2022)

IOSCO's fintech study covers DLT that underpins the workings of Bitcoin and other cryptocurrencies.[110] DLTs are technologies used to implement distributed ledgers. DLT attracts the interests of financial services for various reasons, including the possibility that permissioned DLT present an opportunity to save costs when they are employed to replace legacy systems and associated back office processes. Permissionless DLT, on the other hand, could potentially present risks when they are applied to disintermediate financial institutions and central counterparties.

DLT has grown significantly in the marketplace. Over US$11.5 billion venture capital (VC) investments were made in DLT in 2024 alone.[111] Also, 13,854 patents have been filed between January 2013 and October 2023.[112] However, there has been an ongoing decline in volume since 2020.

Proofs of concepts in the securities industry include keeping corporate records, making corporate actions processes more efficient, revamping post-trading operations of exchange-traded equities, or trading and settling OTC derivatives, facilitating loan syndications, tracking repo transactions and rehypothecation, trading short-term debt, automation of KYC, and AML compliance processes among financial institutions, individual digital ID, and alternative financing. Extending from these, the more frequently cited potential benefits as they apply to financial services include cost reduction in settlement, faster speed of settlement, reliability and traceability of records, automatic and real-time filings to regulators, inclusion of new asset classes, efficiency enhancement, and enhancement in security.

DLT implementation in the securities markets could raise various technological, operational, business, and regulatory challenges.[113] Technological challenges involve matters such as scalability, interoperability, and cyber resilience. Operational challenges involve matters such as governance and smart contracts. Trading- and settlement-related challenges involve matters such as management of the cash leg of transactions, recourse mechanism, position and collateral netting, and transparency. The implementation of distributed ledger technology and smart contracts in the securities markets may raise several legal questions, including but not limited to the validity of tokens as a representation of ownership and legal finality of smart contracts.

Though DLT is still evolving, various authorities have issued their views.

In June 2016, ESMA[114] issued a discussion paper while, concurrently, the European Parliament[115] enacted a law that allows some securities vouchers to be

---

110 IOSCO (2017), "IOSCO research report on financial technologies (Fintech)", *IOSCO Research Report*, February 2017, accessed 26/03/2018.

111 https://galaxy.com/insights/research/crypto-blockchain-venture-capital-q4-2024/, accessed 02/03/2025

112 www.mintz.com>insights center>viewpoints, accessed 02/03/2025

113 Ibid note [110], IOSCO (2017)

114 ESMA (2016), "Discussion paper: The distributed ledger technology applied to securities markets", *ESMA/2016/773*, 02/06/2016, www.esma.europa.eu/sites/default/files/library/2016-773_dp_dlt.pdf, accessed 20/12/2023

115 EU Parliament (2016), "European Parliament resolution of 26 May on virtual currencies", *Texts adopted 26/05/16 European Parliament*, www.europarl.europa.eu/doceo/document/TA-8-2016-05-26_EN.html, accessed 20/12/2023

issued and exchanged on a DLT. The US Financial Industry Regulatory Authority (FINRA), in January 2017, issued a paper[116] as its contribution to the ongoing dialogue about their use in the securities industry. It requested comments on matters for which it would be suitable to consider additional guidance, consistent with the principles of investor protection and market integrity based on the applications and their implications for FINRA rules.

While firms can operate globally, regulation is overseen within national or sub-national borders. This could generate challenges in terms of regulatory consistency, as well as cross-border supervision and enforcement. It also generates risks of regulatory arbitrage. The global nature of fintech could therefore contribute to challenges that might be addressed by international co-operation and the exchange of information among regulators.

Regulators have engaged in greater multilateral collaboration on the topic of digital innovation at IOSCO, FSB, and the BIS. Regulators could additionally continue to enter into bilateral memoranda of understanding to collaborate, thereby enabling regulators to share information about financial services innovations in their respective markets, including emerging trend and regulatory issues. Emerging, new fintech activities, such as DLT and cryptocurrencies, sometimes cut across different industries within the wider economy, thereby having an impact on current regulatory perimeters within jurisdictions. Many jurisdictions have engaged in greater national regulatory coordination. For instance, in Japan, a new working group of the Financial System Council was formed. This is the advisory body of the Japan Financial Services Agency that helped spawn major legislative amendments to the Payment Services Act and the Banking Act.[117]

As early as 18 January 2018, IOSCO issued an ICO cautionary note.[118] It described ICOs, also known as token sales, or coin sales, as typically involving the creation of digital tokens using DLT and their sale to investors by auction or through subscription, in return for a cryptocurrency, such as Bitcoin or Ether, or, more rarely, for official fiat currency. The IOSCO does not consider these offerings as standardised, and as such, their legal and regulatory status is likely to depend on the circumstances of the individual ICO and the relevant jurisdiction. The IOSCO further cited clear risks associated with these offerings. ICOs are deemed as highly speculative investments wherein investors are putting their entire invested capital at risk. Though some operators are providing legitimate investment opportunities to finance projects/businesses, the enhanced targeting of ICOs to retail investors via online distribution channels by parties often

116 FINRA (2017), "Distributed ledger technology: implications of blockchain for the securities industry", *FINRA*, 21/01/2017, www.finra.org/sites/default/files/FINRA_Blockchain_Report.pdf, accessed 20/12/2023

117 Ibid note [110], IOSCO (2017)

118 IOSCO (2018), "IOSCO board communication on concerns related to initial coin offerings (ICOs)", *IOSCO Media Release*, 18/01/2018, www.centralbank.ie/regulation/markets-update/iosco/markets-update-issue-2-2018/international-organization-of-securities-commissions-(iosco)/iosco-board-communication-on-concerns-related-to-initial-coin-offerings-(icos), accessed 20/12/2023

located outside an investor's home jurisdiction raises concerns. Crucially, they may not be subject to regulation or the issuer could be operating illegally in breach of existing laws, and this raises investor protection concerns. There have been instances of fraud, and as a consequence, investors are cautioned to be very careful when considering whether to invest in ICOs.

In a related development, the IOSCO cautioned its member countries over the regulation of cryptocurrencies, saying that such regulation might confer undue legitimacy on the products. At a meeting in Madrid, Spain, the gathering of regulators with IOSCO leadership opined that regulating virtual currencies would deceive the general public into believing that there is a regulatory faith in the products.[119] The gathering reached a consensus to conduct a deep analysis of the nature of the products to enable a clear appreciation of the depth of regulation required to ensure adequate protection of investors. They further agreed to launch intensive public awareness initiatives to boost investor education and understanding and accelerate the development of the right regulatory framework as may be necessary. Regulators, especially in emerging markets, are further advised to better prepare for the incursion of cryptocurrencies into their markets, by putting in place the appropriate regulatory frameworks that would ensure transparency, efficiency, and protection for investors.

The IOSCO's consultation report of 28 May 2019 described the risks and issues that it has identified pertaining to cryptoasset trading platforms (CTPs). The report outlined key considerations that are intended to assist regulatory authorities when evaluating CTPs within the context of their regulatory frameworks.[120] These primary matters to be addressed include access to CTPs, safeguarding participant assets, conflicts of interest, CTPs operation, market integrity, price discovery, and technology. Many of these are also common to conventional securities trading venues but could be heightened by how CTPs are operated. Where regulatory authorities have determined that a cryptoasset is a security and falls within their remits, the basic principles or objectives of securities regulation would apply. The IOSCO seeks to continue monitoring the evolution of the markets for cryptoassets to ensure the issues, risks, and key considerations identified in the report remain pertinent and appropriate. Its approach therefore aligns with the G20's 2018 communiques calling on international standard-setting entities to continue their monitoring of cryptoassets and their risks according to their respective mandates and assess multilateral responses as required.[121]

The IOSCO considered the comments and issues raised and received from its consultation report and came out with its final report in February 2020. This

119 Nnorom, N. (2018), "IOSCO warns on regulation of virtual currencies", *Vanguard*, 27/02/2018, www.vanguardngr.com/2018/02/iosco-warns-regulation-virtual-currencies/, accessed 03/03/2018.

120 IOSCO (2019), "Issues, risks and regulatory considerations relating to crypto-asset trading platforms", *IOSCO Consultation Report CR02/2019*, May 2019, www.iosco.org/library/pubdocs/pdf/IOSCOPD627.pdf, accessed 20/12/23

121 Ibid note [120], IOSCO (2019)

describes issues and risks identified that are associated with the trading of cryptoassets on cryptoasset trading platforms. Pertaining to the issues and risks raised, the report describes key considerations and toolkits deemed as useful for each consideration, as these are intended to assist regulatory authorities evaluating such platforms within the contexts of their regulatory frameworks. The key considerations examined included access, safeguarding participant assets, conflicts of interest, market integrity, price discovery, and technology. The operational model adopted by a trading platform and the existing regulatory framework could ascertain the degree to which issues or risks exist, are pertinent, or have already been mitigated.[122]

Acknowledging that this market is new and evolving quickly, the IOSCO further clarified that the key considerations and toolkits proposed are not intended to suggest or mandate any particular regulatory action or requirement. These constitute specific niches that the IOSCO believes jurisdictions could explore in the context of the regulation of crypto trading platforms, while the toolkits are illustrations that could be adopted by regulatory authorities to deal with the key considerations and the associated risks and issues.[123] The IOSCO, in consideration of these insights, would continue to monitor the evolution of the markets for cryptoassets, with the aim of ensuring that the issues, risks, and key considerations identified in the 2020 final report remain pertinent and appropriate. The report, though, does not include analysis of the criteria applied by regulatory authorities to ascertain whether a crypto falls within their remits but instead focuses on the trading of cryptos on platforms when the regulatory authority has ascertained that it has the legal authority to regulate those assets or the specific activity involving those assets.[124] The IOSCO, in July 2024, updated its principal themes going forward. These included technology and digital finance, cryptoassets, sustainable finance, fraud and scam prevention, investor resilience, and the basics of investing.[125]

The IOSCO final report in November 2023 published its recommendations on how to regulate the crypto and digital assets markets.[126] These recommendations are targeted at cryptoasset service providers, including trading, operating a market, custody, lending, and the promotion and distribution of cryptos on behalf of others.[127] The IOSCO advised regulators to achieve equivalent outcomes for investor protection and market integrity, such as those mandated in

122 IOSCO (2020), "Issues, risks and regulatory considerations relating to crypto-asset trading platforms", *IOSCO Final Report FR02/2020*, February 2020, www.iosco.org/library/pubdocs/pdf/IOSCOPD649.pdf, accessed 20/12/2023

123 Ibid note [122], IOSCO (2020)

124 Ibid note [122], IOSCO (2020)

125 IOSCO (2024), "IOSCO announces themes for its 8th edition of world investor week", *IOSCO Media Release IOSCO/MR/14/2024*, 10/07/2024, www.iosco.org/news/pdf/IOSCONEWS740.pdf?v=3, accessed 18/07/2024

126 IOSCO (2023), "Policy recommendations for crypto and digital assets markets: Final report", *IOSCO Final Report FR11/2023*, 16/11/2023, www.iosco.org/library/pubdocs/pdf/IOSCOPD747.pdf, accessed 20/12/2023

127 Ibid note [126], IOSCO (2023)

conventional financial markets, so as to facilitate a level playing field between cryptoassets and conventional financial markets to curtail the risk of regulatory arbitrage. It further advocated the importance of enhanced regulatory co-operation to resolve cross-border matters, including the need for all members to implement its recommendations consistently.[128] The 18 recommendations set out six domains consistent with IOSCO standards, namely, conflicts of interest arising from vertical integration of activities and function; market manipulation, insider trading, and fraud; cross-border risks and regulatory co-operation; custody and client asset protection; operational and technological risk; and retail access, suitability, and distribution.[129] These recommendations are directed at all kinds of cryptos, including stablecoins.

Pertaining to prudential standards, in December 2023, IOSCO published its nine recommendations applicable to decentralised finance products, services, systems, and activities.[130] Decentralised finance (*DeFi*) pertains to financial products, services, activities, and arrangements that deploy distributed ledger or blockchain technologies (DLTs), including self-executing codes, known as smart contracts. It seeks to run in a disintermediated and decentralised way, thereby cancelling some conventional financial intermediaries and centralised institutions, while facilitating particular direct investment activities.[131] It is still an evolving, as well as expanding, technological innovation.

It may have the upside of boosting financial innovation, enhanced efficiencies, and improved access to financial products, services, and activities. Blockchain business cases proposed include those pertaining to primary market issuance, secondary market trading, asset servicing, as well as life cycle management. The IOSCO promotes responsible innovations of benefits to investors and markets. It boosts prioritised focus on analysing and responding to market integrity and investor protection concerns, including those emerging from technological advancements in DeFi.

IOSCO's nine recommendations for DeFi address market integrity and investor protection originating from DeFi by supporting greater consistency of regulatory frameworks and oversight in member jurisdictions. These are complementary to the Crypto and Digital Assets (CDA) markets policy recommendations.[132] They adopt a "lifestyle approach" in resolving the main risks identified in the report and are principles-based and outcomes-focused and are targeted at DeFi products, services, activities, and systems through

128 Ibid note [126], IOSCO (2023)

129 Ibid note [126], IOSCO (2023)

130 IOSCO (2023), "Final report with policy recommendations for Decentralised finance (DeFi)", *IOSCO FR/14/2023*, December 2023, www.iosco.org/library/pubdocs/pdf/IOSCOPD754.pdf, accessed 30/12/2023

131 Ibid note [130], IOSCO (2023). There is as yet a generally accepted definition even among industry participants.

132 IOSCO (2023), "Policy recommendations for crypto and digital asset markets: Final report", *IOSCO Final Report*, November 2023, www.iosco.org/library/pubdocs/pdf/IOSCOPD747.pdf, accessed 20/12/2023

deploying IOSCO's widely accepted global standards for securities markets regulation.[133]

Among the IOSCO's mission is the enhancement of greater consistency pertaining to the regulation and oversight of cryptoasset markets within the context of the cross-border nature of these markets, the potential for regulatory arbitrage, and significant risk of harm to retail investors, apart from seeking to promote consistency in the manner cryptoasset markets and securities markets are regulated within individual IOSCO jurisdictions in accordance with the principle of "same activity, same risk, same regulation/regulatory outcome".[134]

The recommendations include the covering for expanded co-operation among regulators to coordinate and respond to cross-border challenges in enforcement and supervision and to deal with regulatory arbitrage concerns that originate from the cross-border nature of global cryptoasset activities undertaken by DeFi participants who offer their products, provide their services, and partake in activities across multiple jurisdictions. Though the recommendations are not directly aimed at market participants, all cryptoasset markets participants are advised by the IOSCO to seriously consider the expectations and outcomes fleshed through the recommendations and the supporting guidance in the undertaking of regulated and cross-border activities.

6.8 Financial Action Task Force (FATF)

In October, the FATF 2018 adopted changes to its pre-existing recommendations to explicitly clarify that they applied to financial activities pertaining to virtual assets and also provided definitions for *virtual asset* and *virtual asset service providers*.[135] Recommendation 15 requires that VASPs be regulated for AML/CTF purposes, licensed or registered, and subject to effective systems for monitoring purposes. Subsequently, in June 2019, the FATF adopted Interpretative Note to Recommendation 15 to further clarify how the FATF requirements should apply pertaining to virtual assets and their providers, especially with regard to the application of the risk-based approach; supervision or monitoring for AML/CTF purposes, licensing, or registration; preventive measures, such as customer due diligence, record keeping, and suspicious transaction reporting, among others; sanctions and other enforcement measures; and international co-operation.[136]

The FATF also adopted the present guidance on the deployment of a risk-based approach to virtual assets and virtual asset providers in June 2019.[137] The intention is to assist both national authorities, in understanding and developing

133 Ibid note [132], IOSCO (2023)

134 Ibid note [132], IOSCO (2023)

135 FATF (2019), *Guidance for a risk-based approach and virtual asset service providers*, Paris, FATF.

136 Ibid note [135], FATF (2019)

137 FATF (2021), *Updated guidance for a risk-based approach: virtual assets and virtual asset service providers*, Paris, FATF

regulatory and supervisory responses, and private sector businesses engaging in relevant activities, in understanding their AML/CTF obligation and how they could effectively comply with these requirements. The guidance further demonstrates how virtual asset activities and virtual asset service providers fall within the scope of these recommendations.

It analyses the five kinds of activities covered by the definition of *virtual asset service providers* and gives instances of virtual assets related activities that fall within the definition and that would be excluded from the FATF scope. As such, it highlights the key elements required to qualify, namely, acting as a business on customers' behalf and actively facilitating virtual asset related activities. The guidance also clarifies the application of the FATF recommendation to countries and competent authorities, including virtual asset service providers and other obliged entities that partake in virtual asset activities and including financial institutions like banks and securities broker dealers. The G20 in the June 2019 Osaka Summit reaffirmed that cryptoassets do not pose a threat to global financial stability and requested further work done by standard-setting bodies like the FATF.[138]

A FATF study[139] highlighted that 75% of the 98 jurisdictions evaluated are only partially or non-compliant with the requirements, while 73% of these are not undertaking sufficient risk evaluations. Also, some 30% of the 151 survey respondents have not yet decided if and how to regulate the virtual asset service providers niche, 60% have decided to permit them, 11% report electing to prohibit them, but with only one jurisdiction evaluated as largely complaint with the requirements.[140] Additionally, the study further highlighted that implementation of the travel rule requiring financial institutions to share data on transactions exceeding a threshold is inadequate, as over 50% of respondents have not initiated steps towards the implementation.[141]

The FATF cautioned that decentralised finance and unhosted wallets, including person-to-person transactions, pose money laundering, terrorist financing, and hiking of financing risks, including abuse by sanctioned participants. The FATF lamented that some jurisdictions faced difficulties in mitigating these risks, including identifying particular natural or legal persons responsible for virtual asset service obligations in decentralised finance procedures. Accordingly, the FATF expects jurisdictions to quickly implement and operationalise the travel rule,[142] sufficiently identify risks, install mitigation measures, including the monitoring or supervising of the virtual asset

138 Helms, K. (2019), "G20 leaders issue declaration on crypto assets – A look at their commitments", *Bitcoin*, 01/07/2019, https://news-bitcoin-com.webpkgcache.com/doc/-/s/news.bitcoin.com/g20-leaders-declaration-crypto-assets-commitments/, accessed 16/07/2019.

139 FSTF (2023), "Methodology: For assessing technical compliance with the FATF recommendations and the effectiveness of AML/CFT systems", *FATF*, Updated June 2023, www.fatf-gafi.org/en/publications/Mutualevaluations/Fatf-methodology.html, accessed 20/12/2023

140 Ibid note [139], FATF (2023)

141 Ibid note [139], FATF (2023)

142 This is Recommendation 16 (INR16), requiring the relevant financial institutions to gather information on the payor and the beneficiary in an electronic transfer of funds.

service providers niche with enforcements against non-compliance, as well as evaluating illicit finance risks of DeFi processes and unhosted wallets, and to consider how those fit into their AML/CFT arrangements, including sharing such practices globally.[143]

6.9 A brief comparative note regarding multilateral cryptoasset regulators

This chapter has demonstrated how economic blocs/global leadership forums, such as the G20 and G8, look at the potential risks posed by cryptoassets to the conventional financial system, to businesses, and to investors. It also examines how international financial standards-setters, like the IMF, the BIS, the FSB, and the IOSCO, approach this issue. In particular, the impact of ICOs on the capital markets as perceived by the IOSCO and other large national regulators, such as the SEC and the FCA, were also analysed.

It appears that economic blocs, such as the G20 and G8, are taking the position that cryptoassets are not posing a threat to global financial stability and are focusing on close monitoring of existing and emerging risks in the context of consumer and investor protection and AML/CTF considerations. Their goal is to use the multilateral approach effectively applied to help quell the 2008 global financial crisis. To this end, they have directed the FSB and other standard-setting bodies to advise on further multilateral responses when appropriately needed. Of late, they have become concerned over the risks posed by the wider employment of new kinds of cryptoassets for retail payment purposes that might necessitate close examinations by the competent authorities to ensure compliance with high standards of regulation. On this issue, FSB's September 2019 report on stablecoins and tokenisation is likely to get a response from them with regards to these items. In the meantime, they confirm adherence to FATF reporting standards for cryptoassets.

Drawing from previous experiences, other than the 2008 global financial crisis, G20 and G8 summits are unlikely to focus enough on the cryptoasset risk threat to the global financial system as other high profile agendas are likely to draw greater attention. These happened during the recent 2019 Osaka Summit and the earlier summit in France. However, the G20 and G8 forums do provide the platform for multilateral solutions to potential cryptoassets issues in relation to the global financial system. In contrast, the EU takes a more disciplined approach to the potential harm posed to market participants and financial systems and the main reason they have, under the guidance from the FSB, taken initiatives to gather an early appreciation of how blockchain innovation unleashed through the cryptoassets industry could transform markets and financial institutions to be ready with risk containment measures, including serious reflections on how the industry is to be regulated in the EU.

143 Ibid note [139], FATF (2023)

The OECD acknowledged both the benefits and the risks from the deployment of cryptoassets and has called for a balanced and harmonised approach to deal with the problem. The OECD's larger membership base enables it to reach out to more economies with its various guidance, the latest of which included the call for the use of blockchain technology to support and assist the further growth of SMEs. Other than these, it has a relatively lower profile than the G20 or G8, both of which enjoy greater global attention.

The FSB, though, focuses more on the issue of financial stability and in this has the ear of the G20 and G8 and other forums. It continues to provide helpful insights onto the workings of cryptoassets covering both the perils and the opportunities they bring. The BIS, the central bank for central bankers, initially took a very conservative stand on cryptoassets. Rightly so, from the perspective of their mission, as the success of private money globally could suggest the potential end for central banking. Lately, they have shifted their position when the IMF and some central banks started to explore the potential of using CBDC, the latest of which came from the governor of the Bank of England.

While the IMF urges caution with regards to the cryptoasset industry, it has, in recent years, become slightly more positive towards it. The IMF has even called upon governments and central banks around the world to take a more balanced approach that takes into account both perils and the innovation opportunities unleashed by cryptoassets and the blockchain technology that underpins it. In contrast to all the others, the FATF issued specific guidance focusing on AML/CTF reporting precautions that most policymakers and regulators take seriously. Compared to the others that tend to take general stands, AML/CTF is a high-priority agenda for the FATF. Most regulatory institutions tend to follow FATF standards, as deviations from these tend to attract blacklisting response in the global financial arena.

The potential heightened cryptoasset AML/CTF risks aside, all the multilateral global regulators discussed here agree that the blockchain technology behind cryptoassets could extend its value to areas where trusted authority is mandatory for the coordination of socio-economic activities as it could offer the supporting infrastructure in substitution for these activities. This suggests a set of protocols and code-based rules inserted on top of blockchain based networks for deployment in financial institutions, capital markets, online operators, and content providers – and including government systems. This technology, therefore, enables the on-setting of new self-contained and autonomous systems of rules that install order without law in the direction of private regulatory frameworks, referred to as "lex cryptographica", that enable people and institutions to organise, communicate, and exchange value on P2P format without intermediary actors.[144]

144 Davidson, S., De Filippi, P. & Potts, J. (2016), "Disrupting governance: The new institutional economics of distributed ledger technology", *SSRN Electronic Journal*, January 2016, www.researchgate.net/publication/323980958_Disrupting_Governance_The_New_Institutional_Economics_of_Distributed_Ledger_Technology, accessed 18/08/2018; Wright, A. & De Filippi, P.

Though "lex cryptographica" is similar in some respects to other conventional means of regulation by code, it nevertheless differs from current code-based regimes, as it runs autonomously of any centralised authority. Blockchain's decentralised systems and applications could therefore be governed almost entirely by code rules, unlike other current technological systems in use on the internet. These could portend various risks, as they operate by going around conventional systems of control. Blockchain technology, however, does not necessarily suggest the end for the rule of law as, despite its potential widespread deployments, governments still maintain their holds over laws, codes, social norms, and market forces that could ultimately indirectly or directly regulate this emerging technology.[145]

Both conventional systems and the blockchain decentralised system have their fair shares of constraints, ambiguity, and uncertainty. Conventional technological systems in employment on the internet and blockchain systems have their fair share of constraints, ambiguities, and uncertainties. As blockchain widens its applications and grip on the economy,[146] the option for the world could opt for the conventional rules of legal systems that are not entirely suitable. Alternately, the world could opt for the benefits of liberation from the tyranny of centralised intermediaries and trusted authorities via decentralised blockchain technology, but that could also bring with it a tyranny of codes. In the meantime, with pilots going into production, expansion of real-world smart contract applications, and preparations for state-backed digital currencies, blockchain is arguably ready to leave the hype behind and transition to a more mundane but useful phase.[147]

All in all, multilateral policymakers and regulators, for the most part, call for a balanced approach when dealing with cryptoassets. At the same time, owing to several high-profile illicit deployments of cryptoassets, FATF crypto related AML/CTF standards are now in place for the world to follow. These are unlikely to diminish innovation flowing from the cryptoasset industry. It is also likely that regulatory response would converge gradually as multilateral institutions continue to have an impact on the views of national institutions. For the moment, though, the regulatory response across the world is split into three camps, namely, the wait and see camp, the camp for the deployment of new cryptoassets law, and those relying on the tweaking of existing rules to deal with the emerging technology.

(2015), "Decentralized blockchain technology and the rise of lex cryptographica", *Cryptocurrency Research Group (CRG) Paper*, 12/03/2015, www.researchgate.net/publication/314892724_Decentralized_Blockchain_Technology_and_the_Rise_of_Lex_Cryptographia, accessed 18/08/2018.

145 De Filippi, P. & Wright, A. (2018), *Blockchain and the law: The rule of code*, Cambridge, MA, Harvard University Press.

146 Hacker, P., Lianos, I., Dimitropoulos & Erich, S. (2019), *Regulating blockchain: Tecno-social and legal challenges*, Oxford, Oxford University Press; Finck, M. (2019), *Blockchain regulation and governance in Europe*, Cambridge, Cambridge University Press.

147 Wlasawsky-Berger, I. (2019), "Blockchain, yesterday's hype, transitions into something else", *Wall Street Journal*, 07/03/2019, https://blogs.wsj.com/cio/2019/03/07/blockchain-yesterdays-hype-transitions-into-something-else/, accessed 08/08/2019.

Indeed, the global best pathways to the regulation of cryptoassets that are borderless, open source, decentralised, and constantly evolving persist as the perennial question policymakers, industry, and users are still grappling with as the cryptoasset ecosystem develops.[148] Over the past few years, these various international standard setting entities have undertaken a range of initiatives to generate evidence based research including high-level frameworks to evolve a global approach. Against this, some jurisdictions have opted to focus on certain key aspects of the ecosystem frequently accompanied by the objective of ensuring consumer protection, prevention of illicit financing and financial stability, but deploying various approaches, extending from principles based, risk-based, agile regulation, self- and co-regulation, and ultimately, regulation by enforcement.[149]

To ensure a wide and global treatment of this phenomenon, diverse stakeholders as constituents of the Digital Currency Governance Consortium were consulted to design recommendations for the international organisations and national/regional authorities, including industry stakeholders, while duly acknowledging the pivotal roles of the academia, civil society organisations (CSOs), and most importantly, users in evolving a responsible ecosystem.[150] It is worth noting that the recommendations appreciate that the distinct opportunities and risks presented by cryptoassets will also require an innovative approach, while developing from insights and best practices advanced in other sectors as well. The need, though, for a global approach is merited owing to the borderless nature of technology, as well as the potential of interconnectedness within the cryptoasset ecosystem and with the conventional financial system.[151] Though the global approach is an ideal pathway, various barriers may impede it. These pertain to the lack of harmonised taxonomies/classification, to regulatory arbitrage, and to fragmented monitoring, supervision, and enforcement, including the lack of coordination among various law enforcement agencies, which leads to inconsistent enforcement and lack of coherence in regulatory approaches.[152]

---

148 World Economic Forum (WEF) (2023), "Pathways to the regulation of crypto-assets: A global approach", *WEF White Paper*, May 2023, https://www3.weforum.org/docs/WEF_Pathways_to_the_Regulation_of_Crypto_Assets_2023.pdf, accessed 20/12/2023

149 Ibid note [148], WEF (2023)

150 Ibid note [148], WEF (2023)

151 Ibid note [148], WEF (2023)

152 Ibid note [148], WEF (2023)

CHAPTER 7

Cryptoasset regulatory policies in selected advanced Western economies

7.1 Introduction

In general, almost all advanced Western economies are marked by strong, well established banking systems. This chapter focuses on cryptoassets regulatory policies in the advanced economies of the United States, UK, Australia, Canada, EU, and Switzerland. The two national economies of the United States and the UK are selected for study as they play dominant roles in the advancement of fintechs in general and the crypto industry in particular. The United States leads the world as the most active fintech hub. The implications flowing from Brexit make the UK an interesting country for case study as the country leans on fintech start up developments to spur growth. Australia and Canada are selected mainly because of their general aggressiveness toward cryptoassets development in general and Bitcoin to some extent. Both economies are also part of the UK-led Commonwealth of Nations adhering to common law practices. The EU is selected as it is one of the largest economic blocs in the world with substantial global influence on financial regulatory development. Switzerland is one of the world's leading financial enclaves with strong banking and finance traditions. It would be interesting to see how it copes with the global impact of the crypto industry. Therefore, how regulators deal with cryptoassets in these respective national and regional economies is of interest to the world as these economies are sophisticated and generally well-regulated.[1]

The analysis regarding regulatory approaches for an emerging and potentially private global currency starts with a discussion on the evolution of sovereign or fiat currencies. Fiat money has a hierarchical nature.[2] It is a promise to pay and stands as the ultimate form of money, and it achieves this as it has the most credible promise. Rather than having any kind of natural value, money's value depends on the credibility of its issuers, and that credibility relies upon an elaborate institutional infrastructure. Where confidence in that institutional structure

1 Blandin, A., Cloots, A. S., Hussan, H., Rauchs, M., Saleuddin, R., Allen, J. G., Zhang, B. & Cloud, K. (2019), *Global cryptoasset regulatory landscape study*, Cambridge, Cambridge Centre for Alternative Finance (CCAF).

2 Johnson, M. (2015), "Is money in your pocket same as money in the bank?", *Investopedia*, 24/12/2015, www.investopedia.com/../money-your-pocket-worth-same-bank.asp, accessed 02/02/2018.

DOI: 10.4324/9781032667416-7

is disturbed, so would the value of money. Cash and bank deposits are examples of different forms of money. An exchange rate is involved when switching from one form of money to another. In all these alluded to advanced economies, money could be exchanged between cash and deposit amounts, one for one, or at par rate. This, however, might not always be the case, as US history and events in Greece in 2015 confirmed.

7.2 Historical background

When capital controls were imposed in Greece in 2015, the value of a euro in a Greek bank account was reduced.[3] This resulted in merchants offering discounts from customers paying in cash. The cause of this were the capital controls which made euro deposit accounts less liquid than euros in cash notes. Liquidity is one of the essential features of money and the value it claims to hold. Restrictions arising from capital controls demonstrate how the liquidity of different forms of money cause the value to deviate. Apart from the matter of liquidity, another factor that can have this effect is the credibility of the issuer.[4]

In times of crisis, such loss in liquidity becomes more apparent, as occurred in Greece and elsewhere recently.[5] In the US antebellum period, from the adoption of the US Constitution in 1789 to the commencement of the Civil War,[6] the United States used gold and silver coins as government sanctioned forms of money, alongside notes issued by banks and only of value if the bank survived. In Greece, paper note euros are liabilities of the ECB, rather than euro-denominated Greek bank deposits or liabilities of private Greek banks.

The hierarchical nature of money[7] is reflected by the differentiation between the liabilities of public institutions and those of private institutions. During the time of the gold standard, when gold functioned as the means of final payment, with everything else merely a promise to pay, gold sat at the top of the hierarchy. For a fiat-backed monetary system, the state-issued currency is at the top of the hierarchy. It is money by decree which has value because the state is promising to enforce its exchangeability for goods and services, and its ability to store value is bestowed to it by law.

For the general public, the ability to make payments directly from their deposit accounts at par value with cash transactions implies that these are equivalent forms of money, where bank deposits are deemed a more secure storage for cash.

---

3 Kambas, M. & Gregorio, D. (2017), "Greece to further ease restrictions on individual bank withdrawals", *Reuters*, 04/08/2017, www.reuters.com/../greece-capital-controls/greece-to-furtherease-restrictions-on, accessed 02/02/2018.

4 Ashton, M. (2016), *What's wrong with money? The biggest bubble of all*, New York, John Wiley & Sons.

5 Ibid note [4], Ashton (2016).

6 Bodenhorn, H. (2015), "Antebellum banking in the United States", *Economic History Association Paper*, www.eh.net/encyclopedia/antebellum-banking-in-the-united-states, accessed 02/02/2018.

7 Kelton, S. A. (1998), "The hierarchy of money", *Levy Economics Institute of Bard College WorkingPaperNo. 231*, April 1998.

Banks, in contrast, see the same deposit account as their own ability or promise to pay the state-issued currency. In practice, banks need to hold only a fraction of their customers' deposits in the form of that currency.

Thus far, cryptoassets are treated as a private digital money or a commodity, depending on the jurisdiction concerned. Digital money exists only in digital form and does not have any physical equivalent in the real world, but it can have the key essential characteristics of conventional or fiat money, as it can be obtained, transferred, or exchanged for another currency or used to transact in goods and services. Above all, it is not geographically restricted.[8] A *cryptoasset* is an asset that can be used as a means of exchange. It is deemed reliable as it is based on cryptography, which primarily seeks to make communications secure. Its mathematics based and algorithmic protocol ensures reliability. Cryptoassets use blockchain and a decentralised ledger that operates without any supervisory authority controls. They therefore differ from the conventional digital money in being decentralised and being anonymous in nature but are transparent.[9]

Digital currencies are a non-physical representation of money. This contrasts with *cryptoassets*, which represent a truly online asset that does not have value other than in its virtual world.[10] Notable examples of virtual currency are Poké-Coins found in the Pokémon Go game, Facebook credit for in platform game, and K-star within the Kardashian game app. In each of these, traditional fiat currency in digital form must be exchanged for the virtual currency, but it is a one-way flow as there is no easy way to exchange these items back to traditional fiat currency or use to buy things in the real world, as their use and value reside within the platform they have been created in.

A *digital currency*, by comparison, is a digital representation of a physical asset, such as money in a PayPal wallet that can be used to buy K-stars. Importantly, digital currency is owned and controlled by central banks and governments. Virtual currency, on the other hand, is decentralised and can be created by any corporate app maker or individual. It thus falls under a bespoke set of creation and usage rules external to national fiscal policy.

Bearing in mind the aforementioned, cryptocurrency regulatory policies would depend on how particular economies view it. Since the treatment of Bitcoin appears to differ between economies, their regulatory approach is likely to differ until, perhaps, when a more universal consensus is achieved. This chapter focuses on regulatory policies in the United States, UK, Australia, Canada, the EU, and Switzerland for the reasons mentioned earlier.

8 Tar, A. (2017), "Digital currencies vs. cryptocurrencies", *Coin Telegraph*, 13/12/2017, www.cointelegraph.com/expllained/digital-currencies-vs-cryptocurrencies-explained, accessed 02/02/2018.

9 Annison, T. (2017), "Virtual vs digital currency-What's the difference?", *The Market Mogul*, 22/07/2017, www.themarketmogul.com/difference-virtual-digital-crypto-currencies, accessed 02/02/2018.

10 Ibid note [9], Annison (2017).

7.3 The US cryptoasset regulatory policy

On 24 April 2025, the US Federal Reserve withdrew its previous guidance that had previously required banks to provide advanced notification or receive advance authorisation before engaging in many cryptocurrencies or assets. From then on, they have categorised crypto as part of its general safety and soundness regime. A notification requirement by the banks remains. The Federal Deposit Insurance Corporation (FDIC) and the Office of the Comptroller of the Currency (OCC) have also removed guidance requiring banks to obtain advanced approval before engaging in digital asset activities.[11]

The then outgoing chair of the Federal Reserve, Janet Yellen, said that cryptocurrencies are highly speculative assets, are not a stable store of value, do not constitute legal tender, and for now play a very small role in the payment system. She appeared to downplay cryptoassets' ability to have an impact on the wider financial markets.[12]

The US SEC has modernised the rules relating to exchange-traded funds (ETFs). By May 2024, it had given the green light for ETFs that hold Ether, the world's second largest crypto, some 6 months subsequent to the launch of Bitcoin ETFs that witnessed some of the most successful debuts in the industry's history. In combination, the funds have attracted more than US$6 billion of net inflows, led by the iShares Bitcoin Trust (IBIT).[13] Pertaining to ICOs, the SEC stated that whether or not a particular token or cryptocurrency falls foul of securities laws depends on the facts and circumstances of each case. According to Joshua Ashley Klayman, Chair of the Wall Street Blockchain Alliance's legal working group, this means that existing facts- and circumstances-based enquiries, and not bright line tests,[14] should continue to apply to token sales. The SEC states that whether a particular investment transaction would constitute a security offering would depend on the case's facts and circumstances, including the economic realities of the transaction, regardless of the terminology or technology used.[15] So far, its enforcement actions against ICO sponsors included halting one[16] and exposing alleged frauds.[17] The then SEC chairman, Jay Clayton, articulated concerns about market participants who extend customers'

11 www.mondaq.com/unitedstates/fin-tech/1619658/federal-reserve-board-wthdraws-guidance-regardingh-digital-asset-activities, accessed 05/05/2025.

12 Disis, J. (2017), "Fed chair calls Bitcoin highly speculative", *CNN*, 13/12/2017, www.cnn.com/2017/12/13/investigating/Bitcoin-janet-yellen-federal../index.html, accessed 02/02/2018.

13 Pound, J. (2024), "Eher ETFs appear set to launch on Tuesday, six months after massive debut for bitcoin funds", *CNBC*, 22/07/2024, www.cnbc.com/2024/07/22/ether-etfs-seem-set-to-launch-on-tuesday-six-months-after-bitcoin-funds-debut.html, accessed 24/07/2024

14 These are strictly interpreted legal or regulatory rules which have little or no scope for flexible interpretation.

15 SEC (2017), "SEC exposes two initial coin offerings purportedly backed by real estate and diamonds", *SEC Press Release 2017–85*, 29/09/2017, www.sec.gov/news/press-release/2017-186-0, accessed 02/02/2018.

16 SEC (2018), "SEC halts alleged initial coin offering scam", *SEC Press Release 2018–8*, 30/01/2018, www.sec.gov/news/press-release/2018-8, accessed 02/02/2018.

17 Ibid note [16], SEC (2017). Here, the SEC charged REcoin, a cryptocurrency-backed real estate company and DRC World, a diamond company with fraud.

credit and ICO gatekeepers, such as lawyers,[18] and celebrities who help promote ICOs.[19] On 25 July 2017, the SEC issued an investor bulletin regarding ICOs, stating that these could be fair and lawful investment opportunities but might be used improperly.[20] In an effort to advance ICO development, the SEC has provided a dedicated ICO guide.[21] The contents basically mirror the SEC's ICO perspective discussed earlier. Jay Clayton, in an earlier testimony to a US Senate hearing, has stated that most ICOs he came across previously were essentially securities requiring SEC registration.[22] The SEC further mentioned that the delay thus far in framing crypto regulation would provide more time for the industry to advance on its own.[23] As alluded to earlier, SEC surprised the crypto community with giving approval to Blockstack,[24] a start up exploring to design a new version of the internet using blockchain that gives users control over their personal data. Blockstack would be allowed to raise US$28 million via token sales that would comply with Regulation A+, which is applicable only to small companies.

The CFTC confirms that Bitcoin and other digital currencies are commodities covered by the Commodity Exchange Act (CEA), specifically under Section 1a (9) of the CEA. This defines *commodity* as including "all services, rights, and interests in which contracts for future delivery are presently or in the future dealt in".[25] New York Law School professor Houman Shadab, an expert in cryptographic technologies, cautioned, however, that the CFTC's oversight of the technology is limited to these applications, but this puts to rest any notion that all virtual currencies qualify as securities, as otherwise the SEC would have taken the action against Coinflip, a provider of ATMs that enable people to trade cash

---

18 Zinman, D., Walker, J. Q., Myers, M. W. & O'Byrne, W. (2018), "SEC issues warning to lawyers on ICOs", *Big Law Business*, 23/02/2018, www.biglawbusiness.com/sec-issues-warning-tolawyers-on-icos/, accessed 25/02/2018.

19 SEC (2017), "SEC statement urging caution around celebrity backed ICOs", *SEC Public Statement*, 01/11/2017, www.ec.gov/news/public../statement-potentially-unlawful-promotion-icos, accessed 02/02/2018.

20 SEC (2017), "Investor bulletin: Initial coin offerings", *Investor Alerts and Bulletins*, 25/07/2017, www.sec.gov/oiea/investor-alerts-and-bulletins/ib_coinofferings, accessed 02/02/2018.

21 Suberg, W. (2019), "US SEC highlights dedicated ICO guide amid ongoing regulatory debate", *Coin Telegraph*, 11/02/2019, www.cointelegraph.com/news/us-sec-highlights-dedicated-ico-guide-amid-ongoing-regulatory-debate, accessed 5/03/2019.

22 Clayton, J. (2018), "Testimony on 'Oversight of the U.S. Securities and Exchange Commission'", *SEC's Chairman's Testimony before the U.S. Senate Committee on Banking, Housing, and Urban Affairs*, 11/12/2018, www.sec.gov/newsroom/speeches-statements/dec-11-2018-testimony-oversight-us-securities-exchange-commission, accessed 05/03/2019.

23 Berman, A. (2019), "SEC 'crypto mon': Delay in crypto regulation may allow more freedom for technology", *Coin Telegraph*, 10/02/2019, www.cointelegraph.com/../sec-crypto-mom-delayin-crypto-regulation-may-allow, accessed 5/03/2019.

24 Erlich, S. (2019), "Blockstack prepares for its true test following SEC approval to raise $28 million on a blockchain", *Forbes*, 16/07/2019, www.forbes.com/sites/stevenehrlich/2019/07/16/blockstack-prepares-for-its-true-test-following-sec-approval-to-raise-28-million-on-a-blockchain/, accessed 18/07/2019.

25 CFTC (2015), "Order instituting proceedings pursuant to sections 6 (c) and 6(d) of the Commodity Exchange Act, making findings and imposing remedial sanctions", *Order CFTC Docket No.15–29*, 17/09/2015.

to cryptocurrency and vice versa. This entity is said to have violated Section 4c of the CEA and Part 32 of the CFTC's regulations.[26]

The CFTC, therefore, claims jurisdiction over fraud and manipulation involving Bitcoin traded in interstate commerce and the regulation of commodity futures linked directly to Bitcoin. The CFTC allowed the Chicago Mercantile Exchange (CME)[27] and Chicago Board Options Exchange (CBOE)[28] to launch Bitcoin futures. It also approved a platform for the trading and clearing of virtual currency derivatives for LedgerX,[29] a swap execution facility and derivatives clearing organisation.

The US IRS Virtual Currency Guidance treats Bitcoin as property for federal tax purposes. This means that a capital gain or loss should be recorded as if it were a transaction involving property. If held for resale, it should be treated as an inventory, and therefore an ordinary gain or loss recorded. When used for payment, Bitcoin should be treated like a foreign currency that must be converted, and its fair exchange value verified on an exchange. The IRS thus appears to treat Bitcoin as a hybrid, depending on the manner of use or intention.[30]

The United States is a federal republic comprising 50 states, a federal district (namely Washington, DC), five major territories, and various minor islands. Federal regulations and state-led legislation are in play where virtual currencies such as Bitcoin are concerned. Several US states plan to approve the acceptance and promotion of the use of Bitcoin and blockchain technology. From 1 January 2025, Arizona has allowed payment of local taxes in Bitcoin by cryptocurrency service providers,[31] while Vermont[32] has recognised blockchain as evidence and Delaware has authorised the registration of shares in Delaware[33] companies in blockchain form.

The National Conference of Commissioners on Uniform State Laws approved a model Act providing for the regulation of digital currency businesses at the

---

26 Rizzo, P. (2015), "CFTC ruling defines Bitcoin and digital currencies as commodities", *Coin Desk*, 18/09/2017, www.coindesk.com>Regulation, accessed 02/02/2018; Brito, J., Shadab, H. & Castillo, A. (Fall 2014), "Bitcoin financial regulation: Securities, derivatives, prediction markets, and gambling", *The Columbia Science & Technology Law Review*, XVI: 144–221.

27 Price, M. & McCrank, J. (2017), "U.S. regulator says it will allow CME Group, CBOE to list Bitcoin futures", *Reuters*, 01/12/2017, www.reuters.com/../Bitcoin/u-s-regulator-says-it-willallow-cme-group-cboes-to, accessed 02/02/2018.

28 Ibid note [28], Price & McCrank (2017).

29 CFTC (2017), "CFTC grants DCO (Derivatives Clearing Organization) Registration to LedgerX LLC", *CFTC Press Release pr7592–17*, 24/07/2017.

30 IRS (2014), "IRS virtual currency guidance: Virtual currency is treated as property for U.S. federal tax purposes; General Rules for property transactions apply", *IRS Notice IR-2014–36*, 25/03/2014; IRS (2014a), "IRS Notice 2014–21", *IRS Notice 2014–21*, 14/04/2014.

31 Arizona State Senate Fact, Sheet for SB, www.azleg.gov/legtext/56leg/2R/summary/S.1128FICO.DOCX.htm, accessed 05/05/2025.

32 Higgins, S. (2018), "Vermont could collect taxes in crypto under proposed law", Coin Desk, 08/01/2018.

33 Roberts, J. J. (2017), "Companies can put shareholders on a blockchain starting today", *Fortune*, 01/08/2017, www.fortune.com>Tech>Blockchain, accessed 02/02/2018.

state level.[34] The Uniform Law Commission (ULC) defines *virtual currency* as a form of electronic value that depends on the market. It is not backed by a government, which means it lacks status as a legal tender. Interests in cryptocurrencies have grown because of the belief that they are relatively safe from hacking, often are cheaper and faster, and have finality of payment. Cryptocurrencies have legitimate purposes and can be bought, sold, and exchanged with other kinds of virtual currencies or fiat currencies. Responding to the absence of an overarching federal payments regulatory framework, state laws in play needed to be harmonised to the extent possible. The model Act as approved by the National Conference of Commissioners on Uniform State Laws covers licensing requirements, reciprocity, consumer protection, cybersecurity, anti–money laundering, and supervision of licensees.[35] More recently, they have produced a Virtual Currency Consumer Protection Act in 2024.[36]

The preceding are regulatory initiatives at the federal and state levels in the United States. Regulatory watchers are eagerly awaiting further initiatives from the SEC and the CFTC following the joint authorship of a paper[37] looking at cryptocurrency rules, much of which is still relevant. The paper's key points are as follows:

1. Transparency, investor protection, and market integrity are critical to ensuring that innovation continues.
2. The collective market capitalisation of cryptocurrencies by US investors in cryptocurrencies is significant, although the Federal Reserve takes the view that for now market participation in cryptocurrencies has yet to reach a level warranting a response. Cryptocurrencies' prices are set by trading on spot platforms. Many of these platforms are based offshore, where none of them are registered with either the SEC or CFTC.
3. A cryptocurrency is initially designed as a payment facilitation alternative to fiat currencies, but it lacks the sovereign backing available to the latter. A cryptocurrency also lacks other fiat currencies' hallmarks, such as governance standards, accountability, and oversight, and regular and reliable reporting of trading and related financial data. Importantly, cryptocurrencies are now being promoted, pursued, and traded as investment assets, with their purported utility as an efficient medium of exchange being a distant secondary characteristic.

34 Uniform Law Commission (ULC) (2017), "Regulation of virtual currency businesses act", *ULC*, 14/07/2017, www.uniformlaws.org/../regulation%20of%20virtual%20currencies/URVCBA_Final_, accessed 02/02/2018.

35 Ibid note [35], ULC (2017).

36 www.uniformlaws.org/viewdocument/2024-june-26-meeting?CommunityKey=4ba1acad-6816-49a7-84c8-018a850d535f, accessed 05/05/2025.

37 Clayton, J. & Giancarlo, J. C. (2018), "Regulators are looking at cryptocurrency: At the SEC and CFTC, we take our responsibility seriously", *The Wall Street Journal*, 24/01/2018.

4. For some areas, the federal authority to police cryptocurrencies is clear. The Bank Secrecy Act and its implementing regulations set up federal anti–money laundering obligations that apply to most activities in the business of accepting and transmitting, selling, or storing cryptocurrencies. In other areas, though, federal authority obligations are unclear. Some would point to the absence of US and other government market regulations on the matter.
5. Two large CFTC regulated exchanges were permitted to self-certify and commence trading futures products without CFTC approval. They do now expend considerable time engaging with CFTC staff and have agreed to implement risk mitigation and oversight measures, including heightened margin requirements and a further requirement that the exchanges have information sharing agreements in place with underlying Bitcoin trading platforms. This enabled the CFTC to gain oversight over the US Bitcoin futures market and access to data that could facilitate the detection and pursuit of bad participants in underlying spot markets.
6. The SEC does not have direct oversight of transactions in currencies or commodities, though some products tagged as cryptocurrencies have the characteristics of securities. Where this is the case, the offer, sale, and trading of such products must be undertaken in compliance with existing securities laws. The SEC has shown that it will vigorously pursue those who seek to evade the registration, disclosure, and anti-fraud requirements of US securities laws. The SEC additionally monitors the cryptocurrency related activities of the market participants it regulates, including broker dealers, investment advisers, and trading platforms.
7. The SEC is dedicating a significant portion of its resources to the ICO market. The SEC has made it clear through various announcements that federal securities laws apply irrespective of whether the offered security is tagged as coin, utility token, rather than a stock, bond, or investment contract. The SEC has cautioned market participants of its concerns over many examples of form being elevated over substance. The use of such form based arguments has deprived investors of mandatory protections.
8. The CFTC, SEC, together with other federal and state regulators and criminal authorities, will continue to collaborate to ensure transparency and integrity in these markets and, importantly, to deter and prosecute fraud and abuse.
9. Going by past tech journeys in the United States, distributed ledger technology is likely to be followed by many more major innovations, but the SEC, CFTC, and others with similar obligations will not allow it or any other tech advancements to disrupt regulators' commitment to fair and sound markets.

10. The CFTC has also approved a platform for the trading, that is, a swap execution facility and derivatives clearing organisation. It is now requesting industry feedback so as to better comprehend the markets, mechanics, and technology for cryptoassets beyond Bitcoin and, in particular, the Ether and Ethereum networks.[38]

At the 6 February 2018 Senate Hearing, the SEC provided the following testimony, of which the following parts are still relevant today:[39]

1. The SEC's mission is to protect investors, maintain fair and orderly and efficient markets, and facilitate capital formation. These are achieved through the SEC's enforcement of the federal securities laws and oversight of the securities markets and their participants. The SEC regulates securities transactions and certain individuals and firms participating in the securities markets, but it does not have direct oversight of transactions in currencies or commodities, including currency trading platforms.
2. The emerging cryptocurrency and ICO markets have grown rapidly and attracted significant capital from retail investors. These can benefit the economy and investors, but when laws are not adhered to, the risks to all investors are high. Such risks include risks caused by or related to poor, incorrect, or non-existent disclosures, extreme price volatility, manipulation, frauds, and thefts from hackings.
3. Regardless of the promise of technology, those investing in opportunities falling within the scope of federal securities laws deserve full protection under those laws. Enthusiasms get heightened by the "missing out" syndrome. Fraudsters and others prey on such enthusiasm.
4. The SEC, together with the CFTC as federal market regulators, is charged with establishing a regulatory environment for investors and market participants that fosters innovation, market integrity, and ultimately, confidence. The SEC, in relation to cryptocurrencies, ICOs, and related assets, has taken various initiatives and actions. A cornerstone of such initiatives is to ensure that investors make informed decisions, a core principle of federal securities laws embodied in the SEC's registration requirements. It is worth adding that over recent years, security token offerings (STOs) have become much more popular and largely replaced ICOs. STOs represent real financial assets, such as shares, land, or investment funds. These require legal and regulatory approval and are much safer from the point of view of consumers.

38 CFTC (2019), "CFTC's technology advisory committee to meet on 27th March 2019", *CFTC Press Release*, 27/02/2019, www.cftc.gov/PressRoom/PressReleases/7880-19, accessed March 2019.

39 Written Testimony of Jay Clayton, Chairman of SEC Before the Senate Committee, Washington, D.C., 06/02/2018.

5. These market products span national boundaries, and significant trading may occur on systems and platforms outside the United States, meaning, that the funds involved might migrate quickly overseas without notice of investors' knowledge. This means risks could be amplified, including the risks that US market regulators, such as the SEC and state securities regulators, may not be able to effectively pursue participants who do not follow the rules or recover funds. There are also significant security risks arising from the loss of investment and personal information due to hacks of online trading platforms.
6. Many cryptocurrencies are touted as having the same functions as fiat currencies, but without the backing of governments. Their beneficial features generally claim to include the ability to make transfers without an intermediary and without geographic limitations and with lower transaction costs compared to other forms of payment. Critics counterclaim that these benefits are unproven, while the other touted benefits such as the anonymity of buyers and sellers, and the absence of government oversight could also facilitate illicit trading. The proliferation and popularity of cryptocurrency markets gives rise to questions as to whether the country's historical regulatory approach could deal with such financial products that look and sound like conventional financial products. In reality, investors trading on such crypto platforms are not protected by market protections that they have taken for granted when transacting through broker dealers on registered exchanges or alternative trading systems such as best executions, prohibitions on front-running, short sale restrictions, and custody and capital requirements.
7. It seems that many US based cryptocurrency trading platforms have elected to be regulated as money transmission services. Such predominantly state-regulated payment services are traditionally not subject to direct oversight by the SEC and CFTC. Traditionally, such money transfer services have not quoted prices or offered other services similar to securities, commodities, and currency exchanges. The current applicable regulatory framework for cryptocurrency trading was not designed with trading of the kind seen today. The SEC, together with the CFTC, is open to exploring with Congress, as well as other federal and state agencies, whether increased federal regulation of cryptocurrency trading platforms is necessary or appropriate.
8. Currently, the SEC is monitoring the crypto-related activities of the market participants it regulates, including brokers, dealers, investment advisers, and trading platforms. Participants that allow for payments in cryptocurrencies, allow customers to purchase cryptocurrencies, including on margin, or otherwise use cryptocurrencies to facilitate securities transactions are expected to exercise caution, including ensuring that their cryptocurrency activities are not undermining their anti–money laundering and know your customer obligations.

9. Financial products linked to digital assets, including cryptocurrencies, could be structured as securities products subject to federal securities laws even if the underlying cryptocurrencies are not themselves securities. Market participants have sought SEC approval for new products and services of this type that are focused on retail investors, including cryptocurrency linked exchange-traded funds, of which 11 spot price Bitcoin ETFs entered the market in January 2024.
10. Various market professionals have touted the utility or voucher like characteristics of their proposed ICOs to differentiate them from conventional securities, by elevating form over substance. The SEC considers the rise of such form based arguments as a disturbing trend depriving investors of mandatory protections that clearly are required as a consequence of the structure of the transaction. The SEC cautions that merely calling a token a utility token or structuring it to provide some utility does not prevent the token from being a security. It is particularly more troubling when promoters of such offerings emphasised the secondary market trading potential of these tokens or the ability to sell them on an exchange for profit. This implies that prospective investors are being sold on the potential for tokens to increase in value and with the ability to lock in those increases by reselling the tokens on a secondary market or otherwise profit from the tokens based on the efforts of others. The SEC considers all these as key hallmarks of security and securities offerings.
11. Gatekeepers and others, including securities lawyers, accountants, and consultants, are cautioned to focus on their responsibilities and be guided by the principal motivations for SEC registration, offering process and disclosure requirements, and investor protection. Engaging in the business of selling securities generally requires a license. Experience suggests that excessive touting in thinly traded and volatile markets could be indicators of scalping, pump and dump, and other manipulations, and frauds. Those who operate systems and platforms that effect or facilitate transaction in crypto-products could be operating unregistered exchanges or broker-dealers in violation of the Securities Act of 1934. The SEC acknowledges the responsible steps taken by social media platforms, such as Facebook, to restrict the ability of users to promote ICOs and cryptoassets on their platforms.
12. The SEC's Division of Enforcement set up a new Cyber Unit focusing on misconduct involving distributed ledger technology and ICOs, the dissemination of false information through electronic and social media, brokerage account takeovers, hacking to obtain nonpublic information, and threats to trading platforms. The Cyber Unit collaborates closely with the cross-divisional Distributed Ledger Technology Working Group.
13. The SEC has taken enforcement proceedings, in one case against an individual for defrauding investors in a pair of ICOs purportedly

backed by investments in real estate and diamonds, when neither company had real operations. The SEC obtained an emergency asset freeze to halt an alleged ICO fraud operated by a recidivist securities law violator that purportedly raised up to $15 million from thousands of investors in August 2017. Another company in December 2017 halted its ICO after being told by the SEC that its ICO was an unregistered offering and sale of securities. More recently, the SEC halted an allegedly fraudulent ICO that targeted retail investors promoting what it claimed as the world's first decentralised bank. The SEC is also increasingly concerned with recent instances of public companies without a meaningful record in pursuing distributed ledger technology or blockchain technology changing their business models and names to reflect a focus on these without adequate disclosure to investors about their business model changes and the risks involved. The SEC is therefore now monitoring this closely, especially as to whether the disclosures comply with federal securities laws.

The CFTC chairman submitted the following testimony to the Senate Banking Committee:[40]

1. Virtual currencies or cryptocurrencies are a digital representation of value that function as a medium of exchange, a unit of account, and/or a store of value. Cryptocurrencies may be all things to all people; for some, potential riches through rapid increase in value; for others, the next big thing, a technological revolution, and an exorable value proposition; but for some others, a fraud, a new form of temptation and allure, and a way to take the money of the unsuspecting.
2. The total value of all outstanding Bitcoins on 5 February 2018 was about $130 billion against a Bitcoin price of $7,700. Bitcoin's market cap or even digital currencies' market cap of US$365 billion is relatively much smaller than the US stock market cap, or that for gold, estimated at some $8 trillion. Yet despite being a relatively small asset class, virtual currencies present novel challenges for regulators.
3. The CFTC's mission is to foster open, transparent, competitive, and financially sound derivatives markets. By working to avoid systemic risks, the CFTC aims to protect market users and their funds, consumers, and the public from fraud, manipulation, and abusive practices related to derivatives and products subject to the CEA.
4. The CFTC began with the oversight of agricultural commodities, but gradually, its organised commodity future markets evolved to include those for energy and metals commodities collectively, including crude oil, heating oil, gasoline, copper, gold, and silver. The CFTC also now

40 Written Testimony of J. Christopher Giancarlo, Chairman Commodities Futures Trading Commission (CFTC) Before the Senate Banking Committee, 06/02/2018.

oversees commodity futures markets for financial products, such as interest rates, stock indexes, and foreign currency. The CEA's definition of "commodity" is broad. It can mean physical products, such as agricultural products; or natural resource, like gold or oil; a currency or interest rate; or all services, rights, and interests in which contracts for future delivery are presently or in the future dealt with. The Dodd–Frank Act of 2010 empowers the CFTC to oversee most of the US swaps markets[41] in addition to exchange-traded futures markets.[42]

More than 90% of Fortune 500 companies use derivatives[43] to manage commercial or market risks in their worldwide business operations. When properly used, derivatives serve the needs of society to help moderate price, supply, and other commercial risks to free up capital for economic growth.

5. The CFTC regulates derivatives market participants and activities. It oversees a variety of individuals and organisations. These include swap execution facilities, futures commission merchants, commodity pool operators, and other entities. The CFTC prosecutes derivative market frauds and manipulations, including misconduct in underlying spot markets for commodities. The CFTC has stipulated that those cryptoassets, such as Bitcoin, met the definition of "commodity" under the Commodity Exchange Act 1936 (CEA). However, the CFTC does not have regulatory jurisdiction under the CEA over the markets or platforms undertaking cash or spot transactions in virtual currencies or other commodities or over participants in such platforms. Current US laws, in fact, do not provide any US federal regulator with such regulatory oversight authority over spot[44] virtual currency platforms operating in the United States or abroad. Nevertheless, the CFTC does have the jurisdiction to enforce civil enforcement actions concerning fraud and market manipulation in virtual currency derivatives markets, and in underlying virtual currency spot markets, through subpoena and other investigative powers. The CFTC, in contrast to the spot markets, has both regulatory and enforcement powers under the CEAs over derivatives on virtual currencies traded in the United States. For derivatives on virtual currencies traded in US markets, the CFTC conducts comprehensive regulatory oversight, including

41 These are markets made up of parties engaged in contracts for differences. These are contracts where the two parties pay or receive money from each other according to the amount by which a price or value has gone up or down. They are primarily used to hedge a financial risk.

42 A *futures contract* is one where a party pays or receives money according to whether an underlying asset goes up or down in value. These can be traded privately (OTC) or on an exchange, as though it were a share.

43 A generic term to cover futures, options, and contracts for differences which are all contracts where parties can trade against the change in value of an underlying asset, currency, or interest rate.

44 The current price for an asset, that is, one quoted for the next 48 hours as opposed to a price for future delivery.

imposing registration requirements and compliance with a full range of requirements for trade practice and market surveillance, reporting and monitoring standards for conduct, capital requirements, and platforms and systems safeguards.

6. The CFTC has been direct in asserting its area of statutory jurisdiction concerning virtual currencies derivatives. They have taken enforcement action to prohibit wash trading[45] and prearranged trades on a virtual currency derivatives platform. They have also taken action against a Bitcoin futures exchange operating in the United States that failed to register with it. The CFTC has also issued proposed guidance on what a derivative market is, and what is a spot market in the virtual currency context. They also issued warnings about valuations and volatility in spot virtual currency markets, besides launching an unprecedented consumer education effort.
7. The CFTC has been especially assertive of its enforcement jurisdiction over virtual currencies. Its virtual currency enforcement task force garners and deploys relevant expertise in this evolving asset class and shares information with counterparts at the SEC with similar virtual currency expertise. The CFTC took enforcement action against a virtual currency Ponzi scheme. Between January and February 2018, the CFTC filed a series of civil enforcement actions against perpetrators of fraud, market manipulation, and disruptive trading involving virtual currency. These include My Big Coin Pay Inc., the Entrepreneurs Headquarters Limited, and Coin Drop Markets.
8. As for Bitcoin futures, at one point the open interest at CME of 6,695 Bitcoins at CBOE Futures Exchange is relatively small. At a price of around $7,700 per Bitcoin, the notional value came to about $94 million. By comparison, the notional amount of the open interest in CME's WTI crude oil futures was more than a thousand times larger, or about US$170 billion, as of 2 February 2018, while the notional amount represented by the open interest of Comex gold futures was about $74 billion.
9. Futures exchanges may self-certify new products on 24-hour notice prior to trading under CEA and CFTC regulations and related guidance. This is to enable futures exchanges to quickly bring new products to the marketplace. Prior to their certifying and launching of Bitcoin futures in December 2017, both the CME and CBOE had numerous discussions and exchanged numerous draft product terms and conditions with CFTC over some months. CFTC staff also secured the voluntary co-operation of CME and CBOE with a set of enhanced monitoring and risk management steps.

---

45 A *wash trade* is an artificial trading activity where a participant simultaneously buys and sells the same investment to create an artificial price. In some states, for example, the United States, the UK, the EU, and Hong Kong, this will amount to market manipulation.

10. Subsequent to the launch of Bitcoin futures, criticisms were directed at the self-certification process by market participants. They questioned why the CFTC did not hold public hearings prior to the launch. However, the CFTC focus is on how the futures contract and cash settlement indices are designed to bar manipulation and the appropriate level of contract margining to meet CEA and CFTC regulations, rather than seeking to solicit and address stakeholder concerns in new product self-certification, appropriately the function of the futures exchanges and futures clearinghouses. The CFTC's response to the self-certification of Bitcoin futures has been a balanced one that has culminated in the world's first federally regulated Bitcoin futures market. Blocking self-certification would not have stopped the rise of Bitcoin or other virtual currencies; it would instead ensure that virtual currency spot markets continue to operate without effective and data-enabled federal regulatory surveillance for fraud and manipulation.
11. The CFTC has sufficient authority under the CEA to protect investors in virtual currency derivatives. With regards to virtual currency spot markets, the CFTC has only enforcement jurisdiction to investigate and, where appropriate, conduct civil enforcement actions against fraud and manipulation. Any extension of the CFTC's regulatory authority to virtual currency spot market would require statutory amendment of the Commodity Exchange Act.
12. The CFTC believes that the responsible regulatory response to virtual currencies must begin with consumer education. The CFTC has produced an information primer on virtual currencies, consumer and market advisories on Bitcoin investing and other virtual currencies, a dedicated CFTC Bitcoin webpage, several podcasts regarding virtual currencies and underlying technology, the weekly publication of Bitcoin futures, and analysis of Bitcoin spot market data. The CFTC's Office of Consumer Education and Outreach (OCEO) engages actively with responsible outside partners to educate consumers on Bitcoin and other virtual currencies. The OCEO is in working partnership with the Consumer Finance Protection Bureau, the American Association of Retired Persons, the North American Securities Administrators Association (NASAA), the National Attorneys General Training and Research Institute, and the Federal Reserve Bank of Chicago.
13. The CFTC's enforcement jurisdiction over virtual currencies is not exclusive. This means that the US approach to oversight of virtual currencies is evolving into a multifaceted, multi-regulatory approach that includes the SEC, state banking regulators, the IRA, and the Treasury's Financial Crimes Enforcement Network (FinCEN). The CFTC also actively communicates its approach to virtual currencies with other federal regulators, including the Federal Bureau of Investigation, the Justice Department, and the Financial Stability Oversight

Council. Additionally, the CFTC is in communication with overseas regulatory counterparts through bilateral discussions and in meetings of the Financial Stability Board and the IOSCO.

14. DLT has the potential to enhance economic efficiency, mitigate centralised systemic risk, defend against fraudulent activity, and improve data quality and governance. It is also likely to have a wide and lasting impact on global financial markets in payments, banking, securities settlement, title recording, cybersecurity, and trade reporting and analysis. When attached to virtual currencies, it aims to serve as a new store of value, facilitate secure payments, enable asset transfers, and power new applications.
15. Distributed ledger technology might enable financial market participants to manage the significant operational, transactional, and capital complexities brought about by the many mandates, regulations, and capital requirements stipulated by regulators in the United States and elsewhere in the context of financial stress. Distributed ledger technology could, according to one estimate, eventually enable financial institutions to save some $20 billion in infrastructure and operational costs annually. Blockchain could also cut trading settlement costs by a third, or some $16 billion, annually, and trim capital requirements by some $120 billion. Migrating from systems of record at the firm level to an authoritative system of record at the market level is an enormous opportunity to improve existing market infrastructure. Beyond financial services, distributed ledger technology can benefit international trade, charitable initiatives, and social services. Other distributed ledger technology applications include legal records management, inventory control and logistics, charitable donation tracking and confirmation, voting security, and human refugee identification and relocation.
16. The "do no harm" approach for the development of the internet over the last two decades is well recognised, as is the fact that the enlightened regulatory underpinning of the internet helped bring about many profound changes to society. It was without doubt the right approach for the development of the internet, and the rest is history. This could also be the right approach for distributed ledger technology. Virtual currencies nevertheless require more attentive regulatory oversight in key areas, especially to the extent that retail investors are attracted.
17. The risks of cryptocurrencies and ICOs to all investors are very high, and caution is merited. A key concern is whether the historic approach now in play for the regulation of currency transactions is suitable for the cryptocurrency markets.
18. The CFTC, together with the SEC, would support policy initiatives to review existing frameworks and ensure that they are effective and efficient for the digital era. Consideration should be given to shortcomings of the current approach of state by state money transmitter licensures

> that leaves gaps in protection for virtual currency traders and investors. Proposed federal regulation of virtual currency platforms would need to adjust to the risks posed by relevant trading activity and enhance the efforts to prosecute fraud and manipulation. Suitable federal regulatory oversight could include data reporting, capital requirements, cybersecurity standards, measures to prevent fraud and price manipulation, and anti-money laundering and know your customer protections. The resulting rationalised federal framework may be more effective and efficient in ensuring the integrity of the underlying markets.

Interestingly, previous announcements by the SEC and CFTC on fintech financial products gave the message of the intention to apply a light touch approach to provide space for experimentation and innovation. Both these testimonies give a clear indication that the SEC and CFTC intend to facilitate the expansion of federal oversight on primary and secondary cryptocurrency markets. It is likely that the sway is prompted by the extreme price volatility of cryptocurrencies, the expansive participation of retail investors, the significant thefts and hackings of Bitcoin in cryptocurrency exchanges across the world, the perceived increase of Bitcoin use in illicit activities, the signals of failing economies relying on cryptocurrencies, the avoidance of sanctions and other challenges, as well as the periodic surging of cryptocurrency capitalisation, suggesting its potential evolution into a mainstream asset class that might pose a threat to sovereign fiat currencies.

7.4 Potential cryptoasset regulation in the US

The price volatility of cryptocurrencies, together with the risk of theft for retail investors and allegations of price manipulation, as well as the lack of regulatory oversight, prompted regulatory intervention in the United States. Recent steps have been the congressional hearings of 2025. The title gives a feel of the content: "A Golden Age of Digital Assets: Charting a Path Forward".

The differing perceptions of intrinsic value inevitably have an impact on people's assessment of whether cryptocurrencies as a whole are a fundamentally positive or negative phenomenon, and hence whether they should be regulated with a light or heavy touch.[46] The SEC's view essentially is that although there is some public pressure for a cryptocurrency based on international exchange, it is not yet seeing those benefits manifesting themselves in the marketplace. The CFTC, however, points out that economists posit that there is a relationship between Bitcoin value and the difficulty or cost of mining, and that there is thus a floor price where the level set is above zero. The CFTC stance differs

46 Felsenthal & Overall (2018), "The Regulation of Bitcoin: The role of the CFTC". *Clifford Chance*, https://www.cliffordchance.com/content/dam/cliffordchance/briefings/2018/01/regulation-of-bitcoin-the-role-of-the-CFTC, accessed 05/08/2025.

philosophically from the SEC's in three ways.[47] Firstly, the CFTC believes that cryptocurrencies are CFTC jurisdictional commodities which constitute a fundamentally new asset class. Cryptocurrencies are not simply old wine in new bottles but instead a commodity unlike any the CFTC has dealt with in the past, and hence a genuinely new phenomenon, not just cosmetically, but substantively. Secondly, the CFTC is of the opinion that because Bitcoin and other virtual currencies are a genuinely new economic and financial phenomenon, their characteristics are not captured by and not subject to existing laws. Since existing laws were not designed with cryptocurrencies' unique properties in mind, the jurisdictional deficit applies not just to the CFTC but to all federal regulatory agencies as well.[48] The CFCT believes that a change in the law is needed for it to be able to comprehensively regulate the cryptocurrency spot markets where trades are for prompt delivery, the same way that it regulates the cryptocurrency derivatives market where trades are made for future delivery or may never result in physical delivery, settling instead by cash or netting. As of May 2025, such laws have not been put into effect.

Pertaining to the derivatives markets, the CFTC can impose liability on entities for failing to register or to obey business conduct requirements. In the spot markets, the CFTC is restricted to policing fraud and manipulation, and this impacts on the kinds of enforcement actions the CFTC can take. This view implicitly recognises that such markets are not presently illegal under existing laws. If new laws are required to regulate them, then the applicable law currently in effect could not declare them wholly illegal.[63]

Thirdly, the CFTC holds that the optimal regulatory regime for spot markets for cryptocurrencies is one involving the lightest possible regulatory touch, to avoid stifling the market for digital assets through excessive regulation.[49] Unlike the SEC's preference for declaring virtually the entire ICO market illegal and the apparent focus on policing registration and marketing violations whenever taking place even in the absence of fraud, the CFTC believes that a lighter touch approach is appropriate, though with enhanced protection for retail investors for blockchain-based assets. This resembles the laissez-faire attitude adopted during the birth of the internet. It may also reflect the ongoing turf war which arises from time to time between the two institutions.

Following the Senate Banking Committee hearing, there is an inter-agency conferral between the CFTC, SEC, Federal Reserve, Treasury, IRS, and state banking regulators to identify gaps in their respective regulatory frameworks and whether new legislation is needed. Another observation of the Senate cryptocurrency hearing is the open admission by the CFTC that the cryptocurrency hearings are having an impact on those currencies' price movements. The prices of Bitcoin and other cryptocurrencies rose during and after the Senate hearing, reflecting the widespread sense that it brought the asset class one step closer to

47 Ibid note [54], Felsenthal & Overall (2018).
48 Ibid note [54], Felsenthal & Overall (2018). 63 Ibid note [54], Felsenthal & Overall (2018).
49 Ibid note [54], Felsenthal & Overall (2018).

mainstream adoption, even if legal strategies around token issuance may have to shift. It suggests that the industry is finding ways of meeting the demand from both the general public and Wall Street.[50] Meanwhile, rumours have been circulating in the media that US regulators have sent a number of subpoenas to firms they suspect might be violating securities laws.

A review of federal and state laws that might have an impact on cryptos is necessary. This is to ascertain whether they could be regulated under existing provisions. Foremost, as cryptocurrencies operate as an alternative currency with individual users, banking concepts and regulations appear feasible. There are close similarities between some cryptos, such as Bitcoin, and money transmission services as defined under federal and state laws, electronic fund transfers as dictated by the Federal Reserve Board's Regulation E, and the applicability of US legal tender laws with respect to state contract law.[51]

Foremost, people use cryptocurrencies as a banking device or pseudo-bank account, while money under modern banking times is issued by a central bank and/or created by a central bank via monetary policies or by licensed commercial banks. The general consensus is that a bank is, firstly, a financial establishment for the deposit, loan, exchange, or issue of money and for the transmission of funds. Secondly, under securities laws, a *bank* includes any financial institution, whether or not incorporated, doing business under federal or state law if a substantial portion of the institution's business consists of receiving deposits or exercising fiduciary powers equivalent to those permitted to national banks.[52] Thirdly, the business of banking includes discounting and negotiating promissory notes, drafts, bills of exchange, and other evidences of debt, receiving deposits, buying and selling exchange, coin and bullion, loaning money on personal security, and obtaining, issuing, and circulating notes.[68]

The key concept of a bank under US federal and state law is that it is an institution, accepts deposits, and provides loans. A cryptocurrency, for example, Bitcoin, has to demonstrate these three key characteristics to fall under the general requirements to be a bank. Bitcoin is not an institution, business, or person but primarily a collection of users making use of a payment mechanism. This makes Bitcoin simply a medium of exchange. The Federal Reserve, being in charge of the US dollar, conducts the monetary policy for the country. In contrast, Bitcoin conducts its monetary policy through software without the intervention of a central institution. Its value is secured by users and not by government, business, or any kind of institution. When it comes to accepting deposits, the Bitcoin software just distributes currency. Bitcoin is stored in personal computers or in an online wallet, not on the Bitcoin network, and hence, the notion of using Bitcoin

50 Eha, B. P. (2018), "Crypto exchanges welcome regulators as they woo institutional clients", *American Banker*, 21/02/2018, www.americanbanker.com/news/crypto-exchanges-welcome-regulators-to-attract-institutional-clients, accessed 25/02/2018.

51 Kaplanov, N. M. (2012), "Nerdy money: Bitcoin, the private digital currency, and the case against its regulation", *Temple University Legal Studies Research Paper*, 22/07/2012.

52 *Black's Law Dictionary (2014)*, Tenth Edition, Eagan, Thomson West. 68 12 U.S.C. S.24 (West Supp. 2010).

as a kind of offshore bank account is unworkable. Bitcoin is acquired through mining, through exchange, or by purchase, and not through loan making. Taking these three Bitcoin characteristics into consideration, it is likely that federal and state banking laws are inapplicable to Bitcoin and other cryptocurrencies.

Bitcoin transfers virtual currency between parties through a system managed by other individual users who create blocks and blockchains necessary to carry out the transfer.[53] This could suggest that Bitcoin resembles a money transmitting service which is regulated by the US Treasury and individual states,[54] even though Bitcoin is unlikely to be a money transmitter under federal laws or the US Code. The determination of a money transmission service is similar to that of a money transmission business but is more loosely defined and a subject of facts and circumstances. *Money transmission services* are any operation accepting currency or funds for transmission to another place. A money transmission service, as drawn from statutes and case laws, includes a person or business that controls an operation engaging in funds transfers or other values substituting for currency, frequently for profits, that requires licensing under state law. As such, Bitcoin technology is unlikely to fall within this take on money transmitter services, as Bitcoin is not a legal entity, nor is it operated for profit. However, Bitcoin users controlling and operating the Bitcoin software could fall within the regulator's definition of a person who transfers value that substitutes for currency. Bitcoin miners, though, could potentially satisfy the "for profit on a frequent basis" criterion, as they are rewarded with Bitcoins for their efforts. This is, however, arguable, as they are not directly transferring payments for specific individuals or in charge of an operation transferring funds for others like a conventional money transmission service.

The Financial Crimes Enforcement Network's (FinCEN) position is that it would make no distinction between fiat currency and cryptocurrencies, such as Bitcoin, for the purpose of the money transmission laws.[55] This means that individuals and businesses merely exchanging for goods and services and vice versa are not money transmitters. Businesses that accept cryptocurrency from one person and send it to another or back to the same person are money transmitters and are not exempt from money transmission regulation simply because they do not deal in fiat currencies. Also, any business that exchanges fiat currencies for one kind of cryptocurrency to another is a money transmitter. Payment processors who accept cryptocurrency from a merchant's customers and pass fiat currencies to the merchants are usually money transmitters.

---

53 Vigna, P. & Casey, M. J. (2015), *Cryptocurrency: How Bitcoin and digital money are challenging the global economic order*, London, The Bodley Head.

54 Santori, M. (2015), "What is money transmission and why does it matter? Attorney Marco Santori explains how the current state of money transmission laws in the US can affect digital currency startups", *Coin Center*, 07/04/2015, www.coincenter.org/entry/what-is-money-transmissionand-why-does-it-matter, accessed 02/02/2018.

55 FinCEN (2017), "Important information for Money Services Businesses (MSB)", *FinCEN*, 11/02/2017, www.fincen.gov/resources/financial-institutions/money-services-businesses, accessed 02/02/2018.

As FinCEN regulates money transmitters in accordance with the Bank Secrecy Act, which includes elements of the Patriot Act, money transmitters must consequently register with FinCEN, undergo initial risk assessment, and adopt a written anti–money laundering policy based on those risks. As such, money transmitters have to appoint a qualified compliance officer, train employees on compliance procedures, and undergo regular testing and review of their business's compliance programme.[56]

While federal law requires mere registration, state law requires licensure. Some states, like Texas and Kansas, have published official guidance on whether and how their laws apply to digital currency businesses. The New York State Department of Financial Services (NYSDFS) released its final BitLicense rules in June 2015 and, in April 2022, added that virtual businesses were covered by the assessment framework for banking and insurance purposes. The NYSDFS emphasised that the regulations are not targeted at passive investors, and companies also would not need prior approval from NYSDFS for every new round of venture capital financing. In general, a company will only need prior approval if the investor wants to direct management and policies of the firm as a controlled person. Cryptocurrency businesses only need to obtain prior approval from the NYSDFS for any new material product, service, or activity, rather than for all new products, services, or activities. The final rules eliminate any obligation on them to file currency transaction reports and suspicious activity reports with the NYSDFS, where such reports must already be submitted to the federal governments.

While FinCEN sees itself as money laundering preventers, state regulators see themselves as consumer protectors. This explains why the state license application process seeks to ensure safety, soundness, and solvency and includes a heightened kind of substantial background check and substantial financial reporting obligations.[73]

Financial services in the United States are heavily regulated with regulations written for business models that have not significantly altered for decades. There arise two real world consequences because of this. First, some new business models that could significantly improve businesses either move offshore to innovate elsewhere or simply quit and move on to a different product. For those businesses able to fit into the existing regulations, the costs of determining how these obligations apply, combined with the ongoing compliance costs, act as a barrier to entry for bootstrapped virtual currency software companies. Thus, the reduction of innovation becomes the result of the policy.[57]

The exchange of cryptocurrency might constitute an electronic funds transfer since they function as a medium of online payment, and this is regulated by the Federal Reserve under the Electronic Fund Transfer Act of 1978 (EFTA). The aim of EFTA is to provide a basic framework establishing the rights, liabilities, and responsibilities of participants in electronic fund transfer systems. The

56 Ibid note [55], Santori (2015), 73
57 Ibid note [55], Santori (2015).

statute seeks to provide a framework of law regulating the rights of consumers against financial institutions in electronic funds transfers,[58] and to help bring certainty to an era of banking which is fast becoming faceless.[59]

Under the EFTA, an electronic funds transfer includes any transfer of funds,[60] [61] [62] other than a transaction originated by cheque, draft, or similar paper instrument, which is initiated through an electronic terminal, telephone instruments, or computer, or magnetic tapes, so as to order, instruct, or authorise a financial institution to debit or credit an account.[78] Under the EFTA, a financial institution includes a state or national bank, savings and loan association, mutual savings bank, a state or federal credit union, or any other person who directly or indirectly holds an account belonging to a customer.[79] The regulations implementing EFTA also include access devices and electronic funds transfers into their definition of *financial institutions*.[80] For Bitcoin to come within the Regulation E regulatory framework, Bitcoin has to be an institution conducting electronic funds transfers. While the Bitcoin software would not qualify as a financial institution under Regulation E, as it is not a legally cognisable entity, a digital wallet company, however, might.

Other than financial regulatory provisions as discussed earlier, there are other legal concerns, such as whether the use of Bitcoin causes any contractual problems, whether Bitcoin resembles complementary currencies under the law, or if securities provisions prohibit the use of Bitcoin. In respect of these, there are some useful illustrations.[63] A fiat currency such as the US dollar is legal tender for all debts, public charges, taxes, and dues. If a cryptocurrency is not deemed to be a currency, then any sale of a good or services for Bitcoins would essentially be a barter contract. Barter contracts are covered under the Uniform Commercial Code (UCC).[64]

Other equivalent examples are community currencies, which are notes issued by a non-governmental group within a confined locality that have a monetary value designed to develop local economies. This medium of exchange is then accepted for goods and services within the community according to the parameter of the system. The Time Dollar system[65] and the Ithaca HOURS[66] are good examples of these. These could be considered as bills of credit. The US Constitution prohibits states from issuing these, but the prohibition does not apply to private persons or private partnerships or private corporations. The creator of

58 *Shawmut Worcester County Bank v. First American Bank & Trust*, 731 F. Supp. 57, 61 (D. Mass. 1990).

59 *Spain v. Union Trust*, 674 F. Supp. 1496, 1500 (D. Conn. 1987).

60 U.S.C. S.1693(a)(6).

61 U.S.C. S. 1693a.

62 C.F.R. S. 205.2(i) (2010).

63 Ibid note [52], Kaplanov (2012).

64 Lord, R. A. (1989), *Williston on contracts*, Eagan, Thomson Reuters.

65 Cahn, E. S. (2017), "Time dollars: A new currency in community building", *Time Bank*, September 2017, www.tbmw.org/tag/time-dollar/, accessed 02/02/2018.

66 Ellis, B. (2012), "Funny money? 11 local currencies", *CNNMoney*, 27/01/2012, www.cnn.com/galleries/2012/pf/1201/gallery.community-currencies/3.html, accessed 02/02/2018.

the Liberty dollar was convicted not because he tried to create a new form of currency but because he violated the rules by coining real metal coins and passing them off as US currency.

Since cryptos are purchased and exchanged in person, on online exchanges, and over the internet and are interpreted variously as a currency, an investment, or even a future contract, they could likewise be regulated in a variety of ways. When looking for the meaning and scope of "security" in the Securities Act 1934, form should be disregarded for substance and the stress should be on economic reality.[67] [68] This principle has been applied in many areas within securities by the courts, thereby providing a foundational rationale to approaching financial regulation.[69]

Where cryptos are deemed as a security, then the SEC has wide powers to regulate or even prohibit the exchange of Bitcoins. The US Supreme Court defined the basic test applied to distinguish an investment contract falling within the definition of a security from a traditional commercial transaction. The Howey test, to determine the presence or absence of an investment contract under the securities statutes, is whether the scheme involves an investment of money in a common enterprise with profits to come solely from the efforts of others.[70] Primarily, the distinction is whether the investors are attracted solely by the prospects of a return on their investment. The Court also created a family resemblance test in *Reeves v Ernst & Young*,[71] where it was held that a note is presumptively assumed to be a security and thus regulated under federal law so long as it does not meet one of the Reeves's mitigating factors. As cryptocurrencies are created to be a kind of online currency, it might be best to treat them as such in the securities realm. Foreign currencies are generally not viewed as a security, and there are precedents providing an exception for currency trading under the definition of *security*, as alluded to earlier in the *Reeves v Ernst & Young* case. A cryptocurrency is not a foreign currency in the formal sense, since it is not designed or maintained by a foreign government. It does, however, function like a national currency by facilitating exchange and serving as a store of value in the marketplace.

Cryptocurrencies could also be classified as commodities, and its exchange could therefore be a commodity futures contract. The definition of a *commodity futures contract*, however, is not provided for in the CEA or in CFTC regulations. The CES nevertheless negatively defines "future delivery" to not include any sale of any commodity for deferred shipment or delivery. The Supreme Court held in *Dunn v Commodity Futures Trading Commission*[72] that futures contracts are agreements to buy or sell a specified quantity of a commodity at a particular price for delivery at set future dates, and these are governed by

67 *Tcherepnin v. Knight*, 389 U.S. 332, 336 (1967) (citing S.E.C. v. W.J. Howey Co., 328 U.S.).
68 , 298 (1946).
69 *United Hous. Found., Inc. v Forman*, 412 U.S. 837, 838 (1975).
70 *Securities & Exchange Commission v W. J. Howey Co*. 328 U.S. 293 (1946).
71 *Reeves v Ernst & Young* 494 U.S. 56,57 (1990).
72 *Dunn v. Commodity Futures Trading Commission*, 519 U.S. 465 (1997).

the CFTC. However, even though commodity futures trading is regulated by the CFTC and must be done in compliance with market rules on a designated exchange, the CEA does not include an agreement, contract, or transaction in foreign currency. This means that though the CFTC does have authority to regulate any commodity contracts involving futures contracts, where contracts involving foreign currency are concerned, the CFTC only maintains a limited regulator capacity compared with other commodities.

Whilst cryptocurrencies are technically not a foreign currency, they function in the same manner. The Securities Exchange Act of 1934 exempts currencies from its definition of a *security*, but it is generally understood that currency is not a security. Market participants that conduct a sufficient amount of currency trading are nevertheless permitted to do so off market but may be required to register with the CFTC.[73]

Overall, under US law and regulation, Congress and the executive have the ability to prohibit or limit the use of cryptocurrencies in the markets. However, they fall within a grey area under US law in which they are not necessarily outlawed but still give rise to contractual obligations. Hence, they could be treated as a local or community currency under the law, receiving full authority as a medium of exchange under contract law, requiring taxation on income, and not implicating securities regulations.

The position at case law, unfortunately, remains confused and, so far, at least, is limited to decisions in the lower courts. In the *SEC v Trendon T. Shavers and Bitcoin Savings and Trust Co.*,[74] Texas state attorney Amos L. Mazzant said:

> It is clear that Bitcoin can be used as money. . . . The only limitation of Bitcoin is that it is limited to those places that accept it as currency. However, it can also be exchanged for conventional currencies. . . . Therefore, Bitcoin is a currency or form of money.

The position in New York, however, is less clear. In *US v Failella*,[75] it was determined that Bitcoin qualified as money, but in *US v Petrix*,[76] Judge Hugh B. Scott held that it was not money but private property, along the same lines as special metals. Passing legislation to clarify the point, or a Supreme Court decision, would make matters a great deal clearer.

Those arguing that since any prohibition on cryptocurrencies is unlikely to be effective, outright prohibition on their use would be ill advised and not practical, as they are an open source project, and given their characteristics, there is no cryptocurrency company to raid, subpoena, or shut down. Even if the website and the source code information underlying services were erased, there would

---

73 CFTC (2010), "Final rules regarding retail forex transactions", *CFTC Press Release*, 30/08/2010.

74 2014) 4:13-CU-416.

75 (2014) 39 F Supp 3d 544.

76 (2016) No 15-CR-227A.

be no impact, as the database supporting cryptocurrencies exists only in the distributed P2P network designed by its users, and removing any of the individual computers that constitute the P2P network would have hardly any impact on the rest of the network. Instead, there appears to be a more persuasive case for federal and state officials to develop a familiarity with the technology underlying cryptocurrencies and the nature of their transactions that could provide adequate information to reasonably investigate and counter any illegal activity.[77] Though there is unlikely to be a viable way to outlaw them, policymakers could stop the use and transfer of cryptocurrencies by outlawing the activity itself, by making interstate transactions using Bitcoin invalid.[78] Outlawing the use and distribution of any P2P electronic currency, or any options between these two extremes, could also signal a clear message that it is illegal to use them. The crackdown method as used in China could also be explored, but this ignores the prospect that cryptocurrency, like technology, could be developed that does not have the advantage that they now possess in assisting law enforcement. Such a new system could be solely maintained by foreign users and in a way that does not disclose all transactions publicly.[79]

Better ways of preventing criminal activity involving cryptocurrencies include looking at its public database, as this provides the opportunity to track and locate those using them for illicit activity. The publicly available information inherent to the Bitcoin system is likely to be more effective in tracking criminal activity than a system lacking such information. Such measured investigations could help stop illegal activity without punishing those using the technology in legal ways.

The more important reason to resist prohibiting cryptocurrencies lies in the fundamental notion of the internet itself. Cryptocurrencies are unfettered by substantial regulation and can help contribute to economic growth and job creation. Though in existence for only a few years, many kinds of businesses are flourishing because of cryptocurrency activities or because of their underlying blockchain technology. To a significant extent, cryptocurrencies have drastically reduced the cost of online transactions in a secure, anonymous, and efficient way.

Despite their price volatility, cryptocurrency thefts at exchanges, and some reported links to illicit activities, there are those who prefer a system outside of any government control or influence. Importantly, modern and advanced

77 Ibid note [52], Kaplanov (2012).

78 Johnston, M. E., McGuire, D. & Wiley, N. D. (2008), "The evolution of the peer-to-peer file sharing industry and the security risks for users", *Tuck School of Business Dartmouth College Paper Presented at the Proceedings of the 41st Hawaii International Conference on System Sciences*.

79 Touloumis, T. (2009), "Buccaneers and Bucks from the internet: Pirate Bay and the entertainment industry", *Seton Hall Journal of Sports and Entertainment Law*, 19: 253–258.

economies such as Switzerland[80] and Japan[81] are taking to cryptocurrency in significant ways, while Germany[82] is turning into a development hub for virtual currencies and blockchains, even though they are outlawed in some economies and discouraged in others because of fears of fraud and illegal activity.

Cryptocurrencies cannot survive in a viable form without enforceable contracts and a stable rule of law. When smothered by excessive regulation or an uncertain legal and regulatory environment, the promises and potential benefits would be lost. They present a particularly difficult and unique jurisdictional challenge to existing regulatory and enforcement agencies because of their ability to transcend borders in seconds and their anonymity due to encryption.[83] As said so by so many people, a proper balance between law, regulation, and freedom is essential.[84]

The regulators have become more active with the SEC having set up a collaborative programme with blockchain and cryptocurrency start-ups. It is called FinHub, or the Strategic Hub for Innovation and Financial Technology.[85] At present, both state level and federal bills are being put forward to both regulate and facilitate this new area. It is too early to tell how effective this will be.

Recent research suggests advancing the regulatory path through Congress empowering the SEC or, alternatively, the CFTC with the authority to regulate the offering, distribution, and trading of cryptoassets, including the regulation of trading platforms, custodians (wallets), brokers, and advisers.[86] The expanded powers should also be accompanied by the expansion of resources of both the SEC and the CFTC to enable both to implement more effectively existing as well as new authorities. Also, the congressional legislation should focus on core principles equivalent to those undertaken for the futures industry and crowdfunding. Core principles should, at the minimum, cover the protection of customer assets; governance standards; conflicts of interest; periodic

---

80 The Economist (2018), "Tales from the crypto-nation: Digital currency", *The Economist*, 426(9080): 69; Miller, H. (2017), "Welcome to crypto valley: The Swiss city of Zug embraces digital currency", *Bloomberg*, 09/10/2017, www.bloomberg.com/news/articles/2017-10-10/welcome-to-crypto-valley, accessed 02/02/2018.

81 Yagami, K. (2017), "Japan: A forward thinking Bitcoin nation", *Forbes*, 02/11/2017, www.forbes.com/sites/outofasia/2017/11/02/japan-a-forward-thinking-bitcoin-nation/, accessed 02/02/2018.

82 Turner, Z. (2018), "Bitcoin finds a home in cash-loving Germany: Country is turning into a development hub for virtual currencies and blockchains", *The Wall Street Journal*, 17/01/2018, www.wsj.com/articles/bitcoin-finds-a-home-in-cash-loving-germany-1515330000, accessed 02/02/2018.

83 Trautman, L. J. & Harrell, A. C. (2017), "Bitcoin versus regulated payment systems: What gives?", *Cardoza Law Review*, 38(3): 1041–1097.

84 Eha, B. P. (2017), *How money got free: Bitcoin and the fight for the future of finance*, London, One World Publications Ltd.

85 SEC (2018), "SEC launches new strategic hub for innovation and financial technology", *SEC*, 18/19/2018, https://hackernoon.com/cryptocurrency-regulaion-update-november-2018-d9b17837aeec, accessed 26/02/2019.

86 Massad, T. G. (2019), "It's time to strengthen the regulation of crypto-assets", *Brookings Economic Studies Paper*, 18/03/2019, www.brookings.edu/articles/its-time-to-strengthen-the-regulation-of-crypto-assets/, accessed 25/06/2019.

reporting; pre- and post-trade transparency requirements; prevention of fraud, manipulation, and abusive practices; pertinent disclosures to platform users; risk management, cybersecurity, and AML; KYC; and other relevant measures to minimise nefarious activity risk and to ensure transparency.[87] As for off-shore platforms that offer or provide access to US investors, Congress should empower the relevant agencies with the authority to decide whether such platforms should be required to comply with US standards, or demonstrate compliance with comparable standards, or to disclose explicitly that they do not adhere to such standards.

Developments in the United States in 2024 brought the country closer to having a regulatory framework for cryptos. Since then, federal legislative initiatives have generally stalled. Two bills, though, namely, the Financial Innovation and Technology (FIT) for the 21st Century Act and the Blockchain Regulatory Certainty Act, both help define when a cryptoasset is a security or commodity, expand oversight of the industry, and clarify the roles of different entities in managing the crypto. While these bills have been introduced, they have yet to advance further.[88] The FIT bipartisan legislation seeking to create a new legal framework for digital currencies managed to get approval from the House of Representatives despite an unusual warning from SEC that it could generate new financial risk arising from the creation of new regulatory gaps undermining decades of precedents pertaining to the oversight of investment contracts, thereby putting investors and capital markets at immeasurable risks.[89] Drawing insights from high-profile prosecutions,[90] fraud cases, bankruptcies, and failure, the SEC maintained that cryptos should be subject to the same laws as other assets. The SEC further clarified that under FIT, investment contracts recorded on a blockchain would no longer be treated as securities to deny investors protection under securities laws.[91] Also, FIT would enable as well issuers of crypto investment contracts to certify themselves that their own products are digital commodities not subject to SEC oversight, leaving the agency just 60 days to challenge this.[92]

87 Ibid note [87], Massad (2019).

88 De Nikhilesh (2024), "Congress needs to act on crypto regulations, CFTC Chair Behnam tells lawmakers: The CFTC Chair was testifying on the regulator's 2025 budget request", *Coin Desk*, 09/03/2024, www.coindesk.com/policy/2024/03/06/congress-needs-to-act-on-crypto-regulations-cftc-chair-behnam-tells-lawmakers/, accessed 24/07/2024

89 Reuters (2024), "US House passes crypto bill despite warning from SEC", *Reuters*, 23/05/2024, www.reuters.com/world/us/us-securities-regulator-urges-against-crypto-bill-adoption-2024-05-22/#:~:text=May%2022%20(Reuters)%20%2D%20The,could%20create%20new%20financial%20risks, accessed 22/07/2024

90 Cohen, L. & Godoy, J. (2024), "Bankman-Fried sentenced to 25 years for multi-billion dollar FTX fraud", *Reuters*, 29/03/2024, www.reuters.com/technology/sam-bankman-fried-be-sentenced-multi-billion-dollar-ftx-fraud-2024-03-28/, accessed 22/07/2024

91 Ibid note [90], Reuters (2024)

92 Ibid note [90], Reuters (2024)

7.5 The EU's cryptoasset regulatory policy

EU institutions and some individual member states have issued various statements, guidance, and regulations potentially applicable to blockchain, cryptoassets, and ICOs. For example, the ECB does not regard cryptoassets as a full form of money or currency from a legal perspective. The ECB defines a *cryptocurrency/cryptoasset* as a digital representation of value, not issued by a central bank, credit institutions, or e-money institutions, which in some circumstances could be employed as an alternative to money.[93] The ECB refers to *cryptocurrency* schemes to describe both the aspect of value and that of the inherent or inbuilt mechanisms, ensuring that value can be transferred.

The cryptocurrency systems ecosystem specifically comprises new categories of participants not previously present in the payment's environment. Emerging business models are now developing around obtaining, storing, accessing, and transferring units of cryptocurrencies. Some new systems are built with slightly different characteristics that could improve the functionality or some elements in the ecosystem. For others, the purpose is unclear, as it seems only a few are used or intended to be used for payments. Acceptance of cryptocurrency systems is not widespread, though some e-commerce merchants have announced their willingness to accept payments with Bitcoin. It appears that Bitcoin was used for around 500,000 transactions daily worldwide in 2024, compared to a total of 11.6 million credit card payments.[94]

Users further encounter payment system like risks owing to their direct participation in the cryptocurrency systems, as well as risks associated with their particular characteristics, such as the counterparty risks discussed, price volatility, and the risks of investment fraud associated with the lack of transparency. There are no safeguards for now to protect users against such risks.

On the other hand, the ECB notes that cryptocurrency systems present some advantages as perceived by users. They could pose a challenge to retail payment instruments and innovative payment solutions pertaining to costs, global reach, anonymity of the payer, and speed of settlement. New, improved cryptocurrencies could overcome the current barriers to widespread use more successfully than the current ones, especially for payments within virtual communities closed loop environments like internet platforms and for cross-border payments.[95]

As discussed earlier in Chapter 6, international authorities such as the FATF have taken an interest in virtual currency systems because of the potential risks to the integrity of the international financial system. Various central banks and financial and supervisory authorities across the world have cautioned users of

93 ECB (2015), "Virtual currency schemes – a further analysis", *ECB Paper*, February 2015, www.ecb.europa.eu/pub/pdf/other/virtualcurrencyschemesen.pdf, accessed 02/02/2018.

94 www.statistica.com/statistics/730806/daily-number-of-bitcoin-transactions? accessed 05/05/2025

95 Ibid note [94], ECB (2015)

the risk pertaining to holding and transacting virtual currencies.[96] Some have provided clarifications on the legal status, started regulating certain activities, or issued outright bans. Responses vary depending, in part, on the part of the world from which they originate and on the kind of authority.

The ECB, in advancing further from its 2012 Virtual Currencies Report,[97] suggested that though cryptocurrency systems can have positive aspects in terms of financial innovation and the offer of additional payment alternatives for consumers, they also clearly entail risks. The ECB, with regards to its monetary policy and price stability and related agendas, maintains that the materialisation of these risks depends on the volumes of cryptocurrency systems issued and their connection to the real economy, including their traded volume and the acceptance of supervised institutions involved with them. For now, all these risk drivers remain low, implying no material risks for any of ECB's tasks as yet.[98] However, an incident involving cryptocurrency systems and a subsequent loss of trust in them could also undermine users' confidence in electronic payment instruments, in e-money, and/or in particular payment solutions, like those in place for e-commerce. Therefore, the ECB intends to continue to monitor payment-related developments in cryptocurrency systems. It has been argued that the building of an effective cryptoassets monitoring framework would require caution because of data issues, as well as a stepwise approach to filling gaps.[99]

The ECB Crypto-Assets Task Force (ECBCTF), meanwhile, concluded that present market conditions suggest that cryptoassets risks or potential implications are limited and/or are manageable within the context of existing regulatory and oversight frameworks.[100] It nevertheless cautioned that its evaluation is subject to further insights from its continuous monitoring of cryptoassets and the need to raise awareness and develop preparedness. By way of example, ECB's analysis of different kinds of stablecoins suggests a trade off between the novelty of the stabilisation mechanism applied initiatives extending from mirroring the conventional electronic money approach to the introduction of an algorithmic central bank and their capacity to maintain a stable market value.[101] Stablecoins in general claim to stabilise the value of major currencies in the volatile cryptoasset market. Thus, relatively less innovative stablecoins could offer

96 Ibid note [94], ECB (2015)

97 ECB (2012), "Virtual currency schemes", *ECB Paper*, 12 October 2012, www.ecb.europa.eu/pub/pdf/other/virtualcurrencyschemes201210en.pdf, accessed 02/02/2018.

98 Ibid note [94], ECB (2015).

99 Chimienti, M. T., Kochanska, U. & Pinna, A. (07/08/2019), "Understanding the crypto-asset phenomenon, its risks and measurement issues", *ECB Economic Bulletin*, 5, www.ecb.europa.eu/press/economic-bulletin/articles/2019/html/ecb.ebart201905_03~c83aeaa44c.en.html, accessed 08/08/2019.

100 ECB (2019), "Crypto-assets: Implications for financial stability, and monetary policy, and payments and market infrastructures", *ECB Occasional Paper Series No. 223*, May 2019, www.ecb.europa.eu/pub/pdf/scpops/ecb.op223~3ce14e986c.en.pdf, accessed 08/08/2019.

101 Bullman, D., Klemm, J. & Pinna, A. (2019), "In search for stability in crypto-assets: Are stablecoins the solution?", *ECB Occasional Paper Series No. 230*, August 2019, www.ecb.europa.eu/pub/pdf/scpops/ecb.op230~d57946be3b.en.pdf, accessed 29/08/2019.

reliefs to users seeking a stable store of value, particularly when legitimised by the adherence to standards that are typical of payment services. However, confirmation on the potential future role of more innovative stablecoins outside their core user base is still awaited.

In the meantime, the ECBCTF argues that in the absence of a common taxonomy, uncoordinated regulatory approaches could motivate regulatory arbitrage. It suggests that an EU-level regulation should first target the cryptoasset gatekeepers, like custody, trading, and exchange services, providing the entry point to retail customers and regulated entities.[102] It cautioned of the unsuitability of the approach focusing on intermediaries in the decentralised networks and proposed subjecting these to a minimum set of principles that seek to ensure the network's technological integrity, transparency of algorithms and protocols, cyber resilience, and regulatory compliances. The ECBCTF stressed that unintended consequences could result from regulating gatekeepers only and that decentralised networks should be evaluated in a holistic cost–benefit framework.

The EBA's mandate in Article 9 of its founding regulation covers the monitoring of existing and new financial activities so as to provide guidelines and recommendations with the agenda of promoting the safety and soundness of markets and convergence of regulatory practice. Subsequent to its analysis of virtual currencies, on 13 December 2013, the EBA issued a public warning advising consumers that cryptocurrencies are not regulated, and as such, there are significant risks in using them.[103] The outstanding question at that point of time was whether cryptocurrencies should or could be regulated.

The EBA considers cryptocurrencies as digital representations of value that are issued neither by central banks nor public authorities, are not necessarily attached to fiat currencies, but are accepted by natural or legal persons as a means of payment and could be transferred, stored, or traded electronically.[104] Main participants in the cryptocurrency space are users, exchanges, trade platforms, inventors, and e-wallet providers. Potential benefits attached to virtual currencies include reduced transactions cost, faster transaction speed, and financial inclusion. Such benefits, though, might be less relevant in the EU due to the existing and pending EU regulations and directives that are explicitly targeted at faster transaction speeds and costs and increasing financial inclusion.

Relative to the benefits identified, there is a wide range of risks involved across several categories, including risks to users; risks to non-user market participants; risks to financial integrity, such as money laundering and other financial crimes; risks to existing payment systems in conventional fiat currencies;

102 Ibid note [101], ECB (2019).

103 Central Bank of Ireland (CBI) (2013), "EBA warning and opinion on virtual currencies", *CBI*, 13/12/2013, www.centralbank.ie/consumer-hub/consumer-notices/eba-opinion-on-virtual-currencies, accessed 02/02/2018.

104 EBA (2014), "EBA opinion on 'virtual currencies'", *EBA/Op/2014/08*, 04/07/2014, www.bancaditalia.it/compiti/sispaga-mercati/strumenti-pagamento/normativa/EBA-Op-2014-08-Opinion-on-Virtual-Currencies.pdf, accessed 02/02/2018.

and risks to regulatory authorities.[105] Various casual drivers for such risks were identified, as these suggest regulatory measures that could be employed to contain them. These include the scenario that a cryptocurrency scheme could be created, then its function subsequently altered by anyone and, in the example of decentralised schemes such as Bitcoin, by anyone with an adequate share of computational power; that payer and payee could remain anonymous; that cryptocurrency schemes are not restricted by jurisdictional boundaries and could therefore undermine financial sanctions and seizure of assets; or that market participants lack sound corporate governance arrangements.[106]

The EBA noted that a regulatory approach comprehensively addressing risk drivers would necessitate a substantial body of regulation where some components are untested. Amongst other elements, it would need to comprise governance requirements for several market participants, the segregation of client accounts, capital requirements, and importantly, the design of a scheme governing authorities that are accountable for the integrity of a virtual currency scheme and its key components, including the protocol and transaction ledger.[107] Though such a long-term structural scheme is yet to be available, some of the more pressing needs as identified would need to be addressed in other manners. As an immediate measure, the EBA recommended that national supervisory authorities discourage credit institutions, payment institutions, and e-money institutions from buying, holding, or selling cryptocurrencies.[108]

The EBA further recommends that EU lawmakers consider declaring market participants at the direct interface between conventional currencies and cryptocurrencies, such as virtual currency exchanges, to become obliged entities under the EU anti–money laundering directive and therefore subject to its anti–money laundering and counter-terrorism financing requirements.[124] Such immediate responses could insulate regulated financial services from cryptocurrency schemes and could mitigate those risks arising from the interactions between them and regulated financial services. It would, however, be unable to mitigate those risks that arise within or between cryptocurrency schemes themselves.[125] All things being equal, these immediate responses would enable cryptocurrency schemes to develop outside the financial services sector, including the design of solutions that could comply with regulatory demands of the kind as mentioned.[126] They would also enable financial institutions to maintain a current account relationship with businesses active in the virtual currency space.

The 5th Anti–Money Laundering Directive (5AMLD)[109] extended the scope of the regulations to include electronic custodian wallet providers, cryptocurrency

105 Ibid note [105], EBA (2014).

106 Ibid note [105], EBA (2014).

107 Ibid note [105], EBA (2014).

108 Ibid note [105], EBA (2014)

109 *Directive (EU) 2015/849*, https://finance.ec.europa.eu/financial-crime/anti-money-laundering-and-countering-financing-terrorism-eu-level_en#:~:text=Directive%20(EU)%20 2015%2F849%20(the%205th%20anti,governed%20under%20their%20legal%20framework, accessed 02/02/2018

exchange service providers partaking in exchange services between virtual and fiat currencies, and others. The 5AMLD is expected to strengthen existing directives through the aforementioned, by enabling better identification of politically exposed persons (PEPs), by restricting the anonymous use of virtual currencies, by enhancing information sharing between financial supervisory authorities, and by increasing transparency pertaining to the beneficial ownerships of companies. It remains to be seen how effective this can be.

Additionally, the EU proposes to subject these entities to registration or licensing requirements and to subject those who own or hold a management function in these entities to fit and proper testing. On 8 October 2020, the European Parliament adopted a legislative initiative procedure on emerging risks on cryptoassets and digital finance. They also recommended thus:

1. Moving towards a stronger regulatory and supervisory framework
2. Developing a legislative framework for stablecoins
3. Developing an EU sandbox for developing new products
4. Strengthening anti-laundering and anti-terrorist framework in this context

In 2022, the European Parliament required transparency, disclosure, authorisation, and supervision of transactions which involved issuing and trading cryptoassets. They also indicated a desire to protect consumers and to protect market integrity and financial stability by regulating public offers. It went further and argued for further steps against market manipulation.

Other than national rules, the following key EU rules could be applicable:

1. The Markets in Crypto Asset Regulation (MiCAR)
2. The Prospectus Regulation
3. The Markets in Financial Instruments Directive (MiFID) 1 and 2
4. The Alternative Investment Fund Managers Directive
5. The Fourth and Fifth Anti-Money Laundering Directives

The EU has issued MiCAR scheduled for final implementation in 2025. This categorises three types of cryptoassets: activity-related tokens, electronic money tokens, and other cryptoassets. It also introduces a scheme for providers. The rules apply to issuers and service providers; it does not apply to cryptoassets that are within the definition of “financial instruments”, non-fungible and non-exchangeable tokens and central bank digital currencies.

MiCAR achieved the distinction of being the first cross-jurisdictional regulatory and supervisory framework for cryptos to enter into force. The legislation constitutes part of EU’s mission to set up a regulatory framework for facilitating the adoption of DLT and cryptoassets in the financial services sector. This launched a new milestone into the EU’s Single Rulebook applicable to cryptoassets service providers (CASPs) and cryptoasset issuers (CAIs) operating in and across the EU. This replaces a patchwork of individual member states’ national frameworks on the regulation of crypto, besides seeking to strike a fair balance between resolving different levels of risks generated by each kind of cryptoasset and the need to boost financial innovation. ESMA and the EBA have been entrusted with preparing the regulatory technical standards (RTS) and implementing technical standards (ITS) and guidelines that would further specify the application of the legislation. National competent authorities (NCAs) of the EU are already publishing their own supervisory guidance and expectations of how they will authorise and supervise CASPs and CAIs and/or conventional financial service providers seeking to offer Markets in Crypto-Asset Regulation (MiCAR) regulated activity.[110]

Generally, any business activity pertaining to cryptos that is not tagged as "financial instruments" in the EU is likely to fall under MiCAR. Particular kinds of cryptos are presently exempt from MiCAR but could still be subject to some form or no regulatory requirement stipulated elsewhere.[111] Non-EU crypto enterprises undertaking activities for EU customers have to comply with MiCAR requirements.[112] MiCAR, though, exempts services on the basis of "reverse solicitation", that is, when responding to an initiative from an EU customer under a set of strict terms as prescribed in MiCAR.[113] The bulk of cryptos that are not already in scope of present regulation, like MiFIR/MiFID II, would come under MiCAR. These include asset reference tokens (ART), e-money tokens (EMT), and other cryptos, including utility tokens.[114] Tokens defined as "financial instruments" are subject to the existing financial services rules, in particular, MiFIR/MiFID II, while tokens defined as cryptoassets are subject to the pan-EU regime prescribed by MiCAR that will introduce rules pertaining to regulated crypto services, including authorisation, passporting, and ongoing supervision requirements for CAIs and CASPs.[115]

MiCAR regulatory requirements include the following:[116]

- *Algorithmic cryptos and stablecoins*. Algorithmic stablecoins are not defined in MiCAR, where none of the operative provisions refer to them directly, while recital 41 of MiCAR makes it clear that stablecoins should fall within the scope of regulation regardless of how the issuer seeks to design a crypto, including the mechanism for maintaining a stable value of the crypto. This means that where a stablecoin falls within the definitions of an asset-referenced token (ART) or an

110 EBA (2024), "EBA brings the application of MiCAR to the attention of issuers, consumers, and other relevant stakeholders and announces priorities for the supervision of issuers of ARTs and EMTs for 2024/2025", *EBA*, 06/07/2024, www.eba.europa.eu/publications-and-media/press-releases/eba-brings-application-micar-attention-issuers-consumers-and-other-relevant-stakeholders-and, accessed 18/07/2024

111 Ibid note [513], PwC (2023)

112 Ibid note [513], PwC (2023)

113 Ibid note [513], PwC (2023)

114 Ibid note [513], PwC (2023)

115 Ibid note [513], PwC (2023)

116 Ibid note [513], PwC (2023)

e-money token (EMT), Titles III or IV will be applicable. The same will apply to algorithmic stablecoins. Where the algorithmic cryptos do not seek to stabilise the value of the crypto, by referencing one or several assets, the recital stipulates that offerors or persons seeking admission to trading should in any case comply with Title II of MiCAR.

- *Transferability*. This is a vital element of the definition of *cryptos*. This clarifies that digital assets that cannot be transferred to other holders do not fall within MiCAR scope. Loyalty schemes, for instance, where loyalty points can be exchanged for benefits only with the issuer or offeror of those points. CAIs would have to comply with several obligations before making an offer to the general public in the EU, or in order to seek admission of such cryptos to trade on a trading platform. This includes the obligation to publish a white paper, but that will not apply where the cryptos are offered for free, are generated via mining, are unique, and are not fungible with other cryptos, or where the offering is made to fewer than 150 natural or legal persons per member state, where the aggregate considerations are not more than EUR 1 million over a period of 12 months with the commencing of the offer, or where the offering is addressed exclusively to qualified investors. The white paper needs to describe the technical information of the crypto, approved market communication, legal entity registration, financial conditions and details of natural or legal persons involved in the venture, brief information of the venture, characteristics of the token, key features on utility and information on "tokenomics", business plan, disclosures on risks, any restrictions on transferability on the tokens issued, as well as regular audit or reserves.
- *ART end EMT offerings*. These are subject to further requirements, such as the public disclosure of various policies and procedures, including additional disclosures of safeguards of reserve funds and internal control systems and where additional supervisory expectations could be set by NCAs. CAIs and EMTs are required to be authorised either as credit institutions or as electronic money institutions. MiCAR prohibits yield and interest, with rewards, discounts, or compensations for holding EMTs being treated as offering interest.
- *CASPs*. Those legal entities seeking to become CASPs are required to have a registered office in an EU member state and to have secured authorisation to provide one or more regulated crypto services from an NCA. Authorisation obtained in one member state will allow the CASP to passport its regulated activities across other member states. CASPS have to adhere to the general conduct of business rules. These include the stipulation that a CASP must have at least one director who is resident in the EU, have its place of effective management in the EU, and in compliance with prudential capital and governance, risk stipulations, including internal organisational requirements. Those CASPs providing custody and/or safekeeping of cryptos are required

to set a custody policy with segregated holdings and daily reporting of holdings and have liabilities for loss of clients' cryptos in case of malfunctions or cyberattacks. CASP have to place clients' funds received with a central bank or credit institution at the end of every business day. Trading platforms have to establish operating rules, technical measures, and procedures to ensure resilience of the trading system, with the final settlement taking place within 24 hours of a trade. The level of minimum capital requirements applicable to a CASP varies on the kind of registered activity it undertakes.

- *Market abuse.* MiCAR prescribes rules to prevent market abuse, including via surveillance and enforcement mechanisms. The MiCAR market abuse framework clarifies the definition of inside information applicable to cryptos, the parameters of market abuse regulations, as well as the need for CAIs whose cryptos are permitted to trade on a crypto-trading platform to disclose inside information. The regulation outlaws market manipulation, illegal disclosure of insider knowledge, and insider trading in MiCAR in-scope cryptos.
- *Enforcement and supervision.* Here, NCAs operate as the frontline supervisors and enforcement agents of CASPs and CAIs. They will apply a set of supervisory tools, including on site and off site inspections, thematic reviews, and regular supervisory dialogues to identify, monitor, and request solutions to compliance deficits by CAIs and/or CASPs. The new enforcement powers include powers to suspend CAIs/CASPs' offering of activity, powers to suspend advertisements and marketing activity, powers to publish public censures or notices that a CAI/CASP is failing compliance, powers requiring auditors or skilled persons to undertake targeted on site and/or off site inspections of the CAI/CASP, and/or powers to issue monetary fines, other non-monetary sanctions, and administrative measures to CAIs/CASPs and/or the members of management, including bans.

Thus, the adoption of MiCAR signifies a significant step forward towards creating financial services regulations that are apt for the digital era and contribute to a future-proof economy. The regulation is powered by the idea that cryptos have the potential to usher in significant benefits to market participants, like the streamlining of capital raising processes and providing faster, more cost-effective and efficient payment choices. In responding to the considerable gaps in the regulatory landscape for cryptos in the EU, MiCAR provides a regulatory framework governing the provision of services pertaining to cryptos, including the operation of trading platforms, with the target of providing explicit rules and preventing crypto holders from being exposed to risks, especially in niches not covered by consumer protection rules, including risks to market integrity.

The design of a detailed regulatory framework targeted at cryptos is envisaged to lead to enhanced user confidence, significantly contributing to the development of a market in such assets, including the promotion of the financial stability and seamless operation of payment systems. Simultaneously, MiCAR, in line with the principle of "same activity, same risks, same regulation", sets up a full-fledged prudential framework for CASPs, and ARTs, comprising stringent authorisation, business conduct, integrity and organisational requirements, and complemented by robust supervisory powers of competent authorities.[117]

As a regulation, MiCAR is binding and directly applicable in all EU member states, thereby ensuring maximum harmonisation. This option avoids regulatory fragmentation, safeguarding against competition distortion within the internal market.[118] Further, it facilitates cross-border expansion for CASPs throughout the EU and mitigates the potential for regulatory arbitrage. Put succinctly, MiCAR sets the rules governing the issuance, public offering, and trading of cryptos, including the authorisation and supervision of CASPS, issuers of ARTs, and issuers of EMTs.[119] It also, in essence, provides protection for cryptoasset holders and clienteles of CASPs, while addressing the prevention of market abuse associated with cryptos.[120]

Regulating cryptocurrencies presents formidable difficulties. One reason for their rise is the entry of nefarious users. The way cryptocurrencies, especially Bitcoin, work makes them ideal for money laundering, drug money, and the funding of terrorism. This suggests that, ultimately, new laws would need to end the anonymity of wallet addresses, as well as making exchanges and their users more transparent to the world. Such new laws might not be able to solve the issue of anonymity, as those engaged in tax avoidance or in the criminal world could hold cryptocurrencies under false identities or through third parties[121] and, importantly, the access to expert professional advice, demonstrated clearly in the Panama and Paradise Papers leaks.[122]

The other difficulty that the EU has highlighted is that suspicious transactions made through cryptocurrencies are not sufficiently monitored by the authorities, who are unable to link the transactions to identified persons. This is a serious practical difficulty when implementing the new rules. Blockchain technology, the digital ledger behind them, is virtually tamper-proof and does not require monitoring.[123] This raises the possibility that with the new rules, this might generate the unintended intention of pushing dirty money further behind the firewalls and into the dark web.

---

117 Solomon, M. C. et al. (2024), "MiCAR and Morrison: Navigating opportunities and challenges for U.S. digital assets companies in the EU and in the UK", in Dewey, J. N. (ed.), *Blockchain & cryptocurrency regulation*, London, GLI.

118 Ibid note [120], Solomon et al. (2024)

119 Ibid note [120], Solomon et al. (2024)

120 Ibid note [120], Solomon et al. (2024)

121 Business World (2018), "Will EU regulation of Bitcoin and other cryptocurrencies succeed?", *BusinessWorld*, 30/01/2018, www.businessworld.ie/news/Will-EU-regulation-of-Bitcoin-and-other-cryptocurrencies-succeed-570220.html, accessed 02/02/2018.

122 Yeoh, P. (2018), "Financial secrecy business offshore and onshore", *Company Lawyer*, 39(9): 279–285.

123 Ibid note [124], Business World (2018).

Germany, the most powerful of the EU member states, has taken an attitude towards cryptocurrencies that could offer glimpses of the EU's potential regulatory path. Germany's Federal Ministry of Finance formally recognises Bitcoin as a unit of account – a form of private currency usable for private transactions. It is not treated as a foreign currency or as e-money. It is taxable, although if the cryptocurrency is held for more than 1 year, it can be disposed of tax free.

In a public message, the Ministry subsequently clarified that it would not tax cryptocurrencies such as Bitcoin when they are applied in payments. When used for purchases, they would receive the same treatment as legal tender. Taxes for purchases would be calibrated in accordance with EU's VAT directive. Taxes may be imposed on fees collected by providers of digital wallets and other kinds of services pertaining to cryptocurrencies. Taxes are not imposed on block rewards sent to miners, or those intermediaries facilitating their conversion to or from fiat currencies. The European Court of Justice ruled such kinds of conversion as tax exempt supply of services. Those intermediaries that purchase or sell cryptocurrencies would also be tax-exempt, as would blockchain miners.[124]

Germany's Federal Financial Supervisory Authority (BaFin) treats cryptocurrencies such as Bitcoin as units of accounts within Section 1 (11) of the German Banking Act, last updated 2024. They are financial instruments comparable to foreign exchange, with the difference that they do not refer to a legal tender. Comparable cryptocurrencies and online exchanges are accordingly subject to regulatory supervision. As such, they are not currency, foreign notes, or coins – nor are they e-money within the interpretation of the German Payment Supervision Act. Nor do they constitute a claim on an issuer, as in effect one does not exist. Digital means of payments, in contrast, are backed by a central entity which issues and manages the units. BaFin generally is critical of cryptocurrencies, especially in the context of murky ICOs.

The Bundesbank, Germany's central bank, generally rules out the idea of an official digital money for the Euro zone. It is also concerned over the risks of losses from investments in cryptocurrencies. It argues that any initiative to regulate them has to be a concerted global basis so as to be effective with the greatest possible international co-operation. Germany's call to the G20 for regulatory intervention quickly received support from France and the United States.

As virtual currencies continue to creep into the mainstream through the launch of crypto futures, cryptocurrency index funds, etc., opportunities could continue to flourish. A way to gain control of cryptocurrencies could be via the ending of net neutrality. The United States has started this initiative, but it is not a straightforward process. It is also uncertain whether the new regulations could enable the effective monitoring of those bent on having less government oversight; after all, the very rationale for their introduction was the avoidance of government oversight.[147]

124 *Skatteverket v David Hedqvist*, 22 October 2015. C-264/14.

Additional oversight certainly exists in the form of amendments to the 4th EU Anti–Money Laundering Directive enclosed in the 5th.[125] *Cryptocurrencies* are defined as "a digital representation of value that can be digitally transferred, stored or traded and is accepted . . . as a medium of exchange". Cryptocurrencies and cryptocurrency exchanges are determined to be "obliged entities" for the purposes of anti-laundering and terrorist financing regulations. In addition, the reporting obligations are extended to the cryptocurrency area by financial intelligence units having the obligation to make sure the names and addresses are taken of the owners of cryptocurrency. Finally, the financial regulators in the EU are required to regulate the providers of cryptocurrency exchanges and wallets. Thus, for the purpose of the anti–money laundering laws and financial regulation, cryptocurrency has entered the financial services mainstream.

In its briefing to G20 members in Osaka in June 2019, the FSB recapitulated that the EU, the EBA, the European Insurance and Occupational Pensions Authority, and ESMA are the four regulators for cryptoassets in the EU. This aside, individual member states are passing their own domestic legislation to fill the gap that exists at the EU level. This suggests that the existing EU regulatory framework gives rise to the risks of inconsistent interpretations across EU member states and the potential for regulatory arbitrage despite MiCAR.

7.6 The UK's cryptoasset regulatory policy

The FCA and the regulator which deals with the capital requirements relating to relevant UK financial institutions, namely, the Prudential Regulation Authority (PRA), are primarily responsible for the supervision of financial services in the UK. HM Treasury (HMT) has overall authority regarding financial services and legislation in the country. The FCA, PRA, and Bank of England (BoE) together, in close collaboration, but working independently, maintain and advance UK's financial services and legislative and regulatory framework,[126] which includes cryptoassets and market participants in the industry.

Under English common law, a *cryptoasset* is, in general, a digital form of personal property or a chose in possession[127] where the rights of the owner of that property are derived from the capacity to physically possess it and transfer title to it to others, although these cryptoassets are intangible. As the nature and characteristics of cryptoassets continue to evolve, their legal status would persist in a state of flux. In the absence of a formal statutory definition for

125 Ibid note [124], Business World (2018)

126 Penn, B., "Banking regulation in the UK: Overview", *Thomson Reuters Practical Law*, 01/08/2018, https://uk.practicallaw.thomsonreuters.com/w-008-0211?transitionType=Default&contextData=%28sc.Default%29; Mwenda, K. K. (2018), *Legal aspects of financial services regulation and the concept of a unified regulator*, Washington, DC, The International Bank for Reconstruction and Development/The World Bank.

127 Financial Markets Law Committee (2016), "Issues of legal uncertainty arising in the context of virtual currencies", *FMLC Paper*, July 2016, http://fmlc.org/wp-content/uploads/2018/03/virtual_currencies_paper_-_edited_january_2017.pdf, accessed 26/11/2017.

cryptoassets/cryptocurrencies/virtual currencies, it would be guided by the 5th AMLD, which states that a virtual currency

> is a virtual representation of value that is not issued or guaranteed by a central bank or public authority, is not necessarily attached to a legal established currency, but is accepted by natural or legal persons as a means of exchange, and which can be transferred, stored, or traded electronically.[128]

This therefore would include various kinds of digital representation of value, extending from cryptoassets and others, as almost all these under EU's taxonomy of cryptocurrencies have a digital representation of value, are decentralised, not attached to a legally established currency, not possessing the legal status of currency or money, and are electronically transferable, storable, and tradeable.

Potential controversies could arise with regards to cryptocurrencies having to be a means of exchange. First, it does not say anything about a cryptocurrency that is not accepted as a means of exchange now but where there is no intrinsic limitation preventing them from becoming a means of exchange in the future.[129] This then depends on the willingness of parties to accept the cryptocurrency as a standard of value in their mutual dealings. However, as soon as that happens, they transform it into a means of exchange and it falls under the definition of the 5th AMLD. Thus, from the perspective of combating money laundering, terrorist financing, and tax evasion, the relevant laws will apply as the activity will potentially have been carried out on an exchange. Second, it does not say anything about a virtual currency that is a medium of exchange but which is also an investment instrument.[161] Though cryptocurrencies in general are marked by high volatility, mainstream finance increasingly considers them as a financial asset class. Moreover, the 5th AMLD definition does not say that this should be the only or the predominant function of the cryptocurrency. Cryptocurrencies as such should be covered by the definition provided in the 5th AMLD. In any case, even in the fiat currency framework, a fiat can also be acquired and held for investment or speculation purposes, and this does not alter the fiat's primary status of being a fiat currency. Hence, the 5th AMLD's definition of virtual currencies is adequate to combat money laundering, terrorist financing, and tax evasion through the cryptocurrencies included in the taxonomy in use in the EU[130] and the UK.

Foremost, the FCA final guidance categorises cryptocurrencies into three types: Firstly, exchange tokens such as Bitcoin, which are used as both media of exchange and as investments. Secondly, security tokens, which may entitle the holder to ownership or a share of property rights. These are caught by both the

---

128 Houben, R. & Snyers, A. (2018), "Cryptocurrencies and blockchain: Legal context and implications for financial crimes, money laundering and tax evasion", *European Parliament Paper PE619.024*, July 2018, p. 68.

129 Ibid note [131], Houben & Snyers (2018).

130 Ibid note [131], Houben & Snyers (2018).

Financial Services (Regulated Activities) Order 2001[131] as they are categorised as financial instruments.[132] Finally, utility tokens, which can be redeemed for a specific product using a DLT platform.

Cryptocurrency derivatives[133] will be caught under the financial services' regulatory regime as all three categories of derivative are "specialised investments" under the Financial Services and Markets Act 2000 (Regulated Activities) Order 2001.[134] At the risk of over-simplifying, the three categories are:

- Cryptocurrency futures, which exist where two parties agree that one will transfer an amount equal in value to a cryptocurrency's future price on a stated or determinable future date in return for a determinable payment in the other direction. Essentially, if the cryptocurrency rises in value in the interim, one party (who will normally be holding it) will gain and the other will lose. The converse also applies.
- Cryptocurrency options are, in essence, a variation on this arrangement. Here, one party pays a deposit in return for the right to notionally sell a cryptocurrency to the other party or to buy it from them. In the event of the price moving in favour of the depositor, they will make a profit. In the event of its value moving the other way, they will suffer a loss, but if this exceeds the amount of the deposit, they can forfeit the deposit and their loss will be limited to that amount.
- Cryptocurrency contracts for differences are an arrangement where two parties agree to exchange payments equal in value to the difference between the price of a cryptocurrency and a stated item of other value for a fixed or determinable period of time.

This means that the party arranging, selling, advising, or managing in relation to them will have to be regulated by the FCA.[135] The regulatory concerns, although real, have not yet come to an overall completed regulatory approach. The speed of development of the marketplace, coupled with a realisation by those inside the regulators that significant investment and job opportunities might be tied up in the new developments, has resulted in a considered approach. The Cryptoassets Taskforce (CAT) has been set up, including the FCA, HM Treasury, and the Bank of England, with a view to analysing the impact not only of cryptocurrencies but also of cryptoassets generally and DLT. Their report[136] was carried

131 SI 2001/544 as amended.

132 They will also be caught throughout the EU by the Markets in Financial Instruments Directive II (MiFID II).

133 Essentially, futures, options, and contracts for differences where the underlying "commodity" is a cryptocurrency; Soylemez, Y. (2020), "Cryptocurrency derivatives: The case of bitcoin", in Hacioglu, U. (ed.), *Blockchain economics and financial market innovations: Financial innovations in the digital age*, Basel, Springer, pp. 515–530.

134 SI 2001/544 as amended.

135 And for capital adequacy purposes, the Prudential Regulation Authority (PRA) if they are a bank or insurance company.

136 *Cryptoassets Taskforce: Final Report*, October 2018.

out against a background of not wishing to obstruct innovative developments in these areas.[137] This is evidenced by the government investing over £10 million to support a range of DLT projects, including analysing its potential for use in the public sector and joining the EU Blockchain Partnership, which will require a national approach following the UK's departure from the EU. In addition, £20 million has been made available through the GovTech Catalyst Fund to explore both this and the potential of DLT in the financial services area. There are already 12 cryptoasset spot exchanges in the UK, of which only four post daily trading volumes of over US$30 million equivalent. The 12 only amount to 2.66% of worldwide daily trading, though it should be added that some overseas exchanges have subsidiaries or branches here.[138]

The taskforce determined that key issues were:

- Maintaining the UK's international reputation as a safe and transparent place to do business
- Ensuring that there are high regulatory standards in the financial marketplace
- Protecting consumers
- Guarding against future threats to financial stability
- Allowing those who innovate within the rules to prosper

The FCA has created an "Innovation Hub and Regulatory Sandbox" to allow businesses to test "innovative products, services, business models and delivery mechanisms in the real market, with real consumers".[139] A significant, if currently small, number of firms have used this facility.[174]

The Bank of England has created a fintech hub to consider how the policy implications of the new developments might work out. One development was the work with 18 firms relating to proof of concepts to assist in understanding how the new technologies might be adopted. There has also been an analysis of the existing payments system to see how comparable it will be with DLT-based payment systems. The Financial Policy Committee has also considered the financial stability implications of cryptoassets.

Within the current regulatory regime, certain areas will be relevant for any regulated firms working with cryptocurrency as their business requires these elements from all regulated firms in the carrying out of their business activities.

- The FCA Principles for Business and, in particular, the requirement that a firm maintain sufficient financial resources, maintain adequate systems and controls, and also that they deal with the FCA in an open

137 Department for Digital, Culture, Media and Sport (2017), "Executive summary: Our plan for Britain" *Department for Digital, Culture, Media and Sport*, 01/03/2017, www.gov.uk/government/publications/uk-digital-strategy/executive-summary, accessed 31/01/2020.

138 *Cryptoassets Taskforce: Final Report*, October 2018, p. 15.

139 *Cryptoassets Taskforce: Final Report*, October 2018, p. 5.

and co-operative way.

- The Senior Managers and Certification Regime (SMCR), which means that the regulator can hold senior management of the relevant firms responsible even if the activity concerned was an unregulated one.
- The Systems and Control Provisions, which deal with organisation, risk control, record-keeping, and employee requirements, to name the most important.
- The Financial Promotions Rules, which require that promotions be clear, fair, and not misleading. This requires behaviour to be in line with the Financial Promotions Order 2005.[140]

Essentially, this divides communications with the public into unsolicited real-time, solicited real-time, and non-real-time communications and requires anyone issuing such a promotion to be registered for the purpose by the FCA, unless an exclusion applies. The first of these essentially covers cold calling by speaking to someone in person or over the phone. The second covers doing so after the receipt of evidence that the member of the public wishes to be contacted on the matter, and the final one covers other methods of communication, such as writing, email, and leaving and answering phone message. The further down this list of three communication goes, the less vulnerable the recipient, and therefore the less protection they receive. The nature of the investment concerned is also a factor with those involving longer-term and larger risks, providing greater protection, mostly in terms of the risk warnings that have to be provided.

In addition, a firm which is not licensed to carry on investment business will be committing a criminal offence[141] if they induce anyone to enter into business involving regulated investments, which, as we have seen, will include some of the examples of cryptocurrency. A problem that arises here is that the newness of the cryptocurrency market means that it may not be entirely sure whether some products are going to be caught by the regulators or not. If in doubt, a firm should seek the regulator's view.

The main concern was that there were key risks to the public. They were the risk of large scale losses to the public, losses due to market manipulation, and also that the products might be used as vehicles for financial crime.[142] As yet, though, they are not seen as posing a potential threat to financial stability.

What, then, do the regulators see as their perceived benefits? Firstly, their use as a means of exchange opens up the possibility of increased efficiency in the international financial transfer markets as a result of fewer intermediaries being involved. There is also the possibility that they could improve the traceability and transparency of financial transactions and increase stability, as there would

140 SI 2005/1529 as amended.

141 Section 21 of the Financial Services and Markets Act 2000.

142 Cryptoasset Taskforce (2018), "Cryptoassets taskforce final report", *Cryptoassets Taskforce Final Report* 26/1/2018, https://assets.publishing.service.gov.uk/media/5bd6d6f0e5274a6e11247059/cryptoassets_taskforce_final_report_final_web.pdf, accessed 15/11/2018, p. 41.

be no central system which might be disrupted. It may also lower barriers to entry, encourage competition, and provide an alternative to traditional payment methods.

When cryptoassets are used as an investment, they may also widen access, but subject to what are seen at present as an unacceptable degree of risk. When cryptoassets are used to raise capital, there are potential benefits. ICOs may be supporting new business models and provide incentives for improvements in the traditional process of raising capital. They may also improve efficiency as they directly link issuers with investors, and this is a particular benefit with small issuances. In particular, there could be a benefit in that it can help address the funding gap. Firstly, many high risk projects find it difficult to raise funds in the early stages of projects, and the direct connection may help here. In addition, there is the classic funding gap of between around £1 million and £10 million where funding has traditionally been hard to raise. The new ICO and security token (STO) market could change this. Finally, the international basis of ICOs and STOs will mean that smaller firms can tap into the international financial markets in a way in which they could not have done in the past.

The key risk they found was that there was a concern expressed that money launderers and terrorist financiers would benefit because "of their accessibility online, their global reach and their pseudo-anonymous nature".[143] The UK government's analysis[144] suggested that the risk of this remained low, though a fear was expressed that cryptoassets could assist in crimes related to computer technology. Concerns also relate to the anonymity of cryptoassets ATMs, peer-to-peer exchange facilities, and the relative privacy of some coins. Europol's latest analysis suggests that around £3–4 billion is laundered using cryptoassets, which is only 3–4% of the amount laundered in Europe alone.[145]

The risk of financial losses for investors has already been mentioned, but in addition, there is the risk of products being marketed with poor or unclear pricing material. There will now be recourse to the Financial Ombudsmen Scheme and the Financial Services Compensation Scheme provided the cryptocurrency or asset fits within the definition in the Financial Services and Markets Act 2023 for regulatory purposes.[146] Also mentioned was the lack of clarity of ICO offerings due to the lack of standardisation, such as that exists with regard to prospectuses in relation to the public offering of shares or bonds. Indeed, a recent report suggested that around 25% of ICOs could be fraudulent.[147] Around 46% of those issued in 2017 have already failed.[148] Those derivatives involving cryptoassets

143 Ibid note [146], Cryptoassets Taskforce (2018), p. 33.

144 In the form of the National Risk Assessments of Money Laundering and Terrorist Financing 2015 and 2017.

145 Silma, S. (2018), "Criminals Hide Billions in Cryptocash – Europol", *BBC*, 12/02/2018, www.bbc.com/news/technology-43025787, accessed 15/11/2018; See also the FATF report to the G20 Finance Ministers and Central Bank Governors, Financial Action Task Force, 2018.

146 S.69 Financial Services and Markets Act 2023

147 BIS Annual Report, Bank for International Settlements, 2018.

148 Hankin, A. (2018), "Nearly half of all 2017 ICOs have failed", *Market Watch*, 26/02/2018, www.marketwatch.com/story/nearly-half-of-all-2017-icos-have-failed-2018-02-26#:~:text=Failed%20

could also cause an investor to lose more than the amount they invest, and retail investors may not be cognisant of this.

The London Stock Exchange has not yet approved a listing which references any of these three categories and will only do so where they have confidence in the integrity of the underlying product. That said, there have been 56 ICOs used for raising capital in the UK, which account for 4.3% of the world market during the relevant period.[149] What is also significant is the location of those investing by this means, but unfortunately, this is not known. A comparison with the geographical spread of investors in conventional bond or share issues would be of interest.

As alluded to earlier, the main impediment to the design of new rules and policies could be attributed to the lack of a common lexicon around cryptoassets.[150] Global Digital Finance, an industry grouping, is trying to resolve this issue. Meanwhile, it has been said that countries with a higher level of domestic cryptoasset activity usually have retrofitted regulation.[188] This response is justifiable in the context of the fast moving new space that encountered early signs of fraudulent activity. Malta and Luxembourg have been able to develop crypto-friendly regulatory and tax regimes, but their ability to achieve this is intrinsically linked to their relative lack of cryptoasset activity.

Compared to conventional systems where regulators are able to deal with individual nodes of firms or individuals on a case by case basis, networks premised on DLT, on the other hand, operate according to consensus, and encryption might not be reliant on any one node. Here, regulators have the conundrum of resolving whether node operators have responsibility for the assets traded or the private key holders that made the transaction.[151] This is because a majority group of participants in a distributed network could collude to reach a consensus and undo a transaction or block a particular private key from transacting, thereby making their digital assets useless.

Thus far, this pivotal point has not been resolved sufficiently, and where node operators assumed responsibility, they might have to be regulated. Importantly, when involving cross-jurisdictional transactions, purpose built rules could be needed to counter this. Self-regulated industry led entities, for this reason, play important roles as initiatives for setting up appropriate regulations continue.[152] Meanwhile, the regulatory sandbox is viewed in the UK and many other jurisdictions across the world as a fine example of a collaborative and structured

ICOs%20report%3A%20'A%20Digital%20Graveyard%20of%20Broken%20Promises'&text=According%20to%20a%20survey%20from,as%20%E2%80%9Csemi%2Dfailed.%E2%80%9D, accessed 07/02/2020.

149 Coin schedule market research in association with the Taskforce, 20 August 2018.

150 Bladin, A. et al. (April 2019), *Global cryptoasset regulatory landscape study*, Cambridge, Cambridge Centre for Alternative Finance (CCAF).

151 Marshall, S. (2019), "Cryptoasset compliance in the UK: The story so far", *Torca*, 31/05/2019, https://thefintechtimes.com/torca-cryptoasset-compliance/, accessed 02/06/2019.

152 Ibid note [155], Marshall (2019).

approach to innovation and innovative products. A wide range of entities across four past cohorts have been able to test innovative products, services, business models, and delivery mechanisms with real consumers under regulator monitoring. This is by far FCA's more successful story, as the national regulatory sandbox is now a global regulatory sandbox[153] with the participation of many economies and would soon include the United States too. The willingness of other jurisdictions to join in is due to their recognition that this is probably the best approach to deal with fintech start ups that deal with financial instruments characterised by cross-border features.

Due to the inherent nature of the underlying assets that have no reliable basis for valuation, the prevalence of market abuse and financial crimes in the cryptoasset secondary market, extreme price volatility, and inadequate understanding by retail consumers of cryptoassets, the FCA considers these products as unsuitable for retail consumers.[154]

The UK government has not expanded the FCA's regulatory perimeter and has only assigned it to be the supervisor for the 5th AMLD. As said earlier, the 5th AMLD introduced an anti-money laundering regime for cryptoassets. This will bring within its remit virtual currency exchange platforms and wallet providers. Thus, this will therefore help to dampen some consumer protection and market integrity fears that had emerged exposing users' identities and fund sources.

The FCA Guidance therefore sets out the regulatory treatment of cryptoassets within FCA's regulatory remit. The regulatory perimeter sets the demarcation between regulated and unregulated financial services. Where entities undertake activities falling within the regulatory perimeter within the UK as part of their business, it would probably be required to be authorised by the FCA, or in some other instances by the PRA, except when exempted. Business entities are not able to issue financial promotional activities like inviting persons to partake in investment activities, such as getting them to purchase regulated cryptoassets without FCA approval or a person authorised by the FCA for approving the contents of these communications.

A person undertaking specified activities pertaining to specified investments will fall under the FCA's regulatory perimeter. The FCA in this connection has demarcated two broad kinds of regulated tokens, electronic money (e-money) and security tokens, and unregulated tokens, which are essentially anything else. Examples of these are Bitcoin and Litecoin.

153 FCA (2019), "Global financial innovation network (GFIN)", *FCA*, 09/08/2019, www.fca.org.uk/firms/innovation/global-financial-innovation-network, accessed 10/08/2019; Strachan, D., Nair, S., Gallo, V. & Fouche, M. (2018), "A journey through the FCA regulatory sandbox", *EMEA Centre for Regulatory Strategy Paper 09/10/18*, www.fintechscotland.com/a-journey-through-the-fca-regulatory-sandbox/, accessed 08/08/2019.

154 FCA (2019), "FCA proposes ban on sale of crypto-derivatives to retail consumers", *FCA News Release* 03/07/2019, www.fca.org.uk/news/press-releases/fca-bans-sale-crypto-derivatives-retail-consumers#:~:text=The%20FCA%20has%20published%20final,to%20the%20harm%20they%20pose, accessed 05/07/2019.

Nevertheless, the FCA tells businesses to be aware of the country's intention to extend the requirements of the 5th AMLD to include exchange services between cryptoassets, transfer of cryptoassets, cryptoasset ATMs, and new cryptoassets issued through ICOs.

Regulated security tokens are tokens that provide rights and obligations similar to specified investments, like shares, other than e-money, which will be within FCA's regulatory perimeter. The FCA cautioned that this will depend on the substance or token intention and not the form or labelling used. *Regulated e-money tokens* are tokens that are defined under the Electronic Money Regulations 2011 (EMRs). The EMRs define *e-money* as electronically stored monetary value as represented by a claim on the e-money issuer. *Stablecoins* refer to tokens stabilised through being backed by fiats, cryptoassets, algorithms, other tangible assets, or their combinations thereof subject to their structure and the stabilisation model, and these would remain, for the moment, outside of the FCA's perimeter. Any tokens, though pegged to fiats or other assets deployed for the payments of goods and services on a network, potentially could fall within the definition of *e-money* and therefore within FCA's perimeter.

Utility tokens are tokens providing consumers with access to current or prospective services or products. These are equivalent to pre-payment vouchers and will accordingly fall outside the regulatory perimeter. The FCA narrated various case examples of these.

Mainstream cryptoassets commentators claim that given the popularity of security token offerings, there could be a blurring of the lines between these and utility tokens.[155] This is because utility tokens could be labelled as security tokens to ensure that they do not fall foul of any promotion type restrictions. This raises the question as to whether this actually alters the nature of the token itself when it comes to trading in them. The FCA, though, has clarified that they pay less attention to labelling than the underlying characteristics. The FCA has further clarified that further clarity between types of tokens would be forthcoming, such as demarcating a specific regulated e-money token category and an unregulated category that includes utility tokens.

For this and more, the FCA would need the Treasury to bring more cryptoassets into the law, and that would require serious thinking as to the country's intention for the fintech space. This would need to balance the benefits of innovation with the needs for investors' safety risk and financial stability considerations but taking into considerations what other competitive hubs across the world have done thus far.

Various kinds of market participants and the activities they undertake would probably be required to comply with the Prospectus Regulation or would otherwise require authorisation for the delivery of services, like the forwarding of

155 Allison, I. (2019), "UK finance watchdog issues guidance on regulation for Bitcoin and cryptoassets", *Coin Desk*, 31/07/2019, www.coindesk.com/markets/2019/07/31/uk-finance-watchdog-issues-guidance-on-regulation-for-bitcoin-and-crypto-assets/, accessed 02/08/2019.

dematerialised instructions, the safeguarding and administering of investments, the advising on investments, and dealing, arranging, or operating an OTF or an MTF.

It needs stressing that though the FCA guidance is not binding on courts, entities are generally treated to have complied with FCA rules when they act in accordance with these. The final guidance is therefore applicable to businesses that issue or generate cryptoassets, that market cryptoassets products/services, that transact on cryptoassets, that hold or store cryptoassets, and to financial advisers, professional advisers, investment managers, recognised investment exchanges, and consumers and consumer entities.

The UK, through the FCA, has therefore taken the initial steps in the regulatory treatment of cryptoassets in the country but keeping in mind its mission of dealing with consumer protection, market integrity, and competition issues. The FCA will strive to measure the success in achieving these outcomes via:

- Evaluating feedback from final guidance stakeholders
- Growth in the numbers and accuracies of authorisation submission from businesses undertaking regulated cryptoassets activities
- Fewer referrals to its unauthorised business division and financial promotions team showing that persons and their advisers are clearer about when they need authorisation and when FCA's financial promotion rules would set in
- Fewer calls and/or requests for support via Innovate on issues pertaining to the regulatory application to cryptoassets
- Evaluating feedback from consumers as to whether FCA's regulatory framework has helped consumers better understand the cryptoassets markets, by potentially measuring this through follow-up consumer surveys and analysing calls via the FCA consumer hub.

The final guidance has also informed market participants of FCA's cryptoassets regulatory works in progress, as mentioned earlier, the consultation on potentially banning the sale of derivatives linked to particular kinds of unregulated cryptoassets to retail clients; Treasury's consultation on whether further regulation is required in the cryptoassets markets, especially with respect to unregulated cryptoassets mentioned earlier; and Treasury and FCA's work on the transposing of the 5th AMLD.

Overall, the FCA's final guidance has contributed to an enhanced understanding on how to approach the crypto industry for interested business entities. For investors and retail investors, this enhances clarity of the kinds of risks involved when looking at cryptoassets as an investment class and, importantly, how and why they differ, as well as the regulatory, and hence safety, implications involved.

In any case, the sea of voices, particularly those from the primary stakeholders, not only in the UK, but also across the other main crypto hubs in other parts of the world, could have an impact on the regulatory agenda usually straddling between being ahead in innovation and being too loose on safety, security, and stability measures. This probably helps explain why structures and remits are in flux as regulators and supervisors adapt their agendas and working methods to the rapidly evolving environment.[156] The trend of supervision in the sector is both widening and deepening, with supervisors needing to turn to technology or exponential techs to help them discharge their obligations more efficiently. There has been some new rulemaking in some niches and in some jurisdictions, but supervisory and regulatory missions are increasingly focused on the monitoring and review of major post-crisis rules. Policymakers and regulators are yet insisting on more data, and increasingly also calls from institutional investors and the industry for a rationalisation of requirements and for greater global regulatory convergence. This is not going to be easy, given today's geopolitics.

Meanwhile, for global digital platforms running from outside the EU, regarding the matter of whether they would be subject to the Markets in Crypto-Asset Regulation (MiCAR) is optional in practice, the answer appears to tilt towards a resounding no; if offering their services in the EU, third country cryptoasset service providers will be required to obtain authorisation under the regulation from a competent authority of a member state, and for purposes of such authorisation, they will be required to set up a subsidiary, or at least a branch in such member state. Also, third country enterprises that are issuers of asset-referenced tokens (ARTs) and aim to offer them to the public or request admission to trading in the EU will need to obtain authorisation under MiCAR, which requires an establishment in the EU, while issuers of e-money tokens (EMTs) will have to be legal entities set up in the EU and authorised as banks or e-money institutions in a member state. These conditions imply that global digital asset platforms aiming to provide services in the EU would have no option but to seek one or multiple authorisations under MiCAR and comply with the regulation. Indeed, MiCAR's territorial scope is wide, with little scope for avoidance.

The implementation of MiCAR in the EU on 20 April 2023 coincided with a time of rising scepticism towards risky crypto frameworks that could lead to an anticipation of a highly rigorous implementation of the regulation. The ECB recently pushed the need for robust regulatory standards concurrently with a cautious approach to public support for the crypto business,[157] whereas the EBA urges financial institutions and undertakings seeking to partake in ART and EMT activities to undertake comprehensive legal and risks evaluations while implementing risk mitigation measures. Additionally, the EBA has also urged national competent authorities to inform existing issuers of cryptos about the incoming MiCAR requirements, to provide consumer information, and to motivate alignments to guiding principles incorporating disclosure obligations,

156 Brown, T. & Patterson, J. (2019), "A sea of voices: Evolving asset management regulation report", *KPMG Paper*, June 2019, https://assets.kpmg.com/content/dam/kpmg/xx/pdf/2019/06/a-sea-of-voices-eamr2019.pdf, accessed 08/08/2019.

157 Panetta, F. (2023), "Paradise lost? How crypto failed to deliver on its purposes and what to do about it", *Speech by Fabio Panetta, Member of the Executive Board of the European Central Bank, at a panel on the future of crypto at the 22nd BIS Annual Conference, Basel, 23 June 2023.*, www.bis.org/review/r230628e.htm, accessed 20/12/23

business models evaluations, and adoption of robust governance and organisational arrangements.[158]

Even though the regulatory outcomes sought in the UK resemble those in MiCAR, the UK's approach differs significantly, as instead of electing for a radical, new scheme of regulation, it adopts a phased approach to regulation, whereby the present financial services regulatory framework is amended to also cover for cryptoassets.[159] For instance, its anti–money laundering/counter-terrorist financing framework has included particular crypto businesses, such as crypto exchange providers and custodian wallet providers, since 2020.

The UK's Financial Services and Markets Act 2023 (FSMA 2023) legitimised digital settlement assets or fiat-backed stablecoins for settling payment obligations within the confines of the UK regulatory perimeter with the intention that, in general, they should be regulated under e-money and payments regulation by the FCA, including bringing systemic arrangements within the existing framework for systemic payment systems and service providers that are overseen by the Bank of England (BOE). From October 2023, the country's financial promotion space has been amended so as to regulate "qualifying cryptoassets", or cryptos that are fungible and transferable.[160] This is targeted at improving consumers' comprehension of the risks linked to crypto investments, while also ensuring that crypto promotions are positioned as the standards as the wide financial services.

The UK Treasury has published consultation mapping out high-level proposals for the regulation of various crypto-related activities equivalent in scope to MiCAR, with focus on "high-priority" crypto activities through the amending of FSMA 2000 (Regulated Activities) Order 2001, which, together with its parent statute, the Financial Services and Markets Act 2000, is the primary source of law establishing the perimeter of UK financial services regulation.[161] Overall, the UK seeks to be the jurisdiction marked by the most open, well-regulated, and technologically advanced capital market globally. The UK is of the belief that crypto technologies may have widespread impact across financial services and, accordingly, aims to maximise their potential benefits. Future crypto-linked activities are presently not accorded high priority, examples being validation and governance activities, such as mining or validating transactions, operating a

---

158 EBA Statement 12/07/2023, www.eba.europa.eu/sites/default/files/document_library/Publications/Other%20publications/2023/Statement%20on%20%20preparatory%20steps%20towards%20application%20of%20MiCAR/1057527/Statement%20on%20timely%20preparatory%20steps%20towards%20the%20application%20of%20MiCAR%20to%20asset-referenced%20and%20e-money%20tokens.pdf, accessed 20/12/23

159 Ibid note [120], Solomon et al. (2024)

160 FCA (2023), "Financial promotion rules for cryptoassets", *Policy Statement PS23/6*, June 2023, www.fca.org.uk/publication/policy/ps23-6.pdf, accessed 20/12/23

161 Treasury (2023), "Future financial services regulatory regime for cryptoassets", *Treasury*, 01/02/2023, www.gov.uk/government/consultations/future-financial-services-regulatory-regime-for-cryptoassets, accessed 20/12/2023

node on a blockchain, or applying cryptos to run a validator node infrastructure on a proof of stake network.[162]

While widely similar to MiCAR, the UK Treasury proposals[163] appear to develop from the definition adopted in FSMA 2023 that defines a *cryptoasset* as any cryptographically secured digital representation of value or contractual rights that can be transferred, stored, or traded electronically, and that deploys technology supporting the recording or storage of data, which may include DLT. Unlike MiCAR, though, this definition does not limit cryptos to assets using DLT, or equivalent technology. Importantly, however, whereas MiCAR imposes different levels of regulatory obligations depending on the wide category of cryptos, the UK Treasury at this phase does not envisage systematic distinctions based on the category of crypto involved.[164]

Instead of cryptos accorded specific regulatory treatment based only on their characteristics, as in MiCAR, the Treasury proposals hinge on regulatory obligations applied to market participants, depending on the specific regulated activity in question.[165] While MiCAR imposes regulatory requirements pertaining to the provision of advice on cryptos or portfolio management services pertaining to cryptos, the UK Treasury's consultation is of the view that such services are relatively limited as they are presently being directed towards institutional and high net worth customers with little immediate risk of harm to retail consumers.[166] On the other hand, unlike MiCAR, the UK Treasury proposals seek to bring within its regulatory perimeter lending, borrowing, and leveraging activities, like the running of a crypto lending platform. This appears to be a risk-driven regulatory initiative, as noted in its consultation, as credit risk has been observed as a significant driver of crypto market turbulences; and as such, platforms undertaking lending or borrowing activities should be required to hold adequate financial resources to manage counterparty credit risk and to address liabilities as they fall due.[167] The Treasury's response includes, among others, the following:[168]

- Detail on the regulated activities and tokens which will be in scope for phase 1 of the Treasury's approach to regulating cryptos and how these will be demarcated from phase 2 activities is spelled out in a separate "stablecoins update" policy papers.
- The Treasury clarifies that the intended outcomes for non-fungible tokens (NFTs), utility tokens, security tokens, and other data objects or

162 Ibid note [120], Solomon et al. (2024)
163 Ibid note [120], Solomon et al. (2024)
164 Ibid note [120], Solomon et al. (2024)
165 Ibid note [120], Solomon et al. (2024)
166 Ibid note [120], Solomon et al. (2024)
167 Ibid note [120], Solomon et al. (2024)
168 Weatherill, A. et al. (2023), "HMT publishes final proposals for UK cryptoasset regulation", *Norton Rose Fullbright*, 30/10/2023, www.regulationtomorrow.com/eu/hmt-publishes-final-proposals-for-uk-cryptoasset-regulation/, accessed 20/12/2023

"things" that were of concern to respondents could be captured unintentionally. However, the Treasury advises that its proposed regime does not seek to capture activities pertaining to cryptos that are specified investments and are already regulated, such as security tokens, or activities pertaining to truly unique or non-fungible NFTs that are more similar to digital collectibles or artwork than a financial service or product.

- The Treasury categorically "disagrees" with suggestions that retail trading and investment activity in unbacked cryptos should be regulated as gambling than as a financial service.
- FCA authorisation will not be automatically extended to businesses registered with the FCA under the Money Laundering Regulations.
- The UK government is targeting to set phase 2 secondary regulation for crypto activities in 2024 "subject to Parliamentary time".
- The Treasury recognises the need to mitigate fragmentation of crypto liquidity that could originate from a restrictive location and market access policy and accordingly plans to proceed with an approach that facilitates access to international liquidity pools under particular circumstances.
- With regards to issuance and disclosures, the Treasury believes that recklessness and negligence liability standards will enable market participants to manage their liability provided they initiate reasonable enquiries. IT confirms its support for the use of publicly available information to compile appropriate parts of disclosure and admission documents.
- A modified approach will be adopted towards market abuse obligations on crypto exchanges in view of the potential need for a staggered implementation for cross-venue data sharing obligation.
- And the Treasury has launched an engagement initiative to inform stakeholders of its plan of actions and so on. Importantly, the Treasury is committed to nurturing a regulatory environment where businesses can innovate, besides critically maintaining financial stability and clear regulatory standards, to enable market participants to use evolving technologies reliably and safely.

The Treasury has set out a policy paper[169] providing updates on its legislative approach for bringing fiat-backed stablecoins into the UK's regulatory perimeter for financial services as part of phase 1 of its approach to crypto regulation. This is in addition and subsequent to the UK regulatory approach to cryptos, stablecoins, and DLT in financial markets consultation response that was published in April 2022. Here, the Treasury confirmed its intention to establish a regulatory framework for fiat-backed stablecoins, including when deployed as a means of

169 Treasury (2023), "Update on plans for the regulation of fiat-backed stablecoins", *Treasury*, October 2023, www.gov.uk/government/publications/update-on-plans-for-the-regulation-of-fiat-backed-stablecoins, accessed 20/12/2023

payment that has already been implemented via the introduction of measures in the FSMA 2023. The Treasury also seeks to initiate secondary legislation. Such legislative provisions have brought activities pertaining to fiat-backed stablecoins into the regulatory perimeter to enable FCA. The policy update provides further detail on the objectives of the proposed legislation to facilitate the FCA's regime, besides providing further information pertaining to the BOE's regime, the Payment Systems Regulator regime, and co-responsibility for supervision of systemic fiat-backed stablecoin enterprises.[170] As such, the update seeks to inform the development of the FCA's and BOE's approaches for regulating stablecoin issuers and custodians, and systemic digital settlement assets (DSA) payments systems and service providers, respectively.[171]

Unlike the comparative certainty provided by MiCAR or the UK regulatory framework, US securities laws in general do not apply extraterritorially, whether in the context of conventional securities laws, or in digital assets transactions that could potentially be investment contracts, and therefore securities transactions, unless particular specific circumstances are present.[172] As to whether US authorities seeking to assert jurisdiction over foreign digital asset companies would be informed by what alleged misconduct is at issue and the company's US nexus in the context of the registration provisions of US securities laws, courts have held[173] that the mere location of purchasers in the United States does not satisfy that test.

The probability that a court would apply the US securities laws to claims against a foreign digital asset company would rise where the company allegedly partakes in fraud that was directed at or had an impact on US investors. Where this involves enforcement action alleging fraud, the conduct and effects test, rather than the Morrison's transactional test, would probably apply.[174] This test requires either conduct within the United States that constitutes significant actions to further the breach, even if the securities transactions take place outside the United States and involve only foreign investors, or conduct taking place outside the United States that has a foreseeable substantial impact within the United States.[175] Indeed, the CFTC, the SEC, the DOJ, and private plaintiffs have not hesitated to take actions against foreign digital asset companies that are alleged to have partaken in fraud. US competent authorities and private

---

170 Ibid note [172], Weatherill et al. (2023)

171 Campbell, J. & Furlong, E. (2023), "Provisions relating to digital assets under the Financial Services and Markets Act 2023 come into force", *Pilsbury*, 29/08/2023, www.pillsburylaw.com/en/news-and-insights/financial-services-markets-act-digital-assets.html, accessed 20/12/2023

172 *Morrison v. National Australia Bank Ltd.*, 561 U.S. 247 (2010); *Absolute Activist Value Master Fund Ltd. V. Ficeto*, 677 F. 3d60, 66–69 (2d Cir. 2012); *Stoyas v. Toshiba Corp.*, 896 F.3d 933 (9th Cir.2018); *SEC v. Bio Def. Corp.*, 2019 WL 7578525, at *11–13 (D. Mass. Sept. 6, 2019); *SEC v. Ripple Labs, Inc.*, 2022 WL 762966, at *11 (S.D.N.Y. Mar. 11, 2022); and *Anderson v. Binance*, 2022 WL 97824, at *4 (S.D.N.Y. Mar. 31, 2022).

173 A*bsolute Activist Value Master Fund Ltd. v Ficeto*, 677 F. 3d 60, 69 (2d Cir. 2012); *Anderson v. Binance*, 2022 WL 976824, at *4 (S.D.N.Y. mar 31, 2022)

174 Ibid note [120], Solomon et al. (2024)

175 Ibid note [120], Solomon et al. (2024)

plaintiffs have embarked aggressively with regards to foreign digital asset companies, where there is alleged misconduct that has some alleged nexus to the United States.[176] Emphatically, though, US securities laws do not apply extraterritorially, and foreign companies defending against securities claims may have good persuasive arguments under well settled precedent that plaintiffs have gone beyond the territorial scope of these laws.[177]

7.7 Australia's cryptoassets regulatory policy

Australia's Anti-Money Laundering and Counter-Terrorism Financing Amendment Act 2017 (AMLCTF) was passed in December 2017, amending the 2006 Act.[178] The initiative was aimed at imposing restrictions on digital currencies, especially Bitcoin, due to their continuous growth and adoption in the mainstream financial sector and, importantly, to fight the threat of financial crime in Australia. Australian lawmakers felt the need to make this move after the discovery that one of the country's major banks, the Commonwealth Bank, had violated laws pertaining to money laundering.[179] This was also the response to the Financial Task Force's report that the country's existing laws to combat money laundering have serious flaws that needed amendments to eliminate loopholes. The proposed laws empower AUSTRAC, the country's financial and intelligence agency, to monitor the activities of all cryptocurrency exchanges operating in Australia. The primary aim of the monitoring is to ensure that financial transactions are not related to money laundering or terrorism.

The AMLCTF expands the Act's object to reflect the domestic objectives of anti–money laundering and counter-terrorism financing regulations. It also expands the scope of the Act to include regulation of digital currency exchange providers, clarify due diligence obligations pertaining to correspondent banking relationships, and widen the scope of these relationships. This Act in particular would require businesses offering convertible digital currency exchange services, such as exchanging money for Bitcoin or vice versa, to be registered with and subject to mandatory reporting obligations to AUSTRAC.

If enacted in its present form, the key provisions and their implications are as follows:[180]

176 Ibid note [120], Solomon et al. (2024)

177 Ibid note [120], Solomon et al. (2024)

178 Anti-Money Laundering and Counter-Terrorism Financing Act 2006, No. 169, 2006, Compilation No. 48 Including Amendments up to Act no. 156, 2018 20/12/118, www.austlii.edu.au/au/legis/cth/consol_act/alacfa2006522/, accessed 07/02/2019

179 Althauser, J. (2017), "Australian exchanges now required to register with AML regulatory body", *Coin Telegraph*, 09/12/2017, https://cointelegraph.com/news/australian-exchanges-now-required-to-register-with-aml-regulatory-body, accessed 02/02/2018.

180 Allgrove, A-M., Fair, P., Lawrence, A.J. & Patten, T. (2017), "Bitcoin to be regulated in Australia", *Baker McKenzie*, 01/12/2017, https://blockchain.bakermckenzie.com/2018/01/18/cryptocurrency-to-be-regulated-in-australia-under-anti-money-laundering-laws/, accessed 02/02/2018.

1. Digital currency exchanges would be required to secure registration with AUSTRAC, undertake customer due diligence together with the usual anti–money laundering and counter-terrorism checks, provide suspicious transactions reports to AUSTRAC involving physical currencies of A$10,000 or more, and maintain particular records about transactions and customer identification for 7 years.
2. Offering digital currency exchange services without AUSTRAC registration would be a criminal offence. For a first offence, penalties of up to 2 years' imprisonment and/or 500 penalty units, equivalent to A$105,000, would apply. Significantly higher penalties are applicable for repeat offences. Alternatively, offenders could be pursued through the civil penalty provisions that presently stipulates penalties of up to A$2.1 million for businesses and A$420,000 for individuals.
3. The setting up of a Digital Currency Exchange Register gathering background information and other details on AUSTRAC-approved entities providing digital currency exchange services.
4. When enacted, the AMLCTF brings Australia's AML and CTF law in line with similar measures already in place in the EU, Canada, and the United States. In targeting the activities of Bitcoin exchange providers, the AMLCTF essentially focuses on the "entry" and "exit" points in the digital currency space. This is when a person either uses regular money to purchase digital currency or when seeking to convert digital currency back into regular money. As such, it would not impact on how digital currency could be transferred between users without thereby affecting the privacy of such transactions.

The Australian Taxation Office (ATO), in its taxation guidance for cryptocurrencies, maintains that transacting with Bitcoin is similar to a barter arrangement, with similar consequences.[181] ATO's view is that cryptocurrencies are neither money nor a foreign currency and that their supply is not a financial supply for goods and services tax (GST) purposes. It is, however, an asset for capital gains tax (CGT) purposes. As such, cryptocurrency users need to keep transaction records containing the date of the transactions, the amount in Australian dollars (extractable from reputable online exchanges), what the transaction was for, and who the other party was, even if it is just their crypto address.

When using cryptocurrencies to purchase goods and services for personal use or consumption, any gain or loss from disposal of that cryptocurrency would be disregarded as a personal use asset, provided the cost is A$10,000 or less. When receiving cryptocurrency for goods and services that are provided as

181 Australian Taxation Office (2019), "Tax treatment of cryptocurrencies in Australia- specifically bitcoin", *ATO*, 18/06/2019, www.ato.gov.au/individuals-and-families/investments-and-assets/crypto-asset-investments/what-are-crypto-assets#:~:text=crypto%20assets%20are%20taxed%20as,ordinary%20income%20for%20tax%20purposes., accessed 07/02/2020; McGimpsey, P. (2024), "The crypto tax changes you need to know about", *Forbes*, 19/03/2024, www.forbes.com/advisor/au/investing/cryptocurrency/crypto-tax-change/, accessed 25/03/2024

part of a business, this would be treated as ordinary income, equivalent to the same process as receiving non-cash consideration under a barter transaction. The value in Australian dollars would be the fair market value obtainable from a reputable exchange.

Australian regulation for cryptoassets in the capital markets has advanced. The ASIC announced in their Corporate Plan for 2018–22 that they would focus on the potential "harmful effects" in this area.[182] This means that crypto exchanges are now going to be regulated along the same lines as stock exchanges and financial market operators and will thus be required to register with the Digital Currency Exchange Register.[183] ASIC updated its regulatory guidance (INFO225) in May 2019[184] with details of legal obligations for cryptocurrency firms under Australia's Corporation Act, the ASIC Act, and other applicable laws. This is far more comprehensive and now specifically refers to more business models, with various examples shown to provide market participants with enhanced understanding of how ASIC would regard their use of cryptoassets. Thus, INFO225 has been relabelled to include a consideration of cryptoassets, rather than confined only to cryptocurrency. This suggests a widening of the intended guidance and due notation of the evolving nature of the cryptoassets market away from ICO offerings of cryptocurrencies towards tokenised funds and security token offerings.

Foremost, ASIC's regulatory guide will apply to cryptoassets issuers, cryptoasset intermediaries, cryptoassets exchange and trading platforms, cryptoasset payment and merchant service providers, and wallet providers and custody service providers. Second, irrespective of the labelling used, INFO225 updates previous guidance to provide further details on when ASIC will consider the features of ICOs or tokens to demonstrate that the offer is of an interest in managed investment scheme (MIS), a security, a derivative, or a non-cash payment facility. INFO225 has now revised the previous guidance on MIS significantly. It has provided details pertaining to the requirements of retail and wholesale MIS offerings. It also tells why relying on an appointment as a corporate authorised representative of another Australian Financial Services License (AFSL) will not by itself be adequate to issue interests in an ICO or cryptoassets that have been treated as an MIS.

The INFO225 guidance confirms that ASIC expects businesses to be able to form conclusions that their tokens or ICOs are not financial products, and to know who their investors are, where the business seeks to rely on wholesale/

182 ASIC (2018), "18–260MR ASIC's Corporate Plan 2018–2022", *ASIC*, 07/09/2018, https://download.asic.gov.au/media/4855947/asic-corporate-plan-2018-22-focus-2018-19-published-31-august-2018.pdf, accessed 26/02/2019; ASIC (2022), "ASIC corporate plan 2022–2026", *ASIC*, August 2022, https://download.asic.gov.au/media/v3vhdqiw/asic-corporate-plan-2022-26-focus-2022-23-published-22-august-2022.pdf

183 Suberg, W. (2018), "Australia launches new cryptocurrency exchange regulations", *Coin Telegraph*, 03/04/2018, https://cointelegraph.com/news/australia-launches-new-cryptocurrency-exchange-regulations, accessed 10/02/2020.

184 ASIC (2019), "Initial coin offerings and crypto-assets", *ASIC Information Sheet INFO225*, 30/05/2019.

sophisticated investor exemptions. It cautions that Australian laws cited to apply to particular tokens might not be exhaustive, and responsibility will fall on the entities to ensure compliance with the laws. It has now been further clarified that to operate in Australia, exchanges listing tokens that are deemed as financial products will be required to hold an Australian market license unless exempted. ASIC cautioned that, as of now, there are no licensed or exempt exchanges in the country that could enable investors to transact in cryptoassets treated as financial products. It has also clarified that overseas token categorisations will not automatically translate to equivalent products in the country. ASIC clarified further that the country's definition of *financial products* is wider than those in other jurisdictions. This means extra care on ascertaining whether an entity's token, though not treated as a financial product in other jurisdictions, could be the case. Blockchain ventures not involving the use of cryptocurrencies remain unimpacted by this guidance, even though other jurisdictions have provided clearer pathways.

This again suggests the benefits of taking a global approach when studying the nature of cryptoassets as they continue to evolve and why national regulatory and supervisory authorities need to be vigilant on the current regulatory regimes across the world to avoid being perceived as inhospitable fintech hubs, now that Switzerland, Singapore, and the UK have provided relatively clear categorisation of tokens and paths forward for the issue of cryptographic tokens. Despite these, INFO 225 is argued to represent one small step for man, with a giant leap to be made in regulatory treatment to accommodate blockchain initiatives such as smart contracts.[185] As of May 2025, ASIC has released Consultation Paper 381 proposing updates to INFO 225.

The articulation of Australia's intention to proceed with legislation that regulates cryptos will commence with the defining of asset classes via token mapping, described as the world's maiden token-mapping exercise. This involves categorising digital assets to help determine how they need to be regulated, as crypto tokens and NFTs have a wide range of applications. The then assistant treasurer and minister for Financial Services of the government indicated the jurisdiction's intent to introduce a custody regime for digital assets and licensing for crypto exchanges so as to protect Australians, especially in the context of collapses, misconduct, fraudulent tokens, and scams where Australians have lost millions or have been forced to wait a significant period before repayment. He reiterated that the focal point for regulation would be tougher rules for exchanges which will be required to hold an Australian Financial Services License so as to transact in Australia.[186] Such a license would come with obligations that others in the finance industry are meeting. This means crypto exchanges and other

185 Bacina, M. & Skevington, T. (2019), "ASIC updates crypto-asset guidance-it's one small step for man . . .", *Piper Alderman Paper*, 06/06/2019, https://piperalderman.com.au/insight/asx-updates-guidance-for-cryptocurrency-projects/, accessed 08/08/2019.

186 Jones, S. (2023), "Address to the Australian financial review summit 2023, Sydney", https://ministers.treasury.gov.au/ministers/stephen-jones-2022/speeches/address-afr-super-and-wealth-summit-2023, accessed 20/12/2023

digital asset platforms will need to act honestly, fairly, and efficiently, including the need to manage conflicts, dispute resolution systems, solvency and cash reserve requirements, financial record-keeping requirements, the need to produce disclosure requirements for services offered, and the obligations to monitor and disrupt market misconduct.[187]

The Australian government has already provided certainty on taxation of cryptos, and as an investment asset, they are subject to capital gains tax. This implies that investors will not need to be able to track each transaction when they trade, make a purchase, and gift or sell crypto to ascertain whether they made a profit or loss, provided the overall final profit or loss can be determined.[188] Others are of the view that beyond imposing proper rules around custody, FTX's collapse highlighted the urgent need for basic compliance clarity for the crypto industry, and that issues such as reporting, governance, and treasury management will need to have appropriate checks and balances put in place by businesses.[189] Above all, as the crypto industry is global in nature, all jurisdictions should be extra mindful of the recommendations of global standard-setters, such as the IOSCO, BIS, and so on.[190]

Though there is presently no legislation crafted to address cryptoassets as a discrete rea of law, this does not prevent them from being captured within present regimes under Australian law. The Australian Securities Investment Commission's (ASIC's) regulatory guidance informs businesses of its approach to the legal status of cryptos.[191] This, in turn, depends on how they are structured and the rights attached, which ultimately determine the regulations with which an entity must comply. For instance:[192]

- Cryptoassets forming parts of a collective investment product that is a final product under the Corporations Act 2001 (Cth) (Corporations Act) fall within the scope of Australia's existing financial services regulatory regime.
- Where the rise in cryptoasset lending activities fall within the scope of the credit activities within the National Credit Consumer Protection Act 2009 (Cth) (NCCP Act), the pertinent entities may need to hold an Australian credit license or be otherwise exempt from this requirement.

187 McDonald, J. (2024), "The future of crypto regulation in Australia", *Forbes Advisor*, 09/05/2024, www.forbes.com/advisor/au/investing/cryptocurrency/crypto-regulation-in-australia/, accessed 18/07/2024

188 Ibid note [191], McDonald (2024)

189 Ibid note [191], McDonald (2024)

190 Ibid note [191], McDonald (2024

191 ASIC (2024), "Crypto-assets", *Information Sheet 225* (INFO 225). Obligations under the Corporations Act 2001 (Corporations Act) and the Australian Securities and Investments Commission Act 2001, *ASIC*, 07/03/2024, https://asic.gov.au/regulatory-resources/digital-transformation/crypto-assets/#:~:text=managed%20investment%20scheme%3F-,Australian%20laws%20apply,as%20a%20responsible%20entity%2C%20and, accessed 15/03/2024

192 Reeves, P. (2024), "Australia", in Dewey, J. N. (ed.), *Blockchain and cryptocurrency laws and regulations*, London, Global Legal Insights

- ASIC explained that expectations form part of the underlying assets of exchange trade products (ETPs) and other investment products. ASIC draws out expectations for market operator, retail fund operators, listed investment entities, and Australian financial services license holders dealing in cryptoassets.[193] This mainly revolves around the criteria that ASIC expects market operators to apply when determining whether a specific cryptoasset is a suitable for market-traded products. This generally requires institutional support of the cryptoasset, service providers willing to support the ETPs that invest in or provide exposure to the cryptoasset, maturity of the spot market for the cryptoasset, regulation of the cryptoasset, maturity of the spot market for the cryptoasset, regulation of derivatives linked to the cryptoasset, and the availability of robust and transparent pricing mechanisms for the cryptoasset.
- ASIC, in October 2021, considered that Ether and Bitcoin probably satisfy its criteria for determining suitable underlying assets for an exchange-traded product. ASIC has incorporated good practices pertaining to how fund asset holders are required to custody cryptoassets, including the ensuring adequate risk management systems are in place. Though ASIC has clarified, recent enforcement actions demonstrated that it considers cryptoassets to be an appropriate investment asset for retail clients in very limited circumstances. Presently, though, there are no specific regulations addressing blockchain or other DLTs in Australia.

7.8 Canada's cryptoassets regulatory policy

Canada, like the United States, supports and advances the use of advanced technology. Again, like most advanced economies, it strives to take a balanced regulatory approach that, while protecting consumer welfare, would also promote and not stand in the way of technological innovation, especially when dealing with emerging exponential industries (those using Industry 4.0 technologies that yield faster, cheaper, and higher quality outcomes relative to those using conventional technologies), such as those to do with blockchain and cryptoassets. The country has, in this respect, opted for timely, relevant state action to leverage on the opportunities unleashed by this, while being mindful of the challenges, pitfalls, and risks associated with the virtual currency domain.[194]

193 ASIC (2022), "Info 230", *ASIC November 2022*, https://asic.gov.au/regulatory-resources/markets/market-supervision/exchange-traded-products-admission-guidelines/, accessed 20/12/2023

194 Gerstein, I. R. & Hervieux-Payette, C. (2015), "Digital currency. You can't flip this coin", *Senate Committee on Banking, Trade and Commerce Paper*, 30/06/2015, https://publications.gc.ca/site/eng/9.801699/publication.html, accessed 08/08/2019.

The country's taxation laws and rules are applicable to virtual currencies, including cryptoassets. Like the US CFTC, the Canadian Revenue Agency treats cryptoassets as commodities and not a sovereign fiat. Around 50% of any capital gain is taxable, whereas if the cryptocurrency is owned by a company, 100% is taxable. Under general securities laws, various cryptocurrencies or tokens are categorised as securities. Thus, transactions via cryptoassets in Canada are deemed as barter transactions, and gains and losses have to be reported to the tax authority.[195] Also, Canada amended its Proceeds of Crime (Money Laundering) and Terrorist Financing Act, whereby virtual currencies are treated as money service businesses from the context of anti–money laundering law.[196]

The Canadian Securities Administrators (CSA) issued guidance on how securities law requirements could be applicable to ICOs, initial token offerings (ITOs), cryptocurrency investment funds, and cryptoassets exchanges transacting in these products.[197] Canada's first DLT fund, namely, Blockchain Technologies ETF, was approved on 1 February 2018.[198] To enhance the understanding of how DLT could have an impact on the wholesale payments systems, a collaborative research initiative between R3 (a DLT entity), Payments Canada, and the Bank of Canada, known as Project Jasper, was undertaken in March 2016 along three phases. Its findings for Phase III were released in October 2018.[199] Phase I was built from an Ethereum platform, while Phase II was developed on the Corda platform. Phase III tested digital depository receipts (DDR) as a digital representation of Canadian currency in 2016 and 2017. Project Jasper tested this via CADcoin, with the Bank of Canada issuing DDR. Here, a transfer of DDR is equated with a full and irrevocable transfer of the underlying claim on central bank deposits.[200]

Cryptoassets regulation is essentially regulated under securities laws in line with the regulator's mission to protect the investing public. Securities laws are enacted and regulated under various applicable provincial laws, but these have been largely harmonised via the initiatives of the CSA, which represents all provincially mandated securities regulators in the country.

---

195 Al-Shikarchy, M. & Gheorghiu, L. (2017), "Canadian taxation of cryptocurrency . . . so far", *Gowling WSG Paper*, 14/11/2017, https://gowlingwlg.com/en/insights-resources/articles/2017/canadian-taxation-of-cryptocurrency-so-far/, accessed 08/08/2019.

196 Ahmad, T. (2014), "Regulation of cryptocurrency: Canada", *The Library of Congress*, June 2018, https://maint.loc.gov/law/help/cryptocurrency/canada.php#:~:text=Canada%20allows%20the%20use%20of,also%20apply%20to%20cryptocurrency%20transactions., accessed 07/02/2020.

197 Canadian Securities Administrators (CSAs) (2017), "Cryptocurrency offerings", *CSA Staff Notice46–307*, 24/08/2017, www.osc.ca/en/securities-law/instruments-rules-policies/4/46-307/csa-staff-notice-46-307-cryptocurrency-offerings, accessed 08/08/2019.

198 Milano, A. (2018), "Canadian regulators approve country's first blockchain ETF", *Coin Desk*, 02/02/2018, www.coindesk.com/markets/2018/02/02/canadian-regulators-approve-countrys-first-blockchain-etf/, accessed 08/08/2019.

199 Hendry, S., Lee, J., McCormack, A., Velissarios, J. & Webster, S. (2018), "Jasper Phase III: Securities settlement using distributed ledger technology", *Jasper III Report*, 22/10/2018, www.payments.ca/insights/research/jasper-phase-iii-collaborative-research-initiative-between-payments-canada-bank, accessed 08/08/2019.

200 Ibid note [203], Hendry, Lee, McCormack, Vellissarios & Webster (2018).

Canada used the Investment Contract Test (ICT) to determine whether a financial instrument could be categorised as a security. To fall within this categorisation, four conditions had to be satisfied:[201] First, there must be an investment of money; second, there must be an intention or expectation of profit; third, there must be a common enterprise; and fourth, where the fate of the venture will be significantly affected by the work of others, other than the investor. The courts in Canada would be guided by the substance and not the form of these contracts. The current regulatory trend in Canada involves applying and adapting existing securities laws, including the ICT, to schemes involving blockchain or cryptoassets that mirror conventional securities, without regard to the use of new technology.[202]

The Canadian regulatory approach to blockchain platforms is that they can register for business, and as early as 2025, 11 have done so. However, there is a ban on crypto trading platforms offering margin, credit, and other forms of leverage to any type of client in connection with the trading of cryptoassets on the crypto trading platform. It is necessary for platforms to segregate client funds from the platform's own, and the clients' funds must be held with a third party. Stablecoins cannot be offered unless prior consent is obtained from the regulators.

All in all, Canada shows a positive attitude towards blockchain and cryptoassets and has been in the forefront where the design of regulatory frameworks for these is concerned. This also helps explain why many crypto miners from China have set up shop in Canada. There is a case for optimism in Canada presently because of the rising cryptoasset adoption in the country.[203] Despite not recognising cryptoassets as legal tender, the Canadian Revenue Agency classifies them as commodities. This reflects a cautious approach to cryptoassets, treating it as a potential threat while recognising its growing presence.

Provincial securities and derivatives regulations provide the main regulatory framework for digital assets. Such rules are supplemented by federal anti–money laundering laws requiring certain crypto exchanges and transfer services to register as money service businesses (MSBs). Securities regulation in Canada includes the distribution and trading of securities and derivatives. This entails requirements for prospectuses, registration of dealers and advisers, and rules for exchanges and trading platforms. The Canadian Securities Administrators (CAS), an organisation of provincial and territorial regulators, has issued various guidelines to deal with the evolving crypto market. CAS and the Canadian Industry Regulatory Organisation (CIRO) have guided how existing regulations

201 *Pacific Coast Coin Exchange v Ontario Securities Commission*, [1978] 2 S.C.R. 112 (Pacific Coast).

202 Druzeta, C., Grant, S. & Peters, M. (2019), "Canada", in Dewey, J. (ed.), *Blockchain and cryptocurrency regulation*, 1st edn, London, Global Legal Insights, pp. 243–253.

203 KPMG (2024), "With riasing crypto asset adoption in Canada, there's reason for optimism: Improved infrastructure, regulatory clarity and growth in on-shore trading draws support", https://kpmg.com/ca/en/home/insights/2024/04/rising-cryptoasset-adoption-in-canada.html, accessed 18/07/2024

apply to cryptoassets. Typically, digital assets like Bitcoin and Ethereum are categorised as securities. Nonetheless, where a digital asset satisfies the criteria of an investment contract, it may be regulated as a security. The CSA adopts a wider approach to determine whether an asset is a security, concentrating on the substance of the asset instead of its form. Crypto trading platforms could also be included under securities laws, especially where they provide users with contractual rights to the cryptoasset instead of immediate ownership. For those issuing or distributing virtual currencies deemed securities, it is necessary to comply with prospectus requirements, or using applicable exemptions is necessary. In the meantime, Canada plans to adopt the international cryptoasset reporting framework by 2026. This would impose new reporting requirements for cryptoasset service providers, such as exchanges and brokers, to enhance transparency and compliance in the crypto sector.[204]

7.9 Switzerland's cryptoassets regulatory policy

Switzerland has sustained its reputation as the global centre for the wealth management industry, accounting for some 27% of global offshore wealth, or some US$2 trillion.[205] Switzerland also enjoys being the most blockchain-friendly European country. The UK, on the other hand, is the leading destination for all international movers into the European tech ecosystem, followed closely by Germany, France, Netherlands, Ireland, and Switzerland.

Switzerland was at risk of losing its competitive edge over rival financial markets after being pressured to give up major aspects of its world-renowned banking secrecy laws reputation due to the aggressive moves by the US DOJ and the IRS Criminal Investigations Division. This was demonstrated by the closing down of one of its oldest private banks and the billions in fines on its more prominent banks. Zug, in becoming a global hub for virtual currencies, seems to save the day by helping the country acquire the reputation of being the crypto nation for the digital revolution with a flourishing ICO market.[206] Swiss-based ICOs raised about US$550 million in funding in 2017, accounting form some 14% of the global ICO market.[218] Many Swiss ICOs are designed as foundations applying for non-profit tax status, with money raised in them deemed as donations that might not be returned to ICO investors.[207]

204 Vignesh, S. G. (2024), "Crypto regulations in Canada: Key updates for 2024", *Compedia*, 09/07/2024, https://coinpedia.org/cryptocurrency-regulation/crypto-regulations-in-canada-2024/#:~:text=Canadian%20Crypto%20Regulation%202024%3A%20What's,compliance%20in%20the%20crypto%20sector, accessed 01/08/2024

205 Ozelli, S. (2018), "Why Switzerland is becoming a 'Crypto Nation' with a flourishing ICO market: Expert take", *Coin Telegraph*, 8/01/2018, https://cointelegraph.com/news/why-switzerlandis-becoming-a-crypto-nation-with-a-flourishing-ico-market-expert-take, accessed 08/08/2019.

206 Ibid note [209], Ozelli (2018)

207 Neghaiwi, B. H. (2018), "Top Swiss cryptocurrency law questions 'stupid' ICO structure", *Reuters*, 22/01/2018, www.reuters.com/article/uk-swiss-crypto/top-swiss-cryptocurrency-lawyer-questions-stupid-ico-structure-idUSKBN1FB1TM, accessed 08/08/2019.

The country, via the Swiss Financial Market Supervisory Authority (FINMA), is likely to deploy forward looking regulations via the tweaking of its existing laws to accommodate crypto technology and its financial applications. The regulatory journey began with a cautionary alert to investors about fake cryptocurrency on 19 September 2017. This was followed by a concise briefing on the country's ICO regulatory approach on 29 September 2017, when FINMA drew attention to market participants to comply with some potentially applicable banking, securities dealer, anti–money laundering, and prospectus laws and regulations. Towards this end, FINMA provided a detailed guidance for ICOs setting out various basic features of ICOs. These support FINMA's position that ICOs represent an approach for accessing funds digitally for entrepreneurial ventures. Here, FINMA conceded that the wide range of token and ICO startups made it difficult, if not impossible, to provide clear legal guidance.

As such, FINMA would treat each case on its own merits and demerits, focusing on the underlying economic purpose of an ICO, especially when there are signs of efforts to circumvent existing regulations. These would include evaluating the transferability and economic function and purpose of these tokens, so as to confirm their status as payment tokens, utility tokens, asset tokens, or hybrid tokens.

As to the designation of ICOs as securities, this would depend on evaluation through the Swiss Financial Market Infrastructure Act, where *securities* have been defined as "standardised certificated or uncertificated securities, derivatives, and intermediated securities that are eligible for mass standardised trading, (meaning) . . . being publicly offered for sale in the same structure and denomination or are placed with more than 20 clients".[208] Guided by this, payment tokens would not be treated as securities where these are designed as a means of payments; utility tokens where their sole aim is to give digital access rights to an application or service would also not be deemed as such, while tokens designed for investment purpose at the point of issue would be treated as securities in the same way as asset tokens. Where asset tokens constitute an uncertificated security or a derivative that depends on an underlying asset for its value and these tokens are standardised suitably for mass standardised trading, they would be treated as securities under existing laws. The Swiss Federal Council amended the Swiss Banking Act, whereby businesses that undertake activities beyond conventional banking features, including cryptocurrency- and blockchain-related entities, would be able to accept public funds up to a maximum of CHF 100 million, provided they are authorised or licensed and do not invest or pay interest on these funds.[209] FINMA also issued guidance for those seeking fintech licences.[210]

208 FINMA Guidelines Section 1.2(b).

209 International Monetary Fund (2019), "Switzerland: Financial sector stability assessment programme", *IMF Country Report No. 19/184*, 26/06/2019, www.imf.org/-/media/Files/Publications/CR/2019/1CHEEA2019004.ashx, accessed 08/08/2019.

210 FINMA (2018), "Fintech license: FINMA publishes guidelines", *FINMA*, 10/12/2018, www.finma.ch/en/news/2018/12/20181210-mm-fintech-bewilligung/, accessed 08/08/2019.

FINMA claims that they have taken a balanced approach to handling ICO ventures to enable legitimate innovators to navigate the regulatory landscape to launch projects consistent with Swiss financial services laws while simultaneously protecting investors and the integrity of the country's financial system. Switzerland is also positioning as an attractive destination for ICOs for issuers and investors owing to the country's relatively more favourable tax laws.[211] Switzerland nevertheless has to take on competition from offshore financial centres like the Cayman Islands and Malta.

Thus, in general, cryptoassets are deemed as an asset class and are regulated by the Swiss Financial Market Supervisory Authority (FINMA), which is responsible for issuing four kinds of crypto licenses: fintech, exchange, investment fund, and banking. FINMA further ensures that the jurisdiction's anti–money laundering act is followed. New guidelines, though, have been introduced recently to strengthen the regulation of crypto exchanges and digital asset services to align with FATF's recommendations. Responding to the presence of more than 1,000 blockchain and crypto businesses, Switzerland introduced the Swiss Blockchain Act 2021,[212] incorporating detailed regulations for blockchain-based businesses with good attention on investor protection by distinguishing cryptoassets and providing more legal clarity for bankruptcy situations.[213] The legislation, in effect, maintains Switzerland's principle of technology neutrality, as well as a new license category for trading systems based on DLT, and clarity on how cryptoassets are taxed.

7.10 The Cayman Islands' cryptoasset regulatory policy

The Cayman Islands are seeking to be the preferred global jurisdiction for the formation of investment funds by increasingly investing in cryptoassets and exploiting its investment opportunities in this niche. This is attributed to the jurisdiction's neutral tax treatment, political stability, and generally respectable regulatory framework.[214] Relative to other jurisdictions, the Cayman Islands securities regime is more favourable. Accordingly, the Cayman Islands are growing as a destination of choice for many ICOs and platform development entities, including cryptocurrency exchanges. Physical presence and support personnel are easy to develop in the jurisdiction, made even more attractive with

211 Bohi, R., Wenger, D. & Wandel, S. A. (2017), "Switzerland: Taxation of initial coin offerings in Switzerland", *Prager Dreifuss*, 27/12/2017.

212 SIF (2022), "Blockchain/DLT", www.sif.admin.ch/sif/en/home/finanzmarktpolitik/digitalisation-financial-sector/blockchain.html, accessed 20/123/2023. On 1 August 2021, the Federal Act on the Adaptation of Federal Law to Developments in Distributed Electronic Reister Technology and the associated blanket ordinance came into force.

213 Vignesh, S. G. (2024), "Crypto regulations in Switzerland 2024", *Coinpedia*, 20/07/2024, https://coinpedia.org/cryptocurrency-regulation/crypto-regulations-in-switzerland-2024/, accessed 25/07/2024

214 Gobin, I. & Skotnicki, D. (2018), "Cayman Islands", *The Virtual Currency Regulation Review-Edition*, 01/11/2018, https://thelawreviews.co.uk/edition/the-virtual-currency-regulation-review-edition-1/1176633/cayman-islands, accessed 08/08/2019.

the benefits from Cayman Islands' special economic zone, known popularly as the Cayman Enterprise City (CEC), which came into being in 2012.[215] Together with this, the government has also announced that a technology-neutral regulatory sandbox will be set up to foster and incubate start-ups in the digital niche.

Existing laws are relied on when dealing with the regulation of cryptoassets. These would include dealing with the Proceeds of Crime Law (PCL), the Securities Investment Business Law, the US Foreign Account Tax Complaint Act (FATCA) and OECD's CRS, the beneficial ownership regime, the Money Services Law, the Mutual Funds Law, and the Stock Exchange Companies Law. Section 6 of the PCL specifies that businesses undertaking relevant financial businesses (RFBs) have to comply with AML regulations. Such businesses include those investing, administering, or managing funds on behalf of other people, issuing and managing means of payment, safe custody services, and money or value transfer business. People in violation of AML regulations commit an offence and will be liable on summary conviction to a fine of CI$500,000 or on an indictable conviction to an unlimited fine and imprisonment for two years.

The Cayman Islands Monetary Authority (CIMA) has regulatory powers for designated kinds of funds operating in and from the jurisdictions. No taxation is, however, imposed on Cayman entities, but those implementing cryptoasset-type business would need to take tax advice from their respective jurisdictions, and especially with due considerations for FATCA and CRS obligations. For now, no specific laws are in play in the jurisdiction with regards to cryptoassets, but these could be launched in the future. Overall, the Cayman Islands' ambition to become a global technology hub is well supported by a sound legal framework (reinforced by updated copyright trademark and parent laws passed in 2016, and the 2017 Data Protection Law), modern infrastructure, state of the art communication systems, a 155% mobile penetration rate, and a generally stable political climate.[216]

Aligning with FATF's international standards, the Cayman Islands introduced a new framework for supervising and regulating virtual asset service businesses, referred to as the Virtual Assets (Service Providers) Act 2020 (VASP Act).[217] The first phase of the VASP focuses on anti–money laundering regulations and VASP registration, while the subsequent stage addresses licensing and further matters awaiting implementation. In itself, though, the first phase provides a flexible regulatory foundation, thereby providing certainty for those operating in this space and in alignment with international standards. The VASP

215 Special Economic Zones (Cayman Enterprise City) Order (2019 Revision. Supplement No. 5 published with Legislation Gazette No. 4 of 21st February 2019, https://legislation.gov.ky/cms/images/LEGISLATION/AMENDING/2019/2019-0012/SpecialEconomicZonesCaymanEnterpriseCityAmendmentOrder2019.pdf, accessed 08/08/2019.

216 Colegate, P. & Thomson, A. (2019), "Technology and innovation offshore guide: Cayman Islands", *Appleby Paper*, 20/03/2019, www.applebyglobal.com/wp-content/uploads/2019/05/Appleby-FinTech-Guide-Cayman-Islands-Final-Revised-20-May-2019.pdf, accessed 08/08/2019.

217 Regulated United Europe (RUE) (2024), "Crypto Islands crypto regulations", *RUE*, 18/07/2024, https://rue.ee/crypto-regulations/cayman-islands/, accessed 21/07/2024

Act refers to virtual assets as a digital representation of value traded or transferred digitally for payments or investment purposes. Digital representations of fiat currencies, as well as virtual service tokens lacking transferability or exchangeability with third parties, including tokens solely serving access or service provision functions, are, however, excluded.[218] The Virtual Assets (Service Providers) Regulations (VASP Regulations) were introduced in October 2020 to enhance clarity on the VASP Act. These regulations outline registration application requirements, fee details, and including further guidance on virtual asset issuances. In essence, the VASP Act clearly establishes the legitimacy of digital assets and cryptoassets within the Cayman Islands, besides also regulating businesses providing service link to virtual assets.[219] Generally, virtual assets themselves and entities dealing with them for their internal purposes are not subject to specific regulation in the Cayman Islands.[220] VASP requires VASPS to either obtain a license or register with the Cyman Islands Monetary Authority, secure a waiver, or hold a sandbox license (CIMA). A VASP is an entity incorporated or registered in the Cayman Islands offering virtual asset services as a constituent of its activities.[221] A virtual asset service, as per the VASP legislation, covers the issuance of virtual assets or the offer of specific services for and on behalf of another entity, including exchange between virtual assets and fiat currencies, exchange between one or more other forms of convertible virtual assets, virtual asset custody service involving the safekeeping or administration of virtual assets or related instruments that enable control over virtual assets, and participation in and provision of financial services linked to a virtual asset issuance or the sale of a virtual asset.[222]

Those cryptoassets and other digital asset businesses not caught under these said categories that may still be subject to general regulations that do not target digital assets under the Cayman Islands include the Securities Investment Business Act (SIBA), the Money Services Act, and anti–money laundering regulations. As alluded to earlier, activities such as the issuance of virtual assets, offerings of financial services connected to virtual asset issuance, or the sale and transfer of virtual assets undertaken by a Cayman Islands entity as a business on behalf of another party are likely to fall under virtual assets services, requiring a license or registration with CIMA under the VASP legislation.[223]

Within the VASP Act, any issuance of virtual assets necessitates prior approval from CIMA. *Issuance* here refers to the sale of newly designed virtual assets to the public in exchange for fiat currency, other virtual assets, or alternative consideration. Though the term "public" is not specifically defined, it should be broadly interpreted. The VASP Regulation differentiates a "private sale", that is, not advertised and is sold via private agreements, but to a limited number

218 Ibid note [222], RUE (2024)
219 Ibid note [222], RUE (2024)
220 Ibid note [222], RUE (2024)
221 Ibid note [222], RUE (2024)
222 Ibid note [222], RUE (2024)
223 Ibid note [222], RUE (2024)

of persons, from a sale to the public, potentially exempting certain sales from VASP legislation registration requirements.[224] The sale of virtual service tokens and any transfer without consideration, such as an "airdrop", is also excluded from this requirement.[225] Direct issuances are subject to a prescribed maximum threshold that is yet to be fixed. The threshold exemption applies where the issuance is facilitated by one or more virtual asset trading platforms or obliged entities, provided these platforms are either licensed under the VASP legislation or regulated in another non-high-risk destination.[226]

7.11 Malta's cryptoasset regulatory policy

Malta's quest to be a globally competitive blockchain island that would be the magnet for entities seeking to grow their blockchain-driven enterprises led to a dedicated digital regulatory regime. This comprised the Virtual Financial Assets Act 2018 (VFAA), the Digital Innovation Authority Act 2018 (MDIA),[227] and the Innovative Technology Arrangements and Services Act 2018 (ITAS)[228] and are collectively known as the Digital Innovation Framework.[229] The idea behind this is to offer a relatively high degree of legal and regulatory certainty and clarity for those engaged in blockchain and cryptoassets. Evidently, the Maltese government has taken notice about the regulatory challenges faced by these ventures arising primarily from most other jurisdictions which are either less hospitable or have decided to rely on existing securities, money transmission, and related regulations.

The VFAA addresses virtual financial assets (VFAs) and initial virtual financial assets offering (IVFAO) matters and matters ancillary or incidental to them.[230] Here, cryptocurrency is categorised as a VFA, and the legislation stipulates a list of rules that assist the industry's growth while equally protecting investors' welfare. It covers those initiating cryptocurrencies and service providers, including cryptocurrency exchanges, investment advisers, e-wallet service providers, custodian and nominee service providers, portfolio managers, and brokerages. The IVFAOs are the equivalent of ICOs, or a mechanism for accessing funds wherein issuers will offer VFAs in exchange for funds. The legislation sets out and clarifies the necessary licensing and other conditions that interested parties have to comply with. It also specifies the kinds of VFAs that

224 Ibid note [222], RUE (2024)

225 Ibid note [222], RUE (2024)

226 Ibid note [222], RUE (2024)

227 The Digital Innovation Authority Act 2018, http://justiceservices.gov.mt/DownloadDocument.aspx?app=lp&itemid=29080&l=1, accessed 08/08/2019.

228 Innovative Technology Arrangements and Services Act 2018, www.fff-legal.com/wp-content/uploads/2018/08/Innovative-Technology-Arrangements-and-Services-Act.pdf, accessed 08/08/2019.

229 Falzon, M. & Valenzia, A. (2020), "Blockchain and cryptocurrency regulation: Malta", in Dewey, J. N. (ed.), *Blockchain and cryptocurrency regulation*, London, Global Legal Insights.

230 Chapter 590: Virtual Financial Assets Act 2018, *Act XXX of 2018*, www.mfsa.mt/wp-content/uploads/2018/12/fintech-main-legislation.pdf, accessed 08/08/2019.

could be issued through IVFAOs and admission to trading on a DLT exchange via a registered white paper at the Malta Financial Services Authority (MFSA), or the competent authority for this business in Malta. IVFAOs are treated as DLT-enabled ways for accessing funds by a legal person registered in Malta.

The VFAA and the MDIA define a *DLT* as a digital or electronic database or ledger where data is stored, shared consensually, synchronised through a network of multiple nodes, distributed/decentralised/shared/replicated, public or private, permissioned or permissionless, and immutable and protected cryptographically. A VFA is referred to as any form of digital medium or data asset that is deployed as a digital medium of exchange, store of value, and unit of account that is not a virtual token, financial instrument, or electronic money. Virtual/utility tokens are deemed as DLT assets that have no utility, value, or application outside the confines of their DLT platform and could be redeemed for funds on the platforms directly by the DLT asset issuers. VFA agents obliged to undertake designated reporting and monitoring are to be appointed by ICO issuers and have to be approved by the MFSA. Entities offering VFAs, or treated as VFA service providers, have to be licensed by the MFSA. The MFSA ascertains whether a product/service falls under the financial services regulation or under the scope of the VFA legislation through the use of a financial instrument test (FIT).

This involves 12 tests and is used primarily to determine whether the activities fall within the context of applicable EU or Maltese regulations. The first of these spotlights on virtual tokens, while the remainder covers various financial instruments, such as MiFID. The MFSA, for the purpose of this test, uses virtual asset definitions located in the consultation paper for the FIT. ICOs that are not financial instruments are subject to minimum disclosure requirements, like providing the necessary information to investors through a white paper, and further information when intending to trade the virtual currency on an exchange.

The VFAA provides the regulatory framework applicable to ICOs as well as the regulation for particular service providers engaged in ICO-related activities, such as cryptocurrency exchanges. Thus, cryptocurrencies could be regulated here or in the existing financial services regulation, including, but not confined to, MiFID II, the Investment Services Act, and the Financial Institutions Act, depending on the asset's categorisation.

Where taxation is concerned, there are no set rules for cryptoassets. This means the tax rules and principles in Malta will be applicable, and normally, capital gains tax would apply. Money transmission laws and anti–money laundering requirements in Malta will be applicable to cryptocurrency issuers and related service providers and, as stipulated under the VFAA, will cover issuers, VFA licence holders, and VFA agents.

The Malta Gaming Authority (MGA) provides guidance for the use of DLTs and the acceptance of virtual currencies in the gaming sector via its sandbox environment.[231] Both single-wallet systems and multiple-wallet systems are allowable under specified conditions. The Malta Stock Exchange in 2018 launched its Binance- and Thomson Reuters–endorsed MSX fintech Accelerator.[232] This is offered to mentor and help start-ups in the blockchain and crypto niche by matchmaking them with global technology and well known business players, as well as office space, state of the art communications, and training facilities. Other stakeholders sharing and collaborating to advance the industry include, among others, the Malta Information Technology Agency, University of Malta's Blockchain Research Group, the Blockchain Malta Association, and BitMalta. The Maltese jurisdiction is also a member of the European Blockchain Partnership,[233] which seeks to foster collaboration between EU member states through the exchange of experiences and know how in this and related areas.

All in all, the cryptoassets regulatory regime in Malta supports innovation while ensuring the effective achievements of high level objectives set by global standard setters like the IOSCO, these being financial stability, investor protection, and market integrity, and addressed via a predominantly principles-based approach that ensures technology neutrality without stifling innovation.[234] Thus, while the EU is pondering and reflecting on what and how to regulate virtual currencies, big individual member states like France and Germany are in final stages of cryptoassets legislation, and smaller states like Luxembourg and Malta, as well as many Baltic economies, have initiated legislations. Malta is said to be by far the boldest with its wide regulatory framework that seeks to enable the jurisdiction to be Europe's crypto hub, as this addresses all key risk areas, such as risks to consumers, market integrity, financial crimes, and cybersecurity. These came about in response to earlier investigations of several gambling firms and banks in the jurisdiction that exposed weak enforcement by local authorities. Malta uses insights from these to strengthen the quality and effectiveness of its financial services regulations and enforcements.[235]

The Maltese Parliament deliberated on the proposed amendments to the Virtual Financial Assets Act (VFA) so as to align with the EU Markets in

231 Malta Gaming Authority (2018), "Guidance on the use of Distributed Ledger Technology and the acceptance of Virtual Currencies through the implementation of a Sandbox Environment", *MGA*, 04/10/2018, www.mga.org.mt/the-mga-publishes-guidelines-on-its-sandbox-framework-for-the-acceptance-of-virtual-financial-assets-and-the-use-of-distributed-ledger-technology--within-the-gaming-industry-at-the-delta-summit-2018/, accessed 08/08/2019.

232 Shen, M. (2018), "The Malta Stock Exchange announced today that Binance is backing the exchange's newly launched program to support fintech startups and entrepreneurs", *Coin Desk*, 19/06/2018, www.coindesk.com/markets/2018/06/18/binance-backs-malta-stock-exchanges-start-up-accelerator/, accessed 08/08/2019.

233 Davila, E. (2019), "Standards supporting BC/DLT interoperability EU initiatives", *ITU-T ITU Workshop on Distributed Ledger Technology Scalability and Interoperability*, Geneva, 02/08/2019, www.itu.int/en/ITU-T/Workshops-and-Seminars/201908/Documents/Emilio_Davila-Gonzalez%20_Presentation.pdf, accessed 08/08/2019.

234 Buttigieg, C. P. & Efthymiopoulos, C. (2019), "The regulation of cryptoassets in Malta: The virtual financial assets act and beyond", *Law & Financial Markets Review*, 13(1): 30–40.

235 Guarascio, F. (2019), "Malta leads on cryptoassets regulation while EU ponders", *Reuters*, 26/02/2019, www.reuters.com/article/business/malta-leads-on-cryptoassets-regulation-while-eu-ponders-idUSKCN1QF1SW/, accessed 08/08/2019.

Crypto-Assets (MiCA) regulation. These amendments are envisaged to streamline existing framework with the comprehensive rules established by MICA, thereby ensuring consistency and coherence in the regulatory landscape for cryptoassets.[236] MiCA is directly applicable to all EU member states, thereby creating a uniform standard for the cryptoassets markets across the EU market from the end of 2024.[237] Malta's VFA framework[238] is already substantially aligned with MiCA, particularly subsequent to the recent VFA legislation amendments. Malta's MiCA Act 2024 seeks to further solidify this alignment, thereby establishing a comprehensive framework governing the issuance and trading of cryptoassets, besides outlining the requirements for public offerings and the admission to trading of various cryptoassets trading, including asset-referenced tokens (ARTs), or tokens whose value is pegged to one or more assets, like commodities or fiat currencies; other cryptoassets, like various kinds of digital assets that do not fall into the previous categories but require regulation; and e-money tokens (EMTs), or tokens that represent fiat money and are employed for payment transactions.[239] The Maltese legislation also introduced amendments to the Banking Act to include references to MiCA and the issue of ENTs and ARTs, as well as the provision of cryptoasset services, to the list of additional activities that entities authorised under the Banking Act may undertake. Additionally, the Maltese legislation will set the tone for the necessary conditions to be fulfilled by crypto service providers to ensure that these operate within a robust legal framework.[240]

7.12 A comparative note

The general analysis of regulatory approaches in these selected advanced economies, including offshore financial centres that operate as protected parts of advanced economies, suggests that cryptoassets can run through the full gamut of regulated financial products. The various kinds of cryptocurrencies are driven commonly by a DLT with inherent encryption, but the more noticeable feature is the fluidity of the terminology deployed, as they could be labelled differently in these different jurisdictions. Australia uses "digital currency", Switzerland uses "payment tokens", the UK uses "cryptoassets", while the United States uses

236 Borg, J. et al. (2024), "Malta's MiCA Bill", *WH Partners*, 04/07/2024, www.lexology.com/library/detail.aspx?g=abc80d8b-e2b8-418d-a934-0bc1e7219c96#:~:text=MiCA%20will%20apply%20directly%20to,in%20the%20implementation%20of%20MiCA., accessed 19/07/2024

237 Schickler, J. (2023), "MiCA, EU's comprehensive new cryopto regulation, explained", *Coin Desk*, 07/09/2023, www.coindesk.com/learn/mica-eus-comprehensive-new-crypto-regulation-explained/, accessed 0/12/2023

238 Malta Financial Services Authority (MFSA) (2023), "Prioritising transparency and consumer safety: Malta's journey in crypto-asset regulation", *MFSA*, 12/12/2023, www.mfsa.mt/publication/prioritising-transparency-and-consumer-safety-maltas-journey-in-crypto-asset-regulation/, accessed 20/12/2023

239 Malta Parliament (2024), "Markets in crypto-assets Bill", Bill No. 107 01/07/2024, www.parlament.mt/14th-leg/bills/bill-107-crypto-assets/, accessed 15/07/2024

240 Ibid note [241], Borg et al. (2024)

"cryptocurrency" or "virtual commodities", depending on the federal agencies involved. Also, while global cryptoassets standard setters like the FATF uses virtual currencies, the BIS uses cryptoassets. For these reasons, this book is not overly particular about the preferred terminology choice. To maintain the flow and clarity of discussions in this book with the formal commentaries used in different jurisdictions, these various terminologies are used here interchangeably, whether they be *cryptoassets*, *virtual assets/currencies*, or *cryptocurrencies*, according to context and jurisdiction, as they mean almost the same thing.

A *cryptoasset* could be typically a consumer credit product, an insurance product, a MIS, a share, a debenture, a derivative, or a payment system. Relatively less common, they could be a miscellaneous risk facility, a purchased payment facility, a foreign exchange product, a banking product, or an interest in a superannuation fund. Many of these jurisdictions look at the substance rather than the form when deciding on the regulatory treatments of these items. These selected advanced economies are not the only ones facing the problem, and as mentioned earlier, most other jurisdictions are encountering a very similar set of problems as cryptoassets are cross-border financial products. This is why the OECD has called upon global regulators to collaborate quickly to provide clarity and a suitable global supervisory framework.[241] IOSCO has acknowledged the potential need for this but, thus far, has only issued cautionary notices and acting as a repository of the regulatory regimes in different countries.

The advanced economies reviewed here appear to embrace certain common regulatory concerns and approaches. In general, they are all mindful of the threats and risks posed by cryptoassets to the investing community and the impacts on the stability of their respective financial systems. These explain why they tend to focus on money laundering and related issues, as well as contagion effects on their financial systems. However, given the background nature of their respective economies and their legal systems, it is inevitable that variations in terms of their regulatory approaches are not unexpected in some areas. This could be problematic, as blockchain and cryptoasset impacts are not confined to national borders.

The United States, the biggest economy in the world, appears to be relying on existing financial securities and related financial services rules and regulations to police cryptoasset products and activities. This has heightened complexity, as federal regulatory agencies like the SEC, the CFTC, and others will get or not get involved depending on how each respective agency treats the various kinds of cryptoassets. The United States' fragmented approach is less followed by the UK, as it relies primarily on the FCA to do the job. Though the FCA has come out with its final guidelines, it has left some gaps that it says are outside of its regulatory perimeter, and this gives rise to some legal uncertainty. The EU is still reflecting and pondering on the approach to take, even as some of its bigger

241 Kelly, J. L. (2019), "Do you know how your token is regulated?", *Investor Daily*, 10/09/2019, www.investordaily.com.au/analysis/45657-do-you-know-how-your-crypto-token-is-regulated, accessed 12/09/2019.

members states, like France and Germany, and some bolder smaller member states, like Malta and Luxembourg, have gone some distance. Mata deserves special mention as its comprehensive virtual assets regulatory regime is by far the boldest in Europe.

Following this, in some respects, are Australia and Canada. While Australia and Canada tweak their respective financial securities and banking regulations to deal with the various kinds of cryptoassets, others, like the UK, have left various gaps. The potential significance of these for issues relating to innovation agility, protection of investor welfare, and financial system stability remains to be seen. Various offshore financial centres have suffered from the impact of scandals disclosed in the Panama and Paradise Papers revelations and have taken steps to improve on their reputations and regulatory system to avoid being blacklisted as financial pariahs by global regulatory financial standards setters like the FTAF, the IOSCO, and BIS, as well as multilateral development agencies like the OECD, the World Bank, and the IMF.

CHAPTER 8

Cryptoasset regulatory policies in selected Asian economies

8.1 Introduction

This chapter examines regulatory initiatives in both large and small Asian economies particularly known for their active participation in cryptoasset activities. These include the large emerging economies of China and India and the advanced economies of Japan, South Korea, and Singapore in the region. They are selected as they are perceived to be cryptoassets hotspots with the resources and willingness to advance the progression of cryptoassets.

In the last three or more decades, Asia has emerged as an important global pole. Hitherto, world attention has been drawn on the United States and the EU, with an occasional spotlight on Japan as it ebbs and wanes in the global economic corridors. Asia as a regional economic powerhouse of global proportion is not by accident. First, it houses five of the world's ten most populous nations, namely, China, India, Indonesia, Pakistan, and Bangladesh, which together account for some 44.5% of the world's total population of more than 7.951 billion.[1] Asia has a good mix of advanced economies (South Korea, Taiwan, Singapore, and Hong Kong), middle income economies (Malaysia, China, Indonesia, Philippines, Vietnam), and low income economies (Afghanistan, Pakistan, Bangladesh, Laos, Cambodia). It includes very large economies, like China, Indonesia, and India. It has very fast growth economies, such as Malaysia, Philippines, and Vietnam. It has a good mix of economies with generally reliable and modern banking systems, like those in Singapore, South Korea, and Malaysia, but also relatively less modern banking systems, like those in Laos, Cambodia, and Afghanistan. The quality and state of physical infrastructures within the region also differ considerably, including the state of communication systems.

With regards to financial systems, the more economically aggressive and competitive economies, like South Korea, Japan, and Singapore, are also fintech hotspots. These fintech hotspots in these more advanced subsets have very aggressive and fast moving blockchain and cryptoassets enclaves. The less well endowed economies in the region are, on the other hand, looking at ways to assist high-technology businesses to help to both develop their economies and

1 Worldometer (2023), "Countries in the world by population (2024)", *Worldometer*, 16/07/2023, www.worldometers.info/world-population/population-by-country/, accessed 08/08/2019.

DOI: 10.4324/9781032667416-8

foster financial inclusiveness. Insights from both are important from a global perspective. The advanced economies of the region engaged with these can potentially pose a competitive threat to those in advanced Western economies, and there are already indications that they can with the likes of Tencent and Alibaba. Insights from crypto engagements by the less-affluent economies in the region are also useful as they could potentially show how the lower-income groups in advanced economies could use the emerging techs to raise their economic position. How each of these selected Asian economies deal with the potentials from the crypto space will now be discussed. This commences with China, potentially the second biggest economy in the world.

8.2 China's cryptoasset regulatory policy

The People's Bank of China (PBOC) has been researching a virtual currency for some time already, and this suggests the possibility of the PBOC becoming the first central bank to issue one. But as long as it remains centralised, that is, endorsed and controlled by the central bank, it would merely be just traditional money with a digitisation vessel that could work well for intra-bank operations but difficult for it to become widespread.[2] However, the initial plan is to issue the digital yuan in association with a group of Chinese banks, named Digital Currency Electronic Payment (or DCEP for short), but only in a few cities, including Shenzhen, Chengdu, and Suzhou. For all other purposes, cryptocurrencies are covered by the general legal ban imposed earlier by the Chinese government, as discussed later.[3]

The Chinese government started to advance its campaign against cryptoassets from mid-September 2017.[4] Rumours simultaneously began circulating about pending shutdowns of all local exchange platforms in the country. At that time, Jihan Wu, co-founder of Bitcoin hardware firm Bitmain, claimed that the rumours were hinting of tougher regulations and temporary closure instead of an outright ban.[5] China's National Internet Finance Association (NIFA) claimed that any cryptoassets exchange currently operating in China has no legal authorisation to engage in this kind of business.[6] There were also no clear warnings or threats that individual Bitcoin traders would be prosecuted. NIFA is a state-backed self-regulatory organisation set up by the PBOC, the country's central bank, with members comprising banks, brokerages, consumer finance companies, and funds.

2 Lunn, B. (2018), "We interviewed somebody in China to find out what is happening in this critical market for blockchain, Bitcoin, and crypto", *Daily Fintech*, 03/03/2018.

3 Seth, S. (2019), "Is bitcoin banned in China?", *Investopedia*, 25/06/2019, www.investopedia.com/news/bitcoin-banned-china/, accessed 07/02/2020.

4 Froelings, L. (2017), "China moves towards tougher Bitcoin regulation, but not to outright ban: Jian Wu", *Coin Telegraph*, 15/09/2017, https://cointelegraph.com/news/china-moves-towards-tougher-bitcoin-regulation-but-not-to-outright-ban-jihan-wu, accessed 02/02/2018.

5 Ibid note [4], Froelings (2017).

6 Ibid note [4], Froelings (2017).

The implication of a complete ban on virtual currency trading in China would have significant outcomes, as the country is home to one of the most active cryptocurrency trading activities around the world. It has, for example, been reported that a large scale mining farm in China accounts for about one-twentieth of the total daily virtual currency production worldwide.[7] Owing to the magnitude of virtual currencies in China, Liu Xiaolei, a Guanghua University professor, suggests that a total ban in the country is neither feasible nor realistic.[8] Hu Bing, FINA researcher, claims that a possible ICO ban may only be temporary and not permanent, and that a ban would only be until the Chinese authorities are able to locate effective solutions on how to regulate the new technology.[9]

In all fairness, the Chinese authorities do have particular problems to deal with. There is a very strong cultural propensity towards gambling in China, often for large amounts of money, and it is illegal. The population can save up and fly to the Special Administrative Region of Macau, where gambling is legal and there is an assortment of very large casinos. Apart from the Jockey Club's gambling facilities in Hong Kong, there is nothing else that is legal apart from the Chinese government's official lotteries.[10] That said, one recent analysis suggests that over 1 trillion Chinese yuan is illegally gambled in China every year.[11]

It is in this context that the Chinese government banned all online poker applications and adopted an extremely cautious approach to cryptocurrencies, and in addition, ICOs were banned. The PBOC demanded in its website on 5 September 2017 that all Chinese ICO activities be stopped immediately,[12] with those already using ICOs to raise funds from Chinese buyers required to make refunds.[13] The aim was to protect the legal rights of investors, to reduce financial risk, and to stop people from evading the country's exchange control restrictions by using cryptocurrencies as the vehicle. The PBOC statement is based on the law of the country, PBOC's laws, commercial banking and securities laws, cybersecurity and telecommunications law, and financing and financial

7 Li, C. & Marchi, G. (2017), "In China's hinterlands, workers mine Bitcoin for a digital fortune", *New York Times*, 13/09/2017, www.nytimes.com/2017/09/13/business/Bitcoin-minechina.html, accessed 02/02/2018.

8 Ibid note [4], Froelings (2017).

9 Konash, M. (2017), "Chinese official: ICO ban in China is temporary", *Coin Speaker*, 11/09/2017, www.coinspeaker.com/2017/09/11/chinese-official-ico-ban-china-temporary, accessed 02/02/2018.

10 The Chinese Sports Lottery and the China Welfare Lottery.

11 Eimer, D. (09/01/2010). "China's secret gambling problem". *Daily Telegraph*, Shenyang, accessed 01/05/2015.

12 Technically this was in the form of a notice issued by seven government agencies of China, that is, the PBOC, the Central Cybersecurity and Information Technology Lead Group of the Communist Party of China, the Ministry of Industry and Information Technology, the State Administration for Industry and Commerce, China Banking Regulatory Commission, China Security Regulatory Commission, and China Insurance Regulatory Commission, jointly issued on 14 September 2017.

13 Zhao, W. (2017), "China's ICO ban: A full translation of regulator remark", *Coin Desk*, 05/09/2017, www.coindesk.com/chinas-ico-ban-a-full-translation-of-regulator-remarks, accessed 02/02/2018.

activities law.[14] Other matters highlighted in the announcement included the following:[15]

1. An ICO, by its nature, is an unauthorised and illegal financing activity involving financial crimes, such as the illegal distribution of financial tokens, the illegal issuance of securities and illegal fundraising, financial fraud, and pyramid schemes. Relevant authorities, as such, would closely monitor the latest market status and collaborate with the justice department and local governments.
2. Organisations and individuals are prohibited from starting illegal token fundraising activity. Commencing from the date of the announcement, all kinds of fundraising activity through tokens are required to cease immediately. Entities and individuals that have completed token fundraising previously would have to refund investors to protect investor rights and to deal with risks properly.
3. Supervision on platforms that provide exchange services for tokens issued during the fundraising would be reinforced. Henceforth, token exchange platforms should not be involved in offering exchange services between fiat currency and tokens, buying or selling tokens for cryptocurrencies, acting as a central party facilitating the trading of tokens for cryptocurrencies, or providing price bidding or middleman service for the exchange of tokens for cryptocurrency.
4. No financial institution or non-banking payment institution shall operate businesses that deal with token fundraising. As such, they shall not directly or indirectly provide account opening, registration, trading, clearing, and settlement services for token fundraising activities.
5. The PBOC cautioned the public on the multiple risks posed by token fundraising, including fraudulent assets, business operational failure, and speculation.
6. Different financial industry entities should study the regulations well. Member companies should voluntarily fight against any illegal financing activity that relates to token and cryptocurrency fundraising, keep a distance form this market chaos, improve education for investors, and jointly help maintain financial stability.

China previously banned Bitcoin by barring Chinese financial institutions from associating with Bitcoin companies as early as 2013,[15] followed by the shutting

14 Ibid note [13], Zhao (2017), p. 15

15 Hern, A. (2013), "Bitcoin plummets as China's largest exchange blocks new deposits", *The Guardian*, 18/12/2013, www.theguardian.com/technology/2013/dec/18/bitcoin-plummets-china-payment-processors-digital-cryptocurrency, accessed 02/02/2018; Hern, A. (2013a), "Bitcoin price tumbles after warning from Chinese central bank: The People's Bank of China has issued a warning that the currency is not legally protected and has no 'real meaning'", *The Guardian*, 05/12/2013, www.theguardian.com/technology/2013/dec/05/bitcoin-price-tumbles-chinese-central-bank-warning, accessed 02/02/2018.

down of cryptocurrency exchanges in 2014.[16] At that time, the PBOC ordered banks to close all accounts opened by operators of websites that trade the currency by 15 April 2014, essentially forcing all Bitcoin exchanges in China to shut down. This meant that the only way out for Bitcoin websites was by moving their servers abroad and using the service of foreign banks and payment companies. This also suggests that Chinese investors would only be able to buy Bitcoin with cash. As for the other market participants, almost all of them, extending from mining, trading, to storage, have moved their operations overseas because of the general ban for all Bitcoin business activities.

Back then in 2014, China enjoyed a strong competitive advantage in Bitcoin mining, accounting for around 50% of the global Bitcoin network mining power. Trading is also said to be the most important financial application of Bitcoin. There are said to be more than 100 Bitcoin trading platforms across the world, of which the top ten are based in the United States, Eastern Europe, and Asia (including China, Japan, and South Korea), and these accounted for more than 90% of global trading volume. Since 2015, regulatory compliance became the primary focus of BTC/US$ exchanges. US based exchanges Coinbase and ItBit received relevant business licence from US authorities, but in China, the relevant government departments have not enacted a licence for digital currencies, thereby making compliance a major issue.[17]

Since then, the Chinese government has become increasingly alarmed at the increase in corporate, personal, and government debt in the economy and has taken a number of steps to keep it under control. Ongoing controls on ICOs can also be seen in that context. Debt to GDP is rising very quickly at 255% in 2016, 300% by the end of 2017, and now 329%. This is very high when compared with other countries with the same level of income per head. Household debt has risen from 40% of disposable income in 2008 to 106% in 2016. Overall debt has risen from 20% to 43% of GDP at the same time: It now exceeds 80%. A significant part of this consists of people financing buying their homes, but there is considerable evidence that prices in many cities are significantly overinflated – meaning, a 2008 Western style financial crisis is a real possibility.

Non-performing bank loans in the United States at the start of the 2007–8 financial crisis were 6%; in China, it already exceeds this. Local government debt was meant to be scaled back over recent years by using bond swaps, but the reforms were used to hide increases in borrowing, which then rose by 20% over 2 years! On top of that, there is no certain way of measuring the effect on lending on the activities of the shadow market. This is such a source of concern to the Chinese government that they have changed the system of financial regulation. Banning ICOs makes sense as part of this process.

---

16 Hern, A. (2013), "Bitcoin price tumbles after warning from Chinese Central Bank", *The Gurdian* 05/12/2013, www.theguardian.com/technology/2013/dec/05/bitcoin-price-tumbles-chinese-central-bank-warning, accessed 02/02/2018.

17 Li, L. (2015), "Bitcoin in China: An insider view", *Coin Desk*, 22/08/2015, www.coindesk.com/markets/2015/08/22/bitcoin-in-china-an-insiders-view/, accessed 02/02/2018.

Huobi, Okcoin, and BTC China are the three Chinese Bitcoin exchanges running alongside several smaller exchanges. Some 3.6 million Bitcoin wallet service providers have emerged to enable mainstream users to send, receive, and store Bitcoin easily and securely. The growth potential of Bitcoin wallets is significant in the United States, but for China, due to the lack of merchants accepting Bitcoin payments and regulatory uncertainty, Chinese users tend to keep their Bitcoin funds on Bitcoin exchanges.[18] Other than Bitcoin trading, payments and international money transfers are the next most important significant applications of Bitcoin. There are more than 100,000 businesses accepting Bitcoin payments, including big companies, like Microsoft, Dell, Expedia, BitPay, Circle, and Newegg.

Bitcoin development could take four, though not necessarily mutually exclusive, directions. It could develop as a global financial asset, as a financial tool for improving money transfer, as a payment network, and as non-financial technology powering decentralised autonomous organisations, smart contracts, prediction markets, and the internet of things. Given this, and for China to find a niche at the forefront of international finance and innovation, the country could differentiate between cryptocurrency and blockchain technology, regulate via existing laws, observe and learn from actions of others, and by supporting research and innovation.[19]

As regulations develop, China is slowly permitting Bitcoin transactions, but under certain restrictions that users need to follow.[20] Bitcoin trading is booming in China despite the official clampdown on centralised exchanges, as traders take to investing in the virtual currency through P2P exchanges. In P2P Bitcoin trade, buyers interact directly on a one-to-one basis with sellers on deals instead of in a centralised marketplace or exchange. This kind of over-the-counter trading is booming (according to China's National Committee of Experts on Internet Financial Security), increasing from 4 previously to 21 currently, while there is enhanced use of messaging platforms like WeChat and Telegram Bitcoin for users to connect.[21] Subsequent to a period of caution after the September 2014 actions, the China blockchain community appears to be back in business.

Similarly, it is expected that China's current ban on ICOs would be similarly followed through with regulation. At present, the government appears to favour the Ethereum based tokens commonly used by tech start-ups to raise funds. This suggests a direction toward niche token sales – in other words, allowing the sale of tokens in a format the authorities deem safe and more measured.[22]

18 Ibid note [17], Li (2015).

19 Ibid note [17], Li (2015).

20 Cuen, L. (2017), "China bans initial coin offerings while Paris Hilton promotes Lydian coins", *International Business Times*, 09/04/2017, www.ibtimes.com/china-bans-initialcoin-offerings-while-paris-hilton-promotes-lydian-coins-2585985, accessed 02/02/2018.

21 Barclay, A. (2017), "China's crackdown raises cryptocurrency demands as they move to peer-to-peer platforms", *South China Morning Post*, 22/12/2017, www.scmp.com/tech/innovation/article/2125282/chinas-bitcoin-crackdown-raises-cryptocurrency-demand-they-move-peer, accessed 02/02/2018.

22 Ibid note [20], Cuen (2017).

Rumours of late are, however, saying that China will officially decide to crack down on all Bitcoin and cryptocurrency trading, not just commercial exchanges. Such a wider clampdown could include blocking mainland access to websites of foreign exchanges, such as Coinbase in the United States and Bitfinex in Hong Kong. Nevertheless, irrespective of China's official position on Bitcoin, the Bitcoin community in China has already reacted by transferring much of their activities to Japan, where regulations are less strict,[23] and by Chinese miners relocating to Canada.[24]

It has been reported that when the terms in Chinese of Bitcoin, cryptocurrency, and ICO were searched on Chinese search engine Baidu and microblog Weibo, no obvious paid sponsored content came up alongside the expected results. Baidu and Weibo are said to have banned cryptocurrency-related advertising,[25] moving in synchronisation with Facebook's[26] banned advertising of cryptocurrencies at that time. The latter justified its action, citing the large number of fintech companies on its platform not operating in good faith.

The Bitcoin community is, however, not unduly perturbed, as there were plenty of other ways to reach both the mass market and virtual currency enthusiasts. Bitmain, which runs China's two largest Bitcoin mining collectives, is setting up regional headquarters in Singapore and has mining operations in the United States and Canada, while Bitcoin.com, the third largest mining pool, is operating a facility in Canada, and ViaBTC, ranked fourth, has operations in Iceland and the United States. They also promote their brand names on popular digital asset news site like Digital News Asia, while Reddit and Twitter have also been deployed as viable alternatives.[27]

When ordered to shut down in September 2017, Chinese cryptocurrency exchanges BTCC China, Huobi, and Okcoin relocated their businesses to Hong Kong, rebranding, respectively, as BTCC, Hiobi Pro, and OKEx. It is relatively easy for Chinese investors to move their funds from their Chinese bank accounts to Hong Kong bank accounts, thereby enabling them to start trading

23 Buck, J. (2017), "China will heavily crack down on all Bitcoin trades", *Coin Telegraph*, 18/09/2017, https://cointelegraph.com/news/china-will-heavily-crack-down-on-all-bitcoin-trades, accessed 02/02/2018.

24 Lampert, A., Harney, A. & Goh, B. (2018), "Chinese Bitcoin miners eye sites in energy- rich Canada", *The Independent* 12/01/2018, www.independent.co.uk/tech/bitcoin-latest-china-miners-canada-target-energy-cryptocurrency-bitmain-a8155446.html, accessed 02/02/2018.

25 Zuckerman, M. J. (2018), "With China tightening regulations, crypto-related Ads reportedly gone from local websites", *Coin Telegraph*, 04/02/2018, https://cointelegraph.com/news/with-china-tightening-regulations-crypto-related-ads-reportedly-gone-from-local-websites, accessed 18/02/2018.

26 Marshall, A. (2018), "Facebook bans cryptocurrency, ICO ads because of 'deceptive promotional practices'", *Coin Telegraph*, 30/01/2018, https://cointelegraph.com/news/facebook-bans-cryptocurrency-ico-ads-because-of-deceptive-promotional-practices, accessed 02/02/2018. Subsequently, Facebook changed this policy.

27 Lee, A. (2018), "Bitcoin ads disappear from social media in China after central bank bans cryptocurrency fundraising", *South China Morning Post*, 06/02/2018, www.scmp.com/tech/china-tech/article/2131419/bitcoin-ads-disappear-social-media-china-after-central-bank-bans, accessed 18/02/2018.

cryptocurrencies more actively and effectively, bypassing China's restrictions.[28] Hong Kong's exchanges have also integrated widely used fintech applications in China, like Alipay and Tencent's WeChat Pay. The integration of these two fintech payment networks has increased the accessibility of Hong Kong–based cryptocurrency exchanges for Chinese investors, thereby easing the process of investing in the cryptocurrency markets. The Chinese government and the PBOC have asked local banks to disclose any suspicious transactions linked to Hong Kong–based markets, but even this move might not be able to prevent Chinese investors from accessing Hong Kong based markets because of apps like Alipay and WeChat Pay.[29]

So far, China has banned ICOs, stopped local Bitcoin exchanges from trading, outlined proposals to discourage Bitcoin mining, and stopped Chinese listed companies abroad, avoiding its domestic ban on ICOs. It is now said to be planning to block domestic access to online platforms and mobile apps offering exchange like services for cryptocurrencies, targeting platforms that allow investors to trade digital assets on overseas exchange, while domestic stock exchanges are scrutinising companies that are promoting themselves as blockchain related to boost their shares.[30] This is a concerted effort by the PBOC, the Cyberspace Administration, and the Ministry of Industry and Information Technology to clamp down on cryptocurrencies and, in particular, Bitcoin. Despite this, China is not necessarily anti-cryptocurrency. The PBOC has conducted trials of its own prototype cryptocurrency, taking China a step closer to being the first major central bank to issue a virtual currency. The country's aspiration, however, seems to be based more on taking full control of such transactions in contrast to the libertarian aspirations of Bitcoin.

For the last two years, China's current government mantra has focused on cleansing risk from financial markets. Among the country's primary concerns are the booming shadow banking sector, a potential source of unregulated loans to speculators in whatever the latest financial risk happens to be. Virtual currencies provide an avenue to move money out of China, potentially adding to outflows that Chinese officials have set about aggressively stemming. According to Mark McFarland, Chief Economist at Union Bancaire Privée, UBP SA, Hong Kong, a longer-term process of tightening the scrutiny of activities that are not in the normal sort of monetary realm is underway.[32] Arising from these developments, Bitcoin is traded in over-the-counter markets in China, which is a relatively slower process that some say would increase credit risk.

For the cryptocurrency world at large, these moves are reshaping the Bitcoin mining industry and driving up costs. Miners initially headed to China because

28 Young, J. (2018), "How Chinese Bitcoin buyers are getting around government ban", *Coin Telegraph*, 27/01/2018, https://cointelegraph.com/news/how-chinese-bitcoin-buyers-are-gettinga-round-government, accessed 02/02/2018.

29 Ibid note [28], Young (2018).

30 Clark, G. & Chen, L. Y. (2018), "How China's Stifling Bitcoin and cryptocurrencies: Quick take", *Bloomberg*, 08/01/2018, www.bloomberg.com/news/articles/2018-01-09/how-china-s-stifling-bitcoin-and-cryptocurrencies-quicktake-q-a, accessed 02/02/2018

of its inexpensive power, local chip-making factories, and cheap labour. In early 2013, China's state-run TV, CCTV (renamed CGTN), aired a short documentary of Bitcoin technology. During this period, more Bitcoin wallets were downloaded by computers in China than in the rest of the world combined.[31] This was because speculating on Bitcoin constituted one of the few investment options available for retail investors in China's heavily regulated financial environment. Up to September 2017, more than two-thirds of Bitcoins were mined in China, where most of the computers used for mining are manufactured.[32] Bitcoin uses a great deal of computing power, and some Chinese computer clusters used for the process enjoyed access to relatively cheap electricity, especially in provinces powered by hydroelectricity, but the political environment soon began to change.

As the speculative fervour threatened to get out of hand, China became concerned about the yuan leaving the country. Though the country limits yuan outflow at $50,000 per person per year, the potential was there, as Chinese people could buy Bitcoins in yuan, sell them on an American exchange, and then withdraw the sum in dollars. In late 2013, the Chinese authorities responded by banning financial services companies from dealing with Bitcoin exchanges.[33] Following this, people could no longer withdraw yuan from their bank accounts to directly buy Bitcoins on Chinese exchanges. Now, Bitcoin miners, and other Chinese Bitcoin businesses, have to look towards Canada, the United States, Australia, Switzerland, and Singapore. This is because China did not just impose a limit on virtual currencies; it shut down the entire highway despite the fact that most of the 2016 Bitcoin trades were done in Chinese yuan.[36]

As mentioned earlier, Chinese people found ways around this by using cash to buy vouchers that could be traded on the exchanges, or by sending money to the personal bank account of someone who worked at an exchange. When the authorities later shut down cryptocurrency exchanges, people turned to online and offline P2P trading. Others could also buy and sell virtual currencies on the encrypted messaging app Telegram, which though blocked in China could be accessed by virtual private networks that could get around the Great Firewall. People already owning coins could also just go online and trade them on an exchange that is based overseas, with even some trading on WeChat, China's massively popular but heavily monitored messaging app.

This capacity to avoid the restrictions arose because China did not ban Bitcoin itself, nor did it explicitly ban P2P trading, and, importantly, has not officially banned the mining of Bitcoin. Words such as *cryptocurrency*, *Bitcoin*, and *ICOs* now verge on being taboo words in China, but *blockchain* or *distributed ledger technology* have not. This was why and how a Chinese university professor who initially had his Bitcoin course cancelled was able to get approval when

31 Kapron, Z. (2014), *Chomping at the Bitcoin: The past, present and future of Bitcoin in China*, Hong Kong, Penguin Books China.

32 Parker, E. (2018), "Can China contain Bitcoin? It is trying. But the cryptocurrency is bigger than any country, even the one where it has been most popular?", *MIT Technology Review*, January/February 2018.

33 Ibid note [32], Parker (2018), 36

launching it under the more politically correct title of "The Smart Economy and Blockchain". This is because Chinese authorities clearly see blockchain as a technology of the future. The country counts blockchain technology as part of its 13th five-year plan and a useful tool for advancing its regional interest in trade. China wants to use blockchain to ensure the trustworthiness of public and administrative data, but according to Ben Kook, an engineering professor at Tsinghua University, it does not want people to print their own money.[34]

Since the changes in Chinese law, many exchanges launched peer-to-peer trading platforms that support direct transactions between investors without the exchange simply acting as a central counterparty. This means that the investors can buy a cryptocurrency and then pay separately by whatever payment method the exchange will accept. The key issue here is the potential long-arm reach of Chinese criminal law even where the exchanges are outside China. This will only be the case if the founders or investors are Chinese citizens or operational decisions are made in the jurisdiction. At present, the Chinese authorities have not been active in this regard, but if they become so, an exchange overseas run by people inside China would seem to be the most at risk.

China's crackdown on cryptocurrencies suggests that no one country can stop them.[38] China first banned ICOs, then exchanges, and subsequently started blocking foreign currency sites from Chinese people with a firewall. In the decentralised network of cryptocurrencies, when one country bows out, another picks up the slack. Hence, when China clamped down, much of its crypto activity migrated to Japan and South Korea. Different functions seem to work in different economies. No longer able to accept cash deposits, these exchanges now provide crypto-to-crypto exchanges along with some futures and index derivatives. Despite the tight regulation, crypto exchanges in China have managed to survive and flourish, but ICO initiatives or frauds have faced tighter regulation because of the risks they posed to the financial system. China's largest cryptocurrency exchange, Huobi, besides relocating its operations to San Francisco, Hong Kong, Korea, and Japan, has turned tighter regulation imposed into a blessing by seizing the initiative to launch user security and protection initiatives, like the User Protection Funds and the Security Reserve, as well as launching the world's first autonomous token listing exchange.[35]

As for blockchain technology, in October 2016, China's Ministry of Industry and Information Technology issued a white paper for its development and application.[40] The Chinese government remains extremely positive about the potential uses of blockchain itself. Hangzhou, the e-commerce city of China, is the first city in the country to include blockchain in its government report. Blockchain maintains its stature alongside artificial intelligence, virtual reality, quantum technology, and commercial aerospace technology. Technology giants

34 Ibid note [32], Parker (2018), 38

35 Pollock, D. (2018), "Why we shouldn't pay too much attention to regulation in China, at least for now", *Coin Telegraph*, 26/02/2018, https://cointelegraph.com/news/why-we-shouldntpay-much-attention-for-regulation-in-china-at-least-for-now, accessed 02/03/2018

like Alibaba and Ant Financials have been implementing blockchain applications since 2016, including charity platforms, mailbox verification, food production tracing, and medicals. Wanxiang Blockchain Labs, another big blockchain player, plans to invest US$30 billion over 7 years to implement smart cities initiative, where blockchain would be the major driver.

Those seeking a technology community would do well to go to the United States, while those seeking friendly laws could consider Japan and Switzerland, and those seeking customers might go to South Korea. Bitcoin now presents China with the same challenge that the internet once did. The country was initially suspicious of the web, as letting it in would mean relinquishing some degree of control, but keeping it out would cut China off from the global economy. This time around, it is too late to isolate the country from the rest of the world, for as long as there is one cable available from the country to the outside world, Bitcoin could then survive.[36]

Bitcoin appears to have passed the China test, as it did not break after China banned it. Cryptocurrencies have delivered on the promise that they could not be defeated by any government, even one as large and powerful as China's.[37] They seem to become stronger each time they are held down by regulations and other barriers. The famed financial adviser and cryptocurrency champion Ronnie Moas argues that if China bans cryptocurrencies, 190 countries around the world would not hesitate to buy them especially in a fire sale. He sees the fear and damage that regulation brings as only noise and would worry only when China, Russia, the United States, and South Korea come out with destructive policies simultaneously.[38]

In summary, the PBOC Circular 2013 and Circular 2017 constitute the primary regulatory frameworks for cryptoassets. Within these, cryptocurrencies are treated as virtual commodities, while ICOs are banned, with resulting civil, administrative, and criminal liabilities.[39] Some of these liabilities fall under existing law. The undertaking of the illegal issuance and sale of tokens is, for example, mentioned under Article 20 of the Chinese Securities Law, and under the said law, individuals and institutions issuing and selling tokens would be required to terminate the illegal transaction immediately and can face fines of up to 200,000 Chinese yuan. Where an ICO is treated as illegally fundraising, the issuer could be sentenced to more than 10 years' imprisonment and faced with a fine of 50,000 to 500,000 Chinese yuan. Despite the prohibition of ICOs and trading platform services for cryptoassets, Chinese authorities have not forbidden the existence of cryptoassets.[40]

With cryptoassets being treated as virtual commodity, there are no particular or explicit restrictions on its acquisition, ownership, or trading by individuals.

36 Ibid note [32], Parker (2018).
37 Ibid note [32], Parker (2018).
38 Ibid note [35], Pollock (2018).
39 Gong, L. & Yu, L. (2019), "China", in Dewey, J. (ed.), *Blockchain and cryptocurrency regulation*, London, Global Legal Insights.
40 Ibid note [39], Gong & Yu (2019).

Generally, China has been implementing further restrictions regarding cryptoassets, extending from banning ICOs, discouraging Bitcoin miners, to a countrywide ban on internet and mobile access to cryptoasset trading platforms. Relative to other major economies, China emerges as one of the strictest regulators with regards to private cryptoassets.

Blockchain companies, on the other hand, would have to follow the guidelines provided by the country's internet regulator, the Cyberspace Administration of China, commencing on 19 February 2019. These include requiring companies to record and log user activity, along with maintaining backups, for a minimum of 6 months, as well as the verification of users based on their national ID and phone number.[41] These aside, blockchain service providers are required to register with the authorities within ten days of providing the service. Those companies developing new products are required to report these to the authorities to undergo safety assessment in line with relevant regulations. Companies involved are also required to implement necessary changes so as to issue warnings to users, then restrict and close accounts, while users violating administrative laws and regulations would have to be reported to the relevant authorities.[42]

China banned non-government-approved cryptoassets in September 2021.[43] The country adopts a strict approach on cryptoassets as it takes the position that cryptos will destabilise its fiat currency at a time the country is striving to expand its economy. The People's Bank of China (PBOC), the central bank of China, and four other authorities jointly released the Circular on the Prevention of Risks from Bitcoin in December 2013, making it compulsory for all financial institutions not to engage in Bitcoin-based businesses.[44] Following this, in September 2017, the PBOC and other authorities issued an Announcement on Preventing Initial Coin Offering risks.[45] This advised that initial coins or virtual currencies will not have legal status as official currencies and cannot, as such, be used as currency in the market. It also prohibited all kinds of ICO activities and exchange services for token financing and trading platforms. Arising from this, Binance relocated away from China. In September 2021, the PBOC and nine other central authorities released the Circular on Further Preventing and Resolving the Risks of Speculation in Virtual Currency Trading (Circular 237). This regulatory document seeks to develop the country's approach to managing risks linked to virtual currencies. Circular 237's key provisions include the stress on the illegality of virtual currency linked activities; the targeting of offshore virtual currency exchanges providing services to Chinese residents and

41 Alex, T. (2019), "China to enforce regulation for blockchain companies in February", *Yahoo Finance*, 11/01/2019, citing a report from CNN, https://finance.yahoo.com/news/china-enforce-regulation-blockchain-companies-083048347.html, accessed 07/02/2020.

42 Ibid note [41], Alex (2019).

43 Elena, R. (2024), "Cryptocurrency regulations in China", *Coinpedia*, 20/03/2024, https://coinpedia.org/cryptocurrency-regulation/crypto-regulations-in-china-in-2024/#:~:text=It%20states%20that%20virtual%20currencies,provide%20services%20to%20Chinese%20residents., 25/03/2024

44 Ibid note [43], Elena (2024)

45 Ibid note [43], Elena (2024)

mandating the authorities involved to block them and punish all those involved; directing financial institutions and payment service providers to refrain from offering any services linked to virtual currency transaction; and references to enhanced supervision and monitoring of virtual currency targeting and speculation.[46] The National Development and Reform Commission issued the Circular on Regulating Virtual Currency Mining Activities.[47] The PBOC, in turn, intensified its scrutiny of cryptos in its recent 2023 Financial Stability Report. This report drew attention to the rapid growth of the global crypto market, while stressing on the importance of consistent oversight, including an alert to crypto regulations across the world.[48] The PBOC advocated for uniform regulation across the board, arguing on the principle of "same business, same risks, same supervision".[49] No tax regime is applicable for cryptos in China, owing to their illegal status.

8.3 India's cryptoasset regulatory policy

For now, there is no precise definition for *cryptoassets*, *cryptocurrencies*, or *virtual currencies* in India. The Reserve Bank of India, the country's central bank, curtails regulated finance and banking channels from partaking in the sales and purchase of virtual currencies. This guidance circular, though, is being challenged by the Internet and Mobile Association of India. There are hints that the government would not allow the use of cryptoassets as currency or to allow its use in the country's payments system. It would also take steps to eliminate the illegal use of cryptoassets. Nevertheless, there could be a concession for those seeking to treat them as a financial asset class, and to this end, the appropriate regulations would be put in place to make these transactions transparent and legal. Cryptocurrency exchanges would likely be regulated via new regulations requiring KYC procedures and record-keeping for transactions.

Up to now, pertinent authorities in the country have been sending mixed signals pertaining to the regulatory approach for cryptoassets. The Finance Ministry has been saying that cryptocurrencies are not legal tender and that it would crack down on the deployment for illegal activities. The Tax Department has issued notices to thousands of crypto investors, alleging tax evasion. The Reserve Bank of India ordered all regulated institutions to stop providing services to businesses and individuals transacting in cryptoassets within 3 months of its notice. There have also been calls from within the corridors of powers that Bitcoin has a place in the country. Suits against these have been scheduled for court hearings, including one at the Supreme Court.

In general, stakeholders in the cryptoasset industry are up in arms against the current and soon-to-be official stand of the Indian authorities to criminalise

46 Ibid note [43], Elena (2024)
47 Ibid note [43], Elena (2024)
48 Ibid note [43], Elena (2024)
49 Ibid note [43], Elena (2024)

cryptoasset investment, thereby putting the country as the first large democracy to ban what is viewed as an innovative technology.[50] They argued that shunning the industry would result in massive job losses and a brain drain and, more importantly, disrupt the country's goal to have a US$5 trillion economy, given that the crypto industry is envisaged to be a US$10 trillion industry over the next five years. They further specifically stressed that India would lose about US$12.9 billion worth of the market if cryptocurrency is eventually banned in the country. By way of example, former domestic exchange Bitbns found the inhospitable regulatory condition too troubling and is now an Estonian-based operation even though their original stand was to operate from out of India.[51]

India is globally acclaimed as a global powerhouse when it comes to IT assets and related skills. They have produced global giants. They have contributed world class talents to many multinational corporations across the world, especially Microsoft. Many of their talents have been helping many economies across the world, especially in the fintech space, including even the United States and the UK. Bangalore in India, for example, is globally recognised as the main source for such talents. While China makes huge strides in computer hardware, India is, in contrast, very powerful in software engineering. While China makes impressive achievements in the fintech space, and in particular electronic payments, India is now fast catching up. While China officially bans cryptoasset transactions, India is apparently still as yet to formalise its stand on the matter. China fears the threats of private cryptocurrencies on its authoritarian regime, while India fears their deployment in its very large informal economy, thereby potentially enlarging the incidence of deployment in illicit activities rather than the risks to its democratic form of government, incidentally the world's biggest democracy.

Though India has not enacted any specific legislation for the regulation of virtual currencies (VCs), the country has contemporised statutes like the Companies Act 2013, which requires the reporting of virtual digital assets (VDAs) in a move to reflect the emerging dynamics of the financial space.[51] The jurisdiction has further widened the scope of the Prevention of Money Laundering Act (PMLA) 2002 through incorporating transactions linked to VDAs, including various exchanges, transfers, and administrative measures linked with VDAs, as well as including participation in and the provision of financial services connected to an issuer's offering and sale of a VDA.[52] Together with this, the country's income tax laws have undergone significant modifications to cover for the taxation of VDAs and, in the process, recognises the fiscal implications of the evolving VC market.[53]

50 Huillet, M. (2019), "Bitcoin ban means massive brain for India, crypto industry warns", *Coin Telegraph*, 16/09/2019, https://cointelegraph.com/news/indias-proposed-Bitcoin-ban-is-already-driving-a-crypto-exodus, accessed 18/09/2019. 51 Ibid note [51], Huillet (2019).

51 Anand, N. et al. (2024), "India", in Dewey, J. N. (ed.), *Blockchain & cryptocurrency laws and regulations 2024*, London, Global Legal Insights

52 Ibid note [52], Anand et al. (2024)

53 Ibid note [52], Anand et al. (2024)

VDAs achieved substantial traction in the legal space to further legitimise the business. Also, enforcement actions under the present tax regime are being initiated, while anti–money laundering (AML) laws have concurrently been expanded to address the rising Web3/VDA business.[54] The common attention extended by financial and regulatory authorities globally reflects the evolving significance and acceptance of the VDA business space. On the other hand, the government's approach towards VDAs can only be better understood when the awaited Cryptocurrency and Regulation of Official Digital Currency Bill 2021 is put into effect.[55] As of May 2025, it remains pending.

Glimpses from statements of senior public officials suggest the potential replacement of a domestic facing law regulating VDAs in preference for a globally aligned, internationally synchronised approach. As the current G20 leader, India influences the international direction of crypto regulation in conjunction with the IMF, WEF, and other stakeholders, while accommodating views from emerging and developed economies. India, in this connection, has released the Presidency Note as input for a Roadmap on Establishing a Global Framework for Crypto Assets for deliberations by G20 member economies. To gain a better understanding of the country's approach for cryptos, it is helpful to evaluate the contemporaneous actions drawn up and/or implemented by the country's various ministries, departments, and representatives.[56]

The more notable of these being the released December 2021 updated version of the National Strategy on Blockchain; the 28 June 2023 Reserve Bank of India's (RBI's) Chapter III Report: Regulatory Initiatives in the Financial Sector; the 28 April 2022 directives under Sub-section (6) of Section 70B of the Information Technology Act 2000 pertaining to information security practices, procedures, prevention, responses, and reporting of cyber incidents for safe and trusted internet issued by the Indian Computer Emergency Response Team (or CERT Guidelines); the successful initiation of the Rupee CBDC pilot via an enabling legal framework achieved through amendments to the Reserve Bank of India Act 1934; the Ministry of Finance's 7 March 2023 PMLA notification that brought every entity partaking in the transactions of VDAs, including exchanges, custodians, and wallet providers, under the purview of the PMLA and rule; and the amendment of the Income Tax Act 1961 (IT Act) that introduced an income taxation regime for VDAs.[57] The amendments in the latter, in a wide sense, introduced the definition for *virtual digital assets*, including non-fungible tokens (NFTs), but excluding closed-system instruments, such as gift cards or vouchers, mileage points, reward points, or loyalty cards and subscriptions to websites, platforms, or applications; a 30% tax on income from the transfer of a VDA; a withholding tax on the transfer of VDAs from one entity to another; treatment of VDAs that are received as gifts; guidelines for VDA

54 Ibid note [52], Anand et al. (2024)
55 Ibid note [52], Anand et al. (2024)
56 Ibid note [52], Anand et al. (2024)
57 Ibid note [52], Anand et al. (2024)

exchanges on how to effect the amendments to the IT Act; and guidelines for peer-to-peer transactions.[58]

Finally, individuals and entities are allowed to hold, invest in, and transact VDAs, as long as they adhere to existing laws. Banks and other RBI-regulated entities, though, have to abide to established due diligence processes to comply with financial services regulations.[59] Nonetheless, the country does not recognise cryptos as legal tender or coin and intends to curb their use in financing illegitimate activities, or within the payment system. In this connection, it is helpful to note the 2020 Supreme Court of India's judgment that acknowledged the dual nature of VDAs, its not being recognised as legal tender but performing many functions of fiat currency.[60] This judgement reflects on the evolving global nature of VDAs that highlights the necessity of developing suitable regulatory mechanisms.[61]

8.4 Japan's cryptoasset regulatory policy

Cryptocurrencies are generally treated as assets in Japan, but the country's amended banking laws, via the Payment Services Act on 1 April 2017, informally dubbed as the "Virtual Currency Act", together with an amendment Act passed in 2022, in effect, launched a regulatory regime for cryptocurrency businesses, thus making Japan probably the first advanced Asian economy to do so. Subsequent to the amendment, 15 business operators registered under this regime. This amended statute recognised that, in effect, cryptocurrencies are a legal form of payment.

These rules stipulate that cryptocurrency exchanges seeking to operate in Japan would henceforth come under the regulatory supervision of the Japan Financial Services Agency (JFSA). As such, they would be subject to annual audits and KYC verifications so as to strengthen the country's anti–money laundering initiatives. Effectively, they would operate through a system of self-regulatory bodies that would have stricter impositions on them than required by law.[62] Cryptocurrency exchange businesses all now have to be registered. Regulation in this context covers registration, maintaining internal controls, segregation of customers' cryptocurrency from that of the exchange, and publishing response policies to hacking and the retention of funds for payment.[63]

The *regulatory regime* is defined as the financial value that may be employed to perform obligations in compensation for purchasing or borrowing of goods,

58 Ibid note [52], Anand et al. (2024)

59 Ibid note [52], Anand et al. (2024)

60 https://main.sci.gov.in/supremecourt/2018/19230/19230_2018_4_1501_21151_Judgement_04-Mar-2020.pdf, accessed 06/08/2024

61 Ibid note [52], Anand et al. (2024)

62 www.globallegalinsights.com/practice-areas/blockchain-laws-and-regulations/japan, accessed 08/08/2019.

63 Helms, K. (2018), "Japan publishes draft report of new crypto regulations", *Bitcoin.com*, 17/12/2018, https://news.Bitcoin.com/japan-report-new-cryptocurrency-regulations/, accessed 24/02/2019.

or receiving services, against unspecified persons, which may be purchased from or sold to unspecified persons and are transferrable by an electronic data processing system, provided that such value is limited to those recorded on an electronic device in an electronic form, and does not include Japanese or foreign currencies, or assets denominated in such currencies. These as described are known as type 1 virtual currencies.[64] In contrast, type 2s are those that can be exchanged with type 1s and with unspecified persons and also viewed as transferable by an electronic data processing system.

Since Bitcoin became recognised as an official form of legal payment in Japan in April 2017, more than 4,500 stores in the country began accepting cryptocurrencies, with one financial newspaper estimating that this could increase fivefold by the end of 2017.[65] The variety of stores accepting Bitcoin, including electronic giant Bic Cam, as well as Bitcoin BTMs, which exchange fiat for Bitcoin and utilities, has greatly increased. Despite the liquidation of Mt. Gox, the then largest Bitcoin exchange in the world, the Japanese enacted regulations focusing on relevant exchanges so as to protect consumers. The country's regulations on this are spelt out in what follows:[66]

1. Going by this classification, the present major type 1 virtual currencies are Bitcoin, Ethereum, or Litecoin, while type 2s are counterparty coins, known as XCP, or tokens that can be exchanged to type 1s. Reward points granted under a particular point initiative are not deemed to be cryptocurrencies, where the points could only be employed at a specified number of shops or cannot be exchanged with real currencies without any limitation posed by a point issuer. Cryptocurrencies must be convertible to fiat currencies and accepted in an open community or freely exchangeable with other virtual currencies without any limitation posed by the issuer.
2. *Cryptocurrency exchange business* refers to those entities purchasing or selling cryptocurrencies; exchanging them with other cryptos; engaging in intermediation or brokerage or acting as agents for them; acting as a defined cryptocurrency exchange; or administering customers' cash or "virtual currency" as defined.

64 Koinuma, M., Ohashi, K. & Sakamoto, Y. (2017), "New law and regulations on virtual currencies in Japan", *Greenberg Traurig*, 24/01/2017; Ishida, M., Mears, E. & Takeda, R. (2017), "Japanese regulatory update on virtual currency business", *DLA Piper Paper*, 29/12/2017, www.dlapiper.com/en/people/t/takeda-ryutaro, accessed 02/02/2018.

65 Sedgwick, K. (2017), "Japan teaches Western government a lesson in cryptocurrency regulation", *Bitcoin Magazine*, 13/11/2017, https://news.bitcoin.com/japan-teaches-western-governments-lesson-cryptocurrency-regulation/, accessed 02/02/2018.

66 Financial Services Authority (FSA), "Details of screening new registration application as virtual currency exchange service provider", *FSA*, 30/09/2017, www.fsa.go.jp/en/news/2017/20170930-1/02.pdf, accessed 02/02/2018; Yeoh, P. (2017), "The brave new world of Bitcoin and blockchain: From 'no-go' to 'go beyond'", *Asia & The Pacific Policy Society (APPS) Policy Forum*, 02/08/2017, www.policyforum.net/no-go-go-beyond, accessed 02/02/2018.

3. Bitcoin users would be subject to the "know your customer" rules by Japanese cryptocurrency exchanges.
4. Such exchanges would be subjected to minimum capitalisation rules to avoid liquidity risks troubling some crypto exchanges across the world. Providers have to have a minimum of ¥10 million, not in possession of assets with negative values, and have the necessary legal compliance to operate a cryptocurrency exchange appropriately and securely. The provider must not have had its registration in Japan as a cryptocurrency exchange service provider revoked, or registration as a similar operator based on provisions in a foreign law deemed equivalent of this Payment Services Act in the past five years. The provider must never have violated the Payment Services Act, the law controlling contributions, money deposits, and interest, or equivalent provisions of foreign laws, and never have been fined in Japan or penalised under foreign laws as a result in the past five years. Other businesses operated by the provider must not harm public interest. The provider's directors must not include disqualified individuals.
5. The provider's organisation system must be verified that they have protective measures in place for service users. These include, for instance, whether the provider is equipped with systems to ensure that users are informed about the characteristics of cryptocurrencies, such as the fact that it is not legal tender or that it carries the risk of loss due to price volatility. Providers must maintain separate management of money or cryptocurrencies deposited by users. The provider must also confirm whether they have established a risk management framework giving sufficient consideration to the possibility of risk materialisation, and whether the IT system risk management system is based on objective criteria.
6. Foreign currency cash service providers are allowed to operate their business in Japan, but they have to be corporations that have a representative in Japan.
7. Cryptocurrency trading is not subject to the 8% consumption tax in Japan. However, Japan's tax agency declared that profits derived from its trading are subject to income tax under miscellaneous income, in contrast to dividend income, real property income, business income, and employment income. The tax agency has not mentioned corporate taxation measures, but it is highly likely that corporate profits generated by virtual currency trading could also be subject to corporate tax.

Tokens can only be sold through a cryptocurrency exchange service provider. This also covers ICOs (discussed in what follows), as there must already be an exchange market for the tokens.[67]

67 Umeda, S. (2018), "Regulation of cryptocurrency: Japan", *Library of Congress*, June 2018, www.loc.gov/law/help/cryptocurrency/japan.php, accessed 07/02/2020.

Japan's FSA cautioned investors of two risks associated with ICOs.[68] The first concerns price volatility, as a token's price may decline or become suddenly worthless. The second refers to their potential for fraud. The JFSA further cautioned that goods and services outlined in the ICOs' white papers might not be realised. Importantly, investors should invest at their own risk, after understanding the relevant risks, the content of the ICO project where the purchase of tokens is being considered, and have given enough attention to the suspicious solicitation of ICOs.

In Japan ICOs are regulated as securities, including where the ICO is contributing to a collective investment scheme.[69] In addition, it is possible that businesses launching ICOs should be aware that they may fall within the scope of the Payment Services Act (PSA) and/or the Financial Instruments and Exchange Act (FIEA), depending on how they are structured.[70] Where tokens fall under the virtual currency provisions of the PSA, then businesses providing virtual currency exchange services regularly must be registered with each local finance bureau. So far, 11 such exchanges have been approved by the JFSA. Where, however, an ICO bears the characteristics of an investment and the purchase of a token by a cryptocurrency is practically deemed as equivalent to that of legal tender, the ICO becomes subject to regulations under the FIEA. The FIEA defines an interest in collective investment schemes (CISs) as securities and would, as such, have to register as a financial service operator unless certain exemptions apply. Generally, an interest in a CIS would be an interest in specified legal vehicles contributed by investors that have rights to receive dividends or distribution of assets arising from businesses that use cash, securities, or other specified assets.

In August 2017, Japanese Bitcoin exchange Zaif operator Tech Bureau launched a platform known as Comsa, which has since seen large-scale investment. This is a one-stop solution that includes the creation of a multi-language white paper, pre-configured token sale dashboard, blockchain integration services, and PR services dedicated for ICOs.[71] Singapore-based Bitcoin exchange Quoine, with a strong presence in Japan, launched a global ICO known as the Qash. Both Quoine and Zaif were among the 11 Bitcoin exchanges approved by the FSA in September 2017.[63] Japanese Bitcoin exchange Coincheck has also received hundreds of requests from Chinese start ups and elsewhere asking it to list their tokens subsequent to the ICO ban in China.[72]

68 Helms, K. (2017), "Japan's Financial Services Authority clarifies stance on initial coin offerings", *Bitcoin Magazine*, 29/10/2017, https://news.bitcoin.com/japans-financial-authority-initial-coin-offerings/, accessed 02/02/2018.

69 Financial Instruments and Exchange Act of Japan 2019

70 Ibid note [69], Helms (2017).

71 Ibid note [69], Helms (2017)

72 Ibid note [69], Helms (2017).

JBA's self-regulatory standards include the maintenance of a cold wallet under the consent of its related members.[73] The JBA noted with concern that maintenance of the cold wallet was delayed, causing an illegal outflow of funds. The JBA further observed that the JFSA had alerted representatives of each cryptocurrency exchange regarding their security based on the possibility of cyberattack. For the future, the JBA, in order to appropriately secure the security of cryptocurrency exchange traders, will establish stricter voluntary regulations and seek compliance with members.

Despite the latest Coincheck hacking and the earlier Mt. Gox scandal, Japan has not retreated when it comes to virtual currencies, and, in particular, Bitcoin. The country responds with stringent KYC requirements and new ICO guidelines. It tempers this with an open invitation to exchange owners, entrepreneurs, crypto pioneers, and Bitcoin enthusiasts that the county is open for the cryptocurrency business.[74] Japan's crypto regulatory position is therefore in sharp contrast to that in China, where regulators have cracked down on the market. This enables Japan to become the powerhouse of the cryptocurrency market.[75]

Japan has also shown that it is capable of a rapid response to new technological innovation. Responding to the Coincheck hack, the JFSA ordered the FSHO and Bitstation exchanges, based in Yokohama and Nagoya, respectively, to halt their operations for a month, and another five other exchanges, including Coincheck (already facing sanctions and told to submit a report by 22 March 2018), to improve on their business practices. The stolen NEM coins in Coincheck were stored in online hot wallets, as against the more secure offline cold wallets generally recommended. Though Coincheck has pledged to reimburse around US$400 million (as against the US$530 million lost) to all those affected, it is unclear how and at what point in time the reimbursements would occur.

In the PSA, Japan became the first country to provide a legal definition of *cryptocurrencies*, namely:[76]

> (1) [P]roperty value that can be used as payment for the purchase or rental of goods or provision of services by unspecified persons, that can be purchased from or sold to unspecified persons, and that is transferable via an electronic data processing system; or

73 Helms, K. (2018), "Japanese crypto exchanges strengthen self-regulation following Coincheck hack", *Bitcoin Magazine*, 29/01/2018, https://news.bitcoin.com/japanese-crypto-exchanges-self-regulation-coincheck-hack/, accessed 02/02/2018.

74 Ygami, K. (2017), "Japan: A forward-thinking Bitcoin nation", *Forbes*, 02/11/2017, www.forbes.com/sites/outofasia/2017/11/02/japan-a-forward-thinking-bitcoin-nation/, accessed 02/02/2018

75 Graham, L. (2017), "As China cracks down, Japan is fast becoming the powerhouse of the Bitcoin market", *CNBC*, 29/09/2017, www.cnbc.com/2017/09/29/bitcoin-exchanges-officially-recognized-by-japan.html, accessed 02/02/2018.

76 Comply Advantage (2018), "Japan cryptocurrency regulations", *Comply Advantage*, 04/07/2018, https://complyadvantage.com/insights/cryptocurrency-regulations-around-world/cryptocurrency-regulations-japan/, accessed 08/07/2018

(2) property value that can be mutually exchangeable for the above property value with unspecified persons and is transferable via an electronic data processing system.[77]

The Act also states that *cryptocurrency* is limited to property values that are stored electronically on electronic devices; currency and currency-denominated assets are excluded.[78] Additionally, under the PSA, only business operators registered with a competent local finance bureau are allowed to operate cryptocurrency exchange businesses.[79] "Deemed dealers" must register, and existing ones cannot expand until registered. Their websites must disclose their registration status.

The FSA has adopted an essentially positive approach. To quote Toshihide Endo[80]: "We would like to see it [cryptocurrency] grow under appropriate regulation". Additionally, for now, Japan appears to be exploring a CBDC.[81] Research has begun evaluating the options between account-based and token-based CBDCs, what other central banks such as from China are doing, and the potential of CBDC.[82]

Interestingly, many facets of the country's new legislation were incorporated in the IOSCO document and circulated in the G20 June 2019 meeting. The G20 leaders jointly issued a declaration on cryptoassets at the end of the June 2019 Osaka summit, reaffirming that cryptoassets do not pose a threat to global financial stability and that further work would be undertaken by standard-setting bodies. The Virtual Asset Service Providers summit, or V20, held in Osaka at the same time, announced that a group of national trade associations representing virtual assets service providers executed an MOU to establish an association to provide a global, unified voice for the virtual asset industry that would assist in establishing mechanisms to engage with government agencies and the FATF to ensure that their best interests are understood and valued globally.[83] The communique pertaining to cryptoassets evidently suggests that the G20, as a whole, has not taken on board Japan's regulatory framework and opted to wait

77 Payment Services Act Article 2, para 5.

78 Ibid note [78], Payment Services Act Article 2, para 5.

79 Payment Services Act Articles 63–2 & 63–3. The FSA is the regulatory agency that handles cryptocurrency transactions as a result of the cabinet delegating its authority over most of the relevant matters under the Payment Services Act, that is, Article 104. See also "Details of screening for new registration application as virtual currency exchange service provider", *FSA*, 10/02/2017, www.fsa.go.jp/en/news/2017/20170930-1/02.pdf, accessed 24/02/2019.

80 Yakubowski, M. (2018), "Japan's financial regulator wants crypto industry to 'grow under appropriate regulation", *Coin Telegraph*, 23/08/2018, https://cointelegraph.com/news/japans-financial-regulator-wants-crypto-industry-to-grow-under-appropriate-regulation, accessed 05/03/2019

81 Fintech News HK (2019), "Japan's central bank explores a central bank backed digital currency", *Fintech News Hong Kong*, 01/03/2019, https://fintechnews.hk/8652/blockchain/japan-central-bank-backed-digital-currency/, accessed 05/03/2019.

82 Yanagawa, N. & Yamaoka, H. (2019), "Digital innovation, data revolution and central bank digital currency", *Bank of Japan Working Paper Series No. 19-E-02/02/19*

83 Helms, K. (2019), "V20 summit concludes with promises for crypto industry", *Bitcoin.com*, 30/06/2019, https://news.bitcoin.com/v20-summit-promises-crypto-industry/, accessed 02/07/2019.

for further guidelines from the global standard setters like the FATF or the BIS. This is unsurprising. Other than the common unified stand to follow FATF's guidance for safeguards against money laundering and other related risks, most G20 members still prefer to map out their own regulatory position, despite conceding that cryptoassets are cross-border financial products requiring international co-operation to ensure effective policing.

There is no omnibus regulation governing blockchain-based tokens. The legal status of tokens under Japanese law is determined based on their functions and uses.[84] For instance, cryptoassets and utility tokens like BTC and ETG are regulated as cryptos under the Payment Services Act (PSA). Businesses operating in the business of buying, selling, or exchanging cryptoassets, including in the intermediation of such activities or in the management of cryptos for the benefit of others, are required to undergo registration as a provider of Crypto Asset Exchange Services (CAES) and a provider of CAES (CAESP).[85]

Currency-denominated stablecoins, like USDC and USDT, are regulated as electronic payment instruments (EPIs) under the PSA. Businesses partaking in the business of buying, selling, or exchanging EPIs, including in the intermediation of such activities or in the management of EPIs for the benefit of others, are required to undergo registration as an electronic payment instruments exchange service provider (EPIESP).[86] Though so-called algorithmic stablecoins that are not collateralised by fiat currency but whose values are linked to fiat currency through algorithms do not fall within the category of EPIs, as they do not qualify as currency-denominated assets,[87] these algorithmic stablecoins instead will constitute cryptoassets where they are transferable or tradeable vis-à-vis unspecified parties on a blockchain.[88]

So-called "security tokens" that represent shares, bonds, or fund interests in tokens are regulated under the Financial Instruments and Exchange Act (FIEA) as electronically recorded transferable rights (ERTRs) to be indicated on securities (ERTRIS) and so on. Businesses partaking in the business of offering, including in the handling of such offers, buying, selling, or exchanging ERTRIS, including in the intermediation of such activities, is required to undergo registration as type 1 financial instruments business operator (type 1 FIBOs).[89] Other than those alluded to earlier, tokens like non-fungible tokens (NFTs) that have no economic function as a means of payment, owing to their unique characteristics, will not be regulated in principle under the present regulatory framework.[90]

84 Nagase, T. et al. (2023), "Blockchain & cryptocurrency regulation 2024 (Japan Chapter)", *Anderson Mori & Tomotsune*, 10/11/2023, www.mondaq.com/fin-tech/1386476/blockchain-cryptocurrency-regulation-2024-japan-chapter, accessed 20/12/2023

85 Ibid note [85], Nagase et al. (2023)

86 Ibid note [85], Nagase et al. (2023)

87 Ibid note [85], Nagase et al. (2023)

88 Ibid note [85], Nagase et al. (2023)

89 Ibid note [85], Nagase et al. (2023)

90 Ibid note [85], Nagase et al. (2023)

8.5 Singapore's cryptoasset regulatory policy

Singapore's central bank, the MAS, has advised the public to act with extreme caution and understand the significant risks they take on where they so choose to invest in cryptocurrencies. This advice came in the back of a recent sharp rise in Bitcoin's and other virtual currencies' prices. Other pointers set out their views, including thus:[91]

1. Cryptocurrencies are not legal tender and are not issued by any government and are not backed by any asset or issuer.
2. The recent strong price surge in cryptocurrencies is driven by speculation. The risk of an equally sharp drop in prices is high. This implies that virtual currencies' investors run the risk of losing all their capital.
3. The MAS does not regulate cryptocurrencies, and there is no regulatory safeguard for investments in them. MAS regulations do not extend to the safety and soundness of virtual currency intermediaries or the proper processing of their transactions.
4. It is difficult to verify the authenticity or credibility of most operators of platforms where virtual currencies are traded, as they do not have a presence in the country.
5. Cryptocurrency transactions are generally anonymous. This makes them vulnerable to being misemployed for unlawful activities. Where a cryptocurrency intermediary is found to have used them illegally, its operations could be shut down by law enforcement agencies. There is also the risk of loss should that intermediary be hacked, as it may not have sufficiently robust security features.
6. Investors who lose money from investing in cryptocurrencies would not be able to rely on any protection afforded under legislation administered by MAS. Therefore, before investing, the public should carefully consider the claims being made about the products being offered. Where the touted ease of making significant profits sounds too good to be true, it probably is. Investors should carefully evaluate whether an investment in a virtual currency is suitable for their investment objectives and risk appetite.
7. Investors and other members of the public suspicious of fraudulent investments involving cryptocurrencies should report such cases to the authorities.

At one point,[92] Singapore's largest bank, DBS, argued, through Chief Information Officer David Gledhill, that Bitcoin was a Ponzi scheme. The CEO

---

91 Monetary Authority of Singapore (MAS) (2017), "MAS cautions against investments in cryptocurrencies", *MAS Media Release*, 19/12/2017, www.mas.gov.sg/news/media-releases/2017/mas-cautions-against-investments-in-cryptocurrencies, accessed 02/02/2018.

92 Chandran, N. (2017), "One of Asia's largest banks says Bitcoin is 'a Ponzi scheme'", *CNBC*, 15/11/2017, www.cnbc.com/video/2017/11/15/one-of-asias-largest-banks-says-bitcoin-is-aponzi-scheme.html, accessed 02/02/2018.

of the MAS highlighted cryptocurrencies' potential beyond a store of value applications, such as cross-border payments.[93] He clarified, though, that where cross-border remittance was going through a blockchain using cryptocurrencies, it could yield benefits. He further clarified that this ought to be the question, rather than whether Bitcoin or Ether was rising or falling in value. He insisted that very few jurisdictions regulate cryptocurrencies, and most have taken the approach that the currency itself does not pose the risk that warrants regulation. Instead, it is the activity around it, such as Bitcoin exchanges or trading platforms, that would see regulation. This is why the central bank's focus is to look at the activities surrounding virtual currencies and ask the questions on the kind of risks they pose and which risks would require a regulatory response.

The CEO of MAS further argued that it is a known fact that cryptocurrencies are often abused for illicit financing purposes. Consequently, the MAS wants to have anti–money laundering controls and controls to counter the financing of terrorism in place. Singapore already requires cryptocurrency intermediaries, such as exchange operators, to comply with requirements to combat money laundering and terrorism financing. MAS will probably formalise this in the forthcoming Payment Services Regulation.[81] MAS further mentioned that where ICOs include the promise of a dividend or other economic benefits, they resemble regular securities offerings and would therefore be covered by Singapore's Securities and Futures Act. Other business models might avoid these security issues, and it would need to be examined case by case to ascertain which ones would come under regulatory ambit and which ones could stay outside.

An early example of a Singapore ICO is TenX,[94] which raised S$80 million in June 2017. This Singapore-based start-up pitched its debit card as an instant converter of multiple digital currencies into fiat money, including dollars, yen, and euros. MAS ICO guidelines say that offers or issues of digital tokens may be regulated by MAS where the digital tokens are capital market products under the Securities and Futures Act (SFA).[95] Capital markets products include any securities, derivatives contracts, and contracts or arrangement for purposes of leverage foreign exchange trading.

Other aspects of the MAS ICO guidelines include the following:[96]

1. The MAS will examine the structure and characteristics of, including the rights attached to, a digital token in ascertaining if that digital token is a kind of capital market product under the SFA.

93 Chanjaroen, C., Tan, A. & Amin, H. (2017), "Singapore won't regulate cryptocurrencies, central bank chief says", *Bloomberg*, 24/10/2017, www.bloomberg.com/news/articles/2017-10-24/singapore-won-t-regulate-cryptocurrencies-remains-alert-to-risk, accessed 02/02/2018.

94 Ellis, J. (2017), "Singapore startup raises $80m in cryptocurrency sale; another follows suit", *Tech in Asia*, 29/06/2017, www.techinasia.com/tenx-crosscoin-ico, accessed 02/02/2018.

95 Sundarajan, S. (2017), "Singapore's central bank outlines when ICOs are and aren't securities", *Coin Desk*, 15/11/2017, www.coindesk.com/singapores-central-bank-outlines-icos-arent-securities, accessed 02/02/2018.

96 MAS (2017), "A guide to digital token offerings", *MAS*, 16/11/2017, www.mas.gov.sg/regulation/explainers/a-guide-to-digital-token-offerings, accessed 02/02/2018.

2. A digital token, for instance, may constitute a *share* when it confers or represents ownership interest in a corporation, represents liability of the token holder in the corporation, and represents mutual covenants with other token holders in the corporation; a *debenture* where it constitutes or evidences the indebtedness of the issuer of the digital token in respect of any money that is, or may be, lent to the issuer by a token holder; or a *unit* in a CIS, or an option to acquire a right or interests in a CIS. Offers of digital tokens which constitute securities or units in a CIS are subject to the same regulatory regime under Part XIII of the SFA, as offers of securities or units in a CIS, respectively, through traditional means.
3. An offer may nevertheless be exempt from the prospectus requirements where the offer is a small offer of securities of an entity or units in a CIS[97] not exceeding S$5 million or its equivalent in foreign currency within any 12-month period, the offer is a private placement offer made to not more than 50 persons within any 12-month period, the offer is made to institutional investors only, or the offer is made to accredited investors. The exemptions for a small offer, a private placement offer, and an offer made to accredited investors are, respectively, subject to certain conditions which include advertising restrictions.
4. Intermediaries who facilitate offers or issues of digital tokens include a person who operates a platform on which one or more offerors of digital tokens may make primary offers or issues of digital tokens known as a primary platform, a person who provides financial advice in respect of any digital tokens, a person who operates a platform at which digital tokens are traded, known as a trading platform. Persons operating a primary platform in Singapore in relation to digital tokens which constitute any kind of capital markets products may be carrying on business in one or more regulated activities under the SFA and, as such, must hold a capital markets services license for that regulated activity under the SFA, unless otherwise exempted. A person who provides any financial advice in respect of any digital token must be authorised to do so in respect of that type of financial advisory service or be an exempt financial adviser under the Financial Advisers Act (Cap.110) (FAA). A person who establishes or operates a trading platform in Singapore in relation to digital tokens which constitute securities or futures contracts may be establishing or operating a market. Those establishing or operating a market or holding himself as such

97 *Collective investment schemes* are defined under Section 2(1) of the SFA, where "capital market products" include any securities (which include shares, debentures, and units in a business trust) units in a collective investment scheme. For the purpose of the digital token offerings guide, the securities laws refer to the SFA and the Financial Advisers Act (FAA). MAS, on 1 August 2017, clarified that where a digital token constitutes a product regulated under the securities laws administered by it, the offer or issues of digital tokens must comply with the applicable securities laws.

must be approved by MAS as an exchange or recognised by MAS as market operators under the SFA, unless otherwise exempted.

5. Where a person operates a primary platform, or trading platform, partly in or partly outside of Singapore, the requirements of the SFA may nevertheless apply extraterritorially to the activities of that person under Section 339 of the SFA. Where a person who is based overseas engages in any activity or conduct that is intended to or likely to induce the public, or a section of the public, in Singapore to use any financial advisory service provided by the person, the person is deemed to be acting as a financial adviser in Singapore.
6. MAS emphasises that the relevant MAS notices on prevention of money laundering and countering the financing of terrorism may apply (AMT/CTF Requirements). Digital tokens performing functions which may not be within MAS's regulatory purview could be subject to other legislation for combating money laundering and terrorism financing. There are obligations to report suspicious transactions with the Suspicious Transaction Reporting Office or the Commercial Affairs Department of the Singapore Police Force.
7. MAS's new payments framework would include rules to address money laundering and terrorism financing risks relating to the dealing or exchange of cryptocurrencies for fiat or other cryptocurrencies. Such intermediaries would be required to put in place policies, procedures, and controls to address such risks. These would include requirements to conduct customer due diligence, monitor transactions, perform screening, report suspicious transactions, and keep adequate records.
8. Six illustrations are provided to further clarify the application of securities laws to offers or issues of digital tokens.
9. Entities looking to apply technology in an innovative way to provide new financial services that are, or are likely, to be regulated by MAS can apply for the regulatory sandbox. MAS would provide the appropriate regulatory support to those approved by relaxing specific legal and regulatory requirements prescribed by MAS which the applicant would otherwise be subject to for the duration of the sandbox.

MAS thus appears not to be seeking to regulate virtual currencies, except when their activities directly fall under its purview. To mitigate the challenges posed by virtual currencies being used for illicit purposes, MAS could seek to impose anti–money laundering and anti–terrorist financing requirements on intermediaries that exchange fiat for virtual currencies, such as exchanges and brokers,[98]

98 Haig, S. (2018), "Singapore to extend regulatory mandate regarding cryptocurrencies", *Bitcoin Magazine*, 12/01/2018, https://news.bitcoin.com/singapore-extend-regulatory-mandate-regarding-cryptocurrencies/, accessed 02/02/2018.

through the PSA[99] that could empower MAS to have greater jurisdiction over relevant exchanges and brokerages.

In November 2018, the MAS put forward a new regulatory framework for payment service providers. The is set out in what is now in the Payment Services Act 2019. Amongst other things, it requires crypto service providers to be treated as those providing the same services for currencies.[100] The definition of *e-money* is being extended to *e-wallets* to provide greater security for the public.

Finally, as part of an ongoing attempt to create a regulatory environment that facilitates blockchain and cryptocurrency development, a regulatory sandbox has been created along the same lines as the UK. This means that those developing new products can submit details and determine the probable regulatory position in advance.

In this connection, MAS released a consultation paper on the creation of pre-defined sandboxes, known as Sandbox Express, to complement the existing fintech regulatory sandbox launched in 2016.[101] The objective is to enable firms seeking to undertake regulated activities to embark on experiments more quickly, without having to go through existing bespoke sandbox application and approval process. Apart from co-operating with other countries similarly using regulatory sandboxes, the MAS has also joined, together with 19 other countries, the Global Financial Innovation Network initiated by the FCA in the UK.[102] The idea behind this is to help global firms interact with regulators, scale ideas, and design a framework for co-operation between financial services regulators. More recently, MAS has also urged the blockchain community from Singapore and across the world to target viable use cases for blockchain technology with deep economic or social impacts and work towards bringing them to life.[103]

Singapore's tolerant approach towards cryptoassets was demonstrated when Binance, the world's largest crypto exchange, announced on 10 July 2019 the official launch of Binance Singapore in partnership with Vertex Ventures China and Vertex Ventures Southeast Asia and India. Binance concurrently mentioned that the Singapore government exhibits an in depth understanding of

---

99 passed 22/02/19

100 Fries, T. (2019), "Monetary authority of Singapore to introduce a regulatory framework for cryptocurrency exchanges", *Tokenist*, 19/01/2019, https://tokenist.com/monetary-authority-of-singapore-to-introduce-a-regulatory-framework-for-cryptocurrency-exchanges/, accessed 25/02/2019.

101 MAS (2018), "MAS proposes new regulatory sandbox with fast-track approvals", *MAS*, 14/11/2018, www.mas.gov.sg/news/media-releases/2018/mas-proposes-new-regulatory-sandbox-with-fasttrack-approvals#:~:text=14%20November%202018-,MAS%20Proposes%20New%20Regulatory%20Sandbox%20with%20Fast%2DTrack%20Approvals,that%20was%20launched%20in%202016, accessed 5/03/2019.

102 Trulioo (2018), "A global regulatory sandbox – Collaboration, policies and solutions for cross-border compliance", *Trulioo*, 24/10/2018, www.trulioo.com/blog/global-regulatory-sandbox, accessed 5/03/2019.

103 Menon, R. (2019), "'Is the block chain a solution looking for a problem?' – Keynote Remarks by Ravi Menon, Managing Director, Monetary Authority of Singapore at CordaDay Singapore 2019 on 7th March 2019", *MAS*, 07/03/2019, www.mas.gov.sg/news/speeches/2019/is-the-blockchain-a-solution-looking-for-a-problem, accessed 8/03/2019.

cryptocurrency and is open towards financial innovation that would enable the city state to lead the next financial revolution. The city state has also prepared proposals that explicitly state that it intends to remove double taxation on various major cryptoassets, which include Bitcoin, Ethereum, and Litecoin,[104] and plans[105] to issue up to two full digital banking licences and three digital wholesale licences that would cater to SMEs and other non-retail segments. Singapore's carefully crafted, forward looking regulatory approach towards financial digital assets and so on has not gone unnoticed by the world. As mentioned earlier, the founder of the World Wide Web very recently mentioned Singapore could be one jurisdiction that could contribute to the design of appropriate regulations to deal with matters in the digital world.

Singapore thus appears to adopt a pragmatic, cautious, and tailored approach toward cryptos.[106] The country recognises the economic and social benefits of cryptos and seeks to have in place a conducive regulatory environment for its adoption within the jurisdiction's financial landscape. Concurrently, the country exercises caution in also recognising the risks arising, especially in the contexts of consumer protection and anti–money laundering/counter-financing of terrorism.[107] Accordingly, its stance is to manage these risks in a proportionate way, including through licensing, where applicable.

Cryptoassets are not treated as the equivalent of money in the jurisdiction. Cryptos, depending on their characteristics, may be treated as a regulated product, like capital market products, including securities, e-money, or a digital payment token (DPT), or as an unregulated digital token that is strictly employed for utility purposes.[108] The Monetary Authority of Singapore (MAS), or the country's central bank, thus far has not issued or backed any cryptoassets for retail use, other than partnering with participants in the industry to undertake a collaborative project (known as "Project Ubin"), to explore the use of blockchain and DLT for the clearing and settlement of payments and securities.[109] The payments network prototype developed through this initiative is envisaged to facilitate the development of a cross-border payments infrastructure, including customer applications. The completed collaborative Bank for International Settlements (BIS) innovation hub and central banks, including MAS

104 Young, J. (2019), "Exclusive: Binance officially launches crypto exchange in Singapore, sees rapid growth", *Forbes*, 09/07/2019, www.forbes.com/sites/youngjoseph/2019/07/09/exclusive-binance-officially-launches-crypto-exchange-in-singapore-sees-rapid-growth/, accessed 11/07/2019.

105 Fintech News Singapore (2019), "Monetary Authority of Singapore to issue up to 5 virtual banking licenses", *FNS*, 28/06/2019, www.mas.gov.sg/news/media-releases/2019/mas-to-issue-up-to-five-digital-bank-licences, accessed 02/07/2019.

106 Pereire, K. & Lin, Y. X. (2024), "Singapore", in Dewey, J. N. (ed.), *Blockchain & cryptocurrency laws and regulations 2024*, London, GLI

107 Ibid note [107], Pereire & Lin (2024)

108 Ibid note [107], Pereire & Lin (2024)

109 MAS (2022), "Ubin+: Advancing cross-border connectivity with wholesale digital currencies", *MAS*, 15/12/2022, www.mas.gov.sg/schemes-and-initiatives/ubin-plus, accessed 20/12/2023; MAS (2024), "Project Ubin: Central Bank Digital Money using distributed ledger technology" www.mas.gov.sg/schemes-and-initiatives/project-ubin, accessed 05/08/2024

initiative "Project Dunbar", announced earlier on 22 March 2022, is said to have demonstrated that central bank digital currencies (CBDCs) could be employed by financial institutions to transact directly with each other through a common platform.[110] Potentially, this would reduce the need for intermediaries, as well as the costs and time needed for the processing of cross-border transactions.

Aside from the November 2022 Ubin+ initiative, MAS has also implemented "Project Orchid".[111] This aims to establish the technical infrastructure for the design and development of a retail CBDC system. However, MAS has been concentrating relatively more on wholesale instead of retail CBDCs, as the issue of financial inclusion is not urgent in Singapore. It is also testing the potential of asset tokenisation across further types of financial assets, such as digital structured products, tokenised investment instruments, tokenised asset-backed securities, tokenised bonds, and tokenised bank liabilities, via industry pilots in co-operation with financial institutions, and under the more recent "Project Guardian".[112] This is envisaged to contribute to enhancing liquidity and inclusivity in the financial markets, apart from improving the efficiency, affordability, and accessibility of financial services. Singapore, as alluded to earlier, has issued crypto trading guidelines, approved amendments to the Payment Services Act (PSA) 2019, as well as the Financial Services and Markets (FSM) Act, to address additional risks, including those to retail investors and money laundering. With regards to judicial evolution, the Singapore High Court held in a 2023 landmark case[113] that a cryptoasset is a personal property right that can be claimed or enforced by action besides being capable of being subject to a trust.

Under Singapore's Payment Services Act 2019, cryptos are either regulated or unregulated. However, owing to cryptos having a wide menu of attributes, characteristics, and features, some cryptos could fall beyond the confines of the said legislation, while yet others could be subject to the purview of Singapore's Securities and Futures Act (SFA) 2001, where their characteristics and features are adequately similar to those of capital markets products or securities as defined

110 El Dimachki, M. (2024), "The Singapore innovation hub centre ", *BIS Innovation Hub Centre Singapore*, 30/05/2024, www.bis.org/about/bisih/locations/sg.htm, accessed 06/08/2024

111 MAS (2022), "Project Orchid", *MAS*, 31/10/2022, www.mas.gov.sg/schemes-and-initiatives/project-orchid, accessed 30/05/2024; King, J. (2023), "Singapore's Project Orchid lets interoperable currency blook: Is purpose bound money a game changer for the future of digital money? James King reports", *The Banker*, 11/07/2023, www.thebanker.com/Singapore-s-Project-Orchid-lets-interoperable-currency-bloom-1689068489, accessed 20/12/2023

112 , MAS (2024), "Project Guardian", *MAS*, 27/06/2024, www.mas.gov.sg/schemes-and-initiatives/project-guardian, accessed 18/06/2024

113 Cramer, S. et al. (2023), "Singapore High Court recognizes cryptoassets as property", *Clifford Chance*, 01/08/2023, www.cliffordchance.com/insights/resources/blogs/talking-tech/en/articles/2023/08/singapore-high-court-recognises-crypto-assets-as-property.html, accessed 20/12/2023. The Singapore High Court, in *ByBit Fintech Ltd v Ho Kai Xin and others (2023)*, held that Singapore law will recognize cryptoassets as a form of property capable of being held on trust. This provides clarity on the legal nature of cryptoassets to confirm that parties in cases involving cryptoassets may apply conventional common law doctrines to protect their assets. This court decision aligns with the ruling in other common law jurisdictions, including that of *Re Gatecoin Limited (2023) HKCFI 914* at the Hong Kong Court of First Instance.

in the SFA.[114] Hence, it would be prudent for those embarking on crypto-linked activities to seek legal opinion whether and how these activities would be regulated under Singapore law.

The PSA, for instance, requires a person engaged in the business of providing payment service to secure a payment license. The legislation defines seven payment services, namely, money changing services, digital payment token (DPT) service, merchant acquisition service, domestic money transfer service, cross-border money transfer service, and e-money issuance service.[115] A crypto could fall within the definition of "e-money" or "digital payment token", and therefore, a person partaking on a business of providing a payment service pertaining to such a crypto would need to secure a license under the PSA. *E-money* is defined as

> any electronically stored monetary value that is denominated in any currency, pegged by its issuer to any currency, has been paid for in advance to enable the making of payment transactions through the use of a payment account, is accepted by a person other than its issuer and represents a claim on its issuer, but does not include any deposit accepted in Singapore, from any person in Singapore.[116]

Where a person issues e-money for the purpose of enabling another person to effect payment transactions, the former would be undertaking an e-money issuance service.[117]

A *digital payment token* (DPT) is defined as

> any digital representation of value (other than an excluded digital representation of value) that is expressed as a unit, is not denominated in any currency, and is not pegged by its issuer to any currency, is, or is intended to be a medium of exchange accepted by the public, or a section of the public, as payment for goods or services or for the discharge of a debt, can be transferred, stored or traded electronically, and satisfies such other characteristics as MAS may prescribe.[118]

A *DPT service* may be a service of engaging in DPTs or a service of enabling the exchange of DPTs. "Dealing in digital payment tokens" refers to transactions of that DPT in exchange for any money or any other DPT other than enabling the exchange of DPTs and accepting or using any DPT as a means of payment for the provision of goods and services.[119] "Facilitating the exchange of DPTs" refers to

> establishing or operating a DPT exchange in case where the person that establishes or operates that DPT exchange, for the purposes of an offer or invitation to buy or sell any DPT in exchange for any money or DPT, comes into possession of any money or any DPT, whether at the time that offer or invitation is made or otherwise.[120]

114 Ibid note [107], Pereire & Lin (2024)
115 Ibid note [107], Pereire & Lin (2024)
116 Ibid note [107], Pereire & Lin (2024)
117 Ibid note [107], Pereire & Lin (2024)
118 Ibid note [107], Pereire & Lin (2024)
119 Ibid note [107], Pereire & Lin (2024)
120 Ibid note [107], Pereire & Lin (2024)

The preceding stipulations aside, certain cryptos that fall within the definition of limited-purpose DPT should not be regulated under the PSA.[121] A *limited-purpose DPT* means

> any non-monetary customer loyalty or reward point, any in game asset, or any similar digital representation of value that cannot be returned to its issuer, transferred or sold in exchange for money and may only be used in the case of a non-monetary customer loyalty or reward point for the payment or part payment of, or in exchange for goods or services, or both, provided by its issuer or any merchant specified by its issuer or in the case of an in game assets for the payments or in exchange for, virtual assets or virtual services within an online game, or any similar thing within that is part of or in relation to an online game.[122]

In this connection, a *non-monetary customer loyalty or reward point* means

> any digital representation of value, by whatever name called, that is not denominated in any currency, is issued as part of a scheme, the dominant purpose of which is to promote the purchase of goods, or the use of services, provided by its issuer or any merchant specified by its issuer, is issued to a person upon the purchase of goods, or the use of services, provided by its issuer or any merchant specified by its issuer, is used for the payment or part payment of, or in exchange for goods or services (or both) provided by its issuer or ant merchant specified by its issuer and is not part of a financial product.[123]

There are two kinds of licenses applicable pertaining to cryptos under the PSA. These refer to the standard payment institution license (SPIL) and the major payment institution license (MPIL).[124] A person required to obtain a license for certain payment services under the PSA would need to obtain an MPIL where the average over a calendar year of the total value of all payment transactions that are accepted, processed, or executed by the licensee in a month is more than S$3 million or its equivalent in a foreign currency for any of those payment services, or S$6 million or its equivalent in a foreign currency for two or more of those person services.[125]

A person required to obtain a license for an e-money issuance service would need to obtain an MPIL where (1) the sum of the average, over a calendar year, of the total value in one day of all e-money that is stored in any payment account issued by the licensee to a person whom that licensee has determined, according to such criteria as MAS may specify by notice in writing, to be a resident in Singapore and the average, over a calendar year, of the total value in one day of all e-money that is issued in Singapore and is stored in any payment account issued by the licensee to any person whom the licensee has not determined, according to such criteria as the authority may specify by notice in writing, to be

121 Ibid note [107], Pereire & Lin (2024)
122 Ibid note [107], Pereire & Lin (2024)
123 Ibid note [107], Pereire & Lin (2024)
124 Ibid note [107], Pereire & Lin (2024)
125 Ibid note [107], Pereire & Lin (2024)

a resident outside Singapore exceeds S$5 million, or (2) the average over a calendar year, or the total value in one day, of all specified e-money that is issued by the licensee exceeds S$5 million or its equivalent in foreign currency.[126] Except for the alluded to circumstances, the payment service provider would only need to obtain a SPIL.[127] Eligibility requirements as prescribed by the PSA include a minimum base capital of S$100,000 for the SPIL and S$250,000 for the MPIL. The license applicant is also required to have at least one executive director who is a Singapore resident or permanent resident and at least one non-executive director who is a Singapore citizen or permanent resident and at least one executive director who is a Singapore employment pass holder.[128] Also, the license applicant must have a permanent place of business or a registered office in Singapore, at which it must keep books of all transactions pertaining to the payment services it provides.[129] Additionally, a payment institution needs to appoint at least one person to be present at its permanent place of business or registered office to address any queries or complaints.[130]

Cryptos could potentially have similar features with the traditional kinds of capital market products, such as securities, units in collective investment schemes, derivative contracts, and spot foreign exchange contracts, for the purposes of leveraged foreign exchange trading. *Securities* refer to shares, units in a business trust, or any instrument conferring or representing a legal or beneficial ownership in a corporation, partnership, or limited liability partnership and debentures.[131] Therefore, traditional requirements could also apply to such cryptos, depending on the kind of activity that is being undertaken pertaining to such cryptos. For instance, for cryptos that are perceived as capital markets products, a person who, whether as principal or agent, carries on or holds himself as carrying on a business, "making or offering to make with any person, or inducing or attempting to induce any person to enter into or to offer into any agreement for or with a view to acquiring, disposing of, entering into, effecting, arranging, subscribing for, or underwriting any capital market products", would need to hold a capital markets services license for dealing in capital markets products, while a person who makes an offer of cryptocurrencies that constitute securities or securities-based derivatives contracts would need to prepare and lodge a prospectus with MAS.[132]

For cryptos that are asset-backed in nature, there is the potential of trading in such cryptos constituting spot commodity trading under the Commodity Trading Act 1992, and a license would need to be obtained so as to engage in such an activity.[133] Cryptos that demonstrate the feature of products regulated under

126 Ibid note [107], Pereire & Lin (2024)
127 Ibid note [107], Pereire & Lin (2024)
128 Ibid note [107], Pereire & Lin (2024)
129 Ibid note [107], Pereire & Lin (2024)
130 Ibid note [107], Pereire & Lin (2024)
131 Ibid note [107], Pereire & Lin (2024)
132 Ibid note [107], Pereire & Lin (2024)
133 Ibid note [107], Pereire & Lin (2024)

Singapore laws are not prohibited in the jurisdiction, but the parties that undertake activities pertaining to such cryptos would have to ensure compliance with the applicable laws.[134] Parties that engage on business activities pertaining to cryptos that do not indicate features of the products regulated under Singapore law would be able to do so without restriction, subject to compliance with other general laws of Singapore.[135]

To keep abreast of developments in the global crypto industry and account for the opportunities and risks that accompany these developments,[136] MAS continually updates, refreshes, or reboots the jurisdiction's regulations. For example, MAS issued on 3 July 2023 a consultation paper to invite public feedback on the draft amendments to the Payments Services Regulations (PSRs) 2019 that would require DPT service providers to safekeep customer assets under a statutory trust and restrict DPT service providers from facilitating lending and staking of DPT tokens by their retail customers.[137] The former seeks to enable the recovery of the customers' monies in the event of the service provider's insolvency. Another consultation paper proposing requirements for DPT service providers to address unfair trading practices was also issued on 3 July 2023.[138]

8.6 South Korea's cryptoasset regulatory policy

South Korea has a population of around 50 million people and a GDP of about US$1.52 trillion, or GDP per capita of US$29,806, making it the thirteenth largest in the world.[139] It is estimated that the Japanese and South Korean cryptocurrency markets account for about 40% of global Bitcoin trades and 10% of global Ethereum trade.[140] Cryptocurrency exchanges in both economies have millions of active traders. Some 80% of South Korean investors are estimated to have profited from investments in cryptocurrencies, with almost one-third of salaried Koreans having an average of US$5000 in crypto, a relatively huge adoption of an untested investment vehicle based almost solely on speculation.[141]

---

134 Ibid note [107], Pereire & Lin (2024)

135 Ibid note [107], Pereire & Lin (2024)

136 Ibid note [107], Pereire & Lin (2024)

137 MAS (2023), "Consultation paper on proposed amendments to the payment services regulations", *MAS*, 03/07/2023, www.mas.gov.sg/-/media/mas/news-and-publications/consultation-papers/2023-consultation-paper-on-proposed-amendments-to-the-ps-regs/consultation-paper-on-proposed-amendments-to-the-payment-services-regulations.pdf, accessed 20/12/2023

138 MAS (2023), "Consultation paper on proposed measures on market integrity in digital payment token services", *MAS*, 03/07/2023, www.mas.gov.sg/publications/consultations/2023/consultation-paper-on-proposed-measures-on-market-integrity-in-dpt-services, accessed 20/12/2023

139 Global Finance (2018), "South Korea GDP and economic data", *Global Finance Magazine*, 08/03/2018, www.gfmag.com/global-data/country-data/south-korea-gdp-country-report, accessed 09/03/2018.

140 Young, J. (2018), "China's largest Bitcoin exchange heads to Japan and South Korea with major bank deal", *CCN*, 04/31/2018, www.ccn.com/chinas-largest-bitcoin-exchange-is-reallocating-to-japan-and-south-korea-with-major-bank-deal/, accessed 02/02/2018.

141 Jo, H. (2017), "In a country known for its 'Bitcoin zombies', one-third of workers are crypto investors", *Quartz*, 28/12/2017, https://qz.com/1166103/a-third-of-south-korean-workers-have-invested-in-cryptocurrencies-like-bitcoin, accessed 02/02/2018.

The hype in cryptocurrency/asset investing and trading in South Korea started with the government officially legalising Bitcoin service providers in July 2017 to facilitate payments, transfer, and trade.[142] It was also envisaged at that time that the country was on the verge of providing a regulatory framework for Bitcoin trading platform and exchanges. A South Korean lawmaker proposed a bill that aims to revise the Electronic Financial Transactions Act such that traders, brokers, or other business entities involved in cryptocurrency transactions would be required to get regulatory approval from the Financial Services Commission (FSC). A key requirement includes the retention of capital of at least $436,300 and data processing facilities.

Thus, while the country's cryptocurrency industry has not been fully regulated, the government officially legalised Bitcoin service providers to facilitate payments, transfers, and trades. *The Korea Herald*, meanwhile, reported that the newly revised South Korean Foreign Exchange Transactions Act started to facilitate fintech companies and cryptocurrency service providers to be approved by the Financial Supervisory Service, the financial regulator in South Korea.[143] The Bitcoin-approved remittance method allows fintech companies to process up to $20,000 worth of South Korean won in Bitcoin for users. This contributed to significant growth in the demand for virtual currency trading in the country, as it did in neighbouring Philippines. Already, according to market data sources, the South Korean Bitcoin exchange processes over 14% of global Bitcoin trades, the third largest market, behind the United States and Japan.[99]

News broke in August 2017 of North Korean hackers targeting South Korean cryptocurrency exchanges in retaliation to new sanctions imposed by the UN.[144] It appears that North Korea has repeatedly acted this way to circumvent the new sanctions, so as to obtain funds to finance its nuclear and related initiatives. A security firm, FireEye, revealed in a threat research paper that it has found evidence to link various cryptocurrency exchange hacking attacks to North Korea, including the one that bankrupted Youbit VC Exchange.[145] By the second week of December 2017, rumours started to emerge of the South Korean government planning to impose stricter regulations. There were then rumours that this would escalate into an outright ban on cryptocurrency exchanges as a way to cool down the digital currency craze, especially after the prime minister's warning that it might corrupt the nation's youth and that crypto could operate as a gateway

142 Young, J. (2017), "South Korea officially legalizes Bitcoin, huge market for traders", *Coin Telegraph*, 21/07/2017, https://cointelegraph.com/news/south-korea-officially-legalizes-bitcoin-huge-market-for-traders, accessed 02/02/2018.

143 Ibid note [143], Young (2017).

144 Althauser, J. (2017), "North Korean Hackers reportedly attack Bitcoin exchange in South Korea", *Coin Telegraph*, 28/08/2017, https://cointelegraph.com/news/north-korean-hackers-reportedly-attack-bitcoin-exchange-in-south-korea, accessed 02/02/2018.

145 Young, J. (2017), "North Korea accused of hacking South Korean Bitcoin exchange Youbit", *Coin Telegraph*, 21/12/2017, https://cointelegraph.com/news/north-korea-accused-of-hackingsouth-korean-bitcoin-exchange-youbit, accessed 02/02/2018.

to pyramid schemes and speculative investment when left unchecked.[146] However, by this time, South Korea had already surpassed its neighbour China in cryptocurrency trading.[147] The government groups represented in the Virtual Currency Task Force and the FCS were apparently divided on the matter, with some fearing the stifling of cryptoassets and fintech innovation. However, the FCS chairman confirmed that any decision to prohibit transactions must have a legal basis.[148] Investors welcome the idea of regulation as they expect this to help the government process what is happening while simultaneously making it more legitimate for bigger financial institutions to put funds into cryptocurrencies. The country presently bans financial institutions from dealing with them.

As far as ICOs are concerned, it is clear that their ban remains. In the meantime, six safeguards are being pushed forth for operating exchanges. Such conditions include confirming the user's real name, submitting proof of income, doing face-to-face interviews for compliance with KYC requirements, as well as providing cryptographic keys to set up anti–money laundering systems, including separating fiat currency accounts and supplying sufficient investment warnings.[105] These are expected to weed out criminal participants and may thus assist in making cryptocurrencies part of the marketplace. The country demonstrated considerable crypto enthusiasm compared to other South-East Asian states, as Bitcoin was trading at a $3,500 premium in South Korean exchanges compared to the rest of the world. This could partly be due to the limited liquidity or supply of Bitcoin, coupled with the strong demand from the finance sector.[106]

The news of a complete cryptocurrency ban surfaced again after a statement from the Ministry of Justice that the government was preparing a bill to ban trading of cryptocurrency on domestic exchanges.[149] Responding to the market's sharp reaction to the announcement, the Presidential Office said hours later that a ban on the country's cryptocurrency exchanges had not yet been finalised, though it was one of the measures being considered.[108] Subsequently, the Finance Ministry clarified that discussions were proceeding on how the government could reasonably regulate cryptocurrency trading. It clarified further that a balanced perspective is necessary, as blockchain technology has high relevance to many industries, including security and logistics. Even were there to be an agreement to move forward with a draft bill to ban cryptocurrency trading, this would require a majority vote in the country's National Assembly before it could be enacted into law, and such a process could take a considerable time.

146 Ambler, P. (2017), "South Korea is not banning Bitcoin trade, financial regulators clarify", *Forbes*, 12/12/2017, www.forbes.com/sites/pamelaambler/2017/12/12/south-korea-is-not-banning-bitcoin-trade-financial-regulators-clarify/#:~:text=Don't%20panic%20just%20yet,down%20the%20digital%20currency%20craze, accessed 02/02/2018.

147 Pauw, C. (2018), "South Korea and crypto regulations, explained", *Coin Telegraph*, 06/02/2018, https://cointelegraph.com/explained/south-korea-and-crypto-regulations-explained, accessed 10/02/2018.

148 Ibid note [147], Ambler (2017).

149 Kim, C. & Kim, D. (2018), "South Korea plans to ban cryptocurrency trading, rattles market", *Reuters*, 11/01/2018, www.reuters.com/article/technology/south-korea-plans-to-ban-cryptocurrency-trading-rattles-market-idUSKBN1F0, 02/02/2018.

South Korea is the third largest Bitcoin trading market in the world, after Japan and the United States. There is a particular concern in that cryptocurrency trading in South Korea is highly speculative and their prices are slightly higher than elsewhere in the world. South Korean authorities have taken steps to limit speculation in the market, including prohibiting cryptocurrency exchanges from issuing new trading accounts, as well as talk of taxing capital gains arising from trading.[150]

The South Korean government later announced that they would be taxing cryptocurrency exchanges at 24.2%, in line with the South Korean tax code for all corporations that make an annual income of over 20 billion Korean won. Apart from banning anonymous trading, there would also be a ban on foreigners and minors from opening new accounts.

It is worth mentioning in this respect that major South Korean banks provide local cryptocurrency exchanges with virtual bank accounts that traders and investors could use to deposit or withdraw large amounts of Korean won without having to use actual bank accounts, which are costly and time-consuming. This was one of the factors that fuelled the crypto craze in the country. The government has frozen the opening of new virtual accounts, and virtual currency traders will not be allowed to make deposits into their cryptocurrency exchange wallets unless the name of their virtual currency exchange matches that of their bank accounts.[151] The financial authorities have also requested relevant exchanges to overhaul their KYC and AML systems.[111]

Meanwhile, South Korea's Financial Services Commission (FSC) confirmed that new measures to tackle cryptocurrency speculation have been implemented on 23 January 2018 via a newly released document that, amongst others, include the following:[152]

1. The guideline requires financial institutions to conduct enhanced due diligence (EDD) in transactions with cryptocurrency exchanges to ensure users' money are in safe hands. The EDD requires banks to verify additional information for cryptocurrency exchanges, the purpose of financial transactions and the source of money, details about services that the exchanges provided, whether the exchanges are using real-name accounts, and whether the exchanges verify their users' identifications.
2. The guidelines identify types of financial transactions deemed money laundering using virtual currencies. For example, a user makes deposits or withdrawals of more than KRW 10 million or KRW 20 million per week, or a company or organisation deposits or withdraws their

150 Ibid note [150], Kim & Kim (2018).

151 Ibid note [148], Pauw (2018)

152 Financial Services Commission (FSC) (2018), "Financial measures to curb speculation in cryptocurrency trading", *FSC Press Release*, 23/01/2018, www.fsc.go.kr/eng/pr010101/22173, accessed 02/02/2018.

money from bank accounts to trade virtual currencies. These all constitute a kind of suspicious transaction for money laundering, which prompts banks to submit a suspicious transaction report to the Korea Financial Intelligence Unit.

3. The guidelines mandate banks to refuse to offer accounts to cryptocurrency exchanges if they do not provide their users' ID information. Banks can also reject transactions if they are deemed to be having a high risk of money laundering.
4. The guidelines require financial institutions to strengthen their internal controls relating to cryptocurrency and share information regarding cryptocurrency exchanges with each other.
5. The FSC expects the measures as announced to reduce room for cryptocurrency transactions to be exploited for illegal activities, such as crime, money laundering, and tax evasion. These measures are expected to have the effects of forcing out those exchanges with high risk of money laundering and prevent speculative money or illegal funds from flowing into cryptocurrency trading through bank accounts.
6. The FSC stresses that the guidelines are not intended to formally institutionalise cryptocurrency exchanges or facilitate virtual currency trading through the exchanges.

After initially drifting towards strict cryptocurrency regulation, South Korea now appears to be tilting towards normalisation, as if in response to recent US regulators' comments that they are some distance from developing a complete regulatory framework for cryptocurrencies and the view of EU lawmakers that a holistic cryptocurrency regulation is fairly low priority. In almost all parts of the world, its regulation as a general asset class has still not evolved. This is mainly because they do not fit neatly into any one category, with some crypto issues appearing to be currencies, some debt paper, some equities, some commodities, some derivatives, and others not fitting easily into pre-existing legal categories.

Participants in the cryptocurrency space in South Korea said the steps taken by the authorities were positive. Julian Hosp, co-founder and president of VC start-up TenX, stated that this could be the start of a crackdown on anonymity and the illegal use cases that some cryptocurrencies have faced.[153] John Sarson, managing partner at Blockchain Momentum,[154] is of the view that protocols to protect investors have been what the cryptocurrency markets have been missing, and this is what the South Korean legislation seeks to implement.

There seems to be a dichotomy between the extremely cautious view of the government so far and that of the population. In January 2018, 200,000 people

153 Cheang, M. (2018), "New cryptocurrency rules just came into effect in South Korea", *CNBC*, 30/01/2018, www.cnbc.com/2018/01/29/south-korea-cryptocurrency-regulations-come-into-effect.html, accessed 02/02/2018.

154 A firm investing in cryptocurrencies and blockchain-based businesses.

signed a petition asking that the government's crypto regulatory approach be ended. Matters relaxed on 30 October 2018, when the FSC cleared banks to work with crypto exchanges by providing virtual bank accounts. Banks were only permitted to reject exchanges if they failed to satisfy the money laundering laws. In early 2019, 7 of the 21 cryptocurrency exchanges who applied had their security policies approved.[155]

There has already been one legal dispute. In *Coins Exchange v Nongyhup Bank* (2018),[156] the bank had unilaterally terminated the banking facilities of the exchange, claiming that in so doing they had followed FSC guidelines. The court disagreed and determined that the banking facilities had to be continued. The same bank also had a legal dispute with a crypto exchange, Bithumb, withdrawing facilities after the exchange suffered two hacking attacks. This was amicably resolved after the exchange overhauled its security and internal management systems.

Therefore, as shown in the regulatory shift in South Korea, a tilt towards a light-touch regulatory approach or the use of self-regulatory initiatives in other situations could be the way forward. That said, there is still a blanket ban on ICOs, though in what may be a sign that the wind is starting to change direction, Min Byung-du, Chairman of Korea's National Policy Committee, called for their adoption "with practical, positive and efficient regulatory frameworks".[157]

South Korea is progressing with regulation for crypto and other virtual assets subsequent to the passing of the Act on the Protection of Virtual Asset Users (Act No. 19563) (VAUPA),[158] promulgated on 18 July 2023. The legislation provides stronger protections for users by including requirements around recordkeeping and transparency.[159] The financial authorities have published guidelines[160] for listing virtual assets. South Korea's Financial Services Commission (FSC) announced that the legislation is intended "to establish a sound order in the virtual asset market and ensure protection for users". Cryptoasset exchanges responded by strengthening their compliance control systems to prepare for the

155 Tomasicchio, A. (2019), "South Korea: 7 crypto exchanges and their security policies have been approved", *The Cryptonomist*, 11/01/2020, https://en.cryptonomist.ch/2019/01/11/south-korea-crypto-exchanges-security-policies/, accessed 07/02/2020.

156 Central District Court's 50th Civil Affairs Division, South Korea.

157 Young, J. (2018), "State of regulation in South Korea: Banks required to provide fair services to crypto exchanges", *Coin Telegraph*, 14/11/2018, https://cointelegraph.com/news/state-of-regulation-in-south-korea-banks-required-to-provide-fair-services-to-crypto-exchanges, accessed 25/02/2019

158 https://perma.cc/6VMU-AYVP, accessed 17/07/2024

159 Shine, I. (2024), "Cryptocurrency regulations are changing across the globe. Here's what you need to know", *World Economic Forum (WEF)*, 02/05/2024, www.weforum.org/agenda/2024/05/global-cryptocurrency-regulations-changing/, accessed 15/07/2024

160 Park, HY (2024), "If there is a history of hacking, listing is prohibited" . . . Authorities' coin listing standards are released. Authorities to release virtual asset listing guidelines in late April to early May. Some criteria can be 'skipped' if traded on a 'legitimate' overseas exchange for more than 2 years", *News1 Korea*, 04/05/2024, www.news1.kr/finance/blockchain-fintech/5375227, accessed 15/07/2024

law going into effect.[161] The legislation features four key aspects, namely, what are "virtual assets covered by the statute; protection of users' assets; regulation of unfair trade practices; and supervision, sanctions and penalties".[162]

The said legislation defines *virtual assets* broadly as "electronic certificates (including all associated rights) that have economic value and that can be traded or transferred electronically" but excludes certain assets, like products regulated under other statutes, and digital currencies issued by the Bank of Korea.[163] With regards to non-fungible tokens (NFTs), the FSC and the Financial Supervisory Service of South Korea announced new guidelines to clarify the application of the Virtual Asset User Protection Act 2024 (VAUPA) to NFTs.[164]

The new statute prohibits the use of material nonpublic information (Art. 10, Para. 1), market price manipulation (Art. 10, Paras. 2, 3), and acts of unfair trading that would disturb market order (Art. 10, Para. 4). These provisions are similar to the provisions in the Financial Investment Services and Markets Act.[165] Further, the new statute prohibits discretionary blocking of deposits or withdrawals of virtual assets (Art. 11) and will need crypto exchanges to create mechanisms to monitor and report suspicious activities to financial authorities (Art. 12).[166]

The legislation imposes responsibilities on virtual asset service providers (VASPs) to protect users' deposits by managing separate accounts and a user list (Arts. 6, 7). According to the guidelines, VASPs will thus be responsible to enrol in insurance or mutual aid programmes in the event of incidents like hackings and computer failures (Art. 8). They will also need to retain virtual asset transaction records for 15 years from the time the pertinent transactional relationship is ended.[167] Article 13 of the statute empowers the FSC to supervise VASPs' acts and inspect their business affairs and financial status. There are also provisions for investigation of and measures in response to unfair trade practices (Art. 14) and measures against breaches (Art. 15). Available enforcement mechanisms include penalties for unfair trade practices (Art. 17), entrustment of supervisory authority (Art. 18), general penalty provisions (Art. 19), confiscation and collection (Art. 20), joint penalty provisions (Art. 21), and administrative fines (Art. 22).[168] The law also provides for a one year minimum sentence for specified breaches (Art. 19(1)).

---

161 I., EB (2024), "Crypto exchanges step up compliance as investor protection law takes effect", https://perma.cc/4ZLF-AA2V, accessed 29/07/2024

162 Umeda, S. (2024), "South Korea: Act to regulate cryptocurrency markets goes into effect", *Law Library of Congress*, 19/07/2024, www.loc.gov/item/global-legal-monitor/2024-07-18/south-korea-act-to-regulate-cryptocurrency-markets-goes-into-effect/, accessed 21/07/2024

163 VAUPA art. 2, para. 1

164 Asia Law (2024), "FSC announces guidelines on determining NFTs' status as virtual assets", *Asia Law*, 12/07/2024, www.asialaw.com/NewsAndAnalysis/fsc-announces-guidelines-on-determining-nfts-status-as-virtual-assets/Index/2023, accessed 19/07/2024

165 Act No. 19263

166 Ibid note [163], Umeda (2024)

167 Ibid note [163], Umeda (2024)

168 FSC (2024), "Authorities introduce guidelines for determining when non-fungible tokens qualify as virtual assets", *FSC*, 10/06/2024, www.fsc.go.kr/eng/pr010101/82419?srchCtgry=&curPage=&srchKey=&srchText=&srchBeginDt=&srchEndDt=, accessed 18/06/2024

The FSC confirms that the following would likely be treated as virtual assets:

- When identical or similar kinds of NFTs are being issued in large quantities or in a series
- When it is possible to split an NFT into factional units
- When it is possible to use an NFT as a direct or indirect method to pay for certain goods or services
- When it is possible to use an NFT as a means of exchange for virtual assets among unspecified individuals, or when it is possible to be used as a means of payment for goods or services linked to other kinds of virtual assets.

8.7 A comparative note

This chapter's review of cryptocurrency regulations in these large, highly competitive Asian economies suggests varied responses. These extend from the hard stance taken by China that includes the outlawing of cryptocurrency exchanges, to the more hospitable Japanese stance that allows cryptocurrency activities subject to various regulatory rules that are not overly restrictive, to the more rigid stance taken in India, where they are expected to fall under very strict regulatory rules or even subject to some kind of ban. It appears that such varied responses might be linked to each respective economy's state of health, the financial system in place, the cultural traditions of regulation in those states, and the level of risks they see from cryptocurrency activities.

It has been argued that the evolution of cryptocurrencies resonates with insights arising from the 1997 Asian financial crisis. This, as well as the subsequent 2008 global financial crisis (GFC), stresses the importance of early warning systems to detect risks and vulnerabilities arising from large and volatile capital flows brought about by excessive speculation. Indeed, the prudence and financial reforms built up by Asian economies after the 2008 GFC insulated most of them from exposures to toxic subprime loans and related financial instruments that induced the 2008 GFC. These provided them with the resilience that enabled them to escape almost unscathed at the commencement of the crisis. The prudence that has, in general, served them well appears to be replicated in their treatment of cryptocurrencies. This could be gleaned from the following table:[169]

Thus, the potential benefits, together with the macroeconomic risks of cryptoassets, raise various questions as to what could be determining the aversion or policy openness. Recent research suggests that a certain level of institutional

169 Bernadette, J. & Shirakawa, R. & Korwatanmasakul, U. (2019), "Cryptocurrency in emerging Asia", *Asia Pathways ADB Institute Paper*, 25/07/2019, www.asiapathways-adbi.org/2019/07/cryptocurrency-in-emerging-asia/, accessed 08/08/2019.

Table 8.1 Relative crypto regulatory status in Asia

Status	**Economy**
Banned	Indonesia, Macau (China), People's Republic of China, Vietnam
Regulated	Democratic People's Republic of Korea, Japan, Myanmar, the Philippines, Republic of Korea, Taiwan, Thailand
Fully liberalised	Brunei Darussalam, Cambodia, Hong Kong, Lao People's Democratic Republic, Malaysia, Mongolia, Singapore, Timor-Leste

quality might be necessary before opening up new kinds of financial technology,[170] such as the blockchain now underpinning the evolution of cryptocurrency.

There is the further need to take cognisance of the different pace in development of institutions and the financial market. The latter tends to outpace the former. It was only three years after the inception of Bitcoin that other cryptoassets made the scene. Thereafter, other market participants joined the fray to exploit the opportunities unfolding. Several legal and security problems then came along. Meanwhile, the pace of strengthening institutions by enhancing bureaucratic effectiveness, or the credibility of legal systems, have not matched up to the demands of financialisation. While some jurisdictions conceded the gap in institutional capacity to regulate and intervene and, ergo, advocate for non-intervention to market development or innovation, others, out of great fear of potential risks to the stability of financial systems and deployment in illicit activities, opted for the ban option. However, it is the quality of governance that would give policymakers the credibility in enforcing their policy choice, irrespective of the decision to intervene, regulate, or let markets be. This is because it is the trust in the system that could facilitate financial development. This suggests that improving institutions could be justifiable moving forward, even if it is outrun by financial development.[171]

Also, the decentralised and global nature of the cryptoassets industry suggests further the need for global co-operation.[172] This is generally recognised across the world, among nations, multilateral developmental agencies, and global standard setters, as discussed previously. Outstanding issues include avoiding potential circumvention of regulation and supervision in the international transactions of cryptoassets, especially for preventing terrorism financing or money laundering. Cryptoassets stakeholders, but especially policymakers, need to be vigilant of potential spillover effects of volatility in the cryptoassets market. Growingly,

170 Shirakawa, J. B. R. & Korwatanasakul, U. (2019), "Cryptocurrencies regulations: Institutions and Financial Openness", *ADB Working Paper 978*, Tokyo, ADB.

171 Ibid note [171], Shirakawa & Korwatanasakul (2019).

172 Ibid note [171], Shirakawa & Korwatansaskul (2019).

macro-financial linkages could render the real sector vulnerable to amplified adverse impacts flowing from new exponential financial technology, more so when cryptoassets become a more significant part of mainstream finance.[173]

Insights drawn from these and the previous chapter covering selected advanced economies suggest that while some regulatory authorities are pondering whether to regulate crypto, some have responded with bans that they now start to review in view of the impact of regulatory arbitrage that result in business and talent migration. For those contemplating how to regulate crypto, they are hesitating or unsure about the use of direct centralised regulation for various reasons, including the lack of adequate skills and knowledge when dealing with the emerging technology.

The "how to" approach could instead rely on the market-based regulation of the activities involved in the business. This formed the basis of the regulatory framework found in some jurisdictions that are relatively more enthusiastic about the potential of the industry. Both these chapters show the difficulties in arriving at a global solution, as national sovereignty issues, cultural issues, legacy issues, economic competition issues, legal system issues, and different perspectives of the nature of market risks stand in the way. The closest to one comes from the FATF, but this focuses mainly on money laundering and related issues. Many regulators from across the world would continue to grapple with this crypto dilemma, but hopefully, as the search goes on for a more global solution, policymakers and other stakeholders would continue to work together to solve the problem.

As the nature and form of cryptoassets are still evolving, the question of treating the phenomenon as a category of financial asset class, form of global payment mechanism, or global virtual/digital currency is still under debate now that big banking institutions like Goldman Sachs and J. P. Morgan and big technology platforms like Facebook and Amazon could be getting potentially more involved in the business.

The issues are complicated by the possible plans of big economies like China and small economies like the Marshall Islands to issue central bank digital currencies. Yes, the crypto world is still evolving despite a decade of market presence, and yes, regulators are still struggling to deal with the opportunities and threats posed by it. This is where researchers, users, and activists can contribute, by interacting with key stakeholders to exchange views and experiences across the world, from small to large economies and from more social to more capitalist economies. In other words, a global perspective is called for.

The diversity of regulatory approaches offers opportunities and challenges for the crypto-crossing border industry. The global trend is gravitating towards

173 Circle/FireEye/Marsh & McLennan (2019), "Crypto-assets and blockchain technology: On the brink of technology?", *Circle/FireEye/Marsh & McLennan Paper*, January 2019, www.marsh.com/content/dam/marsh/Documents/PDF/US-en/on-the-brink-of-legitimacy-mmc-report-january%202019.pdf, accessed 08/08/2019; FSB (2018), "Crypto-asset markets: Potential channels for future financial stability implications", *FSB*, 10/10/2018, www.fsb.org/2018/10/crypto-asset-markets-potential-channels-for-future-financial-stability-implications/, accessed 08/08/2019.

more regulation, à la the bespoke regime in the EU, and also Japan and South Korea, or by regulating via existing frameworks, as in the United States, the UK, and including vibrant small Asian economies, such as Singapore and Hong Kong, or in the wait and see stance as in the rising big Asian economy of India, or practically prohibited in the social economy of China, the second biggest economy in the word.

In what form crypto regulation will ultimately take shape in these economies and, more importantly, whether the world will achieve uniformity or more harmonised regulatory frameworks, and the kind and scale of economic impacts on the industry, remain murky, particularly in the face of geopolitical tensions now affecting the world, as well as including the direction and pace of economic policies in the big influential economies of the world, like the United States, the EU, India, and China. In this connection, empirical research suggests that crypto markets can fuel cross-border capital flight by serving as marketplaces that match counterparts with and without illicit access to foreign exchange.[174]

In those economies where international transactions are restricted, crypto exchanges effectively enable domestic agents to pay a premium to buy foreign currency. The counterparts to these transactions are agents with access to foreign exchange who sell crypto holdings purchased abroad. It has been illustrated that restricted foreign currency and economic imbalances incentivise these transactions via persistent crypto premia in local, relative to global, markets. The associated country case studies undertaken provide empirical support that crypto markets serve as marketplaces for capital flight that already took place, rather than a novel channel for capital flight.[175]

Market participants would need to monitor developments across borders, adapt where necessary, and be aware of risks as regulators seek to prevent another FTX from failing and prosecutors seek justice where it does.[176] These risks aside, the next chapter will assess the technological opportunities and risks as blockchain technology or DLT evolves globally.

174 Von Luckner, C. M. G. et al. (2024), "Crypto as a marketplace for capital flight", *IMF Woking Paper WP/24/133*, www.elibrary.imf.org/downloadpdf/journals/001/2024/133/001.2024.issue-133-en.pdf, accessed 25/07/24

175 Ibid note [175], Von Luckner et al. (2024)

176 Bernard, C. et al. (2024), "Cryptoasset regulatory and risk developments: The global picture", *Freshfields Bruckhaus Deringer*, 01/06/2024, www.freshfields.com/49e193/globalassets/our-thinking/fsnet/pdfs/fs-insights-june-2024.pdf, accessed 25/07/2024

CHAPTER 9

Islamic law and blockchain-based products

9.1 Introduction

One area where blockchain-based products are now operating pertains to the areas of the world covered by Islamic law. It is important to consider the extent to which this is permitted by the different interpretations of Islamic law. The acceptability of such schemes in these parts of the world is important, as some of them are economically underdeveloped, and online, blockchain-based activities offer a potential shortcut to accessing finance and facilities. It is therefore necessary to consider, firstly, the views expressed with regard to Islamic law and, secondly, the steps taken in relevant states to regulate such products by developments in law and regulation.

The analysis will focus on the most widespread school, the Shafiʿi school of Sunni law, considering the following:

- The Islamic law background
- Whether currencies based on blockchain are acceptable
- Whether business structures that are acceptable under Islamic law can be utilised in this context
- Whether debt and equity issues based on blockchain are acceptable.

9.2 The Islamic legal background

There are different schools of Sunni Islamic law: the Shafiʿi, the Hanbali, the Hanafi, and the Maliki. In addition to that, there are also Shia Islamic law[1] and the Ibadi.[2] The Sunni "Islamic law" itself is a generic term covering four main schools of Islamic thought:[3] The schools have an identical approach to certain generally acceptable areas but, on occasion, disparate approaches to certain financial and business arrangements.

1 This is divided into the Ithnā ʿAshariyyah (the most widespread group), the Isma'ilis, and the Zaydis.

2 El-Hawary, D., Grais, W. & Iqbal, Z. (2004), "Regulating Islamic financial institutions: The nature of the regulated", *World Bank Policy Research Paper 3227*, 25/02/2004

3 Four Sunni and one Shia, though if smaller Islamic sects are included, there are a large number of sub-groups. An exact number is a subjective issue, as there are disagreements as to whether some sects are technically Islamic.

DOI: 10.4324/9781032667416-9

All the schools agree that seven general areas are un-Islamic, and as a result, these are prohibited.[4] The areas concerned are interest; excessive uncertainty; gaming; transactions in an unauthorised subject matter; restructuring debts, which provides for an increase in the debt;[5] trading discounted debt (with certain exceptions); and forward rate agreements in currencies. It is necessary to consider whether any of these has an impact on blockchain-based currencies on products.

The analysis of Islamic law involves two different approaches. The so-called "constructionist" approach, which effectively permits the construction of Western-style banking and financial products and determining that they can operate under Islamic law. There is also the "revisionist" approach, which sees the former as being artificial and misusing Islamic law to permit activities that, on reflection, could be seen as un-Islamic and unacceptable.[6] This difference of approach manifests itself in certain blockchain-based activities.

9.3 Are blockchain-based currencies acceptable under Islamic law?

Historically, Islamic law has accepted gold and silver, which were seen as currency. Their inherent value is the same as their trading value, and therefore, they do not fall foul of any of the general principles previously mentioned. Other forms of money and currency are seen as acceptable if used purely as a medium of exchange. Thus:

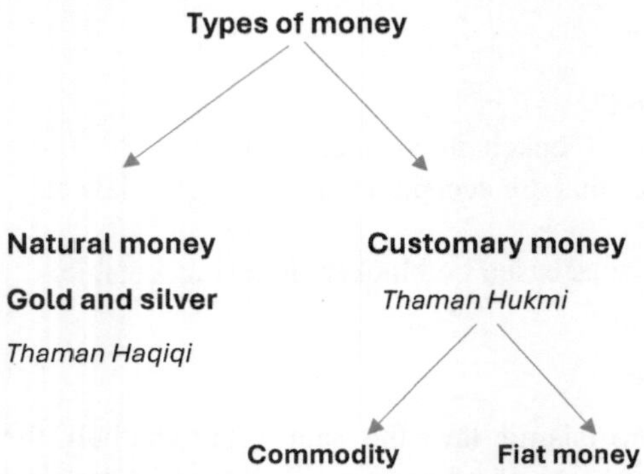

Figure 9.1 Diagram of acceptable types of currency.
Source:[7].

4 Tariq, A. A., "Managing financial risks of sukuk structures", www.Islamicfinance.de, accessed 15/01/2025

5 Abozaid, A. (2021), "Penalty and compensation in financial commitments: A critical Shariah review", *Journal of Sharia and Islamic Studies*, 38(2).

6 Hamoudi, H. A. (2006), "Muhammad's social justice or Islam cant. Langdellianism and the failure of Islamic finance", *Cornell International Law Journal*, 40: 3, ISSN: 0010-8812. See also Professor Al-Rimawi, L. (2024), " 'Shari'a compliance' as the *sine qua non* of the Islamic financial services industry: UK's need for determinacy and jurisprudential clarity", *The Company Lawyer*, 45(7): 244, ISSN: 0144-1027

7 Yunita, P. (2022, January–June), "The evolution of money to cryptocurrency: Are they eligible to be Islamic digital money?", *Journal of Middle East and Islamic Studies*, 9(1), Art 7, p. 7, ISSN: 2242-6946

This distinction between revisionism and constructionism manifests itself in certain aspects of blockchain-based products. Some scholars have declared that all cryptocurrencies are a type of gambling and are therefore *haram* and unacceptable.[8] A different line of argument is that blockchain-based products fail the certainty test, which, as seen above, is one of the seven banned activities.[9] There has been a more general criticism to the effect that blockchain-based products cannot be categorised as money because they have no intrinsic value, the owners cannot be identified, and the value is inherently unstable.[10]

Other scholars have argued otherwise.[11] For example, the Shariyah Review Bureau of Bahrain[12] has accepted blockchain-based currencies, or cryptocurrencies, as money because they are utilised as a medium of exchange for contracts. In addition, blockchain-based currencies possess elements such as assets, benefits, rights (*haq*), and obligations (*dayn*). In addition, it has been argued that such arrangements are transparent, are regulated, and do not fall foul of the rules relating to usury.[13] Another scholar has argued that to satisfy the definition of *money*, three properties must be present: It must function as a medium of exchange, as a unit of account, and as a determinant of value. If it does not satisfy these three elements, it does not satisfy the definition of a *currency*. In such an instance, it is possible that it may still be acceptable as a commodity.[14]

Some have argued that the Islamic scholars concerned have misunderstood the nature of the blockchain product itself and that, as a result, their analysis is flawed.[15] Other factors are the fact that cryptocurrencies do not have an intrinsic value and that they are not regulated by a central bank, resulting in them lacking the necessary social justice to be acceptable. Also, there is an issue with cryptocurrencies in that they have displayed ongoing high price volatility, with the result that they are *gharar* (uncertain in their value), and thus unacceptable.[16] To

8 Mills, D. J. & Nower, L. (2019), "Preliminary findings on cryptocurrency trading among regular gamblers: A new risk for problem gambling?", *Addictive Behaviour*, 92: 136–140. American Psychological Association, https://psycnet.apa.org/record/2019-25445-025, accessed 05/08/2025.

9 Bouri, E., Gupta, R. & Roubaud, D. (2019), "Herding behavior in cryptocurrencies", *Finance Research Letters*.

10 Bakar, A. B., Rosbi, S. & Uzaki, K. (2017), "Cryptocurrency framework diagnostics from Islamic finance perspective: A new insight of Bitcoin system transaction", *International Journal Management Science and Business Administration*, 4(1): 19–28, 1849–5664 (online)

11 Abubakar, M., Hassan, M. K. & Haruna, M. A. (2019), "Cryptocurrency tide and Islamic finance development: Any issue?", *Disruptive Innovation in Business and Finance in the Digital World. International Finance Review*, 20: 189–200. Emerald Publishing Limited.

12 Shariah Review Bureau (2018), *The Shariah Factor in Cryptocurrencies and Tokens*, The Central Bank of Bahrain.

13 Amalin, G. (2018), "The legality of cryptocurrency trade in accordance with the principles of Islamic banking law", Thesis, Indonesian Islamic University, Yogyakarta.

14 Usmani, M. T. (2015), *Fiqh al-Buyu*, Damascus, Syria, Dar al-Qalam.

15 Rabbani, M. R., Khan, S. & Thalassinos, E. (2020), "FinTech, blockchain and Islamic finance: An extensive literature review", *International Journal of Economics and Business Administration*, 8: 65–86, ISSN: 2241-4754

16 Abu-Bakar, M. M. (2018), *Shariah analysis of bitcoin, cryptocurrency, and blockchain*, Oakland, CA, Blossom Labs; Zahudi, Z. M. & Amir, R. A. T. R. (2022), "Regulation of virtual currencies: Mitigating the risks and challenges involved", *Journal of Islamic Finance*, 5: 63–73; Aysan, A. F. & Unal, I. M. (2021, September), A bibliometric analysis of fintech and blockchain

quote Baffa et al., "*gharar* is the Islamic term for transactions or investments that involve uncertainty consisting of two types: Gharar-e-Fahish (excessive) and Gharar-e-Yasir (minor)".[17] As would be expected, the former is unacceptable, but the latter can be accommodated as it is largely an effect of everyday life and is thus unavoidable. In the operation of finance, "the concept of daman in the context of daman al-milkiyyah refers not to risk in the conventional sense but more accurately refers instead to the liability or responsibility arising from ownership".[18] However, the operation of blockchain should not raise issues relating to uncertainty, because its structure, as seen earlier, provides equivalent or arguably greater certainty than pre-existing operating procedures involving written contracts or traditional electronic communication, such as email, due to the difficulty of retrospectively amending the contract.

Some scholars have argued that cryptocurrencies are more acceptable to Islam than fiat currencies and that the underlying structure is not a problem.[19] Others have put forward analyses suggesting an acceptable aspect to cryptocurrencies. For example, "from a *Maslahah*[20] perspective, these coins could help develop Islamic society by increasing wealth and therefore serve the *Maqasid*".[21] It has also been suggested that the risk inherent in cryptocurrencies could be maintained at an acceptable level by utilising partnerships of individuals, which would apply the structure of *Musharakah* (see later) and thus spread the financial risk.[22] Where a crypto-based asset is concerned, matters may be different, as the asset or debt concerned can be more stable and certain in both nature and value. There are less likely to be objections to such structures.[23]

Another factor that needs taking into account in terms of Islamic acceptability is whether blockchain-based products assist in preserving wealth (*Hifz al-Mal*). Factors that are regarded as elements of this are the carrying out of work and

---

in Islamic finance", *FinTech*, 1(398): 51, ISSN: 2289-2109; MPRA Paper No. 109712, Muenchen, https://mpra.ub.uni-muenchen.de/109712, accessed 04/09/2022, 52. Giudici, P. (2018), "Fintech risk management: A research challenge for artificial intelligence in finance", *Frontiers in Artificial Intelligence*, 1: 1.

17 Baffa, I. Jibrin, Sa'id, Abdullahi Doma & Auwal, Garba (2022, December), "Cryptocurrencies from Islamic perspectives: A systematic literature review", *UMYU Journal of Accounting and Finance Research*, 4(1), 8, ISSN: 2795-3823 (online)

18 Razak, Lufti Abul and Saupi, Mohammed Nabil (2017), "The concept and application of Damanal-Milkiyyah (ownership risk). Islamic law of contract perspective", *International Journal of Islamic Finance*, 9(2): 151, ISSN: 2289-4365

19 Böhme, R., Christin, N., Edelman, B. & Moore, T. (2015), "Bitcoin: Economics, technology, and governance", *The Journal of Economic Perspectives*, 29(2): 213–238, ISSN: 1944-7495 (online)

20 Utility. What is good and beneficial. Esposito, J. L. (2003), *The Oxford dictionary of Islam*, Oxford University Press.

21 The goals or purpose of Sharia. Abubakar, M., Hassan, M. K. & Haruna, M. A. (2019), "Cryptocurrency tide and Islamic finance development: Any issue?", in *Disruptive innovation in business and finance in the digital world*, Bingley, UK, Emerald Publishing Limited.

22 Unal, Ibrahim Musa & Aysan, Ahmet Faruk (2022), "Fintech, digitalization, and blockchain in Islamic finance: Retrospective investigation", *Fintech. MDPI*, 388–398.

23 Kirchner, I. K. (2020), "Are cryptocurrencies halal? On the Sharia-compliancy of blockchain-based fintech", *Islamic Law Society*, 28: 76–112, ISSN: 0928-9380. Aysan, A. F., Demirtaş, H. B. & Saraç, M., "The ascent of Bitcoin: Bibliometric analysis of Bitcoin research", *Journal of Risk and Financial Management*, 14: 427, ISSN: 1911-8074.

entering into business arrangements that are themselves Islamically acceptable. Part of the reason that contracts that are unclear in nature, gambling, and charging interest are unacceptable is that they can lead to the destruction of wealth.

The view of Dr Shawki Allam, Mufti of Egypt, is that cryptocurrencies are not acceptable for a range of reasons. Specifically:

> [B]ecause it is not considered as an acceptable medium of exchange by the competent authorities, and because of the damage it entails arising from gharar, ignorance and fraud in its bank, standard and value, as well as the high risks that its practice leads to individuals and countries.[24]

The first of these points is debateable, as a number of Islamic states have legally recognised cryptocurrencies as acceptable and their regulatory systems have been adjusted to deal with them. This is discussed later in the chapter. Dr Allam also believes that cryptocurrencies are not a reliable medium of exchange due to there being high risk in owning them – indeed, the money invested could be lost in full, they reduce the capacity of states to control their currencies and the related risk of the loss of tax revenue, and it is not a reliable medium of exchange. On this last point, it is reliable in terms of it functioning effectively; the issues arise with its volatile value. In addition, he has concerns that cryptocurrencies are separated from other electronic payment methods. This is a more curious objection, as all currencies are separated from each other, but with the exception of non-convertible currencies, they can all be exchanged with each other, cryptocurrencies included. Finally, he is concerned that it cannot be regarded as a currency as it is not issued by a state.

Shaykh Haitham al-Haddad has taken a similar attitude but utilised a different argument, stating that cryptocurrencies have no real value. He qualified this by adding that if their value were based on that of gold, it would be acceptable. It is partly because of this that attempts have been made to provide some type of cryptocurrency with a base in real assets. This would seem to suggest that certain types of asset-backed cryptocurrencies are acceptable.[25] Stablecoin is one such arrangement; another is OneGram, where each crypto coin is backed by a minimum of 1 g of gold, which is arguably the earliest form of currency (along with silver) acceptable to Islam. Likewise, HelloGold was launched on a similar basis in Kuala Lumpur. HalalChain, based in the United Arab Emirates, has a wider asset footprint based on Islamically accessible goods. In the case of shares issued on blockchain, there should be no problem. Initial coin offerings where bonds are based on the blockchain should be acceptable, provided the bond satisfies the principles of Islamic sukuk.[26]

Those who find cryptocurrencies and assets acceptable include Mufti Muhammad Abu-Bakar. He states that there is not a clear definition to be found in the Qur'an or the Sunnah of the Prophet on the issue but indicates that there

24 https://gate.ahram.org.eg/News/1764841.aspx, accessed 15/01/2025
25 حُكمُ التعامُل بالعُملة الإلكترونيَّة المُشفَّرة: (البتكُوين) وأخواتها, accessed 15/01/2025
26 Islam and cryptocurrency, halal or not halal? | Crypto | Al Jazeera, accessed 12/08/2024

are statements in the religious texts which point in that direction. Firstly, he was influenced by the fact that cryptocurrencies can be possessed, be desirable, and be transferred to someone else and be regarded as having value.[27] Therefore, they are within the definition of *property* for the purposes of Islam. He cites a range of academic sources, but of particular significance are the views of Shaykh Taqi Usmani, who stated that if something becomes valuable through customary use, then it amounts to property. Likewise, Shaykh Khalid Saifullah Rahmani stated that a critical factor for property was storability, and this can be done with crypto-based currencies and assets.[28] The only qualifications are that they must be permissible and lawful, capable of being owned and possessed, that they must have some use or benefit and must customarily be regarded as property. In addition, the Qur'an, at 2:282, sanctions and encourages contracts to be established in writing rather than being made verbally.[29] With cryptocurrencies and assets, the fact that there is an electronic record of the contract could be regarded as satisfying these provisions.

Any new application such as blockchain that may be used to execute contracts needs to go through a process of analysis to determine whether it is compatible with Shariah law.[30] As part of this, it will be necessary to review the blockchain mechanism and other related matters that guarantee the safety of the legal side of relevant financial dealings.[31] [32]

Shaykh Khalid Saifullah Rahmani has argued that storability in itself justifies the acceptability of cryptocurrencies and assets, as this helps satisfy the Islamic definition of *property*.[33] The storing of a cryptocurrency or asset can be done on the owner's laptop, which raises no issues. However, storage may take place on an exchange or online. This is effectively a form of financial warehousing, which in common law jurisdictions can be done on the basis of an equitable trust, which can operate as *wadia'h* under Islamic law. This could be structured as a savings arrangement with a guarantee of safekeeping (*wadīʿah yad damanah*) or depositing the asset on the basis of trust (as opposed to a "trust" in the equitable sense), which is referred to as *wadīʿah yad Amanah*.[34] In a *wadīʿah*

27 Abu-Bakar, Mufti Muhammad (2017), "Shariah analysis of Bitcoin, cryptocurrency and blockchain", *Blossom Finance Working Paper*, 5th/04/2017, https://islamicbankers.me/wp-content/uploads/2019/02/2017-analysis-of-cryptocurrency-blockchain-pdf, accessed 15/01/2025

28 Rahmani, Khalid Saifullah (2010), *Jadeed Fiqhi Masail*, Zam Zam Publishers, Karachi.

29 Kunhibava, Sherin, Mustapha, Zakariya, Muneeza, Aishath, AdamSa'ad, Auwal & Karim, MohammadErshadul (2021), "Sukuk on blockchain: A legal, regulatory and Sharī'ah review", *International Journal of Islamic Finance*, 13(1): 119, ISSN: 2289-4365

30 Lacasse, R. M., Lambert, B. & Nida, K. H. A. N. (2018), "Islamic banking-towards a blockchain monitoring process", *Revue de Gestion et d'Économie*, 6(1&2): 33–46, ISSN: 2728-0128

31 Mohamed, H. & Ali, H. (2018), *Blockchain, Fintech, and Islamic finance: Building the future in the new Islamic digital economy*, Walter de Gruyter GmbH & Co KG.

32 Alaeddin, Omar, Al Dakash, Mohanad & Azrak, Tawfik (2021), "Implementing the blockchain technology in Islamic financial industry: Opportunities and challenges", *Journal of information Technology Management*, University of Tehran Research Paper, ISSN: 2980-7972

33 Rahmani (2010).

34 Qaed, I. Q. M. (2014), "The concept of Wadiah and its application in Islamic banking", *Journal of Research in Humanities and Social Science*, 2(11): 70–74, ISSN: 2321-9467

yad Amanah contract, the deposit is guaranteed by the holder, which will bear any losses incurred. In this instance, the holder is not responsible for it, nor can it gain from it. Thus, as there is no profit to be made, no one is going to offer cryptocurrency wallets on this basis, and as there is no responsibility, it would be unattractive to depositors. Alternately, it can be seen as a loan of the asset concerned on the basis that it has to be returned or forwarded on demand. This could equate to a *qard*, which allows the holder to use it for its own purposes. This will work with a bank holding deposits, but it is not useful in the context of a cryptocurrency wallet.

Blockchain-based cryptoassets themselves should therefore not raise any particular issues under Islamic law. It is the nature of the asset itself and its planned use which will require clearance.

9.4 Relevant Islamic business structures[35]

There are six main types of business structure that are deemed acceptable under Islamic law: *Musharakah*, *Mudarabah*, *Ijarah*, *Salam*, *Wakalah*, and *Murabahah*. Of these, five can be set aside as irrelevant in this context. *Ijarah* agreements cover the ownership of property for rent and are used as a source of finance. *Salam* is a commercial contract for future delivery, with payment taking place now. Here the assets must be ascertainable in terms of nature, quality, quantity, and place for delivery. *Wakalah* is an arrangement where a third party provides finance, and *Murabahah* consists of a party buying an asset and reselling it at a profit. It is the remaining one, *Musharakah*, a joint enterprise with a sharing of profit and losses, that is worthy of analysis in this context.

Musharakah translates as "sharing", and it means a Shariah-compliant joint enterprise in which all the partners agree to share the profit or loss of the joint venture.[36] It does so on a similar basis to English statutory and common law relating to partnerships.[37] Each of the parties to the agreement must contribute capital. Once in operation, the share of profit for each partner is determined as a proportion of the final total profit rather than a ratio of the invested capital. The amount of this must be agreed at the outset or the agreement is invalid. If money is drawn from the partnership in the course of the financial year, then this must be calculated as an on-account payment, and an adjustment must be made at the end of the financial year. The parties each has management rights in proportion

35 Also known as "sharikah" structures.

36 See AAOIFI Shariah Standards at No 12, 3.6 See also 5/1/5/6. The AAOIFI is an Islamic international autonomous non-profit-making corporate body that prepares accounting, auditing, governance, ethics, and Shariah standards for Islamic financial institutions. The AAOIFI was established in accordance with the Agreement of Association which was signed by Islamic financial institutions on 26 February 1990. Its requirements are mandatory for Islamic institutions in Brunei, Dubai, France, Jordan, Kuwait, Lebanon, Saudi Arabia, Qatar, South Africa, UAE, and the United Kingdom. They are mandatory generally in Bahrain, Oman, Pakistan, the Sudan, and Syria.

37 See, for example, s. 1 Partnership Act 1890 in England and Wales.

to their investment, although it is acceptable for one or more partner(s) to agree to carry out the management of the operation, and the remainder acting as sleeping partners. It is difficult to see this amounting to a convincing basis for justifying crypto storage facilities as normally structured, but the design could be adapted to try to fit.

9.5 Are debt and equity issues based on blockchain acceptable under Islamic law?

With regard to issuing debt paper on blockchain, *Musharakah* sukuk are defined by the Accounting and Auditing Organization for Islamic Financial Institutions Standard (AAOIFI)[38] as

> certificates of equal value issued with the aim of using the mobilized funds for establishing a new project, developing an existing project or financing a business activity on the basis of any partnership contracts so that the certificate holders become the owners of the project or assets of the activity as per their respective shares, with the musharakah certificates being managed on the basis of participation or mudaraba[39] or an investment agency.

There are issues with this definition in that it potentially blurs the distinction between *Musharakah* and *Mudaraba* and, arguably, without need, as the arrangement traditionally includes the right for the partners to exercise management rights in proportion to their investment.

Provided the debt issue involves the lender in sharing risk in a manner acceptable under Islamic law, debt and, for that matter, equity issues should not face any particular problems merely because they are issued on blockchain. The preceding analysis requiring such contracts to be written, be used for acceptable activities, be secure, and any predictability being minor, should all be easy enough to satisfy in a legitimate debt or equity issue.

Islamic cryptocurrencies and assets have now become a very active market, albeit it is more common in some areas than others. Some of the interpretations of Islamic law inimical to the development of cryptocurrencies and assets have been dominant in, for example, Cairo and Istanbul. Development has thus predominantly taken place in those areas where the contrary view is dominant. In declining order of activity, the big five centres for blockchain-based currencies, debt, and equity issues are Dubai, Malaysia, London, Bahrain, and Saudi Arabia, with others emerging in Doha, Jakarta, Istanbul (despite locally expressed views as to their unacceptability), and Islamabad.

The state regulatory bodies in these areas have both applied new specifically designed laws and regulations to regulate cryptocurrencies and assets and applied pre-existing laws and regulations to areas where there is a pre-existing issue already covered by the law that is relevant here. Examples of the latter tend

38 AAOIFI Shariah Standard No 14 at 5/1/5/6

39 A type of Shariah-compliant partnership arrangement (see earlier text).

to be the laws relating to anti–money laundering, terrorist financing, market abuse, and financial advertising.

9.6 State regulatory bodies

9.6.1 Dubai

The Virtual Assets Regulatory Authority (VARA) governs issuing and trading virtual assets in and through Dubai. The relevant framework is provided through the Virtual Assets and Regulated Activities Regulations 2023. The rule books fall into four categories. Firstly, those relating to the Company Rulebook, which covers the company's structure and governance; fit and proper requirements; rules on outsourcing; environmental, social, and governance issues; the capital and prudential requirements; insolvency; and change of control. Secondly, there is the Compliance and Risk Management Rulebook, covering compliance management, tax, anti–money laundering, client money rules, client virtual assets rules, and anti-bribery and corruption. The Technology and Information Rulebook covers technology, governance, controls and security, personal data, and confidential information. Finally, the Market Conduct Rulebook covers marketing, advertising and promotions, client agreements, complaints handling, investor classifications, public disclosures, market transparency, own account trading, and VA standards. For a close analysis, the contents are all available on the regulator's website.[40] A degree of advice is also offered regarding the interpretation of the rules, although this is non-binding.

The Securities and Commodities Authority and the Central Bank of the UAE also play a key role in regulation and supervision in this area, with the former being responsible for regulating cryptocurrencies and companies active in this area. It is all part of an ambitious plan for the UAE to be a significant player in terms of being a jurisdiction where a significant proportion of blockchain transactions are based.

This all operates in liaison with the UAE's financial free zones, of which there are three: the Abu Dhabi Global Market, aimed at spot trading and providing relevant licenses; the Dubai progressive free zones, for basing crypto companies; and the Ras al Khaimah Digital Assets Oasis, which has financial autonomy with legislative and administrative freedom. Amongst other things, the last of these also has available grants, as well as business advice, marketing, and start-up support.[41] The structure is not hierarchical.

The licensing and regulatory system is therefore quite complex. The UAE's Securities and Commodities Authority licenses exchanges, wallets, and trading platforms and is responsible for cryptos categorised as securities[42] with VARA (see earlier text) responsible for other licensing.

40 https://rulebooks.vara.ae/rulebook/rulebooks, accessed 12/01/2025
41 Cryptocurrency Regulations in the UAE – A Guide for 2025, accessed 14/01/2025
42 UAE, SCA Virtual Assets Regulations 2020

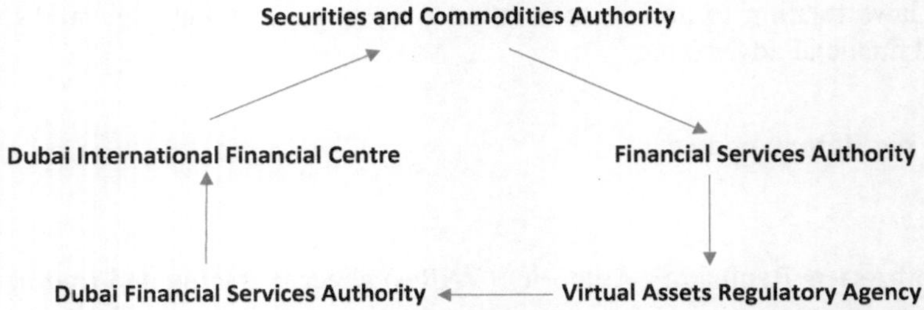

Figure 9.2 Crypto regulatory structure in the UAE.

Cryptocurrencies such as Bitcoin and Ethereum are treated as legal tender.

9.6.2 Malaysia

The country's central bank, Bank Negara Malaysia, regulates cryptocurrencies. The Central Bank of Malaysia Act 2009 (as amended) covers their capacity to regulate. The Financial Services Act 2013 and the Islamic Financial Services Act 2013 deal with financial regulation more generally and money laundering issues, both generally, and, in this context, are covered by the Anti–Money Laundering, Anti-Terrorism Financing and Proceeds of Unlawful Activities Act 2001.

Section 2(1) of the Financial Services Act defines *electronic money* as "any payment instrument, whether tangible or intangible that – (a) stores funds electronically in exchange of funds paid to the issuer; and (b) is able to be used as a means of making payment to any person other than the issuer".

Likewise, there is a parallel definition of *electronic money* in Section 2(1) of the Islamic Financial Services Act, which defines it as

> any Islamic payment instrument, whether tangible or intangible, that – (a) stores funds electronically in exchange of funds paid to the issuer; and (b) is able to be used as a means of making payment to any person other than the issuer.

This does not cover cryptocurrencies or assets, however, and has a much narrower remit. The only other relevant definition is that of *legal tender* in Section 63 Central Bank of Malaysia Act 2009, which is limited to notes and coins issued by the central bank. However, the Capital Markets and Services (Prescription of Securities) (Digital Currency and Digital Token) Order 2019 assists. Regulation 2 defines *cryptocurrencies* as "a digital representation of value which is recorded on a distributed digital ledger whether cryptographically-secured or otherwise, that functions as a medium of exchange and is interchangeable with any money, including through the crediting or debiting of an account". A distinct definition of *crypto-tokens* is added: "a digital representation which is recorded on a distributed digital ledger whether cryptographically-secured or otherwise".

However, this still leaves us in a situation where cryptocurrencies are not regarded as legal tender in Malaysia. Therefore, those operating or dealing with them need a Capital Markets and Services license.

However, the law in Malaysia has recognised their existence. The case of *Luno Pte Ltd & Anor v Robert Ong Thien Cheng*[43] saw an action brought by someone who had mistakenly transferred the agreed number of Bitcoins twice to an exchange. They refused to return the excess, so he sued. On appeal, the High Court agreed that the Bitcoins transferred in excess of the agreed sum had to be returned. Money in its recognised form had been used to purchase the Bitcoin, and therefore, they should be categorised as a commodity. The exchange could not wrongly retain them.

There remain gaps in the Malaysian approach, particularly regarding property rights in crypto, which can be a particular issue in inheritance.[44] There is also the additional factor in Malaysia that much of the population is unbanked, and so crypto offers the opportunity to access financial products and banking that may not have been there before, especially with the rural population.[45] This may be one of the causes of Malaysia being 7th of 27 countries surveyed in terms of usage, with 63% of the population being aware of cryptocurrencies.[46]

The Capital Markets and Services Orders classify certain digital currencies and assets as securities, which brings them within the jurisdiction of the Securities Commission of Malaysia. They are not, however, legally recognised as currencies.

Crucial regulations include anti–money laundering and know-your-client checks, a requirement that information be checked between transferor and transferee in each transaction, all digital asset exchanges must be registered, and platforms must conduct due diligence on initial exchange offerings.

9.6.3 The United Kingdom

The United Kingdom (UK) is the third largest centre for Islamic crypto activity, with the focus, of course, being on the City of London. There is no separate legal or regulatory regime for such products in the UK beyond that which exists for cryptocurrency and assets generally. However, the buyers of such products, if

43 Sessions Court Civil Suit No. BA-B52NCVC-389–12/2017 (Unreported). See analysis in Nawang, Nazli Ismail & Azmi, Ida Madieha Abd Ghani (2020), "Cryptocurrency: An insight into the Malaysian Regulatory Approach", *Hamdard Islamicus*, 43(S.2): 262–271, at 269.

44 Kamis, N. S. & Wahab, N. A. (2022), "Analysing the loopholes on estate administration of cryptocurrency in Malaysia", *International Journal of Islamic Business*, 7(2): 65–77, https://doi.org/10.32890/ijib.2022.7.2.5

45 Susilo, D., Wahyudi, S., Pangestuti, I. R. D., Nugroho, B. A. & Robyanto, R. (2020), "Cryptocurrencies. Hedging opportunities from domestic perspectives in Southeast Asia emerging markets", *SAGE Open*, (10): 4.215824402097160, https.doi.org/10.1177/2158244020971609, accessed 11/04/2025

46 Wang, K. & Crypto.com (2021), "Measuring global crypto users", (Data Report), https.crypto.com/images/202107-DataReport-OnChain-Market-Sizing.pdf

requiring that the products satisfy Islamic law, will need to consider the views of the Islamic scholars of their school of Islam and/or nationality. As seen, there is no overall consistency here, potentially leaving issuers, dealers, exchanges, and wallet providers with more scope to operate in this field than those based in specific Islamic centres. However, it also leaves more scope for disagreement concerning whether a particular arrangement is recognised.

Any financial product subject to Islamic law is regulated by the FCA and the PRA, both of whose aims is to offer a level playing field between Islamic and other products. Despite this, Islamic financial products are a growing part of the market.[47] This is partly because of a significant Islamic population in the country and partly because London is a major financial centre serving overseas as well as domestic markets. By 2023, there were over £38 billion in sukuk issued on the London Stock Exchange. Assets under management in Islamic funds amounted to £250 million.[48] It has been argued that it is the dominant Islamic financial centre.[49] There have been arguments that a new regulatory approach is needed as it operates in the UK at a disadvantage as the relevant regulations are created with a dissimilar approach to that adopted under Islamic law.[50]

9.6.4 Bahrain

The operation of cryptocurrency and assets in Bahrain requires a license from the Central Bank of Bahrain to be able to offer services to the public. Capital requirements are also required, as are cybersecurity risk management with audit procedures. Reporting requirements and an inspection regime are also in place. There has been a thorough approach to regulating crypto,[51] a primary aim of which is to minimise the risk of financial crime and obstructing the illegal use of cryptoassets.

At the level of definitions, Bahrain has subdivided cryptoassets into four different legal and regulatory categories:

- Payment and exchange tokens (i.e. cryptocurrencies)
- Application-specific crypto tokens

47 Rahman, Arshadur (2017), "Islamic banks and central banking", *Q3 Bank of England Quarterly Bulletin*, 155, 156.

48 Fitch Ratings, "2UK maintains Islamic finance western hub status", *Despite Domestic Niche*, 20/06/2023, www.fitchratings.com/research/Islamic-finance/uk-maintains-Islamic-finance-western-hub-status-despite-domestic-niche-2066.2023, accessed 11/04/2025.

49 Hauser, Andrew (2020, December), "Why Islamic finance has an important role to play in supporting the recovery from Covid – and how the Bank of England's new Alternative Liquidity Facility can", *Bank of England Speech*

50 Alkhalifa, Khalifa A. K. (2022), "The regulation of Islamic finance in the UK: A call for change", *LSE Law Review*, VII, at 274, https://lawreview.lse.ac.uk/articles/297/files/submission/proof/297-1-1963-1-10-20220316.pdf, accessed 11/04/2025

51 Vol 6, Central Bank of Bahrain Rulebook, CRA

- Asset tokens, giving a debt or equity claim on the issuer
- Hybrid tokens, combining any of the aforementioned

Once accepted for regulatory purposes, they are categorised as "accepted cryptoassets". The services in relation to these cryptoassets requiring regulation are:

- Receiving and transmitting cryptoassets
- Accepting orders to buy or sell them
- Own account dealing against proprietary assets
- Discretionary portfolio management of cryptoassets
- Cryptoasset custodianship
- Investment advice in relation to cryptoassets
- Cryptoasset exchange, of which there is already one in Bahrain, trading, converting, and exchanging cryptoassets.

Licensing itself falls into the following categories:

Table 9.1 Licensing classification or crypto businesses in Bahrain

Category 1	Category 2	Category 3	Category 4
– Reception and transmission of orders – Investment advice	– Trading in accepted cryptoassets as an agent – Portfolio management – Cryptoasset custody service – Investment advice	– Trading in accepted cryptoassets as an agent – Trading in accepted cryptoassets as a principal – Portfolio management – Cryptoasset custody – Investment advice	– Operate a licensed cryptoasset exchange – Cryptoasset custody service[52]

Capital requirement

BHD 25,000	BHD 100,000	BHD 200,000	BHD 300,000

This is equivalent to approximately

US$66,400	US$265,560	US$531,140	US$796,700

52 Central Bank of Bahrain Issues Regulations governing Crypto-Asset Services – Al Tamimi & Company, accessed 06/02/2025

Importantly, there is a residency requirement. Applicants for licenses must either be incorporated as a joint stock company in Bahrain or be a resident branch in Bahrain of a properly established overseas company. In the latter instance, there must be a suitable resident, such as a lawyer or consultant, to act on their behalf.

Written approval must also be given for approved persons, that is, those considered to be playing key roles in running the firm,[53] and in the case of overseas firms operating through an agent, the relevant parties must be approved in advance. In determining whether the firm and its key personnel have sufficient technological experience, the regulator must be satisfied that there are sufficient anti-laundering and cybersecurity levels, that there is a multi-signature security for hardware wallets, and the firm must be operating either a distinct crypto blockchain architecture or be utilising an existing blockchain.

To engage as an investor, the person concerned must either be an incorporated entity in Bahrain or a citizen over the age of 21.

9.6.5 Saudi Arabia

There is, as yet, no specific legislation in Saudi concerning cryptocurrencies and assets, and the regulator provides what has been described as a *risk-averse*[54] approach by the Saudi Central Bank and the Capital Market Authority. There are a set of implementing regulations on the CFT law covering "electronic currencies", which unfortunately remains an undefined term. It is, however, understood to mean, *inter alia,* cryptocurrencies. Government warnings have been issued in relation to the inherent risks of these products by the Standing Committee for Awareness on Dealing in Securities Activities in the Unauthorized Foreign Exchange Market (Forex), which includes the Saudi Arabian Monetary Authority, and a warning about the lack of regulation,[55] nor can banks engage in crypto-related activities.[56] In addition, the Ministry of Finance issued a similar warning that cryptocurrencies were neither recognised nor regulated in Saudi, but neither are they banned.[57]

The laws relating to anti-laundering[58] and terrorist financing[59] apply to cryptocurrencies, so there is a degree of relevant regulation. In addition, the implementing regulations relating to counter-terrorism laws state that "electronic

53 Directors, chief executives, function heads, chief information security officer, compliance officer, and money laundering reporting officer.

54 US Library of Congress ISSN 2691–6592 FALQs: Elvin Hofverberg. Regulation of Cryptocurrencies in the Gulf Cooperation Council Countries – Part One | In Custodia Legis. Posted 14/01/2025, accessed 05/02/2025.

55 www.sama.gov.sa/en-US/news/pages/News12082018.aspx, accessed 08/04/2025.

56 Kaur, Guneet (2024), "The legal status of cryptocurrencies in Saudi Arabia and Qatar", 10/04/2024, https://cointelegraph.com/learn/articles-legal-status-of-cryptocurrencies-in-saudi-arabia-and-qatar, accessed 08/04/2025.

57 www.mof.gov.sa/en/MediaCenter/news/pages/News20082019.aspx, accessed 08/04/2025

58 The Anti-Money Laundering Law promulgated by Royal Decree No (M/20) on Oct 15th 2017.

59 The Law on Combating Terrorist Crimes and its Financing promulgated by Royal Decree No (M/21) on Nov 1st 2017.r

currencies" are amongst the currencies regulated.[60] It is generally thought that this covers cryptocurrencies, but the definition remains unclear.[61]

Despite this, it is possible to own or set up a company plus apply for a SAGIA license if the applicant is a foreign investor. This is a license issued by the Ministry of Investment of Saudi Arabia, formerly known as SAGIA, and thus the name of the license. Such licenses enable foreign investors to invest in Saudi Arabia. Then it is necessary to apply for a VASP license. The requirements here are a minimum of 3 years unchanged management, 3 years' audited financial statements, relevant management expertise, and SAR 10 million capital.[62] Whilst, as mentioned, cryptocurrencies are not recognised, a range of crypto-related activities are. These are digital banking, processing electronic payments, peer-to-peer lending, asset management, crypto and blockchain applications, and "buy now, pay later" services.[63]

Despite the lack of clarity in legal and regulatory terms, Saudi is now one of the fastest-growing crypto markets in the world, with US$31 billion in transaction value between July 2022 and June 2023, with 18% of the population participating.[64]

9.7 Conclusions

The regulators themselves are, in some instances, created for the purpose of dealing with cryptocurrencies and assets, for example, Dubai's Virtual Assets Regulatory Authority (VARA). However, it is mostly the existing central banks, securities regulators, and financial service regulators that have had their remit extended to apply existing and amended rules to cover the issues raised by crypto. Dubai and Bahrain in particular have engaged in the development of a thorough and well-balanced set of regulations. The former's VARA has issued changes to the Company Rulebook, Compliance and Risk Management Rulebook, Technology and Information Rulebook, and its Market Conduct Rulebook. The UAE's federal structure means that the licensing and regulatory system is quite complex. The UAE Securities and Commodities Authority licenses exchanges, wallets, and trading platforms and is responsible for cryptos categorised as securities,[65] with VARA responsible for other licensing. In Dubai, cryptocurrencies such as Bitcoin and Ethereum are treated as legal tender.

60 Art 1(4) Implementing Regulations of the Law Relating to Terrorist Crimes and its Financing.

61 US Library of Congress ISSN 2691–6592 FALQs: Elvin Hofverberg. Regulation of Cryptocurrencies in the Gulf Cooperation Council Countries – Part One | In Custodia Legis. Posted 14th January 2025, accessed 08/04/2025.

62 Approximately £2 million.

63 el Saghir, Amin, "Navigating the crypto landscape in Saudi Arabia", www.linkedin.com/pulse/navigation-crypto-lanscape-saudi-arabia-amin-el-saghir-ottbf/, accessed 08/04/2025

64 Habadi, Ghaida & Alsamara, Tareck (2025), "The legal nature of cryptocurrencies: Analyzing potential regulatory approaches in the United Arab Emirates and the Kingdom Saudi Arabia", *Journal of Ecohumanism*, 4(1): 2473–2484.

65 UAE, SCA Virtual Assets Regulations 2020

As seen at the level of definitions, Bahrain has subdivided cryptoassets into four different legal and regulatory categories. Once accepted for regulatory purposes, they are categorised as "accepted cryptoassets". The services in relation to these cryptoassets requiring regulation cover all normal aspects of financial services activity.[66]

The development of the law has also seen a common law development in Islamic law with the Malaysian case of *Luno Pte Ltd & Anor v Robert Ong Thien Cheng*[67] discussed earlier. It has been argued[68] that the Malaysian regulatory approach is based on trying to balance the interests of stakeholders who wish to be engaged with the products, creating an environment suitable for growth, protecting consumers, and maintaining financial stability. This accounts for the differences of approach with Singapore, where there appears to be a greater ambition to be a crypto centre.

All in all, the signs are that the majority of the Islamic world is starting to accept or at least tolerate cryptocurrencies and assets. Given that many Islamic states have underdeveloped financial structures, this is important. Populations in remote rural areas can now access financial products online in a manner unthinkable 15 years ago. Those products will include an increasing range of currencies and assets based on digital ledger technology. The future development of Islamic law and regulation in this field will be an important area of study. It suggests that in the struggle between the constructionist and revisionist schools of thought, the former are currently in the ascendancy in the acceptance of cryptocurrencies and assets.

66 Receiving and transmitting crypto, buying and selling, own account dealing against proprietary assets, discretionary portfolio management, cryptoasset custodianship, cryptoasset advice, and operating cryptoasset exchanges.

67 Sessions Court Civil Suit No. BA-B52NCVC-389–12/2017 (Unreported). See analysis in Nawang & Azmi (2020), 262–271, at 269.

68 Nguyen, T. V. & Pham, L. T. (2011), "Scientific output and its relationship to knowledge economy: An analysis of Asean countries", *Scientometrics*, 89(1): 107–117, https://doi.org/10.1007/s11192-011-0446-2

CHAPTER 10

Conclusions

10.1 Introduction

Overall, international economic and financial regulators appear to perceive that there are no significant systemic risks posed by cryptocurrencies as the transactions involved are small relative to mainstream financial products and services. While the BIS stresses the need for regulatory intervention to pre-empt systemic risks from building up until it is too late to avoid the crisis, as with that in 2008, others call for more in-depth analysis of the pertinent issues first. They believe that, for now, the continuous monitoring of the cryptocurrency space will suffice, together with the exchange of information between global agencies and national authorities. Different legal systems have responded to the regulatory enigma posed by cryptocurrencies through four different approaches. [1]

There are economies where no action has been undertaken to regulate cryptocurrencies as such. Some of these require those entities that interface with cryptocurrency transactions to comply with reporting obligations attached to their existing AML/CTF rules, and these are increasing in number because of the growing concerns that cryptocurrencies could be used for illegal activities.

Then, there are those regulating cryptocurrency merely for tax purposes, such that they are subject to VAT or capital gains tax. Then there are those prohibiting or curtailing the use of cryptocurrency, led by China (though they are taking steps to establish a state-run system).

Only a few economies recognise cryptocurrencies such as Bitcoin as a form of currency. By doing so, these jurisdictions appear to be leveraging concepts from traditional financial regulation and adapting them for use with cryptocurrencies.[2] In Brazil, for example, Law No. 2 12,865 of 9 October 2013, Article 6-VI,[3] allows for the creation of electronic currencies. Germany, Japan, and Sweden exemplify economies regulating cryptocurrencies. Germany considers their exchanges as financial service companies that must fulfil strict standards of operation, including meeting initial capital requirements, maintaining certain

1 Boroni, A. (2016), "Bitcoins: Regulatory patterns", *Banking and Finance Law Review*, 32(1): 47–68

2 De Filippi, P. (2014), "Bitcoin: A regulatory nightmare to a libertarian dream", *Internet Policy Review*, 3(2), https://doi.org/10.14763/2014.2.286, www.policyreview.info/articles/analysis/Bitcoin- regulatory-nightmare-libertarian-dream, accessed 02/02/2018.

3 Law 14,478 of December 21st 2022 and Decree 11,563 of June 13th 2023 also apply.

DOI: 10.4324/9781032667416-10

professional qualifications, and reporting transactions to BaFin, the country's financial regulator. Japan is also closely following this approach.

This short review suggests that, thus far, there has been no uniform regulation of cryptocurrencies, which explains the call for direction towards this by the BIS and the IMF. In particular, various regulatory entities have acted independently to provide guidance as to the treatment of cryptocurrencies under the laws within their purview, as exemplified by the CFTC in the United States. This contributed to some clarity, but it also resulted in fragmented and incoherent regulatory frameworks, difficulties in developing frameworks tailored to the unique characteristics of virtual currencies, and failure to give sufficient consideration to the full menu of regulatory issues raised by decentralised cryptocurrencies to result in regulatory frameworks suffering from an unintended lack of oversight in scope.[4]

10.2 Cryptocurrency regulatory issues

Relative to other digital means of exchange that have preceded it, cryptocurrencies face unique challenges. Owing to their decentralised nature, they evade the traditional forms of state regulation and lack a provider or issuer that could be held accountable or a central database. Instead of these, there is a community of users existing operating only in cyberspace. Three potential regulatory regimes could be evaluated for their efficiencies in terms of both cryptocurrency users and national governments. These refer to prohibition, self-regulation, and intermediary regulation.

Regulators are going to take prohibitive measures against cryptocurrencies when used for unlawful purposes, but such might not be the case, as many regulators take care of the integrity aspects by mandating AML/CTF reporting obligations.[5] In any case, cryptocurrencies would be outlawed where they actually posed a threat to an existing fiat currency, especially with respect to the seigniorage income of governments. Further arguments against prohibition include the consideration that they are not yet a major element in mainstream finance and are too insignificant to pose systemic risk.

Besides, a stern regulatory stance against cryptocurrencies could stunt their natural development and growth. This may well drive exchanges to migrate to jurisdictions with low compliance costs in a process of regulatory arbitrage, as already seen in some far-flung, offshore financial centres, and also contribute to a surge in transaction costs. It could be counterclaimed that appropriate regulations could boost market and investor confidence, while the possible increase in transaction costs would be minimal compared to the costs of losing cryptocurrencies and assets from the absence of consumer protection.[6]

4 Tu, K. & Meredith, M. (2015), "Rethinking virtual currency regulation in the Bitcoin age", *Washington Law Review*, 90: 271–347.
5 Ibid note [1], Boroni (2016).
6 Ibid note [1], Boroni (2016).

When faced with the threat of regulation, market participants respond with self-regulation, though this is not something novel. Market participants have consistently argued that the relationships among users within cyberspace should be governed by social norms and market mechanisms without the need for state intervention.[7] However, as over the decades the internet has evolved to become an important medium for commercial exchanges, self-regulation may no longer be the best solution because of the inequities that are bound to arise.

In addition, cryptocurrency transactions are virtually irreversible owing to the computer power which secures them. This ends up benefiting merchants and retailers who are safeguarded against fraudulent practices undertaken by dishonest buyers, but it is concurrently unable to protect buyers from dishonest merchants or retailers. It is generally ineffective to rely on the reputation systems and escrow services available. Cryptocurrency software provides no way to punish its users if they engage in criminal activity, thereby making state intervention necessary. Self-regulation, therefore, appears to have a limited impact and is sustainable only within small groups, which appears to make this solution generally ineffective. The enforcement of existing laws to thwart fraud attempts, as shown in the US FBI's shutting down of Silk Road, appears to support this contention.

Given the difficulties of using the preceding two suggestions, a third intermediary regulation could be reflected upon as cryptocurrency use becomes more widespread. For the most part, operations involving cryptocurrencies are accomplished through virtual currency exchanges. This makes exchanges a good starting point for the implementation of anti-criminal mechanisms concurrently with the use of relevant existing laws. The United States, for example, classifies cryptocurrency exchanges as money transmitters, thereby compelling them to comply with various requirements, including registration with FinCEN; the compilation of reports or records pertaining to criminal, tax, or regulatory investigations; and the implementation of anti–money laundering programmes, along with the need to follow KYC rules.[8] The evident advantage of using pre-existing rules is that no additional undertaking is necessary to design a new and ad hoc regulation of cryptocurrencies, as existing provisions could have achieved the desired aims with a minimal need for amendments.[9] This is, however, unsuitable to address all issues of private international law that may arise with respect to cryptocurrencies, as they are a cross-border phenomenon.[10]

7 Doguet, J. (2013), "The nature of the form: Legal and regulatory issues surrounding the Bitcoin digital currency system", *Louisiana Law Review*, 73(4): 1119–1153

8 Middlebrook, S. & Hughes, S. (2013), "Virtual uncertainty: Developments in the law of electronic payments and financial services", *The Business Lawyer*, 69: 263–273.

9 Ibid note [1], Boroni (2016).

10 Brito, J., Shadab, H. & Castillo, A. (2014, Fall), "Bitcoin financial regulation: Securities, derivatives, prediction markets, and gambling", *Columbia Science and Technology Law Review*, XVI: 144–221.

This shortcoming could, however, be solved partially by the legal interoperability approach.[11] This is a regulatory mechanism that does not require regulation via direct state intervention. It focuses on working together among legal norms, either within the legal system of a nation state or across jurisdictions or nations. Within the context of digitised economies and digitisation, policymakers might have to make initiatives to increase the interoperability of policies and rules as the world heads toward a multilevel governance system, within which the co-operation and interconnection of the various layers are unavoidable elements. The approach's advantages include cost reductions associated with cross-jurisdictional business transactions; the further promotion of innovation, competition, trade, and economic growth; and incentives for the global recognition of fundamental values and rights, such as information privacy and freedom of expression.[12] This suggestion is premised on the notion that an increasing number of legal institutes fall outside the scope of states' regulation and, hence, have to be regulated at the supranational level.

10.3 General regulatory issues

Even as regulation is necessary for the cryptocurrency phenomenon to deter fraud and harm to the global economy and to national currencies, regulators might have to be careful by adopting a delicate approach.[13] This is because excessively restrictive laws might induce innovation to circumvent these controls to foster the development of new virtual currencies and reduce demand for established virtual currencies, with resulting harm to the global economy.[14]

Further, softer laws are also being advocated whereby regulators would not create new rules but instead adapt existing frameworks to render transactions safer and more transparent by promoting enhanced public–private co-operation doing tougher enforcement on non-compliant Bitcoin exchanges and advocating for more active filings of suspicious activity reports (SARs),[15] but not just simply burdening the reporting authorities with massive volumes of SARs.[16]

Yet others, rather than directly regulating cryptocurrencies, opt to facilitate the creation of self-regulatory organisations, non-governmental organisations that formulate and enforce best practices to protect consumers or other kinds of

11 Gasser, U. & Palfrey Jr., J. (2011), "Fostering innovation and trade in the global informational society: The different facts and roles of interoperability", *Swiss National Centre of Competence in Research Working Paper No.2011/39*, June 2011.

12 Trautman, L. (2014), "Virtual currencies Bitcoin & what now after Liberty Reserve, Silk Road, and Mt. Gox", *Richmond Journal of Law & Technology*, 20(4): 1–108.

13 Howden, E. (2015), "The cryptocurrency conundrum: Regulating an uncertain future", *Emory International Law Review*, 29: 741–798.

14 Sonderegger, D. (2015), "A regulatory and economic perplexity: Bitcoin just needs a bit of regulation", *Washington University Journal of Law & Policy*, 47: 175–216.

15 Kirby, P. (2014), "Virtually possible: How to strengthen Bitcoin regulation within the current regulatory framework", *North Carolina Law Review*, 93(1): 189–221.

16 Haynes, A. (2017), "The fourth anti laundering directive: More of the same?", *Company Lawyer*, 38(4): 120–122.

self-regulation. This is because they claim that there is something special about the cryptocurrency that makes it inherently resistant to state control.[17] Bitcoin is uniquely predicated on an open-source protocol that could be modified and regulated by those who use it. Specifically, that system changes have to be accepted by the system users is evidence of the network's self-regulating capability.[18]

Such a display of lack of consensus by regulators over cryptocurrency regulation is muddied further by the widely differing approaches taken recently by national parliaments as well as by ambivalent positions taken by supranational entities. This might not be sustainable in the longer term. At one point, a collective of Bitcoin miners mustered control over 42% of the computer processing power of the Bitcoin network.[19] This is uncomfortably close to the 50% that gives a group of people the power to assume control over the Bitcoin system. Concurrently, though, hundreds of new and competing cryptocurrencies have emerged, such as exemplified by NXT, that rely on a system that makes it impossible for anyone to assert control over most of the processing power within the system.[20] Although these are unlikely to quickly replace Bitcoins, owing to the network effect, namely, the capital investment already incurred by the system's participants, which comprise miners, merchants, and simple users.[24] That said, despite these difficulties, some entity needs to protect consumers and the global economy.

The internet's facilitation of people to communicate and transact with each other across different sectors and across jurisdictions implies that uniform legislation of cryptocurrencies could be more viable. Short of this, cryptocurrencies could well go the way of autonomous vehicles where the need to conform to separate domestic legislation could slow down the implementation of an otherwise beneficial technology.[21] Supranational authorities such as the EU are deemed too regional and have too limited a regulatory scope, while cryptocurrency activities, too, fall outside the ambit of the WTO. This leaves the IMF as the better equipped to engage with them, since the IMF's primary purpose is to ensure the financial stability of the international monetary system.[22] Moreover, the IMF's mandate was updated in 2012 to cover all macroeconomic and financial sector issues that potentially have an impact on global stability. Also, among IMF's original aims was the promotion of exchange stability and, importantly, the establishment of a multilateral system of payments.

However, to put cryptocurrencies under IMF purview would require the necessary amending of IMF's separate currency provisions, but no cryptocurrency

---

17 Papp, J. (2014, Fall), "A medium of exchange for an Internet Age: How to regulate Bitcoin for the growth of E-Commerce", *Journal of Technology Law & Policy*, XV, https://doi.org/10.5195/tlp.2014.155, pp. 33–56.

18 Ibid note [14], Sonderegger (2015).

19 Ibid note [13], Howden (2015).

20 Ziskina, J. (2015), "The other side of the coin: The FECS move to approve cryptocurrency use and deny its viability", *Washington Journal of Law Technology & Arts*, 10(4):306–327.

21 Jeans, E. (2015), "Funny Money or the fall of fiat: Bitcoin and the forward-facing virtual currency regulation", *Colorado Technology Law Journal*, 13(1): 99–128.

22 Ibid note [1], Boroni (2016)

is as yet deemed an official currency by any economy. This would then have to involve empowering the IMF with the competence to amend its charter, something that is extremely difficult to do. The alternative is to respond to the IMF's current call for regulators and others to get together under its banner to carve out a uniform supranational regulation, something previously undertaken before on other complicated issues.[23]

10.4 Public opinion

Where the general stand is to view cryptocurrencies positively, a cleanup of their present image would help, given that they are tarnished by illicit activities,[24] and this should be undertaken together with its endorsement by large businesses, including financial services, accepting cryptocurrencies as alternative means of payment, including by the IMF itself.[25] These concurrent measures could mitigate the impact of Bitcoin on foreign currency markets by bringing Bitcoin within its reach under the categorisation of separate currencies.[26] Then again, the matter is more complicated than this. Opposition to Bitcoin is still very strong within the mainstream economic and financial communities.

Loud voices have been voiced against cryptocurrencies, calling them a scam, a fraud, or a Ponzi scheme.[27] This has turned them into a regulator's nightmare, as whether to prohibit them outright, wait and see, or to regulate them and if so how and by whom. This is because in cyberspace[28] the world is not identified by geographic features and as such might be classified under different legal institutions and governed by specific provisions. This strengthens the case for regulation by supranational organisations or, alternatively, through international instruments.

Novel innovations such as blockchain technology are often accompanied by legal inertia prompted by the initial disorientation pervading the legal domain dealing with them. However, any regulation, once adopted, could quickly become obsolete because of the capacity for high speed evolution amongst the technologies involved.[29] Care and prudence would have to be exercised. Where governments and international organisations over-regulate the cryptocurrency

---

23 Hagan, S. & Mayeda, A. (2018), "IMF calls for global talks on cryptocurrencies" *Bloomberg*, 19/01/2018, www.bloomberg.com/news/articles/2018-01-18/imf-calls-for-global-talkson-digital-fx-as-bitcoin-whipsaws, accessed 02/02/2018.

24 Sirila, D. (2014), *The pleasures and perils of new money in old pockets: M-PESA and Bitcoin in Kenya*, Boston, Harvard University Press.

25 Ibid note [1], Boroni (2016).

26 Plassaras, N. (2013), "Regulating digital currencies: Bringing Bitcoin within the reach of the IMF", *Chicago Journal of International Law*, 14(1): 377–407.

27 Roubini, N. (2018), "The blockchain pipe dream", *Project Syndicate*, 05/03/2018, www.project-syndicate.org/commentary/blockchain-technology-limited-applications-by-nouriel-roubini-and-preston-byrne-2018-03, accessed 06/03/2018; Kharpal, A. (2018), "Blockchain is 'one of the most overhyped technologies ever,' Nouriel Roubini says", *CNBC*, 06/03/2018, www.cnbc.com/2018/03/06/blockchain-nouriel-roubini-one, accessed 08/03/2018.

28 Ibid note [1], Boroni (2016).

29 Ibid note [1], Boroni (2016).

space, the benefits and potential benefits attached to it could dissipate quickly. This is why experts have urged regulators to be prudent and adopt well calibrated policies designed to encouraging resilience and adaptation by existing institutions.[30]

10.5 Regulation – historical issues

As the world reflects on this, it could be useful to take a brief historical snapshot of the general principles behind financial regulation, which is the modern state's approach for guiding markets.[31] In its narrow definition,[32] *regulation* refers to sustained and focused control exercise by a public agency over activities valued by the community and, in its broader definition,[33] refers to all initiatives of the state by whatever means to control and guide the economy and society. Regardless of the width of definition, regulation projects the perception that the state controls private actions through various mechanisms. Regulation is complex as it binds powers of state agencies from the field of public law, with rights of private entities from the field of private law, thereby requiring a balance between values and interests that could clash with one another.[34]

The most prominent model for supervising private sector activities applied in many economies is that of the regulatory state.[35] This is premised on the use of regulation as a means of governance and on professional regulatory agencies supervising the activities of the private sector. The uniqueness of these agencies pertains to the high degree of independence they enjoy compared to governmental ministries that report to ministers and to Parliament.[36] Over time, the regulatory state became gradually more dependent on regulatory tools and policies so as to achieve their objectives. This culminated in a significant expansion of administrative legislation, proliferation of independent regulatory agencies, and expansion of their powers and improvements in the means of supervision.[37]

The regulatory state notion raises the question as to the extent of state involvement that is desirable in the relationship between individuals in society. The

30 Brito, J., Shadab, H. & Castillo, A. (2014), "Bitcoin financial regulation: Securities, derivatives, prediction markets & gambling", *Columbia Science & Technology Law Review*, 16(1): 144–221

31 Majone, G. (1997), "From the positive to the regulatory state: Causes and consequences of changes in the mode of governance", *Journal of Public Policy*, 17(2): 139–167.

32 Selznick, P. (1985), "Focusing organization research on regulation", in Noll, G. N. (ed.), *Regulatory policy and the social sciences*, Berkley, University of California Press, pp. 363–367.

33 Levi-Faur, D. (2011), "Regulation and regulatory governance", in Levi-Faur, D. (ed.), *Handbook of the politics of regulation*, Cheltenham, Edward Elgar, pp. 3–21.

34 Plato-Shinar, R. (2018), "Principles of financial regulation", *Journal of International Banking Law and Regulation*, 33(3): 108–110.

35 Scott, C. (2017), "The regulatory state and beyond", in Drahos, P. (ed.), *Regulatory theory: Foundations and applications*, Canberra, ANU Press.

36 Ibid note [34], Plato-Shinar (2018).

37 Majone, G. (2010), "The transformation of the regulatory state", *Osservatorio sull'Analisi d'Impatto della Regolazione*, https://edisciplinas.usp.br/pluginfile.php/5122391/mod_folder/content/0/MAJONE%2C%20Giandomenico.%20The%20transformations%20of%20the%20regulatory%20State.pdf?forcedownload=1, accessed 02/02/2018.

solution lies not merely on the worldview embraced but also on the particular issues under scrutiny. In general, there seems to be a general consensus that, in democratic societies, there is little space for public supervision of private entities, unless required to entertain a public need. Sometimes, supervision is required to address market failures, or to ensure suitable conditions of the supply of essential services. All such circumstances and matters do not concern only the imposition of supervision but also the extent or intensity of supervision deemed to be appropriate.[38]

10.6 Global co-operation

The 2008 global financial crisis displayed how globalisation served as a catalyst for systemic risk, undermining both the capacity and incentives of national regulators to respond to the relevant risks.[39] Among the many insights that arose from the crisis was the necessity for effective global co-operation and from the application of both soft and hard laws to achieve such co-operation.

While such initiatives are unlikely to change the fundamental nature of the international monetary and financial system, it remains important to design it in a manner that reduces global and domestic imbalances over time, while preserving international stability to support global growth and development. This calls for global co-operation, including a greater legitimacy and, hence, more authority for supranational entities and to protect global stability. It also calls for incentives for market participants and national authorities to align themselves with the promotion of systemic stability. This, in turn, requires policymakers to embrace a systemic perspective and to be ready to implement policies that, while serving national interests, also support a stable international monetary and financial system to contribute to a thriving global economy.[40]

Discourse on financial regulation typically focuses on the issue of the quantity of regulations and the hard choice between regulation and deregulation, best now seen in play in the United States with the ascendancy of the Trump administration.[41] Other insights from the 2008 global financial crisis suggest that regulation could be necessary, but this does not rule out the fact that regulation could be counterproductive. Good regulation serves the public interest through supporting ongoing confidence in the processes, as exemplified by the market process, where the public participates in activities such as auditing. Regulation is therefore necessary to support confidence in the markets and trust in the

38 Ibid note [34], Plato-Shinar (2018).

39 Stiglitz, J. E. (2017), *Globalization and its discontent revisited: Anti-globalization in the era of Trump*, New York, WW Norton & Company.

40 European Central Bank (ECB) (2011), "The financial crisis and the strengthening of global policy co-operation", *ECB Monthly Bulletin January 2011*, pp. 87–97.

41 Zarroli, J. (2017), "Fed Chief Yellen warns against dismantling bank regulations", *NPR*, 25/08/2017, www.npr.org/2017/08/25/546076064/janet-yellen-warns-against-dismantling-bank-regulations, accessed 02/02/2018; Shapiro, S. (2017), "What Trump means for regulation", *Scholar Strategy Network*, https://scholars.org/sites/scholars/files/ssn_regulation_fact_sheet.pdf, accessed 02/02/2018.

reliability of financial reporting and financial services generally.[42] *Good financial regulation* could then be said to be any regulation that protects consumers and users and reduces the extent of fraud and corruption in financial services without imposing excessively high costs on the community.[43]

How faith-based and faith-driven perception, such as Islamic finance, views cryptocurrencies and assets merits attention. A review of relevant analysis (see Chapter 9) suggests that there is no common view amongst Islamic scholars.[44] However, in a number of Islamic states, the industry has demonstrated its ability to develop. Fintechs, within the context of the Fourth Industrial Revolution, can be categorised into automation, disintermediation, and decentralisation.[45] The application of automation and disintermediation by the Islamic Finance industry does not pose any challenge to the established principles of Islamic law and even has the potential of promoting compliance with these principles.[46] The technologies associated with decentralisation, though, are the most challenging to apply in the context of Islamic finance.[47] Also, some of the identifying characteristics of cryptos have also been viewed to be inherently incompatible with some of the established principles of Islamic law.[48]

10.7 The essentials of good regulation

Proposals have also been advanced for the art of designing good regulations that bear the minimum core characteristics of addressing market failures that generate greater benefits than costs and that do not treat businesses differently from one another.[49] Good regulation extending from these needs appear to exhibit the following characteristics:[50]

1. It must actually do good – meaning, it must have a sound rationale and be shown to bring net benefit to society, necessitating costs as well as benefits to be accounted for.
2. It must be better than any alternative regulation or policy tool. In this regard. it is not sufficient to compare a regulation to a counterfactual

42 Thomadakis, S. B. (2007), "What makes a good regulation?", *Paper Presented by Stavros B. Thomadakis, Chairman Public Interest Oversight Board at the IFAC Council Seminar Mexico City, 14/11/2007.*

43 Moosa, I. A. (2018), "Good regulation versus bad regulation", *Journal of Banking Regulation*, 19(1): 55–63.

44 Rabbani, M. R. et al. (2022), "Islamic finance and cryptocurrency: A systematic review", in Hassan, M. K., Rabbani, M. R. & Rashid, M. (eds.), *FinTech in Islamic financial institutions*, Cham, Palgrave Macmillan, pp. 279–306

45 Ibid note [1256], Aldohni (2023)

46 Ibid note [1256], Aldohni (2023)

47 Ibid note [1256], Aldohni (2023)

48 Ibid note [1256], Aldohni (2023)

49 Furchgott-Roth, H. W. (2000), "The art of writing good regulations", *Federal Communications Law Journal*, 53(1): 1–4.

50 Banks, G. (2003), "The good, the bad and the ugly: Economic perspectives on regulation in Australia", *Paper Delivered by Gary Banks Chairman Productivity Commission at the Conference of Economists, Business Symposium*, Hyatt Hotel, Canberra, 02/10/2003.

of no regulation, but to compare outcomes across all feasible policy alternatives.

3. The regulatory evaluation process should take into account the likely outcomes, including a rapid capability for correcting mistakes.
4. It should contain the seeds of its own destruction. Good regulations are not necessarily equated with the presumption of their own immortality but allow for the ongoing appraisal of their risks and continued effectiveness. Where a regulation endures, that should be because it continues to pass stringent tests.
5. It should state (ex ante) what it is going to do and, as far as possible, set up verifiable performance criteria. This evaluates a regulation for precision and relevance and provides a basis for assessment of ex post effectiveness.
6. It should be clear and concise. This implies that it should also be communicated effectively and be readily accessible to those affected by it. Not only should market participants be able to find out what regulations apply to them, but the regulations themselves must also be capable of being readily understood.
7. It should be consistent with other laws, agreements, and international obligations. Inconsistency could create division, confusion, and waste.
8. It must be enforceable. However, it should involve incentives or disciplines no greater than are needed for reasonable enforcement and involve sufficient resources for the purpose.
9. Finally, it needs to be administered by accountable bodies in a fair and consistent manner. This means having good governance arrangements in place. Aside from clear reporting responsibilities and the scope for judicial or administrative review, important features of good governance include clear statutory guidance, transparency of both process and judgement, and public accessibility.

A major failing of previous regulatory approaches was the assumption that where there was a market failure, the appropriate instrument for addressing this was through a non-market approach, usually a command-and-control mechanism that is often highly prescriptive. The general acknowledged aim now is to achieve the desired regulatory outcomes at least cost. This led to a wider menu of regulatory approaches, including recognition of the flexibility and information-laden characteristic of market-based mechanisms that could assume the following forms:[51]

1. Avoid inconsistency between compatible mechanisms, such as taxes and competitive tendering
2. Mandatory information disclosure, with the threat of more heavy-handed regulation and public disapproval

51 Ibid note [50], Banks (2003).

3. Self-regulation, where an industry must devise a workable regulatory approach to achieve accepted performance standards with minimal prescription by regulators.

Markets, therefore, offer the potential for achieving regulatory objectives more efficiently than prescriptive regulations. For instance, it is possible to make a reduction in some undesirable outcomes of a market good in itself. This would bring to bear the inventiveness and cost-consciousness that characterise market competition. Regulations of this nature can allow for the fact that the costs and benefits of regulation vary across businesses and, over time, can allow businesses the freedom to determine what technology is used to achieve a given performance target and, as a consequence, is informationally efficient – meaning, not requiring the regulator to know a lot about the technologies or costs of regulated businesses. A well-designed market generates incentives for individual businesses to act on the information they have. Overall, carefully designed and prudently applied economic instruments offer great potential for achieving better regulatory outcomes at lower cost.[52]

Self-regulation has the benefit of allowing much greater freedom by an industry regarding the detail of regulation, including dispute resolution. It economises on administration costs to governments and uses specialist industry information more efficiently than command and control kinds. Self-regulation is used widely in financial services, telecommunications, and elsewhere. It is inappropriate where performance standards cannot be readily verified, or if penalties are too weak relative to the costs of poor performance or dispute resolution poor. Self-regulation is argued to be a cost-effective alternative to government intervention where these criteria are met.[53] It merits noting that some apparent self-regulation is actually co-regulation in that the government still acts as a monitor and enforcer of some transparent performance criteria.

The reality of regulatory fallibility suggests that there should be appropriate checks and balances and clear statutory guidance for regulators. Regulators also need to consult more widely about the potential impact of regulations, especially regarding compliance costs, and ensure that regulations are regularly tested for continued relevance and cost-effectiveness. Regulatory norms further need confronting. The risks and failures linked to regulatory initiatives should be highlighted so as to avoid having an automatic culture of apparent regulatory fix for every problem arising. Regulatory forbearance could be an apt option for circumstances involving market outcomes that are only a little imperfect.[53]

Finally, it is worth noting the political economy of financial regulation.[54] Research suggests that regulators and policymakers do not always strive to promote public interest but instead could be motivated by a wide menu of

52 Ibid note [50], Banks (2003).
53 Ibid note [50], Banks (2003).
54 Ibid note [34], Plato-Shinar (2018).

extraneous factors, including self interest. This, in turn, could lead to various regulatory failures, such as regulatory capture, regulatory inaction, and regulatory competition, prompting regulatory arbitrage, and so on. Mechanisms such as transparency requirements, independent oversight, constraints on regulators' discretionary powers, and the imposition of institutional and personal liability are fortunately available to hold regulators and policymakers to account.[55]

Given the already difficult agenda and mission of national financial regulators, the advent of Bitcoin and other cryptocurrency equivalents has presented them with a regulatory dilemma as it has for supranational regulators across the world. Cryptocurrencies could be issued privately or by central banks. It could be a cryptocurrency either randomised or tethered. Its scheme might be centralised or decentralised, and its value might be self-anchored or of a specified fiat currency. When facilitating electronic transmission of payment media between distant parties, cryptocurrency schemes, as equivalent to hand-to-hand physical cash delivery, might irreversibly transform the global payments landscape and necessitate novel solutions.[56] Some important aspects of these have been highlighted and discussed.

Ultimately, however, cryptocurrencies will most probably depend on various factors, of which the most significant appears to be whether central banks and governments will regulate it out of existence.[57] However, if they can work in harmony with traditional fiat currencies offering alternative transaction completion methods and investment opportunities, both are likely to be viable. Further, in the absence of intermediation, new solutions would be needed to resolve conflicts of law and other challenges. Legal theorists would need to locate an approach that would avoid fragmentation of internationally issued securities portfolios by identifying a single jurisdiction to which there is sufficient connection to make it reasonable that the law of that jurisdiction should govern an entire portfolio of interests recorded in a distributed ledger.[58] International co-operation for this is crucial, and this means the call by the IMF for co-operation in the treatment of cryptocurrencies merits support.

Blockchain is now increasingly looked upon as foundational and not disruptive. Bitcoin is the first application of this technology but is unlikely to be the last, as major players in just about every sector from finance to health, and utilities to retail, announce that they, too, are getting involved. This will signal a potential shift to the mainstream.[59] Interestingly, a blockchain is now

55 Armour, J., Awrey, D., Davies, P., Enriques, L., Gordon, J. N., Mayer, C. & Payne, J. (2016), *Principles of financial regulation*, Oxford, Oxford University Press.

56 Geva, B. (2016), "Disintermediating electronic payments: Digital cash and virtual currencies", *Journal of International Banking Law and Regulation*, 31(12): 661–674.

57 Anderson, T. A. (2014), "Bitcoin-is it just a fad? History, current status and the future of the cyber-currency revolution", *Journal of International Banking Law and Regulation*, 29(7): 428–435.

58 Kalderon, M., Snagg, F. & Harrop, C. (2016), "Distributed ledgers: A future in financial services?", *Journal of International Banking Law and Regulation*, 31(5): 243–248.

59 Butter, J. (2018), "In FOCUS: Blockchain, foundational not disruptive", *Sustainability RADAR*, https://radar.sustainability.com/issue-16/in-focus-blockchain-foundational-not-disruptive/,

available that not only matches daters based on compatibility, like Match.com, or mutual interest, like Tinder, but also safety, via pre-date video chats, sobriety checks, and "safe" words that the Loly app would listen for. Where the app hears the safe word, it can initiate a call enabling the concerned partner to extricate from the date. This security feature in Loly is claimed to account for those edge use cases where bad participants slip through the cracks onto the platform.[60] Meanwhile, in the shorter term, it looks as though cryptocurrencies and assets are here to stay, but the longer term, it remains a matter of speculation.

Cryptocurrencies and cryptoassets offer a wider potential change for the future. A limitless series of peer-to-peer networks will be created that will disseminate power and control to those using the systems. Suggestions that this will also provide a fairer distribution of wealth[61] remain to be seen, but it is certainly the case that many internet-based facilities, including finance, will be far more readily available to those in parts of the world where direct access to mainstream institutions is inconvenient or impossible. How well law and regulation can keep on top of this remains to be seen. Vitalik Buterin suggested that "there is a large chance that we will never come up with a blockchain governance process that is sufficiently robust that it will be capable of regularly doing things like adjusting fundamental economic parameters".[62] As to the extent to which this will work, time will tell. It may or may not prove to be El Dorado, but regulators of various types will certainly face a dilemma.

Indeed, like various others, the evolution of DLT and cryptos would be subject to the ebbs and flows of the combined impact of the aftermaths of the 2020 Covid-19 pandemic, the global geopolitical tensions, and the acceleration of a multipolar world torn by big power competition, regional wars, and the rising complexities of governance issues. At the global level, the UN provides some degree of global leadership to respond to these said challenges with the UN Sustainable Development Goals (UN SDGs), while the private sector across the world is led and guided on global sustainability by global leaders in the finance industry and coordinated by the Global Compact of 2004.[63] Of late, the environmental, social, and governance (ESG) aspects of cryptos have attracted

accessed 18/03/2018; Iansiti, M. & Lakhani, K. R. (2017), "The truth about blockchain", *Harvard Business Review*, 01/03/2017, https://hbr.org/2017/01/the-truth-about-blockchain, accessed 18/03/2018.

60 Koetsier, J. (2018), "Sex is now on the blockchain. Cue end of western civilization: Men's top fear when going on a blind date is that the woman is fatter than her photo, Women's No.1 fear? Being murdered", *Inc.*, 03/03/2018, www.inc.com/john-koetsier/this-augmented-reality-dating-startup-uses-blockchain-to-verify-consent.html, accessed 08/03/2018.

61 Tapscott, D. & Tapscott, A. (2018), *Blockchain Revolution*, 2nd edn, Penguin, p. 14.

62 Fink, M. (2019), *Blockchain Regulation and Governance in Europe*, Cambridge University Press, p. 209.

63 The Global Compact (2004), "Who cares wins. Connecting to financial markets to a changing world. Recommendations by the financial industry to better integrate environment, social and governance issues in analysis, asset management and securities brokers", www.unepfi.org/fileadmin/events/2004/stocks/who_cares_wins_global_compact_2004.pdf, accessed 19/07/2024

global attention and responses,[64] such as those highlighted in global data exchanges,[65] while the crypto-based approach[66] for a sustainable future has also been proposed. Alluded to earlier, such positive developments would be limited without enhanced global co-operation, and hence the inevitable need for quicker actions globally.

64 Uquehart, A. (2024), "The environmental, social and governance (ESG) aspects of Bitcoin", in Cronqvist, H. & Pely, D. J. (eds.), *The Elgar companion to decentralized finance, digital assets and blockchain technologies*, Cheltenham, Edward Elgar

65 Baynes, M. & Londino, J. C. (2024), "How data center operators can strike a balance with sustainability and rising demand", *Schneider Electric Blog*, 07/05/2024, https://blog.se.com/data-center/2024/05/07/how-data-center-operators-balance-sustainability-rising-demand/, accessed 19/07/2024

66 Meyer, E. et al. (2024), "Regenerative Finance: A crypto-based approach for s sustainable future", in Cronqvist, H. & Pely, D. J. (eds.), *The Elgar companion to decentralized finance, digital assets and blockchain technologies*, Cheltenham, Edward Elgar.

INDEX

Note: Page numbers in *italics* indicate figures, **bold** indicate tables in the text, and references following "n" refer notes.